Affair of the Heart

Affair of the Heart

British Theatre from 1992 to 2020

Michael Billington

methuen | drama

LONDON · NEW YORK · OXFORD · NEW DELHI · SYDNEY

METHUEN DRAMA
Bloomsbury Publishing Plc
50 Bedford Square, London, WC1B 3DP, UK
1385 Broadway, New York, NY 10018, USA
29 Earlsfort Terrace, Dublin 2, Ireland

BLOOMSBURY, METHUEN DRAMA and the Methuen Drama logo are trademarks of
Bloomsbury Publishing Plc

First published in Great Britain 2022

Cover design: Ben Anslow

A catalogue record for this book is available from the British Library.

A catalog record for this book is available from the Library of Congress.

ISBN: HB: 978-1-3502-1477-4
        ePDF: 978-1-3502-1478-1
        eBook: 978-1-3502-1479-8

Typeset by RefineCatch Limited, Bungay, Suffolk
Printed and bound in India

To find out more about our authors and books visit www.bloomsbury.com
and sign up for our newsletters.

CONTENTS

Hopes of Renewal: 2000–9

Bright Spots in the Lost Decade: 2010–19

2019 289

ACKNOWLEDGEMENTS

I must thank *The Guardian* for kindly giving me permission to reprint a selection of theatre reviews that first appeared in its pages. I also owe a deep debt to Richard Nelsson, the paper's information manager, who tirelessly retrieved around 200 of my reviews from the files and saved me an enormous amount of time and labour. And my thanks are due to any number of other people at the paper. First of all the three editors – Peter Preston, Alan Rusbridger and Katharine Viner – who not only employed me but who, in countless ways, gave me support and encouragement. I also worked under a variety of section editors who are too numerous to list but three names in particular stand out: Chris Wiegand who, as theatre editor during the latter years of my tenure, was a constant source of inspiration and advice as well as being a good friend; Alex Needham who, as arts editor at the time of my retirement, graciously said that it was the end of a chapter rather than the conclusion of the story; and Imogen Tilden, the senior arts editor, who was not only a rock of support but also a valued companion at some of the first nights here recorded.

I'd like to thank Martin Crimp, David Greig and Caryl Churchill for their kind permission to reprint their Letters to the Editor about *Blasted*. I was unable to contact the Rev Bob Vernon but I hope he won't mind my reproducing his letter.

I also have to thank my wife, Jeanine, who has been constantly at my side for my half-century or more as a critic, my tech-savvy daughter, Natasha, who put many of these reviews in sequence, her partner Daniel and their son, Samuel, who is a theatregoer of the future.

Finally, and not least, I have to thank Anna Brewer, my editor at Methuen Drama, who commissioned this book, made numerous constructive suggestions and was a model of tact, kindness and sympathy. Technically speaking our contact, because of COVID-19, was often remote but there was nothing remote about Anna's passion for theatre and ability to encourage its author.

Introduction

I have often remarked how plays constantly change their meaning: *Hamlet*, to take the most obvious example, is a different play depending on the historical, geographical and social context in which it is seen. This book has also changed its character because of external circumstances. When I stepped down as *The Guardian*'s theatre critic in December, 2019, I thought it might be of use to record some of the highlights of my experience over the previous 27 years. I chose 1992 as my starting point because in a previous book, *One Night Stands*, I had offered a selection of reviews since I became a full-time aisle-squatter in 1971. The title of this book, *Affair Of The Heart*, suggests that two decades of frantic theatre-hopping settled into a deep, long-term relationship. What I could not have foreseen is that ten weeks after I gave up my job, the theatre itself would be forced to shut down because of COVID-19. When I retired, I felt as if I was stepping off a fast-moving train: I had no idea that the train itself would become virtually stationary for well over a year.

I hope my book will act as proof of the vitality of British theatre over nearly three decades. But it has also become a reminder of a dynamism that was suddenly halted. The book is still a celebration of British theatre but it has now acquired a faint glow of nostalgia and has turned, more than I anticipated, into a record of an irrecoverable, although hyperactive, past. Whatever the financial pressures, the shows still kept coming. In 1992 *Theatre Record* listed 637 productions in London alone: there were almost as many in 2019. But how much has theatre changed in the years between the book's starting and finishing-points?

For a start theatre is now bigger business than ever. SOLT (the Society of London Theatre) published figures for 2019 before the lockdown took effect. They showed a total attendance at SOLT venues of 15.3 million, box-office returns of £799 million and VAT paid to the Treasury of over £133 million: that last figure is a potent reminder of theatre's value to the economy which the Government, during the lockdown, was signally slow to recognise. The commercial theatre, in particular, is like a highly efficient factory and there is much to admire in the work of visionary producers such as Sonia Friedman, who has an admirable faith in new projects, and in Cameron

Mackintosh, who has zealously supervised the refurbishment of the eight theatres he owns. At the same time there was a loss of variety in the period covered by this book. There were never less than 25 musicals at any one time in the West End and, now that they have all but disappeared, I find myself occasionally pining for the star-studded classic revival, the trouser-dropping farce and the kind of intelligent straight play regularly supplied by writers like the late Simon Gray and Ronald Harwood.

The truth is that a critic increasingly looks for sustenance to the subsidised sector: not just the twin battleships of the National Theatre and the Royal Shakespeare Company but the flotilla of smaller venues that offer a new production every few weeks. Their names are well known and their work is reflected in the pages that follow: the Royal Court, Almeida, Donmar, Hampstead Theatre, Bush, Kiln (*nee* Tricycle), Lyric Hammersmith and many more. In the nation at large there are any number of regional theatres that have sustained the highest standards in difficult times: the Royal Exchange in Manchester, the Playhouse in Nottingham, Crucible in Sheffield, Festival Theatre and Minerva in Chichester, Stephen Joseph in Scarborough. The emergence of peripatetic National Theatre companies in Scotland and Wales has also helped to redefine how best to serve a disparate, widespread community. The chief loss is the gradual disappearance of the permanent company, residing at any one theatre, which for decades was the bedrock of regional theatre and which allowed actors, directors, designers and technicians to hone and refine their craft.

I've no wish to sound negative, however. Change is the law of life and many changes in British theatre over the last 30 years have been for the better. Standards of production have become higher, new venues have been discovered, there has been greater attention to audience needs and, above all, a much-needed and long-overdue focus on gender equality and racial diversity. Obviously the Harvey Weinstein scandal and the Black Lives Matter movement have forced every institution to examine its practice, its policy and its past failures. Statistics show that women are still in the minority as playwrights, directors, heads of companies and on theatrical boards. That is something I deplore but figures don't always tell the whole story. In the twentieth century women had to fight for recognition yet, through their pioneering efforts, a number of them changed British theatre for the better. Annie Horniman founded the regional rep movement in Manchester. Lilian Baylis, through her work at the Old Vic and Sadler's Wells, prepared the ground for the National Theatre, English National Opera and the Royal Ballet. Joan Littlewood transformed the Theatre Royal, Stratford East into a place of buoyant experiment and collective endeavour. Caryl Jenner, with the Unicorn company at London's Arts Theatre, proved that there was a year-round demand for theatre for young people. These women were all pathfinders. And, looking back at the period covered by this book, I can see the impact of the growing demand for gender equality. Take playwriting alone. Any list of prominent British dramatists today would be headed by Caryl Churchill but would also include Lucy Kirkwood, Lucy Prebble, Laura Wade, Bryony Lavery, Ella Hickson, Lolita Chakrabarti, Winsome Pinnock and debbie tucker green among many others. You could make an equally long list of women directors, from Katie Mitchell, Deborah Warner and Marianne Elliott to Vicky Featherstone, Indhu Rubasingham and Roxana Silbert who have made a decisive mark either as radical freelances or as heads of permanent institutions. Even if gender parity has still to be achieved, it would be pointless to deny there has been substantial progress.

A similar argument applies to artists of colour. There have always been outstanding plays by individual writers: Errol John's *Moon On A Rainbow Shawl*, Barry Reckord's *Skyvers*, Mustapha Matura's *Play Mas* all made a big impact in the 1950s and 1960s. But, as an article I wrote in 2000 indicates, there have long been questions about the under-representation of artists of colour on stages, behind the scenes and in theatrical board-rooms. Since then things have changed for the better. Plays by BAME writers increasingly take place on big stages, derive from a large talent pool and are wide-ranging in theme. There would also be shock and outrage today if you saw a classic revival with an all-white cast. Even the days when the casting of Clive Rowe as Mr Snow in a National Theatre production of *Carousel* prompted raised eyebrows now seem a thing of the past. Look around today and you find a generation of actors, including Sophie Okonedo, Sharon D. Clarke, Cecilia Noble, Hugh Quarshie, Adrian Lester, David Oyelowo and Chiwetel Ejiofor, who can play anything and everything and who, in some cases, have achieved international fame. Again, there is still much work to be done before we can say that racial equality is firmly embedded in every aspect of British theatre but at least there is acknowledgement of the issue and a hunger for improvement.

If theatre has changed in the period covered by this book, so too has the job of the critic. Some of the changes are obvious. Instead of being banged out on a typewriter, reviews are now filed electronically: a huge bonus in terms of speed of transmission. At the same time, the number of outlets for critics has diminished. What particularly saddens me is that many of the major regional newspapers, in so far as they survive at all, have drastically cut their coverage. I grew up reading *The Birmingham Post* which, in the 1950s, had a major critic in J.C. Trewin who would file 1,000-word reviews of first nights at Stratford or the Birmingham Rep: today the *Post* is a shrunken weekly with a minimal circulation. The only compensation for the loss of print outlets is the exponential growth in digital platforms. *What'sOnStage* and *Exeunt* provide excellent theatrical coverage, established critics such as Libby Purves and Lyn Gardner have created their own websites, there are numerous bloggers with large followings and there is nothing to stop aspiring reviewers from setting one up for themselves. The catch is that, while tyro critics may be able to winkle complimentary tickets out of press agents, no one is likely to pay them for their reviews.

All this has led to doom-laden talk of "the death of the critic." I don't subscribe to this since, for all my concerns about shrinking outlets, the major national dailies have not abandoned criticism: my own paper, *The Guardian*, combines extensive coverage of theatre in print with a website that includes reviews, features and interviews. That is also true of *The Times*, the *Daily Telegraph* and *Financial Times*. As long as theatre is productive, appeals to a sizeable sector of the population and retains its cultural influence, there will be a hunger for criticism. When I stepped down as *The Guardian*'s theatre critic, I quickly scotched any idea that it was the end of an era: I said that in some ways – though not in others – I felt more like Hector in Alan Bennett's *The History Boys* who saw his function as to "pass the parcel." And I was delighted to hand that particular parcel to my gifted successor, Arifa Akbar.

In one respect, however, the role of the critic has changed. We live – or at least we did before the COVID-enforced lockdown – in an age where we are faced by multiple choices. In an average week, prior to 2020, the number of plays, films, books, exhibitions, concerts and gigs competing for attention was bewilderingly large. Criticism, correspondingly, has taken on a more utilitarian function. Part of one's role now is to act as a consumer-guide and a symbol of that is the growth of star-ratings. I have always disliked the star-system because it slaps an instant classification on a work of art and, in the case of theatre, makes no distinction between the text and the performance. But, whenever I questioned star-ratings, I was always told that readers loved them. Even critics now use them as a form of conversational shorthand. I noticed that my colleagues would often ask each other of a particular production "How many stars did you give it?" and then look astonished at the answer if it didn't match their own evaluation.

I accept that a necessary part of the critic's job, especially in a world of high ticket prices, is to offer the reader guidance as what to see or to avoid. But, at the risk of sounding presumptuous, I would argue that it is not one's only function and in this I seek support from higher authorities. One of my favourite works of Oscar Wilde, dating from the early 1890s, is a sustained dialogue, enthrallingly staged by Charles Marowitz in 1971, entitled *The Critic as Artist*. In it one of the speakers argues that criticism is itself a creative act: "It works with materials, and puts them in a form that is at once new and delightful. What more can say of poetry? Indeed I would call criticism a creation within a creation." Even allowing for Wilde's love of paradox, it is fascinating how many people followed in his wake. In 1903 you find A.B. Walkley, the drama critic of *The Times*, writing: "The critics are in the peculiar position of being at once consumers and producers: they are consumers of one art, the art of drama, and producers of another art, the art of criticism." C.E. Montague, a legendary *Manchester Guardian* critic, says something similar in *A Writer's Notes On His Trade* posthumously published in 1930: "The critic is neither a tutor in the techniques of the art which he criticises nor an examiner commissioned to allot marks to its practitioners. He, too, in his humble way, is an artist as they are."

All this sounds a million miles away from today's world. It evokes a society in which the critic was seen as a gentleman – and notice Montague's use of the male pronoun – of relative leisure and as a king, in newspaper terms, of infinite space. Today we are more likely to be men and women rushing between events, expected to come up with instant star-ratings and obliged to cram our thoughts into 450 words. And yet I believe the notion of the critic as artist is an ideal worth cherishing. As critics, we are constantly judged by the validity of our opinions. But, as Wilde said of Ruskin's views on Turner, who cares whether they are sound or not? What mattered was the "elaborate symphonic music" of his prose. None of us can write like Ruskin; nor should we try to. All I'm suggesting is that one of the main functions of the critic is to strain every nerve to write with all the clarity, concision and elegance at his or her command. The critics I most admire – Kenneth Tynan, say, on theatre or Pauline Kael on film – were often erratic in their judgements but were always a joy to read. Whatever my own failings in this regard, I would urge my successors to take pleasure in the act of writing rather than to regard themselves as mere opinion-mongers.

I realise I am offering a hostage to fortune. I would simply add that the following selection of reviews and articles, culled from several million words written for *The Guardian* over nearly three decades, attempts to capture the diversity of British theatre. I recognise that there are many significant omissions and that my choice reveals a metropolitan bias. But the fact is that, although I have spent much of my life driving up motorways and sitting in trains, my home has long been in London which offers a range of activity unmatched in any other theatrical capital. Looking back, I feel that I have led an enviable and privileged existence. But, although I have formally retired, I would echo the words of my colleague, Ben Brantley, who, when he stepped down from *The New York Times* in 2020, said he would never cease being a critic. No more will I; and I look forward to the next chapter in theatre's strange, eventful history with a mixture of nervous trepidation and eager curiosity.

Towards the End of the Millennium: 1992–9

The final decade of the nineteenth century was dubbed "The Naughty Nineties." The end of the twentieth century was more like The Nervous Nineties. Even though there was an air of excitement at the approach of the new millennium, the years before were tinged with apprehension: the result of a stuttering economy that inevitably had its impact on British theatre. When the Conservative Party won the General Election in the spring of 1992, the country was in its longest recession since the Second World War. And although Labour's landslide victory at the 1997 Election was greeted by many with buoyant optimism, the fact is that the decision by Tony Blair and Gordon Brown to stick within pre-set Conservative spending limits meant that there was no immediate uplift for the theatre. In 1999 the National Campaign for the Arts told us that the value of annual Arts Council grants to producing theatres had fallen since 1992 by 13 per cent, that there had been a cumulative loss of £12 million in core funding over the decade and that 33 regional reps had deficits totalling over £10.3 million. What Richard Eyre called "the implicit federation of British theatre" was clearly in jeopardy.

Even in tough times, however, theatre is a resilient medium and there were significant changes of personnel in the 1990s. In 1992 Stephen Daldry took sole charge of the Royal Court and began with a radical look at both the building and its programme. He set about an extensive renovation that meant the Court was closed from 1996 to 1998 and that productions were shifted to the Duke of York's and the Ambassadors. Daldry also reinforced the Court's historic commitment to living writers by launching an avalanche of productions: in 1995 alone there were eight new plays in the main house and nine in the Theatre Upstairs. Out of this creative tumult much important work emerged: Sarah Kane's *Blasted*, Mark Ravenhill's *Shopping and Fucking*, Jez Butterworth's *Mojo*, Conor McPherson's *The Weir* and Martin McDonagh's *The Beauty Queen of Leenane* were all, in different ways, landmark plays but David Eldridge, Joe Penhall, Anthony Neilson, Nick Grosso, Ayub Khan-Din, Phyllis Nagy, Rebecca Prichard and Judy Upton were amongst the new and emerging writers who benefited from Daldry's policy of saturation artistic bombardment. If Daldry proved something of a revolutionary at the Royal Court, Sam Mendes, who with Caro Newling took over the running of the Donmar Warehouse in 1992, was more cautious in his approach. But then the Donmar initially had no subsidy: simply a guarantee from the theatre's owners that they would underwrite the project for three years. Working within strict commercial parameters, Mendes and his team came up with some impressively stylish productions: of American musicals (*Assassins*, *Cabaret* and *Company*), of modern classics (*The Glass Menagerie*, *Glengarry Glen Ross*, *The Front Page*) and revivals of neglected works (*Translations*, *Habeas Corpus*). The real significance of the Donmar is that it showed that in the 1990s there was a ravenous metropolitan hunger for high-quality work in small spaces. Its sister theatre in London was the Almeida which Jonathan Kent and Ian McDiarmid had taken over in 1990 and which balanced new plays (with a bias towards Pinter) with explorations of the world repertory ranging from Euripides, Moliere and Racine to Chekhov, Pirandello and Brecht. The Almeida and the Donmar were class acts. But Mendes, in a startlingly candid introduction to a book about the Donmar's history, said that in an ideal world neither theatre would exist: he saw them both as products of the new freelance culture where few directors had permanent attachments and where actors fitted theatre engagements in between more lucrative film and TV work.

Permanence was always supposed to be the prerogative of the two big national companies but in the 1990s they too were often at the mercy of the freelance culture. Their work was also distinctly variable. Richard Eyre ended his distinguished tenure at the National in 1997 and, in his decade in charge, struck an admirable balance between new work and the classics: he also went out in a blaze of glory with his production of *John Gabriel Borkman* and a revival of *Guys and Dolls*. Trevor Nunn, his successor as director, seemed a safe pair of hands but didn't endear himself to idealists by opening his regime with straight runs of *Oklahoma* in the Olivier and *The Prime of Miss Jean Brodie* in the Lyttelton. Although he went on to do excellent productions of *The Merchant of Venice*, *Summerfolk* and *Troilus and Cressida*, there were justifiable accusations that the National programme was top-heavy with musicals (a total of seven during Nunn's five-and-a-half year tenure) and that he himself failed to gather round him a crack team of associates. The Royal Shakespeare Company, where Adrian Noble had taken over in 1991, also enjoyed fitful success. There were some terrific productions during the Noble years – his own two parts of *Henry 1V* with Robert Stephens, Michael Boyd's radical take on *A Midsummer Night's Dream*, Katie Mitchell's revival of *Ghosts*, Tim Albery's of Schiller's *Wallenstein* – but during the late 1990s Noble made some wayward decisions: amongst them a determination to start the Stratford season in November and to create stand-alone productions that seemed like a negation of the company ethos. It also felt like a sign of the times, and the increasing reliance on sponsorship, that in 1998 Alex Jennings was obliged to promote a Stratford production of *Hamlet* by perching on the bonnet of a Citroen. It's hard to imagine that happening to John Gielgud.

At least the national companies had access to sponsorship through fund-raising departments. It was much tougher for regional theatres at a time of dwindling subsidy. If any single trend became apparent in the 1990s, it was a polarisation in regional theatre. Increasingly there seemed a Premier League of big companies and a Championship group, often situated in the smaller cities or towns, whose existence was precarious: during the 1990s the Salisbury Playhouse and the Everyman Cheltenham both faced temporary closure and the Redgrave, Farnham ceased trading. But there were bright spots around the country as a whole. One of the brightest was Dundee where Hamish Glen, backed by a National Lottery grant, bucked the national trend in 1999 by establishing a 14-strong ensemble in the European manner: Scotland also produced one of the best young playwrights of the decade in the prolific David Greig. Ian McKellen did the state some service by forsaking London and heading a company at the West Yorkshire Playhouse in a three-play season comprising *The Seagull*, *The Tempest* and *Present Laughter*. The Manchester Royal Exchange, after taking the full blast of an IRA bombing attack in the city centre, also defiantly carried on their good work in new premises and there were always good reasons to visit Birmingham, Sheffield, Scarborough or Halifax when Barrie Rutter's Northern Broadsides was at home. If anything struck me about regional theatre it was its capacity for survival in the face of declining subsidy and the lure of a London-based celebrity culture.

You could view British theatre from many different perspectives as we approached a new century. There was a shortage of what David Edgar termed grand narratives, there was far too little attempt to reflect the diversity of the population at large and the exponential leap in funding hoped for from a new Labour government had not materialised. But, in terms of writing, acting and directorial talent, there was still an enormous amount to celebrate. Vladimir Nabokov wrote in 1930 that the coming century's "very designation, a two and three zeros, is so fantastic as to seem absurd."

What had once seemed to Nabokov a fanciful prospect was now about to become a stark reality.

1992

Angels in America by Tony Kushner (UK Premiere) Cottesloe, National Theatre, London: 25 January 1992

Tony Kushner could be accused of un-American activities. In *Angels in America* he has written a big, noisy, public play about the state of the nation; and this is only the first three-and-a-half hour segment of a two-part work. It is far from perfect, but it has a roller-coaster energy that sweeps one along in its wake.

Guilt, I take it, is the theme that plaits together the story's multiple strands. Roy Cohn, Senator McCarthy's former sidekick, may not seem crippled by it except that when, in 1986, he discovers he has Aids, he memorably tells his doctor "Roy is a heterosexual man who fucks with guys." But Joe Pitt, a Cohn protege and a straight-up Mormon with a pill-popping wife, is riddled with guilt on discovering he himself is a closet gay. And Louis Ironson, a word-processing Jewish clerk, is mortified by his own panic-stricken, helpless response to his lover's hospitalisation with Aids.

What Mr Kushner seems to be saying in this hurtling play – subtitled *A Gay Fantasia on National Themes* – is that guilt is part of America's Judaic and Puritan inheritance; and that it has been exacerbated by the society's failure to live up to its Utopian dreams. Indeed, Mr Kushner paints a lurid picture of a country where justice is purchasable, where Cohn and a presidential aide toast the death of liberalism, and where Louis sees everyone as Reagan's children – "selfish and greedy and loveless and blind."

Mr Kushner, who in *A Bright Room Called Day* at the Bush in 1988 equated Thatcher's Britain with Hitler's Germany, is no stranger to exaggeration. But the chief fault of this play is that he seems enthralled by his own virtuosity. Scenes spool on verbosely, particularly those involving Joe's wife, who is driven to Valium by her ecological passion and lack of

marital sex. I also winced at the whimsicality of the episodes where she has
a vision of Antarctica and where a Heavenly messenger arrives to claim Joe's
lover: at these points Kushner seems like a hip J.M. Barrie.

But Kushner's overwhelming virtue is that, unlike most American
dramatists, he is unafraid to link private and public worlds. The scenes
where Louis discovers his lover has Aids are unflinchingly honest; but,
instead of simply wringing our hearts, Mr Kushner develops the point that
society's "bourgeois tolerance" conceals a passionate hatred. Even better, for
my money, is the scene where the power-crazy Cohn denies his homosexuality
to his doctor not so much for fear of social stigma as because gays have zero
clout. Mr Kushner avoids the melodrama inherent in many Aids plays by
constantly relating sex to social attitudes.

You could say he chews off more than he can bite – giving us glimpses of
Mormon morality and the mutual antipathy between many American Blacks
and Jews – but I infinitely prefer a play with too many themes to too few.
And he is beautifully served by Declan Donnellan's direction and Nick
Ormerod's design, which achieve a breathtaking fluidity: scene melts into
scene, the company truck the furniture on and off and the detail feels right,
down to the images of Garbo and Bette Davis that decorate the gay lovers'
bedhead.

Donnellan also has the ability of Bill Bryden to combine ensemble work
with a respect for individual performance. Outstanding here is Henry
Goodman, whose Cohn has a buzz-saw voice, stabbing forefingers and a
close-cut ferocity that suggests power is the most dangerous drug on the
market. But there is also good work from Nick Reding as the shy, closeted
Mormon, Felicity Montagu as his flaky wife, Marcus D'Amico as the guilt-
stricken Louis, and Joseph Mydell as a compassionate Black queen.
Sprawling and over-written as it may be, it is a play of epic energy that gets
American drama not just out of the closet but, thank God, out of the living-
room as well.

Faith Healer by Brian Friel (Revival)
Royal Court, London: 27 January 1992

What is Brian Friel's *Faith Healer*, back at the Royal Court after a gap of 11
years, actually about? Religion? The conflict between fate and faith? Or, as
Fintan O'Toole shrewdly suggests in the programme, some crucial schism
within the Irish psyche? Possibly all of these but, on a second viewing, I was
seized by the idea that it is about the tortured process of creativity itself.

Mr Friel's play is certainly strange, hypnotic and demanding: it consists
of four monologues spoken by three characters. First we hear from Frank
Hardy, the itinerant faith healer who is part-mountebank, part-Messiah
about events leading up to the crucial night in Ballybeg when he tested his
curative powers to the limit. Next comes his wife, Grace, recapping the same

story, including the burial of her still-born child in a lonely Scottish field, from her current vantage point of a Paddington bed-sit. Third on is Teddy, Frank's small-time showbiz promoter and a kind of suburban Danny Rose, who explores his own complex relationship with this miracle-cure roadshow. Finally Frank returns from the grave, as it were, to tell us how on the fatal night in Ballybeg he surrendered his chancy talent to fate.

Formally, the play is taxing but rewarding: each monologue not only gives you a new perspective on past events but shifts the action chronologically forwards. But I suspect the play grips because Mr Friel projects on to the faith healer the writer's own perennial uncertainty about the source of his inspiration. In a pregnant phrase, Grace talks of Frank's "feud between himself and his talent." She also describes his compulsion "to re-create everything around him" by treating the halt and the maimed as fictions. In exploring the tortured character of Frank Hardy, a mix of showman and shaman, Friel is nakedly putting on stage the abiding fear of all creative artists that they will not be able to perform the expected miracle. I am sure it is this element of confession that keeps us in our seats.

Actors also clearly suffer the same doubts about the source and reliability of their magic which may be why, in Joe Dowling's Abbey Theatre production, they respond so warmly to Friel's text. Ron Cook as Teddy, in brown tash and yellow cardigan, brilliantly evokes both the commitment and the sadness of the marginal showbiz figure: a light comes into his eyes as he reminisces about his piping-dog and talking-pigeon acts only to be memorably extinguished as he dwells on his ultimate exclusion from Frank's mystery. Watching Mr Cook, my mind flew back to Olivier's Archie Rice on these boards.

But there is also fine work from Sinead Cusack as Grace, recalling her husband's angst with a loving despair, and from Donal McCann as the square-jawed, slack-tied faith healer who aches to be released from the atrophying terror imposed by his gift. The actors' musical pacing of their monologues, delivered against lightly changing sets by Frank Hallinan Flood, transforms what could be an endurance test into an absorbing theatrical evening.

Moby Dick. Book and Lyrics by Robert Longden, Music by Hereward Kaye and Mr Longden (World Premiere) Piccadilly, London: 19 March 1992

Moby Dick is the latest nail to be driven into the glittering coffin of the West End musical. Lacking logic, style, coherence or sense, it turns Melville's great Dostoyevskyan novel into a campy, vulgar schoolgirl spoof in which lines like "Three years at sea and still no sign of Dick" signal the level of sophistication.

Robert Longden's concept itself poses a problem which his own production never begins to solve. The idea is that we are watching a black-suspendered St Trinian's-style school putting on a home-made version of *Moby Dick* which is a bit like the students of Narkover doing *The Brothers Karamazov*. But the show never makes up its mind whether we are meant to be watching a larky amateur night out or a skilled professional entertainment.

Worse still is the prevailing coarseness of tone. This is, after all, the greatest of American novels in which Ahab is a grand Promethean figure and the white whale symbolises the beauty and terror of the universe. But in this rampantly Philistine cut-up we get endless jokes about dicks, the monomaniac Ahab crying "Obsession is just a perfume" and sex-starved sailors queueing up to enjoy the favours of the cabin-boy, Pip. Not even a belated touch of ludicrous political correctness about Saving The Whale ("When will we ever let our friends of the earth live?" run Mr Longden's lyrics) can prevent the feeling that we are watching a masterpiece being trashed in the spurious name of entertainment. But even on those terms, the show is dire. Without a prior knowledge of the story, the narrative is incomprehensible. And the music by Hereward Kaye and Mr Longden is simply a random assortment of tunes.

Since there are no real characters, one cannot even say the show is particularly well performed. Mr Monopoly as the bosom-twitching headmistress–Ahab figure simply suggests some broad-shouldered, blue-chinned waterfront transvestite. Theresa Kartell as Queequeg displays a nippy pair of pins and Joanne Redman is conspicuous as the spectacled school-swot transformed into Ishmael. But everyone else is subsumed into the air of inane rompery, concluding with a cry "Stuff Art – Let's Dance." As people around me leapt to their feet to acclaim this garbage, I wondered what they would do if confronted by a genuinely spirit-lifting piece of musical theatre by Mozart or Rossini. Presumably, die of shock.

The Rise and Fall of Little Voice by Jim Cartwright (World Premiere) Cottesloe, National Theatre, London: 18 June 1992

Jim Cartwright's new play, *The Rise and Fall of Little Voice,* is his cheeriest yet. It's a Bolton showbiz fairy tale, a back-street Cinderella-story with a built-in kick. You can forgive its stop-go rhythm and its odd, overwrought passages because of its natural warmth and because it affords such generous opportunities to Jane Horrocks and Alison Steadman. Ms Horrocks is the Little Voice of the title: a painfully shy, waif-like agoraphobe with a hidden talent for doing impressions of Garland and Piaf, Cilla and Gracie in the privacy of her bedroom. Ms Steadman meanwhile is her coarse, boozy, widowed mum who is only woken up to her daughter's showbiz potential by her spivvy agent boyfriend.

The play is obviously full of echoes. Pygm*alion*, *A Taste Of Honey*, *Educating Rita* all spring to mind. That matters not a jot: more worrying is the way the story sometimes veers out of control as in a clumsy finale where both the mum and the agent get their come-uppance. But what keeps the play alive is the theatricality of the concept – the dormouse heroine with the freak talent – and the counterpoint between the fairy tale structure and Mr Cartwright's lewd, salty, savoursome language.

Sam Mendes's production needs to be faster and snappier: one scene should dissolve into the next instead of being punctuated by breaks for jazz-drumming. But William Dudley's angled, wallpapered, split-level set is a triumph of bad taste and the two leads are impeccable. Jane Horrocks is like a frail, tiny vessel inhabited by some daemon she doesn't begin to understand: when she turns into Bassey warbling Goldfinger or Gracie Fields yodelling Sing As We Go, she doesn't glow with showbiz unction but simply looks like a naive girl frighteningly possessed. Ms Steadman also subtly avoids turning the situation into a reprise of *Life Is Sweet* where Ms Horrocks was again her daughter. This mum is no good-natured scatterbrain but a wicked witch of the North-West without an ounce of maternal feeling. And there is sterling support from Pete Postlethwaite as the small-time agent, Annette Badland as an illiterate neighbour and George Raistrick as a tatty club owner in a dust-mop wig.

1993

Is There Life after Deptford? An evaluation of Christopher Marlowe 400 years after his death.

3 April 1993

Bernard Shaw, who cordially loathed the Elizabethans, once suggested a statue be erected at Deptford to "the benefactor of the human species who exterminated Marlowe." He based his modest proposal on a dislike of the dramatist's "clumsy horseplay and butcherly rant." With the quatercentenary of Marlowe's death looming on May 30 and with Peter Whelan's speculative Marlovian thriller, *The School Of Night*, transferring from Stratford to The Pit, it seems a good time to ask whether Shaw may have had a point.

We all know the correct line on Marlowe: the "morning star" of English drama (according to Tennyson), the fabled creator of the "mighty line," the Renaissance pioneer who explored the potentialities of man's nature and made Shakespeare possible. But I would argue that we now find Marlowe's mysterious death more exciting than his overweening tragedies – and that he was an infinitely greater poet than dramatist. Having lately re-read the first two sestiads of *Hero And Leander* – all Marlowe lived to finish – I would say it is worth most of the plays put together.

What is extraordinary about Marlowe's life is the fierce passion it still arouses. Last year Charles Nicholl wrote a book, *The Reckoning*, which argued that "sweet Kit Marlowe" was "an atheist, a blasphemer, a dissolute homosexual," a practiced poet-spy who kept sinister company, who possessed an almost pathologically violent nature, and whose death in a tavern fight was connected with political rivalry. But I have just received a spirited, detailed and scholarly 35-page riposte, written by A.D. Wraight for The Marlowe Society, which goes for Nicholl's jugular. Among other things, Wraight suggests Marlowe was not just a loyal servant of the state who gleaned vital information about the Catholic plotters in Rheims, but also "the epitome of Renaissance man who was reaching out to embrace scientific knowledge" and "a lamb led to the slaughter at Deptford."

Wraight may have a point. But methinks he doth protest too much when he describes Marlowe as someone "who hated homosexuality but had compassion for the person who was thus enslaved." This of the man who, in *Edward II*, gave us the first sympathetic portrait of a gay hero (confronted by Gaveston, Edward "smiles in his face and whispers in his ears") in English drama? The man who in *Dido, Queen Of Carthage*, shows Jupiter fumbling with Ganymede, "that female wanton boy"? The man who, in *Hero And Leander*, shows lascivious Neptune stealing kisses from the Hellespont-swimming hero and prying upon "his breast, his thighs and every limb"? You can't just put that down to the filthy gods and goddesses. Marlowe clearly gets a kick out of describing the blatant sex appeal of androgynous boys.

I am not qualified to arbitrate in the Nicholl vs Wraight argument: except to say that I find the image of the gay, tobacco-smoking, atheist spy more intriguing – and more consonant with the plays – than that of the straight, pacific, anti-Catholic monarchist who might have made an ideal head of school at King's Canterbury. What is clear is that there is something magnificently fishy about Marlowe's death in the course of an eight-hour tavern meeting with two espionage agents and a known con man, Ingram Frizer, who was speedily pardoned for the murder. Part of a blitz against free thinkers? A political plot? A le Carre-like dead man switch, as Peter Whelan ingeniously suggests? It remains one of the great unsolved mysteries.

I wish I could get as excited by Marlowe's major plays, all revived by the RSC in the past five years. To be fair, Marlowe escaped from the rigidities of neo-classicism, exploited what George Steiner called "the licentious geography of the Elizabethan theatre" and created grandiose star roles. But *Tamburlaine* is a gloatingly sadistic picture of, in the words of C.S. Lewis, Giant the Jack killer, *Dr Faustus* is a bathetic valley situated between twin poetic peaks and *Edward II*, though sexually pioneering, lacks *Richard II's* intricate political complexity. Oddly, Marlowe's best play is the one that, theoretically, seems least defensible: *The Jew Of Malta*. T.S. Eliot's famous reference to its "savage, comic humour" has been triumphantly vindicated in productions by Clifford Williams and Barry Kyle: even the lurking anti-Semitism pales before Marlowe's exuberantly farcical picture of a world ruled by Machiavellian policy and naked expediency.

But, in the final analysis, I would classify Marlowe as a major poet but a minor dramatist (even Kyd had a better sense of structure). Technically, his one real achievement, as M.R. Ridley pointed out many years ago, was to give a new freedom and flexibility to the grinding monotony of *Gorboduc*-style English blank verse. The point was not that he created a regular, five-stress iambic line, but that he didn't: that he offered infinite variations on the norm. Ridley quotes one of his most famous lines – "See, see where Christ's blood streams in the firmament" – with its five heavy stresses in the first six syllables, as conclusive proof of his liberating nonconformity.

For the real evidence of his genius, however, read *Hero And Leander*. It switches, easily and blithely, as J.B. Steane noted, from heroic and romantic to mock heroic and burlesque. It also makes brilliant use of couplets, both to satirise the nice delays of virginal teasing and to celebrate the giddy raptures of sexual fulfilment. You won't find a much better description of night-before coquetry than:

> She, with a kind of
> granting, put him by it,
> And ever, as he thought
> himself most nigh it,
> Like to the tree of Tantalus she fled,
> And, seeming lavish, sav'd her maidenhead.

Nor will you find many better accounts of morning-after skittishness than:

> But as her naked feet were whipping out,
> He on the sudden cling'd her so about,
> That mermaid-like unto the floor she slid,
> One half appeared, the other half was hid.

Playful, grave, ironic and impassioned, it is one of the best poems about sex in the language. It also suggests that Marlowe's genius was for the lyric-satiric rather than the strenuous demands of dramatic storytelling and characterisation. For dedicated Marlovians, as the quatercentenary of his death approaches, it offers the best possible defence against Shaw's brutal, intemperate iconoclasm.

In retrospect, I feel I was unduly harsh on Marlowe as a dramatist. Edward II is a more subtle play than I make it sound. What is fascinating is that Edward's barons have little problem with his homosexuality: as one of them points out, Alexander, Hercules, Achilles and Socrates all sported with their "minions." What they really object to is that Edward's chosen favourite, Gaveston, is "basely born." In short, this is a play about class as much as sex. It also plays well in the theatre. Over the years I've seen Edward performed by Derek Jacobi, Ian McKellen, Simon Russell Beale and John Heffernan with great skill. What they all brought out – and this is a theme I constantly return to in my reviews – is the essential solitude of monarchy.

Arcadia by Tom Stoppard (World Premiere) Lyttelton, National Theatre, London: 14 April 1993

Tom Stoppard's new play is as intricate, elaborate and allusive as anything he has yet written. It deals, amongst a hundred other things, with determinism and free will, classicism and romanticism, historical reality and academic deduction. But it is also unusually moving in its demonstration of the way genuine discoveries outlive the death of their inventors.

Stoppard makes his point by setting the action in the large room of a Derbyshire country house in two different periods: 1809 and the present day. In the earlier period we see a brilliant young girl, Thomasina, and her tutor, Septimus, and hear of off-stage scandals involving the multiple seductions of a minor versifier's wife. In the present we watch a battle of wits between Hannah, a born classicist studying the history of the house's garden, and Bernard Nightingale, a romantic hare-brained don convinced that Lord Byron was present in 1809, killed the cuckolded poet in a duel and fled the country. At first the two worlds collide; gradually they merge, as in a dream.

As in *Travesties*, Stoppard gets a lot of fun out of showing how we wantonly misconstrue the past. In 1809, for instance, the sparky Thomasina arbitrarily adds a hermitage to the picturesque development plans for her mother's garden; 180 years later the rational Hannah uses this to construct a whole theory about a hermit who expressed "the genius of the place." Again, in 1809 we see the tutor writing an ironic inscription in the poet's rotten volume of verses; for the deluded Nightingale, this becomes proof conclusive of a sinister Byronic intrigue.

All this is good sport. But the play really takes off when Stoppard's ideas and emotions seamlessly coincide. The real heart of the play lies in an exchange between Thomasina and her tutor. She tearfully laments the loss of world civilisation experienced with the burning of the Alexandria library. But her tutor argues that mankind constantly renews itself and that ideas never die. "Mathematical discoveries glimpsed and lost to view," he cries, "will have their time again." And that is precisely what the play proves as we see Thomasina's revolutionary revision of the Newtonian universe outlasting her own tragically foreshortened life.

Many of Stoppard's previous plays, such as *The Real Thing*, have had a strong emotional undercurrent. But here his ideas and his sympathies work in total harness and give the play a strong pulse of feeling. Even the battle between a deterministic and totally random universe takes on an emotional edge. When Valentine, the present-day son of the house and a mathematical wizard, claims that "the unpredictable and the predetermined unfold together to make everything the way it is," he goes on to add that this collusion of disorder and order makes him violently happy. In the past,

Stoppard's plays have shown a kind of panic at the prospect of living in an uncertain world; here he accepts things as they are with a stoical grace.

The danger is that one makes the play sound heavy weather. But, although it is difficult on one viewing to pick up all the play's ideas, Stoppard theatricalises his themes. As always he is liberal with his jokes. Required to give satisfaction for seducing the minor poet's wife, the young tutor cries: "Mrs Chater demanded satisfaction and now you are demanding satisfaction. I cannot spend my time, day and night, satisfying the Chater family." But, beyond the jokes, Stoppard makes something delicately moving out of the way past and present merge as if to cheat the logic of time.

Trevor Nunn's production, set in an elegantly curved room designed by Mark Thompson and backed by Sondheim-ish piano chords by Jeremy Sams, does everything possible to up the emotional ante. And there are good performances in the present tense from Bill Nighy as the quivering, foolish Nightingale and from Felicity Kendal as the would-be-rational, hard-headed Hannah and, in the past, from Rufus Sewell as the Byronic tutor, Emma Fielding as his genius-protege and Harriet Walter as her amorous, Wildean mother. Just occasionally the play lapses into whimsy. But, on the whole, it is a significant breakthrough that shows Stoppard working with tongue in cheek and hand on heart at the same time.

Moonlight by Harold Pinter (World Premiere) Almeida, London: 9 September 1993

Harold Pinter's new play will come as a shock to those who have lately pigeonholed him as a writer of bruising polemic. It emerges, in David Leveaux's fine production as a deeply poignant, raffishly comic, emotion-charged study of the gulf between parents and children and the anguish of approaching death. In its 75 minutes it carries echoes of earlier Pinter plays, including *The Homecoming* and *No Man's Land*, but what stirs the heart is the direct confrontation with mortality.

On stage level we see two adjacent bedrooms. In one room lies Andy: a coarse, brutal former civil servant raging against the dying light. He pines for his absent sons, bullies his wife Bel and is visited by memories of past liaisons: his equivocal friendship with Ralph, an amateur soccer referee, and his lust for Ralph's wife, Maria, with whom he and Bel both had affairs. In another bedroom we see Andy's two estranged sons, Jake and Fred: out-of-work fantasists indulging in parodic, competitive business games but finally denying the call to their father's side. Meanwhile in the space above we glimpse the wraith-like figure of Andy's daughter, Bridget (possibly dead?), who embodies the filial affection for which he desperately yearns.

Beckett, the poet of terminal stages, inevitably comes to mind. What instantly moves one is Pinter's image of a man confronting death in a spirit of rage and uncertainty. Andy's public self has clearly been one of pristine order: in death he lacks the consolation of family or sustaining belief. This, implies Pinter, is the dilemma of modern man. "Rationality," announces Andy, "went down the drain years ago." Or, as his chum Ralph puts it, thinking is no answer to life's meaning. This is Pinter as we've never quite seen him before: nakedly emotional in his presentation of this bedridden, suburban Lear. There is that hunger for an ascertainable past, the sense that love and friendship are subject to betrayal, the feeling that family life is a brutal battleground of sibling rivalry and paternal bullying. But what makes this Pinter's most moving work is the gulf between parents and children.

Ian Holm, returning to the stage after a long absence, gives a superb performance as Andy that reinforces Pinter's emotional impact. Tetchy, ferocious, bullet-headed; he asks with scorching rage, if death is no more than pitch blackness: "What would have been the point of going through all those enervating charades in the first place?" Yet the wonder of this performance is Holm's buried sense of longing for his absent children. I have seen Lears that have moved me less.

Leveaux's production also combines the concrete and the mysterious: the classic Pinter mix. Anna Massey's enigmatic Bel regards her domineering spouse with patient tolerance yet there is no mistaking her hollow-eyed despair when her sons reject her on the phone. Douglas Hodge and Michael Sheen as the two sons, pass the time in name-brandishing games yet somehow suggest, by replicating their father's behaviour pattern, they are still tied to him.

The play is much funnier than I have probably suggested. The piss-taking Pinter humour and the undercutting of verbal pretence are all there. But what makes this an extraordinary play is that Pinter both corrals his familiar themes – the subjectiveness of memory, the unknowability of one's lifelong partner, the gap between the certain present and the uncertain past – and extends his territory. He shows, with unflinching candour, that in an age shorn of systems and beliefs we face "death's dateless night" in a state of mortal terror.

Cabaret. Book by Joe Masteroff, Lyrics by Fred Ebb, Music by John Kander Donmar Warehouse, London: 11 December 1993

Sam Mendes's production of *Cabaret* is the first version I've seen that makes total sense. Even in the Bob Fosse movie you wondered why Liza Minnelli, with that paint-singeing voice and towering presence, wasn't playing the Palace rather than a seedy Berlin niterie. And, where most productions secretly luxuriate in decadence, Mendes memorably exposes its skin-crawling corruption.

We, the audience, sit at cafe-tables, as if customers at the Kit Kat Club; and the floor-show becomes the prism through which we see the characters' lives. Consequently Alan Cumming's excellent Emcee, with rosebud lips and patent-leather hair curling round his ears like quotation marks, is much more than a cabaret host. He pops up in the lodging house scenes like an epicene Puck and comes to embody the spirit of the times: a shape-shifting chameleon who is, at different moments, a satirist of Nazism, its seeming apologist and finally its concentration-camp victim.

What Mendes has done, in short, is to play up the politics in Joe Masteroff's book, Fred Ebb's lyrics and John Kander's durable score. In the past, the show has often seemed like a nostalgic hymn to Berlin hedonism; but emphatically not here. Jane Horrocks is spot-on as Sally Bowles, playing her not as a latent superstar but as a politically naive "gel" from the English shires, who learns fatally late that the Berlin party is over. Thus she renders the title number, devastatingly, not as a triumphal showbiz invocation but as a piece of Brechtian irony: you notice lines you'd never heard before – "Start by admitting the cradle's a tomb" – and reflect that the number coincides dramatically with Sally's aborting of her child.

This is a de-romanticised *Cabaret* that implies late-Weimar decadence was the soil in which Nazism flourished: I was reminded of Luigi Barzini's graphic vision in *The Europeans* of a Berlin full of "listless, apathetic customers titillated and tempted by an outlandish array of horrifying variations." Accordingly Sue Blane's set and costumes – with the chorus girls' black stockings peppered with tiny holes – bring out the tat rather than the sexiness of the Kit Kat Club. But the world of countervailing decency is strongly represented by Adam Godley as the innocent, sexually equivocal writer who acquires moral commitment, and by Sara Kestelman as his solitary landlady and George Raistrick as her shy Jewish wooer. Most of us, if we're honest, go to musicals for escape. But the great thing about Mendes's *Cabaret* – a worthy successor to his *Assassins* – is that it reminds us that, in the context of late 1920s Berlin, escapism was itself a political gesture. The moral, one hopes, is not lost on us today.

1994

The Atheist's Tragedy by Cyril Tourneur
Birmingham Rep: 17 February 1994

Birmingham Rep has stolen a march on the rest of British theatre by reviving Cyril Tourneur's *The Atheist's Tragedy* (1611). You could quibble about details of Anthony Clark's erratically brilliant, modern-dress production – only the second this century – but it is still a sumptuous exhumation that sends the mind spinning back to Trevor Nunn's 1960s rediscovery of *The Revenger's Tragedy*.

Like *Hamlet*, the play is a counter-attack on the revenge ethos. In fact, Tourneur's debt to Shakespeare is considerable. He shows the noble Charlemont returning from a spurious military venture, presumed dead, to discover that his uncle, D'Amville, has murdered his father, inherited his fortune and married off his intended bride to his own sickly son. Cue for action, you might think. But the ghost of Charlemont's father repeatedly warns his son to "leave revenge unto the King of kings." And we see how D'Amville eventually destroys himself – striking his brains out with an axe – through his violation of the universe's moral laws.

Una Ellis-Fermor, one of Tourneur's few advocates, wrote that he appears to accept an inherently evil world order: it strikes me the reverse is true. The play starts with D'Amville arguing that there is nothing to separate man and beast and that, therefore, he might as well indulge his appetites: by the end he has been shamed by Charlemont's stoicism into accepting a higher power. And even the rampant nympho Levidulcia, whose vagabond passion motors the play's farcical sub-plot, ends by stabbing herself and proclaiming "the hatefulness of lust." Tourneur may sardonically anatomise evil but his standpoint is that of a Christian moralist.

That is one reason why I question the modern-dress framework: it not only sits ill with a world of ghosts and charnel houses, but even with Tourneur's residual piety. And the use of continuous on-stage piano accompaniment – music by Mark Vibrans – lends a tongue-in-cheek irony to events as if Billy Mayerl were witnessing a gory Jacobean tragedy. But my purist niggles were overcome by the insolent wit and blazing energy of

Clark's production. He turns a periwig maker, joyously named Cataplasma, into a tattoo-covered madam with a dildo-gnawing sidekick, treats Levidulcia's simultaneous seduction of two men as pure Feydeau and, in the tumultuous final scene, has two judges descend god-like from the panels of Patrick Connellan's overhanging set.

Clark also has a cast our national companies might envy. Gerard Murphy plays D'Amville excellently as an unctuous sober-suited hypocrite finally transformed into a mad, flowing-maned penitent. James Simmons as Charlemont and Katharine Rogers as his intended make virtue interesting. And vice is wickedly well represented by Jane Maud as a glittering, black-basqued Levidulcia, and by Jamie Newall as a false-faced Scottish puritan. A forgotten Jacobean treasure has been exhilaratingly restored: one that argues, like Bacon, that in taking revenge a man is but even with his enemy but, in passing it over, he is superior.

Footfalls by Samuel Beckett
Garrick Theatre, London: 16 March 1994

Beckett is not holy writ. Over the years I must have seen a dozen wildly varying versions of *Waiting For Godot*. But, in a short, late play like *Footfalls*, Beckett uses the stage with the absolute precision of a painter expressing meaning through a single dominant image; which is why Deborah Warner's physically restless production at the Garrick is as absurd as would be a version of *Happy Days* in which the embedded Winnie got up and went for an evening stroll.

Beckett's directions are clear and precise. May, a middle-aged woman with dishevelled grey hair, paces up and down a narrow strip of stage communing with her bedridden mother whom we hear but do not see. It is perfectly possible that the mother's voice exists only in May's unconscious. It is equally possible that May is a ghost reliving the pain of existence. But, however you interpret it, the power of this 20-minute piece lies in the irreducible image of a woman confined to a dimly lit space and accompanied by her echoing footfalls.

It seems to me nonsense, therefore, for May to go walkabout as she does at the Garrick. We first see Fiona Shaw shuffling across the stage in torn, maroon dress, bedraggled, fawn stockings and sandals. She then pops up on a rostrum at the front of the dress circle – the voice of Susan Engel as her mother emanates from the rear – where she precariously paces, clutching the overhanging masonry each time she turns. And for the sequel, in which May recounts the story of Mrs Winter and her daughter Amy which cyclically repeats her own tragedy, Shaw is once more back on stage.

What you lose by all this mobility are the very things that give the play its haunting power. The sense of a woman doomed for all eternity to filial servitude. The idea that May, who has "not been out since girlhood," is the immured victim of her own compulsion. The production even sacrifices Beckett's precise sound score. He insists there must be a clearly audible rhythmic pad: not for any pedantic reason but because May, as a child, rejected the deep-pile carpet on the grounds that "I must hear the feet, however faint they fall." But fiddling around with Beckett is akin to playing the wrong notes in a Beethoven sonata.

I presume the intention is to demystify the piece and to particularise the agony. Fiona Shaw naturally gives May an Irish accent, convulsively clutches and hitches up her dress, claws the air with talon-like fingers when she describes the light as "a faint tangle of pale grey tatters." She squeezes the emotion out of every last phrase. But this is not O'Casey or Synge. It is not the story of one doomed Irish daughter but a timeless image of human suffering. And the meaning lies in the music: in the careful balancing of one phrase with another.

Doing a short Beckett in the West End at reduced prices (£4 for 20 minutes) seems like a brave experiment. But this production will disappoint anyone who remembers the eerie grandeur of the Royal Court original with Billie Whitelaw and will probably puzzle anyone new to the play. The blunt fact is Beckett knew precisely the effect he was after: watching this attempt at roving realism is a bit like seeing someone doodling on a Rembrandt.

This review generated a heated and lively correspondence. Some of it was based on a report, which turned out to be untrue, that the Beckett Estate intended to ban Deborah Warner for life from staging the author's plays. What did happen was that the rights for the production to play in Paris were withdrawn. Edward Beckett, the Estate's executor, wrote to The Guardian *defending that decision and saying that, just as the various recordings of Beethoven's late string quartets are all "based on the same notes, tonalities, dynamic and tempo markings, we feel justified in asking the same measure of respect for Samuel Beckett's plays." The publisher John Calder and the designer Jocelyn Herbert were amongst those who came out in support of the Estate but Fiona Shaw wrote that she had watched the debate with growing rage. Her letter concluded: "By changing the play's spatial relationship, she [Deborah Warner] released a different aesthetic which allows the play to be enjoyed at the heart of experiment where Beckett flourished rather than being banished to the edges of academia and the world of imitative productions which have sadly lessened the impact of the original." I myself argued in a follow-up piece that, while Beckett's earlier work allows for endless reinterpretation, much of his later work "is too unyielding, too fixed in its theatrical demands, to achieve the malleability of a classic." But the debate about the scope for directorial intervention is a healthy one and continues to this day.*

John Gielgud was born on 14 April 1904. This is a celebration of his 90th birthday.

25 March 1994

A new Gielgud story is always a delight; and Peter Shaffer in his recent inaugural lecture as Oxford's Visiting Professor of Contemporary Theatre came up with a treat. As an unknown writer back in 1958, Shaffer was understandably thrilled to discover from H.M. Tennent that his first play, *Five Finger Exercise*, was to be directed by John Gielgud. That delight, however, began to wane when, in the first week of blocking, the famously restless, mind-changing Gielgud gave the actors a wide range of complex, stage-crossing manoeuvres. Came the first end-of-week run-through and everyone was rushing around, in Shaffer's words, with "the galvanic urgency of a circus troupe on cocaine." At the end of the first act, an anguished tenor cry arose from Gielgud in the stalls: "What on earth are you all doing? This is a nightmare." "We're doing exactly what you told us," the actors replied. "You shouldn't have listened to me," said Gielgud. "You know I can't direct."

Needless to say, the production went on to be a flawless, long-running triumph. But it's a good story that helps to explain why Gielgud is easily the most loved and cherished figure in the British theatre. The story reveals his humility, self-deprecating humour and a quicksilver quality that is not merely the source of a thousand gaffes but also a vital clue to his acting. Peter Brook, who first directed him at Stratford in 1950, once perceptively wrote: "Everything in him is moving all the time at lightning speed – a stream of consciousness flows from him without pause; his flickering, darting tongue reflects everything around and inside him: his wit, his joy, his sadness, his appreciation of the tiniest detail of life and work."

That speed, energy and curiosity not only account for his extraordinary longevity but help to define his role in twentieth-century theatre. He is eternally seen as the antithesis to Laurence Olivier: a patrician traditionalist and embodiment of the status quo, in contrast to Olivier the radical experimenter always hungry to ally himself with the new. Tynan, in his early criticism, did a lot to perpetuate the notion of them as aesthetic and spiritual rivals but it has always seemed to me a false distinction. As a Gielgud-watcher for 40 years, I have been constantly struck by his adaptability to change. And Peggy Ashcroft, when I wrote a biography of her, reminded me that it was Gielgud who was the pioneering architect of the company system we take for granted today.

It is true that he was once impetuously dismissive of Brecht and Beckett; that he turned down George Devine's invitation to appear in Beckett's *Endgame* and Osborne's *A Patriot For Me*; that he was shocked by Genet's

Problems only readers have...

LET US KNOW WHAT YOURS IS!

Problem:

Solution:

READERS' PROBLEMS COMPETITION!

Fill the 2 above blanks with your own illustrations.
Tag us on Instagram with #bdloves for a chance
to win **£100** in books.

The Blacks. But this is also a man who appeared in Komisarjevsky's radical Chekhov productions at Barnes in the 1920s, who set up his own West End companies in the 1930s and 1940s, who in his sixties surrendered to the physical demands of Peter Brook's *Oedipus* ("It was rather like being in the army and I dreaded it," he wrote, "but at the same time I knew I wanted to be part of such an experiment"), who has appeared in the plays of Pinter, Bond, Storey and Wood and who regards Alain Resnais's *Providence* as the most exciting film he has ever made. Gielgud has strong familial links with the theatrical past (Ellen Terry was his grandmother's sister): his own mercurial spirit, however, has always been very much in the present.

I first became aware of his reckless audacity when, as a schoolboy, I saw him play King Lear at Stratford in 1955. I'm not sure what I expected from Gielgud other than plangent lyricism. What I saw was a great performance in an astonishingly avant-garde production, co-directed by Gielgud and designed by Isamu Noguchi. The sets were starkly Oriental and the costumes highly symbolic, so that Lear appeared in a gown, as full of holes as a Gruyere cheese, that grew ever more exiguous as he descended into madness. Philistine critics mocked and jeered: I would simply say the production was about 50 years ahead of its time. Any notion I might have had of Gielgud as the remote high-priest of English acting or an ambulatory violincello was instantly scotched.

My admiration for his adventurousness was confirmed a couple of years later when I saw him play Prospero in Peter Brook's production of *The Tempest*. This was no chuntering old schoolmaster four times as old as his brother but a bilious hermit quivering with rage and revenge and lightly clad in a hempen smock revealing a nut-brown torso. Gielgud discovered the essential point: that the drama in the play is internal. And he articulated it perfectly in the speech to Ariel where he achieved a blistering sforzando on "Though with their high wrongs I am struck to th'quick" before descending into pianissimo on "Yet with my nobler reason 'gainst my fury do I take part." This was not Voice Beautiful acting but a brilliant exploration of the psychological tension within the lines.

I am not claiming that every Gielgud performance expanded the frontiers of drama: around this time he could still repair to Noel Coward comedy, such as *Nude With Violin*, where he would appear like an exquisitely furled umbrella. I am simply suggesting that Gielgud has always been much more than the elegant figurehead of English acting: underneath the temperamental fastidiousness, there has long lain a questing and flexible spirit capable of rising to – and seeking out – new challenges.

Everyone was knocked sideways in 1975 by his spectacular physical transformation in Pinter's *No Man's Land*: the chalk-stripe suit, the sandals and socks, the incipient beer-belly, the drawling Bohemian raffishness. It was an astonishing performance. But look at photos of Gielgud's Trofimov in *The Cherry Orchard* exactly 50 years earlier and you discover an almost unrecognisable figure with bleary eyes, steel glasses and pretentious beard. He describes in *Early Stages* how he looked in the mirror and felt he knew exactly how this man would speak and move and behave. And, just as in the Pinter, he seems to have surrendered to the transubstantiation of acting.

But the quality of adaptability that has sustained Gielgud through the decades also applies to his voice. Every possible musical analogy has been used to describe it, of which Alec Guinness's "a silver trumpet muffled in silk" is easily the most eloquent. But the late Ivor Brown got it right when he wrote: "He has cultivated that piece of luck in his larynx with unsparing diligence." At his best, he does not simply chant or sing the verse: he uses it as a precise expression of meaning. Indeed I once heard Richard Bebb on Radio 3 comparing various Gielgud recordings of Richard II over the years and it was fascinating to note how he gradually stripped away the florid excrescences of his youth to achieve a mature hairline precision: acting, as Edith Evans once said, is about cutting away the dead wood.

What is also striking, if you listen to the record of his famous solo Shakespeare show, *The Ages Of Man*, is how he gives the verse an extraordinary physicality. In the great Richard II speech of renunciation you actually get the sense of glass being shattered into a thousand fragments on the mirror – hurling line "As brittle as the glory . . . IS THE FACE" – with a slight caesura before the final cry of destructive despair. When, as Mercutio, he imagines Queen Mab invading a soldier's dreams of "breaches, ambuscadoes, Spanish blades" and drumming in his ears, he vocally reproduces the rattling, vibrating timbre of beaten percussion. And that marvellous sonnet beginning "My mistress's eyes are nothing like the sun" is a masterpiece of wit and irony, with the voice assuming a jocular, leaden emphasis on "My mistress when she walks treads on the ground," conjuring up an image of Rubens-esque substance. That came to mind recently when I watched a physical-theatre group attempting to interpret the same sonnet with maximum blood, sweat and contortion: Gielgud achieved ten times the effect with the use of voice and intelligence alone.

Of course, some parts have always lain outside his range simply because imaginative control cannot make up for physical limitations: as James Agate always used to say: "In acting the envelope is three-quarters of the communication." No amount of burnt cork and vocal richness could persuade me he was one of nature's Othellos and, except on record, one cannot easily imagine him as Hotspur or Antony. What puzzles me, however, in such a rich and full career is that he has almost entirely shunned Ibsen, apart from a brief stab at Oswald in 1928. One would have given a lot to see him as a Machiavellian Bishop Nicholas in *The Pretenders*, a frostily poker-backed Pastor Manders in *Ghosts* or as the guilt-ridden sculptor, Rubeck, in *When We Dead Awaken*, who has destroyed the soul of another to feed his art. Was it just that the chance to play these roles never came up? Or does Sir John, a Chekhovian to his fingertips, have some deep aversion to Ibsen?

But regrets are pointless. What is astonishing is just how much he has achieved. And what, I believe, is still unrecognised is the way the classic seasons he ran at the New Theatre in 1934–35, at the Queen's in 1937–38 and at the Haymarket in 1944–45 paved the way for the work done at Stratford in the 1950s and, ultimately, for the creation of the big national companies. Gielgud, in one sense, was an actor-manager. But he was the least selfish of stars and sought to establish a company of his peers. He famously alternated Romeo and Mercutio with Olivier at the New Theatre in 1935. Peggy Ashcroft was his constant leading lady. And the team of actors he gathered around him – including Michael Redgrave, Harry Andrews, Anthony Quayle and Glen Byam Shaw – became the indispensable pillars of postwar Stratford and, in the case of George Devine, the prime mover behind the Royal Court revolution.

To a young generation, Gielgud is probably best known as a player of stylish cameos in film and television. My contention is that, by fostering the company idea at a time when commercial theatre was utterly star-obsessed, he did more than anyone to change the rules of the game. But if Gielgud is loved, where other actors are admired, it must be for the qualities within the man himself as much as for his contribution to theatrical history. "Acting," as David Hare always says, "is a judgment of character"; and, with the years, Gielgud's own blend of exuberance, soulfulness (possibly inherited from his Slav ancestry on his father's side) and mercurial quick-wittedness seem to have been enhanced rather than diminished. Instead of resting on laurels he has gained new admirers for performances such as his Ryder Senior in *Brideshead Revisited* – "the remorseless tones of false bonhomie masking a chilly indifference," as Derek Granger wrote – or his aristocratic valet in *Arthur* disdainfully crying to Dudley Moore "I suppose I am now expected to wash your dick," or his effete Oxford don in *Inspector Morse*. But the key point, as he approaches 90, is that he is now what he always has been: an artist to his fingertips. Having had a sneak preview of his latest King Lear, which goes out on Radio 3 on April 10, I can safely say that this is not something wistful, embalmed or elegiac but a compelling and urgent study of an imperious tyrant splintering into madness. And that is nothing less than you would expect from Gielgud.

He is not, thank God, some cocooned national treasure but a jobbing actor still experimenting with new readings in one of his greatest roles. Indeed, according to intimate reports, he is anxious to play down his 90th birthday. We, I hope, are entitled to our celebrations. But for John Gielgud, ever ready to catch the next plane to a foreign movie location and probably fretting over the odd blank week in 1995, work is still reassuringly in progress.

The Queen and I by Sue Townsend (World Premiere)/*Road* by Jim Cartwright (Revival) Royal Court, London: 14 June 1994

It was John Osborne who in 1957 famously described the Royal Family as "the gold filling in a mouthful of decay." But the irony of Out of Joint's nifty pairing of Sue Townsend's *The Queen and I* and Jim Cartwright's *Road*, is that even the Windsors are now part of what both authors see as an increasingly lawless, jobless, hopeless society. These are twin conscience-stricken, state-of-the-nation plays that get Max Stafford-Clark's new company off to a buoyant start.

The Queen and I is the jokier of the two. Based on Townsend's bestseller in which the Royal Family is transplanted, in a new republic, to a Leicester council estate, it is rather like an update of Barrie's *The Admirable Crichton*: it deals with the incapacity of the privileged in an alien environment. And it is at its satirical best when the royals are exposed to the same daily humiliations as their former subjects: Princess Di is asked intrusive personal questions by the DSS and the Queen is left tearfully clueless by a Council Tax form.

As Lear says "I have ta'en too little care of this" and Townsend's point is that if only the privileged had any notion of the grisly reality of life in Britain today then change might ensue. Admittedly the inversion-joke runs out of steam in the second act and Townsend leaves you unclear whether she thinks the monarchy should be abolished or drastically altered. But her anger at a Britain of impoverished opportunity comes through and she carefully distinguishes between the various royals. While David Howey's Philip becomes a cantankerous recluse and Doon Mackichan's dim Di pines for her fallen stardom, Pam Ferris's Queen is clearly liberated by her downfall: the moment when, in the course of a drama workshop, she rediscovers herself as a butcher is the highlight of the evening.

But if *The Queen and I* wears its indignation lightly, Cartwright's *Road* confirms its status as one of the best plays of the 1980s: a poetic, if foul-mouthed, evocation of life in a Lancastrian backwater where sex and booze offer the only palliatives to jobless despair. And even though I missed the promenade propinquity of the original production, Max Stafford-Clark's new version underscores the emotional pain: the scene where two bewildered young people – played with quiet intensity by Amelia Bullimore and Pearce Quigley – retire to bed in a suicidal hunger strike is as overwhelmingly moving as ever.

Political theatre, we are constantly told, is dead. These two plays, using the forms of Aristophanic comedy and *Our Town*-like mood piece, remind you it can be rekindled. But, emerging in the interval on Saturday night, it was sadly ironic to find the theatre staff moving a harmless vagrant off the Royal Court's front steps. If you are presenting powerful plays about the plight of the dispossessed, it strikes me as offensive to suggest that compassion stops at your own front door.

Measure For Measure by William Shakespeare Lyric Hammersmith, London: 20 June 1994

Forget Vienna. Declan Donnellan's brilliant Cheek by Jowl production of *Measure For Measure* anchors the play in a specifically English world of sexual guilt, public hypocrisy and punishment-fixation. I would seriously suggest that complimentary tickets be issued to members of the present Cabinet for any night of their choice. Far from narrowing the play down, Donnellan opens it up; and his greatest insight is to realise that the Duke and Angelo, far from being temperamental opposites, are two sides of the same puritan coin. Stephen Boxer plays the former, superbly, as an uptight politician and moral coward who, having presided over 14 years of misrule, leaves it to his deputy to sort out the resulting chaos.

I've also never seen the point so clearly made that the Duke is Angelo's double in his furtive attraction to an Isabella who represents the sexual temptation of corrective chastity. And in the last act, Boxer, in jaunty titfer and camel coat, seems less God's agent than a power-mad fixer pairing off disastrously ill-suited couples in the name of justice and social conformity.

But Donnellan pursues his central idea that politicians who seek to legislate for private morality expose their own internal hypocrisy with rigorous logic. Adam Kotz's Angelo is a sober-suited figure both fascinated and appalled by the itch lurking inside his trousers. And Anastasia Hille plays Isabella marvellously, not as a frigid noviciate but as a passionate woman who nestles in Angelo's arms and who subconsciously equates punishment and sex. The key to this Isabella is not the notorious "more than our brother is our chastity" but the lines where she claims that, were she under sentence of death: "Th'impression of keen whips I'd wear as rubies."

Donnellan and designer Nick Ormerod also create a totally plausible world on stage, one dominated by a central desk, steel chair and an overhanging working light. Only the suspended, implicitly fascist red banner strikes me as gratuitous. But the stage picture is constantly striking so that we are reminded throughout of the imprisoned presence of the doomed Claudio (Danny Sapani) who has to battle against his sister's voluble prayers to plead for his life. There is, in fact, a score of inventive touches, from Malcolm Scates's Elbow misreading his notebook when giving court evidence to an impromptu shriek of "What?" from Marianne Jean-Baptiste's bluesy Mariana when the bed trick is proposed. Veteran Charles Simon, who performed with Frank Benson, intriguingly makes Escalus both a figure of unregenerate humanism and a chain-smoker: clearly some liberties survive even in the world of puritan hypocrisy that Donnellan, staying true to Shakespeare, has so breathtakingly evoked.

Pentecost by David Edgar (World Premiere) The Other Place, Stratford-upon-Avon: 28 October 1994

David Edgar's *Pentecost* is an epic play in a tiny space. It covers a vast array of themes: art history, the refugee crisis, resurgent nationalism, the battle between cultural/linguistic diversity and Eurocentric political ideals. The play eventually buckles under the weight of so much cargo but it is refreshing in these parsimonious times to find a writer taking too much on board rather than too little.

I found the first half entirely gripping. Edgar's setting is an abandoned church near the border of a South-East European country. A hidden fresco is discovered that may be an imitation of Giotto or could be the work of an earlier, unknown genius thereby changing the history of Western art. With great skill Edgar shows how the fresco, re-discovered by a local curator and restored by a British scholar, opens up the divisions within the state and Europe itself: the Orthodox Church, the Catholics, the Ministry of Culture, not to mention art historians and the German–Italian sponsors of the restoration, all have a vested interest in the fresco. It becomes a means of exposing the illusion of the cohesive nation-state.

Edgar has hit on a fascinating dramatic metaphor; and one follows eagerly the conflicting arguments about the fresco's date and authenticity. But in the second half Edgar widens the territory so much as to burst open the dramatic form. An itinerant group of international refugees – led by a Palestinian and including Kurds, Afghans, Sri Lankans, Bosnians and Latvians – take over the church, hold the Western occupants hostage and threaten to set fire to the fresco unless they are granted asylum. At this point Edgar seems to be writing a different play about the refugee crisis, the dangers of an inward-looking Eurocentricity and the elevation of high art above human need. The play eventually returns to its starting point but not without several lurches into melodrama.

Edgar's point seems to be that national identity is itself a myth: as the museum-curator who discovers the fresco puts it, "we are the sum of all the people who invaded us." Given the Babel-like complexity and diversity of Europe, Edgar implies that we should think globally rather than nationally and give basic human imperatives, such as the search for shelter and food, top priority.

It is a powerful argument but it omits certain points such as the danger of multinational companies superseding the idea of the nation-state.

Edgar throws too much into the pot but, at a time when plays are becoming ever narrower in their focus, this is a forgivable fault: it is a big, broad, challenging public work. Michael Attenborough's production also marshals the 20-strong cast with exemplary skill; and there are strongly defined performances from Charles Kay as the drily impassioned British scholar, Jan

Ravens as the local curator, Linal Haft as a sceptical American professor and Katharine Rogers as a vehement Palestinian refugee. Tragical – comical – historical – polemical – political? Edgar's play partakes of all these Polonius-like categories. But, whatever its imperfections, it boldly confronts many of the issues raised by George Steiner in his great Salzburg Festival lecture on Europe last year: above all, the supreme irony that utopian dreams of unity are currently accompanied by the reality of division, fissure and fears of fragmentation.

The life and legacy of playwright John Osborne: born 12 December 1929, died 24 December 1994.

27 December, 1994

One of the most famous stories about John Osborne concerns a meeting with Kenneth Tynan, who had just been appointed Literary Manager of the National Theatre. "Come and join us at the National and make history," said Tynan. "I've already made it," snapped Osborne, turning on his heel. It is perfectly true that if Osborne, who has died aged 65, had written only *Look Back In Anger* his place in the history books would be secure: its premiere at the Royal Court in May 1956 not only put the English Stage Company on the map, but proved to a generation of writers that it was possible to put contemporary Britain on stage. But there was more – much more – to Osborne than that single resonant play.

He was, in my view, a much misunderstood writer. Because of *Look Back In Anger*, he was instantly dubbed an Angry Young Man – a phrase coined by the Royal Court's press officer – and seen as a flame-throwing socialist who eventually turned Right. The truth is that Osborne was a congenital outsider: a truculent individualist with a gift for lacerating invective and with little time for political parties or handed-down truths. I always saw him as a somewhat Byronic figure, viewing the passing world with satirical disdain. He once recorded how one of his wives described him – probably more accurately – as a Welsh Fulham upstart. Either way, he was a compulsive non-joiner whose gift for rhetoric re-charged British drama in the 1950s and 1960s and who ultimately produced two outstanding, self-punishing volumes of autobiography.

As with all writers, his upbringing explains his later attitudes. He was born in Fulham in 1929, the son of an advertising agency copywriter and a barmaid. Describing Christmas get-togethers in *A Better Class Of Person*, he writes that, "What the two families shared was the heart pumped from birth by misgiving. Not a proud misgiving of the spirit but a timid melancholy or dislike of joy, effort or courage." It was a world of lower-middle-class bitterness which Osborne sought to escape, but by which he was always partially claimed.

From the start, he was always a rebel. When a master struck the 16-year-old Osborne at school, he responded by striking back – a gesture for which he was expelled and which suggested his permanent symbol was the untugged forelock. A desultory period as a journalist working for trade papers – *Gas World*, *Nursery World* and *The Miller* – was followed in 1948 by entry into the theatre as assistant stage manager on a 48-week tour of *No Room At The Inn*, and by a long, productive period as a rep actor. He may not have been a brilliant actor – he once described his Hayling Island Hamlet as "a passable impersonation of Claudius after a night's carousing" – but he learned his craft, co-wrote a couple of plays, and married his first wife, Pamela Lane. In a revealing letter about that period, he once wrote to me that he joined his wife in Derby, where she was playing Hester Collyer – a woman almost destroyed by her inability to find an answering passion in her lovers – in Rattigan's *The Deep Blue Sea*. "My notional role in life," said Osborne, "was that of Freddie Page [the object of the heroine's love]. In fact, I was Hester."

It is a revealing remark because it shows Osborne's affection for the older generation of writers – Rattigan especially – whom he was to displace. But it also explains a lot about Osborne's most famous hero: Jimmy Porter in *Look Back In Anger*, which George Devine bravely put on at the Royal Court in 1956. Jimmy is, in some ways, a male Hester: his tragic flaw is that he seeks in others a passionate enthusiasm to match his own. Of course, as memorably incarnated by Kenneth Haigh in Tony Richardson's production, he also became a symbol of angry, alienated modern youth railing at the English class system and the whole gummed-up Establishment. But Jimmy's rage and rhetoric is also part of a quest for what he himself calls "a burning virility of mind and spirit that looks for something as powerful as itself."

However you look at it – as social document or Strindbergian study in self-torment – it remains a great play. It also turned Osborne into an overnight celebrity. The 26-year-old playwright was endlessly interviewed, courted and nibbled at by gossip columnists – one of whom described him, libellously, as "the original teddy-boy."

Amidst all this, he found time to write a second play for the Court, *The Entertainer*, which elicited from Olivier one of his greatest performances as the seedy, third-rate music hall comic, Archie Rice. Those of us lucky enough to have seen it will never forget Olivier's leering, painted public mask or his private howls of self-loathing. What subsequent revivals have shown is that it is also a brutally bitter play about family life: the Rices' endless recriminatory rows must have owed a lot to Osborne's own Fulham origins.

Osborne's life was changed by fame and success. He married Mary Ure. He bought houses in Chelsea and the Kent countryside. He earned a bob or two. But, at heart, he remained a natural dissenter and he soon learned that he had not won the affection either of Fleet Street or the theatre-going public. In 1959, he wrote a musical about gossip columnists, *The World Of Paul Slickey*, which earned vitriolic reviews and which led, on the first night, to Osborne being pursued up Charing Cross Road by parties of irate theatregoers. Osborne's vivid description of the scene in *Almost A Gentleman* suggests he got a high from being so hated.

Through all the private turmoil of the 1960s – in 1963 he married Penelope Gilliatt, and in 1968 Jill Bennett – he continued to write plays and one famously successful, money-spinning film script, *Tom Jones*. But his work was still characterised by unassuaged discontent. In 1961, he wrote a Brechtian chronicle play about the founder of Protestantism, *Luther*, but once again the hero seemed like a projection of Osborne himself. As Tynan shrewdly noted at the time, "Luther in Christendom, like Mr Osborne in the microcosm of the theatre, was a stubborn iconoclast of lowly birth, resentful of authority and blind to compromise."

It was followed in 1964 by an even more remarkable play, *Inadmissible Evidence*, in which Nicol Williamson gave an unforgettable performance as a middle-aged solicitor watching the total disintegration of his life – "a kind of Willy Loman in striped English serge," as Ronald Bryden wrote. But in the hero's blistering rhetoric and punitive self-laceration it was again not difficult to detect something of Osborne's own private rage and sense of being permanently wounded.

But Osborne's biggest play of that period, *A Patriot For Me*, was also one that in 1965 fell foul of the Lord Chamberlain's arbitrary power of censorship. Staged at the Royal Court as a club production for consenting theatregoers, it was a turbulent epic about Alfred Redl, a homosexual spy in the Austro-Hungarian army. It allowed Osborne to write on a big canvas, to pursue the subject of sexual ambiguity – by which he had always been fascinated – and to create one brilliantly theatrical scene in which a group of exquisitely-gowned figures dancing to Mozart turned out, on close inspection, to be men. One of Osborne's richest plays, it had to wait until Ronald Eyre's 1983 Chichester production, with Alan Bates, to achieve the success it deserved.

After the high peak of *A Patriot For Me*, Osborne enjoyed fluctuating fortunes. *The Hotel In Amsterdam* – written in 1968 and scarcely revived since – was an elegant tone-poem about a group of six friends, all fleeing from the influence of a tyrannical film producer. *West Of Suez*, in 1971, was seen by many as the moment when Osborne turned Right. Set in a former British colony, it was widely viewed as a hymn to lost empires: one of the first plays I ever reviewed in these pages, I wrote at the time that it was actually about "the break-up of any civilisation that no longer puts its trust in reason, in respect for other people's values and, above all, in language." It was a view from which I gather Osborne himself did not entirely dissent.

But where Osborne had once been claimed as the spokesman for a generation, he came in later years to be seen as a rancorous theatrical Thersites. *A Sense Of Detachment*, in 1972, with its attack on the corruption of language and the prevalence of pornography, found few supporters. *Watch It Come Down*, staged at the Old Vic in 1976, was an intriguing but intellectually muddled attempt to do a latterday *Heartbreak House*. And *Deja Vu*, a 1992 update on the life and times of Jimmy Porter, while full of vintage Osborne bile, failed to take the West End by storm.

So how important a writer was John Osborne? Without a shadow of doubt, he helped to change the face of postwar British theatre, and nothing can take that away from him. He also wrote at least half-a-dozen plays that will have a claim on posterity. But I suspect he will be remembered as well for his two volumes of autobiography, *A Better Class Of Person* and *Almost A Gentleman*, which reveal him as one of the most incandescent prose writers of his generation. And to those who object to the vicious assault on his former wife, Jill Bennett, I can only quote the remark of a friend who said to me that he must have once loved her a lot to have hated her so much.

As for the man himself, he was a bundle of contradictions. From my slight acquaintanceship, I found he could be as charming and courteous in private as he could be blisteringly rude in print. And in later years, though he achieved domestic happiness with his fifth wife, Helen Dawson, there was something saddening about his alienation from the current theatrical scene. In the course of a very funny letter to me about Terence Rattigan, he reflected on the short period of popularity most dramatists enjoy, and remarked: "I seem to incite only dislike and indifference in whatever I attempt. I never did have much of a following. Now even that remnant is apparently gone. It's a mistake to stick around too long."

But though Osborne fell out of theatrical fashion, the best of his work will survive. He once described his plays as "lessons in feeling." And his unique gift was to create fiercely articulate dramatic heroes who embodied his own wounded and damaged spirit. He was, to the very last, a man with a talent for dissent.

1995

Blasted by Sarah Kane (World Premiere) Royal Court Theatre Upstairs, London: 20 January 1995

Readers of a sensitive nature are warned that the following review may concern words likely to disturb. For, not to beat about the bush, *Blasted* by the 23-year-old Sarah Kane contains scenes of masturbation, fellatio, frottage, micturition, defecation – ah, those old familiar faeces! – homosexual rape, eye-gouging and cannibalism. Far from crying, like the man in front of me: "Bring back the censor," I was simply left wondering how such naive tosh managed to scrape past the Court's normally judicious play-selection committee.

Kane starts in relatively low key. A dying, racist, middle-aged tabloid hack has brought a speech-impaired, seemingly epileptic 21-year-old girl back to his Leeds hotel room for purposes of seduction; and, at first, there is a certain tension as her wariness confronts his intransigence. But absurdity sets in with the revelation that the gun-toting hack is some kind of secret government agent; and it blossoms into full maturity when a pathologically violent, sexually undiscriminating Tommy, a refugee from the civil war raging on the streets, bursts in through the door. I was intrigued to notice, however, that public disorder had not interfered either with room service or with soccer matches at Elland Road. Clearly they're a tough lot in Leeds.

The reason the play falls apart is that there is no sense of external reality – who exactly is meant to be fighting whom out on the streets? – and that Kane's moral disgust at modern civilisation runs up against the law of diminishing returns: by the time the blinded, hungry hack is reduced to digging up the floorboards to devour a dead baby (I did warn you) we have supped so full with horrors that we are reduced to bombed out indifference. James Macdonald directs this farrago with surprising restraint and Pip Donaghy, Kate Ashfield and Dermot Kerrigan are the actors unluckily involved. But after a run of outstanding plays at the Theatre Upstairs based on exact social observation, the good fairies suddenly seem to have deserted this cradle of new drama.

Letters to the Editor about *Blasted*.

From Martin Crimp, Paul Godfrey, Meredith Oakes, Gregory Motton
23 January 1995

Michael Billington's insulting dismissal of Sarah Kane's play, *Blasted* as "naive tosh" (January 20) is extraordinary. His implicit approval only of work restricted to "exact social observation" is an aesthetic which denies a writer the right to create his or her own imaginative world (it also seems to exclude most dramatic works of the last two-and-a-half millennia).

The power of Ms Kane's play lies precisely in the fact that she dares to range beyond personal experience and bring the wars that rage at such a convenient distance from this island right into its heart. She does so not as the bearer of a naive political message, but to precipitate the real theme of her play: that of human relationships in extremis. These she illuminates with wit and an attention to detail which combines pitiless observation with compassionate humanity – qualities emphasised by the fearless acting of this production. Is it perhaps that the savage nature of Ms Kane's play is rare in English art and your critic feels threatened by the unfamiliar? Would he dismiss the writings of Rimbaud, Jarry and Artaud or Goya's images of The Atrocities of War and Los Caprichos in the same way? Mr Billington claims "indifference" towards this play. Why then is his article so condescending? Who is being "naive" here? Who is writing the "tosh"?

From the Reverend Bob Vernon
23 January 1995

Michael Billington is reduced to "bombed out indifference" by Sarah Kane's play. He complains about having to sup full of horror, depraved sex, cannibalism, psychopathology, unexplained civil violence and absurd characterisation. I have not seen the play, but I am inclined to rejoice that a 23-year-old has not been bombed into indifference by the horrors of our time, but taken the time and care to craft her response. Mr Billington writes that "the reason the play falls apart is that there is no sense of external reality – who exactly is meant to be fighting whom out on the streets?" That's a good question. My local shopping centre looks like Grozny, only two out of two dozen shops remain. The rest are reduced to shattered glass and wrecked steel shutters. Some housing estates in our city look like war zones too, burnt out houses, glass- and rubbish-littered streets, dazed, tranquillised people trying to survive. With so many casualties who is fighting whom out there? I don't know either.

Behind the multi-locked doors, we are told, there is depraved sexuality. On the streets, we are told, there are unresolved cases of mental illness. The image of a "blind, hungry hack digging up the floorboards to devour a dead baby" is dreadful, but it rings deep, sad bells.

Sarah's generation has spent much time being told by the Government that everything in our country has improved. Sarah must be living in the best of all possible worlds; until she looks out of her window or turns on her television and sees the ugly, absurd, horrific truths. I don't know what Mr Billington sees out of his window. Maybe shutters have come down. But bombed out indifference will not help. Of course there is joy and beauty, too, in most of our lives, so the picture Sarah has painted cannot be all of the truth (nor is *Coriolanus*), but it sounds as if *Blasted* reflects some of the truth, and whether Sarah was won or lost in artistic or critical terms, I applaud her courage, and that of the Royal Court, in bringing it to our stage.

From David Greig
24 January 1995

I wonder what nerve Sarah Kane must have touched to have found the big guns of the British critical establishment ranged against her so quickly, so violently and so hysterically. Young writers, young women writers in particular, must be used to patronising notices; used to being damned with faint praise. However, no recent play, to my knowledge, has been treated with such a barrage of fear and loathing. Could it be that she is a young woman portraying critically a middle-aged male journalist?

What disappoints me most, however, is to find *The Guardian* reduced to the same prurient level as the tabloids themselves, who have already begun harassing this young author. Michael Billington (January 20), normally a measured, intelligent, critic, has produced a review of astonishingly short-sighted banality.

To describe the play as, "naive tosh," is wrong. Anyone who read Maggie O'Kane's *Guardian* reports from Bosnia knows that such atrocities as Kane describes so powerfully, actually do happen, are happening, under the noses of the same papers which have spewed out their loathing for a mere writer. The review, in mock horror, then lists the play's "outrages" with a barely disguised, slavering glee.

Billington, in his dull, grinding search for "theatre based on exact social observation" criticised the play on the grounds that it contains "no sense of external reality." What about Becket, Artaud, Sartre, Heiner Muller, Howard Barker, Genet, almost all Greek tragedy, come to think of it *A Winter's Tale* contains very little "sense of external reality." An entire, important strand of theatrical writing concerns itself with internal reality, psychological reality.

Drama deals as much in exploring the "reality" of the human psyche through violent or sexual imagery, absurdity and ambiguity as it does in the kind of naturalistic theatre of statistics which one can only assume Billington would prefer. *Blasted* is an extraordinary play. If it weren't it wouldn't have roused so much fearful hatred from the critical establishment. It is a harrowing, difficult and ultimately truthful exploration of abuse. The abuse of women by men, the abuse of the simple by the cynical, the abuse of civilians by soldiers, the abuse of soldiers by war and the abuse of truth by journalists. A sideline in the play shows the journalist ignoring the violence under his nose in favour of prurient "kinky" rape stories. Ironically, in the journalists' treatment of Sarah Kane, her analysis is borne out. On a day when a 15-year-old girl was raped and murdered, both the tabloids and *The Guardian* felt it necessary to devote more space to attacking a young writer who has done nothing more than represent the abuse she sees in the world around her. *Blasted* will last. It's a very good play indeed and after the hysteria dies down it remains to be read and performed for years to come.

From Caryl Churchill
25 January 1995

I was shocked not when I saw *Blasted* but when I was told Michael Billington had said on *Kaleidoscope* that the Royal Court was jeopardising its funding with this production. We all know that funding puts theatre in danger of censorship but I'd have expected him to fight this rather than condone it.

I'm not complaining about his dislike of the play. We're all used to having different opinions from critics. But there's been such a ridiculous outcry about *Blasted* that I'd like to say how much I admire it. Far from its being a mindless string of violent events, as the press has suggested, I found it a coherent story, starting from the social observation Billington requires but able to move into the surreal to show connections between local, domestic violence and the atrocities of war. I find it hard to see why people are so shocked by these things being in a play rather than by the things themselves.

How do we write about a world where all this happens? Sarah Kane has taken it on with a sharp ear for dialogue and a bold imagination for action. Though violent things happen, I found it rather a tender play. Certainly it's a strength not a weakness in the Royal Court season.

Caryl Churchill.

With all due deference to Caryl Churchill, I don't ever recall suggesting on the radio that the Royal Court was jeopardising its funding in presenting Blasted. *My initial reaction to the play was obtuse but I'm not that censorious. It's worth recording that at a public forum some years later in Italy I expressed profound regrets about my review of the play. James Macdonald, who was also on the panel, urged me to stop beating myself up about my review. "I directed the play," said James, "and I got it wrong." His point was that, in his first production, he had failed to intimate in the first half of the play the civil war that was to engulf the characters in the second half. It was a strikingly honest admission. He also rectified the fault in his later, far superior revival of the play at the Royal Court Downstairs. The most striking production of the play I've ever seen, by the Berlin Schaubühne, also made it abundantly clear that the initial, sexually fraught encounter between the young girl and the dying journalist took place against a background of sustained aerial bombardment. I was hopelessly wrong about Blasted on a first viewing. All I can say is that I was not entirely alone.*

Dealer's Choice by Patrick Marber (World Premiere)
Cottesloe, National Theatre, London: 11 February 1995

Poker, said David Mamet, is all about character; which is precisely what makes it a perfect dramatic metaphor. It also explains why Patrick Marber's *Dealer's Choice* – an outstandingly good first play – is not just about the game itself but also about masculine rituals, the nature of obsession and father–son relationships.

It is set in a swank restaurant whose owner, Stephen, organises a weekly poker school involving the staff and his scapegrace son, Carl. With the deft wit of a real technician, Marber sets up the relationships amongst the employees: the divorced chef, Sweeney, torn between the game and the need to see his five-year-old daughter; the flash waiter, Frankie, saving up enough dough to become a Las Vegas gambler; and the born loser, Mugsy, whose hilarious, much-mocked dream is to set up a restaurant in a toilet in the Mile End Road.

Given Marber's background in comedy, it is no surprise that he spins a lot of laughs out of these characters: at one point Mugsy earnestly enquires of a colleague who has gone off to cope with a Boltonian bereavement "Was there much history of death in the family?" But the core of the play lies in the anguished father–son relationship between Stephen and Carl. The former is a strict disciplinarian: the latter is a feckless layabout who owes four grand to a pro poker player, Ash, whom he introduces into the Sunday-night school in the hope that he can clean up with these amateurs.

As movies like *The Cincinatti Kid* long ago realised, any gambling story has a built-in suspense. But Marber's great gift is to use poker not as an end in itself but as a means of exploring character. On a general level, he subtly implies that these are all men who find it difficult to relate to women and who use poker as a sexual substitute.

More particularly, he explores the nature of compulsion and suggests it is nothing to do with winning or losing: it gradually emerges that the most damaged member of the group is the strictest and most apparently controlled, who uses this Sabbath ritual to fill up the cavernous emptiness in his life.

What is astonishing in a young, tyro playwright is the absolute control of form: in the pacing of the story and the playing off of one character against another, Marber scarcely puts a foot wrong. He also directs his own work with total assurance – Bunny Christie's set intelligently uses a revolve in the second act so we see the rotating players in turn – and gets exemplary performances from his actors. Nicholas Day as Stephen exhibits a bourgeois cool that is the supreme bluff, Nigel Lindsay's spaniel-like eagerness as Mugsy is offset by Phil Daniels's rakish charm as Frankie and Tom Georgeson has the sharp watchfulness of the born pro who understands Confucius's point that man cannot hide himself. It is a hugely promising debut in which Marber throughout plays his own hand with consummate dramatic skill.

Skylight by David Hare (World Premiere) Cottesloe, National Theatre, London: 5 May 1995

David Hare once claimed that the question of who sleeps with whom is often of greater dramatic interest than the state of the economy or the decline of the West. But what makes his new play, *Skylight*, such an exhilarating experience is that it unites passion and politics, sexuality and the state of the nation.

At first, it seems to be a small-scale domestic play. Set in a modest flat in north-west London, it consists of a nervous reunion between Kyra, an East Ham teacher, and Tom, a thriving restaurateur. Once they had a six-year-long affair on which Kyra walked out. Now Tom, brooding and guilty after his wife's death of cancer and plagued by a tense relationship with his teenage son, visits Kyra in her lair in an attempt to rekindle past passion.

Hare handles delicately the feints and skirmishes between two people warily circling each other after a three-year gap. But it is in the second act that the play takes wing as the social and political gulf widens to cavernous proportions. Tom, a dynamic 1980s entrepreneur, mocks Kyra for teaching kids at the bottom of the heap. She responds with fury, unleashing a scathing attack on the "right-wing fuckers" who sneer at the teachers, social workers and probation officers who deal with the mess others have created. It is one of Hare's most polemical pieces of writing, but it grows organically out of what has gone before.

I confess I wondered why Kyra had ever fallen for Tom. But Hare, with great skill, shows that you can't legislate for love and that this odd couple are still bound together by a suppressed passion. At the same time, he allows their relationship to become a metaphor for polarised social attitudes. Tom is the kind of Thatcherite man who thinks happiness is something you purchase, as symbolised by the perfect, skylit room he has created for his cancerous wife. Kyra represents the now apparently dated belief that things are worth doing for their own sake regardless of material reward or career progress.

That, however, makes the play sound more loaded than it is. In Richard Eyre's brilliantly tense production you are allowed to see the strengths and weaknesses on both sides. As played by Michael Gambon, who prowls round the stage like a caged bear, Tom is a man of limited vision but sharp intellect: when, for instance, he attacks his wife's proprietary use of the word "spiritual" ("People use it to prove they're sensitive"), or seizes on Kyra's self-punishing desire to live and work on opposite sides of London, he scores direct hits. And Lia Williams, very subtly, makes Kyra a woman of positive convictions and unappeased appetites still tremulously bound to her impossible lover. I wasn't too easy with Hare's typically romantic final flourish involving Tom's son, nicely played by Daniel Betts. But this is still a beautiful piece of writing that deals with the tenacity of love while exposing the awesome divide at the heart of modern Britain.

The Importance Of Being Earnest by Oscar Wilde/*Private Lives* by Noel Coward Old Vic, London/Royal Exchange, Manchester: 10 July 1995

Who said of whom "It is extraordinary that such a posing, artificial old queen should have written one of the greatest comedies in the English language"? The answer, surprisingly, is Noel Coward of Oscar Wilde. And seeing *The Importance Of Being Earnest* and *Private Lives* on successive nights one begins to understand what divides as well as unites these icons of high camp.

Both champion frivolity against false seriousness. Both put style before sincerity. Both mix the artificial and the real. But, if Wilde induces a kind of ecstasy where Coward simply produces pleasure, it is largely because the former seems more open to life. Wilde's masterpiece is, among many other things, a running satire on Victorian society: Coward's play is a perfect theatrical construct but largely unconcerned with anything outside its own goldfish-bowl world.

Terry Hands' hugely enjoyable revival of *The Importance*, fresh from Birmingham Rep, constantly reminds you of Wilde's social satire. Philip Franks's Algernon is a Yellow Book aesthete whose flat is a tribute to chic Orientalism. Roger Allam's excellent Worthing has the priggish insecurity of a man who has invented himself. But the jewel of the production is Barbara Leigh-Hunt's Lady Bracknell which knocks the vulgar arriviste which Maggie Smith lately gave us into a cocked hat. Leigh-Hunt presents a figure of whaleboned, ostrich-feathered snobbery obsessed with rank, fortune and social correctness: hence the now-famous silent mouthing of "a handbag" with a look of appalled horror. But she also makes Lady Bracknell an amused, intelligent ironist who delights in Bunbury's ultimate explosion or Mr Worthing's final discomfiture.

Braham Murray's stylish Manchester revival of Coward's *Private Lives* is also dominated by a frequently underrated actress, Sian Thomas, whose flame-haired Amanda is a spiky, strong-willed woman who proudly proclaims her right to sexual enjoyment, who can wield a lethal adverb and who rams a piano lid hard down on Elyot's fingers in an epic fight scene. And Pip Donaghy accurately suggests that Elyot's studied flippancy masks a murderous temper. There is even a touch of Strindberg about their ferocious combat.

Coward obviously writes scintillating dialogue. But, compared to Wilde, his world seems strangely hermetic: we never learn, for instance, how his characters have come by their obviously sizeable incomes. And where Wilde's philosophy emerges through flickering witticisms, Coward gives us a little hedonistic homily ("Let's blow trumpets and squeakers and enjoy the party as much as we can"). Both were comic stylists. But Wilde is by far the greater artist in that he paints an expansive, multi-hued mural satirising privilege and society, while Coward provides a delicate miniature subtly endorsing it.

Mojo by Jez Butterworth (World Premiere) Royal Court, London: 20 July 1995

Jez Butterworth's *Mojo* marks the Royal Court's most dazzling main-stage debut in years. The fast-paced dialogue and the 1958 Soho gangland setting constantly suggest an Anglicised *American Buffalo*: this is a world in which little men talk big and dirty to disguise their panic and paranoia.

Butterworth takes time to reveal his plot, which turns out to be a mythic power battle among the denizens of Dean Street. We are in a tacky club whose hot property – a 17-year-old rock 'n' roll star called Silver Johnny – has been hijacked by a south London mobster: a point brought home to the club's fear-filled operators when they find its owner chopped up and deposited in two dustbins outside the back door. Under the supervision of their natural leader, Mickey, they barricade themselves in the club for the weekend; only to find, when one of their number stages a daring rescue of Silver Johnny, that all is not what it seems.

Echoes abound: not only Mamet but Cagney gangster movies and even the recent work of Tarantino. But Butterworth is playing a subtle double game. On the one hand, he himself is influenced by the mythic structures of American movies. On the other, he ironically punctures the way small-time Soho drifters, even in the 1950s, modelled themselves on transatlantic icons: they live in Macmillan's drab England but they aspire to Mitchum and Mature and are openly derisive when one of their number invokes the wartime team spirit of his Uncle Tommy.

Butterworth's ability to write scintillating dialogue may, at the moment, outstrip anything he has to say. But he understands perfectly how language can be used to camouflage fear or boost ego. The play starts with a rousing riff between two hangers-on, Potts and Sweets, who hope to get a slice of the action and who compare themselves to the background figures – "Cleaning rifles. Chatting to cherubs" – that you find in a Napoleonic canvas. And later, when the going gets rough, the sweating Potts announces "I am relaxed. I'm talking" – as if words alone could beat back the darkness. It is not, I guess, intended as a real portrait of Soho in the 1950s: it's more *Pulp Fiction* than *Espresso Bongo*. But Butterworth's nightmare vision is beautifully articulated in Ian Rickson's hectic production and the ensemble-playing is first-rate. It is hard to draw a line between David Westhead as the natural boss, Aidan Gillen as his skinnily sycophantic aide, Tom Hollander as the cocky contender for power and Andy Serkis and Matt Bardock as the panic-stricken, Mutt and Jeff minor hoods. At 26, Butterworth already knows how to rhythm a play, write cracking dialogue and build tension: I just pray the movies and cop series don't bag him before he goes on to develop as a dramatist. He's a great find.

1996

Shakespeare on Screen: Reflections on the current bonanza of film productions of the Bard of Stratford-on-Avon.

3 January 1996

William Shakespeare is the most popular screenwriter of the moment. Rarely has there been a period in the history of cinema when so many of the Bard's plays were either being filmed, awaiting release or in preparation.

Oliver Parker's *Othello*, starring Laurence Fishburne and Kenneth Branagh, has already opened in the United States. Richard Loncraine's *Richard III*, jointly scripted by Shakespeare, Ian McKellen and Richard Eyre, opens in Britain later this year. Meanwhile, Branagh is directing and starring in a new version of *Hamlet*, Adrian Noble has just finished shooting his RSC *A Midsummer Night's Dream* and Trevor Nunn's *Twelfth Night* is almost at the starting gate.

Why? Clearly, following the commercial success of the Branagh *Much Ado About Nothing* and the Mel Gibson *Hamlet*, there is a growing conviction that the Bard is no longer box-office poison. The current Bard boom also reflects a shift in our culture. British theatre directors have always desperately wanted to make movies. But whereas in the 1960s they yearned to explore contemporary life, now many of them seek to preserve the classics.

But can it be done? And is it a worthwhile enterprise? The evidence is contradictory. As Eric Bentley wrote, reviewing the Joe Mankiewicz *Julius Caesar*: "The actual filming of Shakespeare never fails to remind us how utterly he belongs to the stage." Even the argument that if the Bard were alive today he'd be writing for the cinema is pretty nonsensical. All one can say with certainty is that if Shakespeare were alive today he'd be extremely old; and that even a work that looks extremely cinematic, such as *Antony and Cleopatra*, with its multifarious short scenes, actually depends upon a sustained rhetorical climax.

That is the key problem with Shakespeare on the screen: the language. How can the cinema cope with this great torrent of words and Shakespeare's matchless gift for verbal scene-painting? Some wondered why Branagh had stripped *Much Ado About Nothing* of Don Pedro's superb lines describing how "the gentle day, before the wheels of Phoebus, round about dapples the drowsy east with spots of grey." The answer may be that Shakespeare, through his vivid evocation of the dawn, pre-empts anything the camera can do.

Adapting Shakespeare to the screen poses a dilemma. Either you offer a fullish text, in which case the film is top-heavy with words, or you cut and slash and run the risk, as the *New Yorker* wrote of the new *Othello*, of sacrificing the volcanic flow of language. The very thing that makes Shakespeare great – his cascading imagery – becomes a cinematic embarrassment.

There is, however, a case to be made for screen Shakespeare. In part, it is purely pragmatic: the films make the plays widely available. I was in Chicago shortly after Branagh's *Henry V* had opened in the States. In Britain it was greeted with polite reviews and modest audiences; in the Midwest it was treated as manna from Branagh. I met people whose lives had been changed by the experience and who regarded Branagh himself as a cultural missionary. Filmed Shakespeare can also enshrine a classic performance. Olivier's *Richard III* is the supreme example: the text is savagely cut, but at least we have a permanent record of Olivier's sublime satanic comedy, of his astonishing physical audacity and of his ability to embody the sheer sexuality of evil. Similarly, future generations who want to know why Gielgud was a great Shakespearean actor need only study the vocal dexterity of his celluloid Cassius in the Mankiewicz movie.

But what can screen Shakespeare do that the stage can't? It can never match the immediacy of the theatre; at its best, however, it can give the plays a vibrant social context. Think of Kozintsev's Russian *Hamlet*, with its unforgettable picture of an Elsinore that is a seething hub of diplomatic activity. Or of Orson Welles's *Chimes At Midnight* where pale afternoon sunlight filters into Henry's court, and where the battle scenes show the declension of honour and chivalry into a muddy chaos where ignorant armies clash by night.

Traditionally, it's the tragedies and histories that have worked best on screen: *Hamlet*, *Macbeth* (at least in Kurosawa's version), *Henry V*, *Richard III* all gain from the cinema's narrative drive, appetite for action and scenic realism. The comedies – with the possible exceptions of Reinhardt's *Dream* and Branagh's *Much Ado* – come off less well. They depend on the creation of a half-real, half-fantasy world and on an imaginative conspiracy between actor and audience that strike me as peculiar to the theatre, though I eagerly wait to be proved wrong by Noble and Nunn.

If Shakespeare is about to make a big-screen comeback, it is for a variety of reasons. It is partly because his plays have social cachet. It is partly because of the missionary zeal of a generation of British theatre folk who want to translate their enthusiasm to the screen. But I also suspect it is because Shakespeare answers some need that the current Hollywood diet of infantile cuteness and depersonalised destructiveness fails to fulfil. Man cannot live by *Home Alone* – or even by Schwarzenegger and Stallone. Shakespeare offers exciting stories and a definition of mankind; and, even though films of his work are a kind of analogue to the original play, they clearly satisfy the humanist instinct that the cinema has in recent years so disastrously denied.

The Beauty Queen of Leenane by Martin McDonagh (World Premiere) Royal Court Theatre Upstairs, London: 8 March 1996

Hardly a week goes by without the emergence of a 25-year-old dramatist. The latest, in a rich period for new writing, is Martin McDonagh, whose *The Beauty Queen of Leenane* – co-produced by Galway's Druid Theatre and the Royal Court – is an astonishingly assured debut. It exploits Irish theatrical tradition and, at the same time, subtly undermines it.

McDonagh's setting is familiar, a rural cottage in the Connemara mountains. And when one is confronted by the 40-year-old Maureen tethered to a vindictive, repressive mother, the nagging Mag, one suspects one is in for one of those plaintive dramas about the denial of life. The impression is confirmed when Maureen has a brief, one-night fling with Pato Dooley, who navvies in London and who is about to leave for Boston and whose invitation to her to join him, we know, is foredoomed.

This is Synge country, a study of solitude and desertion in western Ireland. But McDonagh takes a stock form and reanimates it in several ways. In the first place, by showing that Maureen, far from being a self-pitying spinster, is every bit as ruthless as her exploitative mother. As excellently played by Marie Mullen, Maureen is full of ancient grudges and gets a savage delight out of serving her mum lumpy Complan or even pouring boiling fat over her. Maureen, we gradually realise, is not so much wistful as severely damaged.

McDonagh also brings a post-modern irony to his Synge-song fable. The Galway village has become a global village as the characters moodily stare at Australian soaps on the box. And there is one tremendous scene in which Pato's brother, Ray, delivers a crucial love-letter to the absent Maureen. As the mother greedily eyes the all-important letter, it becomes a plot device straight out of Boucicault. At the same time, as Ray beats his head against the wall in frustration, the scene wittily catches the poleaxing boredom of Irish rural life.

McDonagh, who has Galway forebears but lives in London, where he is attached to the National Theatre Studio, is both exploiting and exposing Celtic myth. This is a world where the radio still spews out Delia Murphy singing The Spinning Wheel, while the young, like Ray, yearn for Mancunian drug culture and regard the passing by of a calf as an event.

Garry Hynes's production expertly catches the play's tension between ancient and modern. Francis O'Connor's cottage set, down to the illuminated crucifix, is a model of rustic realism, and Anna Manahan as the slyly oppressive mother and Tom Murphy as the message-bearing Ray lend their big scene the tension of high comedy. Only Brian F. O'Byrne seems slightly miscast as Pato since he looks a generation younger than Mullen's magnificently entrapped Maureen. But it's an outstanding first play that makes you impatient for more from McDonagh.

Divine Right by Peter Whelan (World Premiere) Birmingham Rep: 25 April 1996

Do we still want a monarchy in Britain? A question largely ignored in the House of Commons is now eagerly debated on the stage of the Birmingham Rep in Peter Whelan's *Divine Right*. But, although it's a fascinating state-of-the-nation play, the paradox is that Mr Whelan, an avowed republican, leaves you feeling strangely sympathetic to the beleaguered royals.

His scenario has an initial plausibility. The year is 2000. The Queen still reigns, New Labour is in power and Prince Charles decides to abdicate his right of succession. As the republican movement gathers steam, Prince William, somewhat less probably, evades his security men, puts on a disguise and goes on a private walkabout through his future kingdom. What he sees leads him to the inexorable conclusion that the English especially are an uncertain people who cling to monarchy to give them "a pseudo-identity": accordingly, with the Royal Family's agreement, he steps down to make way for "a Parliamentary Head of State."

Whelan is writing a play, not a manifesto. But, in his determination to be fair to all sides, he leaves you feeling that there may be a case for monarchy after all. The young Prince is seen not as a calculating schemer like Shakespeare's Hal in Eastcheap but as a troubled charmer with a genuine sense of national responsibility. And the republicans – represented by a fractious alliance of a left-wing Labour MP, a meritocratic Tory and an Irish businessman – are so internally divided that they cannot decide whether they want a figurehead, a moral watchdog or someone with executive power.

It's what you might call *The Queen and I* syndrome: as in Sue Townsend's satire, the very act of dramatising the monarchy seems to produce an intuitive empathy. The young Prince, played with an astonishing mix of shyness and assurance by William Mannering, is much the most compelling character on stage: capable of handling probing TV interviewers and angry republican teachers, yet filled with agonising self-doubt. In fact, Whelan seems to have more of a problem with his potential subjects: the skinhead, Union Jack-toting fascists the Prince meets on the road carry none of the brutish conviction of similar figures in David Eldridge's *Serving It Up* and suggest that the royals may not be the only ones out of touch.

Yet it's a bracing play not least because it rises above royal tittle-tattle to put on stage serious constitutional arguments about the monarchy. An angry teacher goes on television to remind us that the monarchy is curiously exempt from the laws against racial, sexual and religious discrimination and the Irish entrepreneur quotes Disraeli's point that deference has been built into the English character since the Norman conquest.

I doubt that the play will change anyone's mind on the key issue: its very effectiveness as drama invalidates it as propaganda. But it was good to hear a Birmingham audience cheering a state-of-the-nation play in the Hare and Edgar tradition and Bill Alexander's production, staged under Kit Surrey's overarching rusting diadem, matches the sweep of the action. Mannering's superbly unmannered Prince is also strongly backed by Mary Jo Randle as a rare radical survivor in New Labour, by Joe Melia as a rich Irish republican and by Paul Connolly as a PM who has more hair than Blair but all of his vocal emphases.

It is a serious play on a serious subject. But Whelan's skill as a dramatist subverts his own intentions. He clearly sets out to prove that the monarchy is an anachronism that we use to conceal our national uncertainty. What he actually shows is that the republican movement lacks a coherent political agenda and that heirs to the throne, in their isolation and political impotence, are hauntingly tragic figures.

Hedda Gabler by Henrik Ibsen
Donmar Warehouse, London/Minerva Studio, Chichester: 8 August 1996

Two Heddas are better than one. In fact the chance to see two different productions of *Hedda Gabler* – English Touring Theatre's at the Donmar Warehouse and a new version at the Minerva Studio, Chichester – intensifies one's admiration for Ibsen's technical mastery and the mystery of acting. But if Stephen Unwin's Donmar production wins on points over Lindy Davies's at Chichester, it is because it realises a fundamental truth: that Ibsen is providing a portrait of a society as well as of a tormented individual.

The two Heddas themselves are both extraordinary: a mixture of vixen and victim, predator and prey. Alexandra Gilbreath at the Donmar is the more severe, with her hair pressed flat against her skull and her habit of prowling round the parlour. Acutely intelligent and totally unfulfilled, she relentlessly probes her own and other people's weaknesses. What she craves is power over an individual destiny but, when she finally achieves it, she is terrified of the consequences. The great moment in Gilbreath's performance comes when, having sent Eilert Lovborg to certain death, she lets out a cry that starts as triumphant exaltation and turns into gut-wrenching despair.

Harriet Walter at Chichester inevitably makes many of the same points: that Hedda combines innate cowardice with a burning envy of Mrs Elvsted and her capacity to shape another human life. Walter, however, lays more stress on Hedda's suppressed romanticism: she yearns for power but also for an impossible "beauty" in life without the ugly reality of hole-in-corner affairs and an unwanted baby. Both readings are sustainable and prove the polyphonic richness of Ibsen's play. But the key difference is that Unwin uses a wonderfully crisp translation by Kenneth McLeish and brings all the characters into unremittingly sharp focus. Crispin Letts's Tesman, for instance, is no pedagogic ninny but an intelligent scholar who, at the last, angrily and consciously rejects Hedda's cruelty. David Killick's Judge Brack is a suave military-moustached lecher who turns the final screw on Hedda with sadistic relish. And Carol Starks's Mrs Elvsted, although patronised by Hedda and Lovborg, has the selfless passion of the genuine literary muse.

Everything in Unwin's production – one of the best *Hedda Gablers* I've seen – is carefully thought through. When Tesman buries his head in Aunt Julia's lap, you are reminded that he is an orphaned figure constantly seeking mother-substitutes. Even the extraordinary Mercury-winged hat Aunt Julia leaves lying around is clearly an attempt to ingratiate herself with Hedda by mimicking the kind of feathered creation once sported by General Gabler's daughter. Unwin creates a whole world that explains the characters' actions.

Lindy Davies's production lacks that mix of detail and linear clarity. Superfluous music introduces each act, speeches overlap, the text "adapted" by Helen Cooper has odd anachronisms such as "you can say that again." Above all, the surrounding characters are seen from Hedda's viewpoint rather than their own. You can't blame Peter Blythe, gallantly taking over at short notice, for offering only an outline of Judge Brack but where in Nicholas Le Prevost's fusspot Tesman is the obsessive passion of the dedicated scholar? Walter's Hedda aside, the one sharply defined performance is David Threlfall's laconically self-destructive Lovborg.

But the real lesson of this double Hedda is that Ibsen wrote not just a great part but a great play: one in which the protagonist is destroyed not only by her own nature but by the oppressive, interlocking quality of a male-dominated, hypocritical society. At the Donmar you get Ibsen's complete world: at Chichester you get a fine solo performance.

Ashes to Ashes by Harold Pinter
(World Premiere)
Royal Court Theatre Upstairs, London:
21 September 1996

A new Pinter play is always an event: doubly so in the case of *Ashes To Ashes*, which takes place in the relocated Royal Court Theatre Upstairs. A beguiling wraparound 140-seat space has been created from the Circle of the old Ambassadors. In a similar way, Pinter, in this profoundly haunting and disturbing play, builds something new on the foundations of the old.

At first it seems as if we are in familiar Pinter territory. The setting is a smooth, beige-carpeted room in a country house. A man, Devlin, relentlessly quizzes a woman, Rebecca, about a former lover. She describes how the lover would force her to kiss his fist and how her body would bend from his pressure on her throat: what is shocking is her submission to this form of sexual brutality. Devlin is impatient for more details, but the more possessive he becomes – even finally echoing the lover's physical gesture – the more Rebecca eludes his grasp and retreats into another world.

Old Pinter buffs will instantly spot the connections: one thinks of *Landscape*, where a curdled marriage is haunted by the memory of a past lover, or *Old Times*, where a woman remains triumphantly unknowable. But like many artists in their late work, Pinter colonises new territory without sacrificing the old. Here he allies his fascination with isolation and separateness to his instinctive hatred of barbarism; he is exploring the apparent link between sexual and political fascism and the way one echoes, or sometimes even contradicts, the other.

Other writers have made the same connection: not least the South African poet Breyten Breytenbach in *Letter From Abroad To A Butcher*, which asks how the hands that sanction torture can fondle a wife's mysteries, and Sarah Kane in her play, *Blasted*. But where Kane violently juxtaposed the domestic and the political, Pinter, with infinite subtlety, interweaves them. Rebecca talks almost with adoration of her ex-lover. Only gradually does she reveal that he was an overseer of oppressive factories deprived even of toilets (an image drawn from Pinter's reading of Gitta Sereny's book on Albert Speer) and that he tore babies from their mothers' arms. The opening image of the clenched fist slowly expands into a metaphor for Nazism.

But Pinter is not simply exploring the link between sexuality and politics. He also draws a distinction between female resilience and male intransigence. What gives this hour-long play its emotional dynamic is that Rebecca undergoes a profound change while Devlin takes on the lineaments of her lover. As Rebecca describes past cruelties, so they come alive in her imagination: as she envisages a woman whose baby was snatched from her arms in an icy street she takes on her identity. Devlin, meanwhile, for all his invocations of God and moral duty, slowly adopts the persona of the fascist lover.

Pinter's plays are not theses that come beribboned with messages: they operate more like poems, through verbal echoes and repetitions. What he is doing in this spellbinding play is offering a distilled image of experience. How is it, he asks, that men can sanction terrible cruelties and yet be adoring lovers? Is their public monstrosity echoed in their private behaviour? And is there some quality in women, intimately connected with motherhood, that allows them a greater imaginative empathy with suffering? It is fascinating how the word "baby" echoes through the text as if children were the ultimate moral test. It is not a play that yields up all its meaning at one sitting, but it is a dramatic experience of extraordinary intensity. And what it shows is Pinter skilfully marrying private and public concerns. He is as preoccupied as ever by dreams, memories, the looped nature of time: Rebecca describes how her lover claims that his workers "would follow him over a cliff and into the sea" and then imagines the same image glimpsed through a Dorset garden window. But the mystery of existence is here attached to a passionate concern with the cruelties perpetrated in Nazi Germany or modern Bosnia, East Timor or Kurdistan. How, Pinter finally asks, can these things happen? Pinter's own production convincingly makes the transition from England to European history. Every gesture is also freighted with meaning. Lindsay Duncan and Stephen Rea begin by occupying, with relative comfort, two capacious armchairs: by the end, in the gathering darkness, even the chairs have become places for huddled retreat.

Duncan also moves superbly from an English-rose untainted innocence ("Nothing has ever happened to me . . . I have never suffered") into a locked-off world of torment. Rea, for his part, beautifully captures the needling, dogged, persistent quality of a man who believes that truth lies in semantic definitions. In one sense, the play is a contest between the slippery elusiveness of women and the fact-dominated world of men.

But, in the end, *Ashes To Ashes* is a multi-dimensional work that will yield different meanings to each spectator: what it says to me is that Pinter is a radical poet haunted by the mystery of how recognisable human beings, capable of the heart's affections, can at the same time licence unspeakable evil. It is the same question that lies at the heart of *King Lear*; and while Pinter no more has the definitive answer than Shakespeare did, he poses it with mesmeric precision.

1997

Bird and Fortune. A political satire by John Bird and John Fortune (World Premiere) Churchill Theatre, Bromley: 15 January 1997

Satire, according to Broadway legend, is what closes on Saturday night. Not any more: satire is what packs out the Churchill, Bromley, on a January Monday night. Capitalising on their success in the Rory Bremner show, the two Johns – Bird and Fortune – are taking their political double-act on the road. What struck me is how uncannily similar the mood is to that of the early 1960s (the period of TW3, *Private Eye*, the Establishment Club), in that a largely middle-class audience laps up attacks on a visibly disintegrating Government. A sense of national decay is clearly a boon for satirists.

The format in the six sketches is much the same: one or other of the Johns adopts the role of George Parr, who is always a po-faced apologist for some spectacular public ineptitude. They begin with a real belter in which Parr is a health-management consultant, shakily defending, in Bromley's case, the closure of three local hospitals and the use of private finance to build a single replacement. When the interviewer objects that Granada, one of the partners in the new hospital, is a specialist in medical fiction, Parr jauntily replies, "So is the National Health Service." When an audience in Bromley roars its approval of a fierce attack on health privatisation, something is clearly stirring.

What is commendable about Bird and Fortune is that they don't always go for soft targets. Their assaults on the redundant Eurofighter and an oleaginous merchant banker ("If you succeed, you get rewards; if you fail, you get compensation") may be relatively safe. But one sketch, in which Parr becomes a Michael Howard-like spokesman for security units for young offenders, achieves an almost Swiftian cruelty. Reminded that a number of incarcerated youths have committed suicide, Fortune's Parr remarks, with a smoothly purring self-satisfaction, "Well, that's a start, isn't it?"

Bird and Fortune, who came in with the 1960s, are now veterans of the satire circuit; their act, however, seems more barbed, pointed and well researched than anything else around. They also have the gift of pushing a comic premise to absurd extremes. Outlining the Millennium celebrations in the final sketch, Parr envisages the possibility of a 300 foot-high replica of our best-loved national symbol, the Queen Mother, being towed through the air by a Spitfire. It is a surreally lunatic image but not much dafter than some of the ideas already proposed. Indeed, judging by the response at the start of their nationwide tour, Bird and Fortune seem to have caught exactly the public's mood of bitter disillusion with the present regime's waffling apologists.

Ivanov by Anton Chekhov
Almeida, London: 20 February 1997

Ivanov is often referred to as Chekhov's *Hamlet*. But, ironically enough, Ralph Fiennes, who plays the title role in Jonathan Kent's breathtaking revival, seems closer to the great Dane than he did in Shakespeare's play. This is a performance packed with just the right emotional intensity, self-loathing and excoriating candour.

Written in 1887, Chekhov's first major play is closer to melodrama than to the symphonic realism of the later work. But in Ivanov himself Chekhov creates a memorable hero; a bankrupt landowner who, at 35, is tormented by his own lassitude and by his unhappy marriage to his tubercular wife. He seeks nightly refuge on the neighbouring Lebedev estate where the daughter of the house, Sasha, falls headily in love with him. But this only intensifies his guilt and anguish.

As David Hare's excellent new version insists, Ivanov is not really a Russian Hamlet. He is simply acting Hamlet. But the key to the role is that under the self-hatred and cruelty – and at one shocking moment he calls his wife "a dirty Jew" – you should sense what might have been. Fiennes catches precisely this contradiction. He is full of despair and ineffectualness, yet he also implies that Ivanov has an honesty and intellect that has been despoiled by circumstance. Melodrama the play may be in places, but it is also an exuberant social comedy that depicts the pettiness and vulgarity of Russian provincial life with Gogolian fervour. Kent's production releases the play's comic energy through a gallery of memorable performances.

Oliver Ford Davies plays Ivanov's uncle as an embittered misanthrope who craves the excitement of abuse. Anthony O'Donnell is equally unforgettable as Ivanov's mercenary steward. And Bill Paterson makes Lebedev a bulbous soak filled with residual kindness. The scene where the three of them get plastered and are reduced to beating their heads against

walls and tables as they are hijacked by an unstoppable card-bore is as
riotous as anything on the London stage.

Melodrama and farce are juxtaposed, rather than seamlessly mingling as
they do in Chekhov's masterworks. Yet the play has abundant theatrical
vitality and touches deep emotional chords. Ivanov's neglected wife, in
particular, arouses our pity and Harriet Walter plays her beautifully as a
wan, pale figure who cannot quite relinquish her love for her impossible
husband. We see Chekhov's four great plays often enough. What we have at
the Almeida is a joyous resurrection of an earlier work that not only hints at
what is to come but explores the absurdity of Russian life and the human
condition with fizzing satirical energy.

The Weir by Conor McPherson
(World Premiere)
Royal Court Theatre Upstairs at the
Ambassadors, London: 10 July 1997

We all know that English drama is, in Tynan's words, a procession of
glittering Irishmen. But Conor McPherson's *The Weir* is exceptional – a
spellbinder that transfixes you like the Ancient Mariner's tale and proves
that McPherson can combine the monologue form of *This Lime Tree Bower*
and *St Nicholas* with sparkling dialogue.

The less said of the plot, the better: you should discover it for yourselves.
But the action takes place in a small rural bar, complete with smoking stove,
in the Sligo or Leitrim area on a windy, wintry night. The regulars' tippling
is interrupted when Finbar, the local property-owning hotshot, brings in a
fugitive from Dublin, Valerie, who has just bought a house in the area. As
the men show Valerie black-and-white bar-room photographs of the
neighbouring weir and abbey, they start to spin a series of supernatural
tales.

Each story, in classic fashion, reveals something about its teller. Jack, the
crusty bachelor garage-owner, shows his love of language and a fireside
yarn. Finbar displays the insecurity concealed by his cock-of-the-walk strut.
And Jim, Jack's quiet helpmate tethered to his aged mammy, unspools his
own preoccupation with death. But McPherson's play is much more than a
series of hair-raising ghost stories. It offers, in a little over 90 minutes, an
extraordinarily rich picture of Irish rural life, of its superstitions, its solitude,
its strong pecking order, its clannish resentment of outsiders – especially the
German tourists who arrive like swallows each summer.

McPherson is also saying something about sexuality and the nature of the
Irish imagination, about the residual fear of women and about the incapacity
of these tale-telling men – with the exception of the sympathetic barman – to

accept real-life tragedy as articulated by Valerie. No praise, in fact, is too high for a play full of the echoing sadness of disappointed lives or for Ian Rickson's production and Rae Smith's design. Exact in every detail, they turn us into pub-voyeurs perched on rickety chairs. The acting is also perfect. Jim Norton beautifully shows how Jack's flinty spryness conceals a sense of lost happiness. Gerard Horan's blustering Finbar, Kieran Ahern's repressed Jim and Brendan Coyle's taciturn barman have the precise flavour of small-town life. And Julia Ford reveals with great charm and skill the source of Valerie's rapt attentiveness. Along with that other Irish play, *Waiting For Godot*, *The Weir* offers the most exciting evening in theatrical London.

A Six-Point Plan for Theatre.

16 July 1997

The Guardian *commissioned a series of articles on the direction theatre should take. This was my highly personal Six-Point Plan.*

Will theatre survive into the age of digital television, home cinema and the information superhighway? Or will it turn into an increasingly archaic ritual kept alive by a dwindling band of live-action junkies? No one, of course, knows – least of all theatre people themselves. When they tell us that theatre can only survive by "abandoning realism" or "deserting buildings," what they really mean is that that is their own personal preference. But beware global nostrum-peddlers: forecasting the future in Britain itself is difficult enough. Let me, however, offer a few modest proposals as to ways in which our own theatre might, and conceivably should, go as we slither into the next century:

1   Restore the company principle of high productivity and the juxtaposition of new and classic work: everything, in fact, that characterised the RSC in the 1960s and 1970s and that the Old Vic is aiming for today. Pinter's *The Homecoming* in 1965 achieved classic status precisely because it was played by a cast that had just done the Shakespeare Histories; more recently Stephen Jeffreys's *The Libertine*, for Out of Joint, gained extra edge by being played in tandem with a Restoration Comedy, *The Man of Mode*. It is that kind of witty cross-fertilisation we desperately need to recapture.

2   Erode the arbitrary distinction between profit and non-profit theatre. Give each house, not least in London, a style and policy of its own. Already this has begun to happen with the Royal Court's takeover of

two West End sites, the Duke of York's and the Ambassadors, and Peter Hall's tenancy of the Old Vic. But go much further. Play everywhere on Sundays: it works. Open up West End theatres (idle for two-thirds of the day) to a wide range of early-evening activities: talks, debates, poetry-readings, jazz concerts. Allow commercial producers to apply for public funds, on a profit-sharing basis, for genuinely imaginative schemes. How about, for starters, a Millennium season of best British plays of the century?

3   Explore new spaces. I am not of the school that argues all theatre should be site-specific or that conventional auditoria are things of the past. But there is clearly a public hunger for drama that opens up new territory. In the last few weeks alone I've seen Corneille's *The Illusion* staged in Manchester's Upper Campfield Market (a temporary theatre in the round which the Royal Exchange should hang on to), Neil Bartlett's *Poussin* show mounted in a Whitechapel hospital, Eastern Angles's *The Wuffings* presented in a Suffolk garden-nursery. In each case the space had a function and history which helped shape the event. That does not invalidate purpose-built theatres. It simply proves that drama can happen anywhere, that audiences relish buildings that have their own unique resonance.

4   Recognise theatre's endless capacity to reinvent itself. On the simplest level, as Peter Brook reminds us, an empty space can become a bare stage. But theatre also exists in a multimedia, hi-tech world which it would be folly to ignore. Technology has its pitfalls, as shown when Robert Lepage's *Elsinore* failed to open at last year's Edinburgh Festival and led to finger-wagging reminders that theatre was "bare boards and a passion." But, if technology is a bad master, it is also an invaluable servant: witness the fascinating mixture of live action and film in Lepage's own *Seven Streams of the River Ota*, David Farr's *Max Klapper*, Matthew Warchus's current Stratford *Hamlet*. The technology is there to use. A new audience has grown up that is at home with it. It would be self-denyingly stupid for theatre to retreat into a macrobiotic purism.

5   Keep ticket prices cheap. This is at the root of everything. Once seat-prices reach astronomical proportions, you limit the audience in terms of age, class and income-level. But where is the money to come from? Last week I suggested that Lottery funds should be devoted primarily to core funding rather than to capital projects: my postbag implies strong support. Realistic subsidy would enable artists to be paid properly: I recently heard from an actor who wondered politely why he should play Willy Loman for £220 a week in rep. Sensible

subsidy would also increase access. To be fair, the Labour Party is aware of this: it has plans for pay-what-you-can theatre nights (a great success at London's BAC and Tricycle theatres) and for a student Arts Card. But the plans need to be implemented now just as the rules for Lottery funding need to be radically revised in accordance with present needs. PEOPLE BEFORE BUILDINGS, that's the motto.

6   Encourage new talent. Already the Arts Council is advocating mandatory funding of drama students and this is an urgent priority. The Arts For Everyone scheme will eventually use Lottery money to fund new initiatives. But reports from the regions reveal that the current situation is dire: "project" funding, dispensed to new companies, is in some areas (such as the east of England) non-existent. It's precisely the kind of money that in the past gave a kick-start to directors like Stephen Daldry and Deborah Warner. Without it all you have is stasis. In the end, it all comes down to public attitudes. Either we leave theatre to market forces and watch it slowly ossify. Or we acknowledge that theatre is something we're pretty good at, that it defines who we are as individuals and a society and feeds into the whole entertainment spectrum. We can have a theatre, based on scrape-and-save principles, that withers away through inanition or a healthily living one that realises its full potential. The choice, in the end, is up to us and our elected representatives. Death by a thousand cuts or an endorsement of our native genius for drama? Which is it to be?

This was written, three months into a New Labour government, when theatre faced a funding crisis: in particular, the devotion of Lottery money to capital projects rather than core funding seemed insane. But, although my arguments reflect the time, I stand by them today. I still believe that West End theatres should be utilised during the daytime rather than standing empty and that they would benefit from having a coherent artistic policy: it was an idea that was later successfully put into practice at the Theatre Royal Haymarket where Jonathan Kent and Trevor Nunn were allowed to create a programme of their own, at Wyndham's and the Noel Coward Theatre where Michael Grandage produced strongly-cast seasons and, again at Wyndham's, where Kenneth Branagh became an enlightened actor-manager. Sadly, however, the mandatory funding of drama students, which I strongly recommended, did not happen. The result, as we all know, was that students of relatively well-off parents enjoyed a built-in advantage while those who came from poorer backgrounds were often denied access to training.

Playhouse Creatures by April De Angelis (World Premiere)
Old Vic, London: 16 September 1997

What's going to happen to the Old Vic? On Sunday I saw a large audience lapping up April De Angelis's *Playhouse Creatures*. Sad to think that, since the theatre is up for sale, the Peter Hall experiment will come to an end in December. In France, of course, they would simply dub the Old Vic a "national theatre" and purchase it for the state. In Britain, even when Lottery money is available, we prefer to squander it on often-lunatic projects rather than use it to preserve a historic building with a proven company.

The good news is that De Angelis's play, which had an earlier life as a small-scale touring show, expands perfectly to fit its new space. Its theme is the arrival of actresses on the English stage in the 1660s and the way this social and aesthetic advance was vitiated by the players' dependence on aristocratic patrons and leering audiences. But that makes the play sound like a postgraduate thesis when, in fact, it is a robust, earthy, often very funny recreation of Restoration theatrical life.

De Angelis focuses on five actresses, including the statuesque Mrs Betterton, the upwardly mobile Nell Gwyn and the emerging star Mrs Barry. Scenes from the heroic repertory and vignettes of backstage backstabbing are interspersed with reminders of the vulnerability of these pioneer women: the ageing Mrs Betterton is sidelined in favour of glamorous youth, the unemployably pregnant Mrs Farley undergoes a hatpin abortion, and Mrs Marshall, after angering her former patron, is forced to flee amid accusations of witchcraft. Women, De Angelis implies, irrevocably changed the English theatre but were victimised in the process.

Tension ebbs a bit in the final scenes. But there is no denying the sheer exuberance of De Angelis's writing, Lynne Parker's production or, indeed, of the performances. Sheila Gish is unforgettable as Mrs Betterton, faintly absurd in her belief that emotional states can be indicated by clock-hand positions of the arms, histrionically impressive in her Lady Macbeth sleepwalking scene and quietly moving in her memory of having once played the great male roles. Saskia Reeves and Rachel Power are excellent as her bosomy subordinates. Jo McInnes is an engaging Gwyn, and Liz Smith as a wizened stage manager sits in the corner gathering laughs and dispensing wisdom like a strange mixture of Irene Handl and Madame Defarge. A pleasurable evening that reclaims a vital piece of history with wit and passion.

Blue Heart by Caryl Churchill
(World Premiere)
Royal Court, London: 25 September 1997

Experiment and emotion: they rarely go together. But the great thing about Caryl Churchill's *Blue Heart*, co-produced by Out of Joint and the Royal Court, is that it is made up of two subtly interlocking works which play with theatrical form while saying something fascinating about the nature of language, identity and disintegrating family life.

Heart's Desire is the more instantly accessible. A married couple await, with the husband's sister, the return of their daughter from Australia: each time the action starts, it is halted and then replayed with increasingly wild variations. It is a bizarrely funny idea with echoes of Ionesco, Beckett, Ayckbourn and even an old West End comedy called *Big Bad Mouse* in which Jimmy Edwards and Eric Sykes used to stop the action and spool back to the beginning every time a latecomer appeared. But Churchill is not just out to make us laugh. Each time the action is replayed we become aware of the suppurating tensions within the family. It is as if the act of waiting itself releases repressed fears: the married couple's mutual hatred, the sister-in-law's terror of death, and the husband's dream of self-cannibalism leap unbidden to the surface. It is a fiendishly clever and surreal play, timed to perfection, in Max Stafford-Clark's production by Bernard Gallagher, Valerie Lilley and Mary McLeod.

Its full import only becomes clear, however, when you see the second play, *Blue Kettle*. Here we watch a 40-year-old man, Derek, conning a series of vulnerable women into believing he is their long-lost son. But what makes the play so strange is that the words "blue" and "kettle" increasingly take the place of nouns, verbs and adverbs until by the end the characters are conversing in a foreshortened language consisting only of fragmented consonants.

Churchill is clearly suggesting, in line with her recent experiments with physical theatre, that emotion can exist independently of slippery, elusive language. But she allies the formal experiment to a real human dilemma: Derek, whose mother is in a geriatric ward, is driven by a compulsive need for maternal substitutes. And when you put the plays together what comes across is the disintegration not just of language but of family life itself: we are into the idea of what Eliot calls two people who do not understand each other "breeding children whom they do not understand and who will never understand them."

You can argue with Churchill's ideas. But she expresses them with compressed brilliance in two plays that last no more than 40 minutes each. And Stafford-Clark's production stirs up profound emotions, not least in the second play with Jason Watkins as the damaged son and Eve Pearce and Anna Wing amongst the quintet of frustrated mothers. Head and heart, for once in the theatre, work together in perfect synchronism.

1998

An Experiment With An Air Pump
by Shelagh Stephenson (World Premiere)
Royal Exchange, Manchester:
18 February 1998

What is the moral duty of the scientist? Does the quest for truth preclude private passion? Is the notion of progress a myth? Those are the cosmic questions posted by Shelagh Stephenson's new play. And, even if they are only partly answered, it is cheering to find a writer, in only her second stage work, breaking out of the domestic confines.

The play's title derives from a famous picture by Joseph Wright of Derby, its structure from Stoppard's *Arcadia*. The setting is a Tyneside house in both 1799 and 1999. In the former period it is occupied by a crusading physicist and his extended family, in the latter by a genetic scientist and her redundant Eng Lit-teaching husband. And, exactly as in Stoppard, past actions have future consequences.

What Stephenson shows in 1799 is a science driven by utopian fervour. The head of the Newcastle house, Joseph Fenwick, is a passionate republican who believes the task of the scientist is to change the world. Unfortunately he is so bound up in the intoxication of discovery that he neglects his wife, patronises his Scottish servant and is totally unaware that the latter is being treated as a source of cold-blooded experiment by one of his youthful acolytes.

Two hundred years on, the house itself is about to be sold and turned into a branch of the heritage industry. Its co-owner is also being tempted to turn her genetic skill to commercial use. But the discovery of an antique female skeleton in the cellar raises disturbing questions about science's continuing detachment from ethical concerns.

Clearly Stephenson is dealing with a whole raft of scientific, social, sexual and moral issues. One of the key points seems to be that whereas in the past science was partly driven by a spirit of radical inquiry, today it is all too easily appropriated by market forces. The problem is that her chosen dramatic format often short-circuits debate. For instance, the vast issue of genetic detection of foetal abnormality and its possible exploitation by health and insurance companies is reduced to a series of headline arguments. But even if Stephenson's ideas lack room to breathe she is at least questioning in her outlook. She also writes good individual scenes, particularly those involving the highly literate Scottish servant, beautifully played by Pauline Lockhart, and her cruel maltreatment by Tom Mannion's egotistical scientist.

Matthew Lloyd's production fluently manages the transitions from the past, symbolised by floating globes and bird-cages, to the present, denoted by flickering television monitors. David Horovitch as the dominating physicist and Dearbhla Molloy as his cowed wife also neatly show how roles are reversed in 1999. In the end, the play bites off far more than it can chew but what impresses me is the sheer scale of Stephenson's theatrical appetite.

Naked by Luigi Pirandello
Almeida, London: 19 February 1998

Juliette Binoche looks marvellous: the contoured cheeks, the deep-set eyes, the pensive solitude give her the mysterious allure of stardom. She also acts with every fibre of her being in Jonathan Kent's rare revival of Pirandello's *Naked*. But one has to be honest and admit that her eccentric inflections add an extra dimension of difficulty to an already complex play.

All the familiar Pirandello themes are here: the antithesis of art and life, illusion and reality, mask and face, but what makes this 1922 play peculiarly elusive is that we are never quite sure what to make of the heroine, Ersilia. Is she, like Wedekind's Lulu, an essentially innocent creature on to whom men project their varying needs and desires? Or is she a skilful manipulator who constantly reinvents her own identity? Binoche suggests elements of both.

As always in Pirandello, truth is relative. We first see Ersilia, after an aborted suicide, being taken under the protective wing of a famous novelist who wants to fictionalise the account of her life that he has read in a Roman newspaper. We deduce, in fact, that she has been dismissed from the employ of the consul in Smyrna after the death of his child and that she has been rejected by a naval lieutenant in favour of a woman of his own class. But with tormenting skill Pirandello constantly adds new layers to Ersilia's story. First a reporter arrives claiming its veracity is being questioned. Then comes the naval officer who discovers that he may not have been the precise occasion for Ersilia's projected suicide. And finally we get the consul himself from whom we glean more of the truth regarding the death of his baby daughter.

Each of these men, including the novelist, invents his own Ersilia: a mixture of fictive heroine, suicide victim, mistress and whore. Yet she herself conspires in her own re-creation. And this is the point Binoche avidly and intelligently seizes on: at one moment she is all blanched, dress-tearing vulnerability, at another full of masked, berouged assurance. Binoche's performance perfectly captures the character's shifting desperation: all it lacks is a matching vocal technique. But Kent's production conveys Pirandello's ambiguity. Paul Brown's design is an intriguing mixture of the real and the symbolic. A superb performance from Oliver Ford Davies as the novelist, infuriated by his awareness of his own and art's limitations, is also accompanied by good ones from Kevin McNally as the far from honourable consul and Anita Reeves as the voice of Roman respectability. Nicholas Wright's new version of the play adds to the pleasure of a teasingly mysterious evening dominated by the haunting presence of Binoche.

Cleansed by Sarah Kane (World Premiere) Royal Court at the Duke of York's, London: 7 May 1998

How does one write about Sarah Kane? Everyone, including me, so over-reacted to her first play, *Blasted*, that it becomes difficult to judge her with cool clarity. But my initial reaction to her new play is that it displays far greater aesthetic control while remaining mysteriously cryptic.

Kane's theme here is the ability of love to survive fascistic, institutional cruelty. She presents us with a rural rehab centre where the apparent aim is to cure any form of social deviation. Graham, a heroin addict, is incarcerated and ritually purified. His sister, Grace, is punished for her incestuous passion by undergoing a sex-change in which she finally becomes her brother. The gay Carl experiences an even more extreme fate in that tongue, hands and feet are serially removed and his body gnawed by rats. Supervising this grisly cycle of crime and punishment is the Torquemada-like figure of Tinker, a pseudo-doctor who is in total thrall to a peep-show erotic dancer.

Two parallel works come to mind: Orwell's *Nineteen Eighty-Four* and Pinter's *The Hothouse*. Like both those writers, Kane suggests the price of dissent is physical torture and that society has a vested interest in eradicating nonconformity. But invocation of those works also betrays Kane's main weakness. Where Orwell's Ministry of Love and Pinter's psychiatric institution are clearly instruments of the state, you never learn who or what lies behind Kane's hermetic chamber of horrors. If it is meant as a political metaphor, it remains an extremely shadowy one. But it is a measure of Kane's progress as a dramatist that her play seems much more than a catalogue of cruelty. She even goes so far as to suggest that the human spirit is indestructible and that love is a possibility. As a political play, *Cleansed* lacks circumstantial detail in that we never get to know the source of Tinker's authority. But it shows Kane, as a dramatist, is on a learning curve and capable of a lyricism still yearning to find proper expression.

She is excellently served by James Macdonald's production which is as stylised, in its presentation of violence, as Peter Brook's *Titus Andronicus*. It is also astonishingly designed by Jeremy Herbert, who makes Expressionist use of tilted planes and who even, at one point, places the beaten Grace on a vertical wall as if she were a suffering medieval saint. Suzan Sylvester as the amazing Grace, Martin Marquez as her addictive brother and Stuart McQuarrie as the barbarous Tinker, himself pining for love, all perform with total dedication. And, even if the play itself leaves too many questions unanswered, it shows Kane is a fast-developing writer whose moral rage is accompanied by a romantic yearning of which she seems slightly frightened.

Copenhagen by Michael Frayn (World Premiere) Cottesloe, National Theatre, London: 30 May 1998

Michael Frayn has always been a philosophic enquirer, and his dazzling new play is a logical extension of everything he has done before. He starts from a fact and an enigma. In 1941 Werner Heisenberg, who was working on the German atomic bomb project, went to visit Niels Bohr, his private father-figure and Europe's leading quantum theorist, in occupied Denmark. What happened between them? What did they talk about? How did it affect the future of mankind? After all, the German project was unsuccessful, whereas Bohr later went to Los Alamos and participated in the development of the atomic bomb.

It's a brilliant starting point for a play, and Frayn offers neither a docudrama nor a definitive answer but an exploration of what Heisenberg calls "the final uncertainty at the core of things." We meet only Heisenberg, Bohr and Bohr's wife, Margrethe, who acts as our representative in that she demands an explanation of scientific detail in layman's language. What we see are three characters, from the vantage point of eternity, replaying the endless possibilities of the collision between these human particles in wartime Denmark.

What Frayn does superbly is suggest a crucial equation between science and character. Heisenberg is famous for the uncertainty principle: the idea that the more accurately you know the movements of a particle, the less accurately you know its velocity and vice versa. Bohr went on to derive from this the theory of complementarity: that, if I understand it aright, mutually exclusive pairs of measurements are an indispensable part of quantum mechanics.

But the vital point is the dramatic use Frayn makes of this: the two physicists become the embodiment of their theories. Heisenberg's whole position in Denmark is marked by uncertainty: was he there to pick Bohr's brains about nuclear fission, to seek absolution for his work on the bomb, or to show off to his surrogate father? Equally, Bohr recognises the importance of complementary phenomena: in his productive marriage, in his endless research partnerships, in the fissile tensions of his friendship with Heisenberg.

Nothing in the play is abstract or vague. Behind it lurks the question Heisenberg twice puts to Bohr: whether the scientist has the moral right to work on the exploitation of atomic energy. Given today's terrifying headlines about nuclear tests in Pakistan, the question has lost none of its urgency. And, in terms of the drama, Frayn presents us with a fascinating dilemma: was the saintly seeming Bohr, who eventually worked at Los Alamos, morally superior to Heisenberg, whose development of a German bomb was impeded by his failure to apply a crucial diffusion equation to uranium-235? Do we judge people by their motives or the consequences of their actions? Frayn's play poses endless questions, but its dramatic excitement stems partly from the way it uses science as a source of moral debate. While breaking new ground, the play is also is a natural extension of Frayn's previous work for the theatre. He once said that the key philosophical dilemma is that "the world plainly exists independently of us and yet it equally plainly exists only through our consciousness of it." And out of our attempt to impose our ideas upon the world Frayn has created a whole series of philosophical plays. In *Noises Off* we see actors vainly struggling to create order through the complex mechanics of farce: in *Copenhagen* we see physicists seeking to harness the fission properties of uranium isotopes. Significantly, both plays end with an acknowledgement of the power of uncertainty.

Copenhagen finally strikes me as a humanist play about science: one that recognises equally the darkness in the human soul and the preciousness of earthly life, and that suggests that our continued existence may be due to "one short moment in Copenhagen." The play is also directed with exquisite tact by Michael Blakemore, and David Burke's sturdy, paternalistic Bohr, Matthew Marsh's mercurial Heisenberg and Sara Kestelman's inquisitive Margrethe express the ideas with perfect clarity. What Frayn has done is show how theatre can glamourise thought and provide a potent metaphor for the mystery of existence.

The Merchant of Venice/*As You Like It*
by William Shakespeare
Shakespeare's Globe, London: 1 June 1998

Last Friday afternoon I heard a Jew being hissed at in south London. Not, I hasten to add, at a National Front rally but at a performance of *The*

Merchant Of Venice at Shakespeare's Globe. Having heard Orlando's brother, Oliver, prompt a similar reaction the previous evening in *As You Like It*, I began to wonder whether one effect of this new theatre is to morally simplify Shakespeare's plays and turn them into a form of Victorian melodrama.

I should add that Shakespeare's Globe has taught us many lessons. That there is, despite the RSC's claims, a huge summer audience for Shakespeare in the capital. That the plays respond to a bold, frontal style of acting. And that the space itself creates a new actor-audience dynamic. But at the moment the Globe runs the risk of ironing out Shakespeare's ambiguities and turning the plays into simple contests between heroes and villains.

Some, of course, will argue that the hissing that greeted Norbert Kentrup's dignified Shylock in the trial scene merely proves that *The Merchant* is a crude, anti-Semitic play. The flaw in this argument is that we have seen countless modern productions that turn Shylock into a tragic victim by emphasising Venetian ghettoisation of the Jews and rabid Christian intolerance. I would argue that *The Merchant* is still morally complex. It is the Globe style that simplifies it. Proof comes in the treatment of Bassanio, played by Mark Rylance with incisive charm. His wooing of Portia was greeted with "applause and universal shout." Yet modern scholarship and theatrical practice see Bassanio as either a fortune-hunting opportunist or a man agonisingly torn between his new wife and his old male lover. We live, inescapably, in a post-Freudian, post-Holocaust world; you cannot turn the clock back and present *The Merchant* as a play untouched by history.

That said, Richard Olivier's production is not without merit. It proves stillness is a powerful weapon on the Globe stage. It boasts a sardonically intelligent Portia in Kathryn Pogson. It also, incredibly, makes Launcelot Gobbo funny in the manic shape of Complicite's Marcello Magni, who is like Harpo, Groucho and Chico rolled into one. But when you come away from a production of *The Merchant* in which Gratiano has been cheered and Shylock hissed, something disturbing has occurred.

As You Like It obviously presents fewer problems. I also found that in Lucy Bailey's production it offered fewer rewards. It's a straight up-and-down version in which Duke Frederick symbolises his deep-dyed villainy by quaffing from a goblet – at least he doesn't peel a grape – and in which the moral boundaries are clearly set. Its strangest feature is Anastasia Hille's heroine, who at one point strips off doublet and hose to reveal her bare bum and offers us a restless Rosalind determined to illustrate every image. Slightly tiring company, I felt, after a hard day in the forest, but there is a definite erotic charge between her and Paul Hilton's Orlando, and the wrestling scenes come off excellently. But what I'd love to see is a director of the calibre of Deborah Warner or Sam Mendes proving the Globe is capable of transcending moral melodrama.

Via Dolorosa by David Hare (World Premiere) Royal Court at the Duke of York's, London: 9 September 1998

Inside David Hare the playwright there has always been a journalist struggling to get out. But the two merge perfectly in this one-man play, which is both a brilliant piece of reportage about Hare's journey to the Middle East and a cunningly shaped work of art. For good measure, Hare also proves to be a performer of surprising elan.

He starts a little tentatively. Emerging from a door in the back wall of the stripped stage and clad in crisp white shirt and dark flannels, he crosses a narrow bridge like a man about to enter a bear-pit. At first, with eyes fixed in the middle distance, he even seems to be reading off some imaginary autocue. But gradually his confidence builds, his timing grows, and by the end the sardonic observer has been informed by the passion that he encounters in his Middle Eastern journey. This is the real secret of the evening: it is a voyage of discovery in which Hare, coming from a society where faith is a form of social embarrassment, finds dogma, division and despair.

Visiting Israel and Palestine, he doesn't sit in judgement even if the play is pervaded by the plight of the Palestinian refugees. But the question Hare implicitly asks is how much the Western visitor can ever fully understand of a world in which belief is literally a matter of life and death. The big issues, however, grow out of scrupulous observation. In Tel Aviv Hare meets a secular liberal like the theatre director, Eran Baniel, who regards the post-1967 preoccupation with land as profoundly "un-Jewish." But, crossing into the occupied territories, Hare stays with a Jewish family who regard the Oslo peace accord as a betrayal, who see Rabin as a traitor and who engage in hair-splitting arguments over Old Testament texts. Secular and religious Jews barely speak the same language.

In Gaza and Ramallah, Hare encounters a similar mixture of fire and fission. An intellectual poet attacks the Western media's demonisation of the Arabs. But a popular politician is equally scathing about the corruption of Arafat's regime, and a distinguished historian sees Israelis and Palestinians as two peoples inseparably bound up in each other's unhappiness.

This is not, nor does it pretend to be, the whole truth about the Middle East. But it shows Hare's intelligence and irony encountering the volatile passions of Israeli–Palestinian faith and politics. And, while it questions the value of art in confronting the bare facts of the Holocaust, it reinforces one's faith in theatre as a means of communication. Hare, astutely directed by Stephen Daldry, records his subjective impressions, delineates character, fleshes out the issues and shows he has been changed by his Middle Eastern experience. When he returns to the comfort of his Hampstead home, you feel he is both relieved and yet scorched by his encounters with people living in a political crucible. You go expecting to hear a talk. What you get is a deeply moving theatrical mosaic.

1999

The Colour of Justice, edited by Richard Norton-Taylor from the Macpherson Inquiry Tricycle, London: 14 January 1999

What can we do? How can we change the situation? That was the first question asked from the floor at the post-performance discussion after *The Colour of Justice*, Richard Norton-Taylor's edited version of the public inquiry into the death of Stephen Lawrence.

Jon Snow, in the chair, made several telling points. Had cameras been allowed into the original inquiry, he claimed, it would have had a profound effect on British life. It would have exposed us all to the reality of police procedures and the nature of racism in the community. Since that didn't happen, he urged the widest possible circulation of Norton-Taylor's edited version. One broadcasting organisation – not named – has already turned it down. Snow urged us all to write to Alan Yentob at the BBC to request that it be shown. He's right, the more people that see this astonishing work the better.

The Tricycle already has an outstanding record in bringing documentary reality to the stage. It has given us edited versions of the Scott arms-to-Iraq inquiry, the Nuremburg trials and the War Crimes Tribunal at the Hague. But this version of the Stephen Lawrence Inquiry is, in some ways, even more potent. It deals with a developing situation – only this week the Police Complaints Authority absolved the officers involved in the case of racism. It also gives us a vital context in which to assess Sir William Macpherson's findings to be published next month.

The theatre, of course, is an emotional place. But the supreme virtue of this staging by Nicolas Kent and Surian Fletcher-Jones is that it allows the facts that emerged in the inquiry to speak for themselves. Even if one is broadly familiar with the case, one is stunned by the incompetence – to put it at its mildest – with which it was handled. Stephen Lawrence was stabbed to death in Eltham, south London, on the evening of 22 April 1993. But endless questions arise. Why was no attempt made by the police to administer first aid? Why were Stephen Lawrence's attackers not instantly pursued? Why were the suspects, named by a police informant, not put under surveillance till the following Monday? Why have notes of all conversations with the informant gone missing?

All this and much more emerges in the course of the inquiry's patient probing. It is not a court of law but it reveals a forensic appetite for detail, and many of the exchanges are highly dramatic. An ex-detective sergeant, who stolidly denies a racist motive to the attack, cracks under questioning from Michael Mansfield QC and explodes, "He's accusing me of racism in a public inquiry." William Illsley, a now-retired detective chief superintendent, rejects the suggestion that he screwed up a piece of paper from Doreen Lawrence naming the attackers. Ian Johnston, Assistant Commissioner of the Metropolitan Police, apologises for the police's failings and asks forgiveness (from the row behind me came a muttered, vehement cry of "Never.").

The most shocking moment in the inquiry comes when a suspect is put on the stand. He stonewalls in the face of questions from both Mansfield and Macpherson. But we hear about the cache of arms, including knives, guns and swords, found in the house where he lived. We also hear extracts from conversations recorded in the house. "Every nigger," says the suspect's brother, "should have their arms and legs chopped up and left with fucking stumps." As the witness leaves the stand, Macpherson shields his eyes in an involuntary gesture of disgust.

A public inquiry is a form of theatre. But the theatre is not itself a judicial instrument. What this inquiry gains from being staged, even in edited form, is that it forces us to confront the level of racism in Britain today – far worse, according to Neville Lawrence, than when he first came here in the 1960s. It also obliges us to ask what it stems from and how it can possibly be uprooted. As for the police, for all their evasions and apologies, one simple fact emerges: incompetence at this level becomes, whether consciously or not, a form of racism. Had it been a young white male found bleeding to death by an Eltham bus-stop, would they not have reacted totally differently?

After the stunning performance – played by the Tricycle's now regular documentary team including Jeremy Clyde, William Hoyland, Thomas Wheatley and Jan Chappell – it was sobering to confront the actual players in the drama. "Racial hatred," said Michael Mansfield, the Lawrences' QC, "is living amongst us." Imran Khan, their solicitor, claimed "Stephen Lawrence was betrayed by the whole criminal justice system." And Neville Lawrence added, with his customary quiet dignity, "The issues raised by this inquiry are for everybody – not just for one set of the community." Exactly. This inquiry, devastatingly, holds a mirror up to our society; which is why it is not only the most important piece of theatre in London but, as Jon Snow says, should be seen by the maximum number. Over to you, Mr Yentob.

In fact, The Colour of Justice, *directed by Nicolas Kent and produced by Simon Curtis, was filmed for BBC2 and transmitted to great acclaim on 21 February 1999.*

Lift Off by Roy Williams (World Premiere) Royal Court Theatre Upstairs at the Ambassadors, London: 1 March 1999

With racism finally out in the open, Roy Williams's play acquires a pungent timeliness. It deals, however, not with institutions but with individuals. And what it says, with vivid theatricality, is that divisions between Black and white are confused by stock ideas about masculinity and hard and soft behaviour which start in childhood and continue into adult life.

It kicks off in a playground where a white boy, Tone, imitates the patois and aggro of his Black chum, Mal. Both, in striving to be hard, turn on Rich, a dreamy loner who spends his time making paper aeroplanes. Ten years on, in early manhood, Tone and Mal maintain a close friendship based on shared toughness and mutual envy. Tone yearns for his pal's physical confidence and ease while Mal is jealous of the built-in privileges that come with being white. What scuppers the relationship is sex. Mal has a fling with Tone's sister and Tone himself eventually succumbs to the ardent overtures of a female racist.

Williams not only puts on stage something rarely seen – the prickly friendship of young Black and white men – he also, with some subtlety, shows both as victims of inherited notions of masculinity. Even as schoolkids, Tone and Mal talk in aggressively sexual language – "Shut your mum's legs" is a routine insult – and brag about how many times they have been stopped by the police. Williams also reinforces the point that adolescent attitudes die hard by interweaving the playground scenes with those from later life.

Williams's plotting is a bit schematic: when the adult Mal contracts a potentially fatal illness, it is used to prove that there aren't enough Blacks on the medical register to provide a bone-marrow transplant. But this is a genuinely original play: one that shows racial divisions are often muddied by gender politics, cultural imitation and self-loathing. Williams offers no solutions but he dramatises the problem with mordant accuracy. Indhu Rubasingham's excellent production is also finely acted by Michael Price and Alex Wilkinshaw as the mature Mal and Tone, by Ashley Chin and Sid Mitchell as their younger selves and by Laura Sadler and Sarah Cakebread as the female catalysts who expose the precariousness of their friendship.

House and Garden by Alan Ayckbourn
(World Premiere)
Stephen Joseph Theatre, Scarborough:
21 June 1999

Sitting comfortably? I'll begin. Alan Ayckbourn's new play, *House*, set on a Saturday in August, is being staged in Scarborough's proscenium arch McCarthy Theatre. Meanwhile, Ayckbourn's *Garden*, which takes place during exactly the same period, is presented simultaneously in the adjacent theatre. The same characters appear in both, which suggests a third, unseen drama taking place off stage with actors madly commuting between the two venues.

Even by Ayckbourn's standards, this is a mind-boggling technical feat. In *The Norman Conquests* he offered us three perspectives on the same country weekend. But here, because the action is simultaneous, the plays have to be perfectly synchronised. What happens if audience reaction in one house throws the timing? Ayckbourn has even built in adjustable comic business to ensure that the two plays reach their destination on time and enable the actors to take overlapping curtain calls.

The danger is one becomes obsessed by the stopwatch mechanics and ignores the content. But, seen together, the plays offer an extraordinary comic-melancholic vision of married life in which women end up as resilient victims. *House*, in particular, is one of Ayckbourn's best plays – a study in domestic disintegration in which much of the key action happens off stage. It is set in the sitting-room of the wealthy Teddy Platt, a bovine adulterer who is being sounded out by a visiting political fixer about standing as the local MP. The problem is that Teddy's wife refuses to acknowledge his existence, his latest affair with his best friend's spouse is publicly exposed and he becomes embroiled with a dipso French actress who is opening the fete at the bottom of his garden. The play fulfils the definition of farce as the worst day of your life. But it is also a devastating study of differing patterns of destruction.

Teddy, played by Robert Blythe with just the right blundering crassness, is a man who has destroyed his marriage to his well-bred wife (Eileen Battye) through emotional insensitivity. But Ayckbourn introduces a more suave destroyer in the shape of the Tory power-broker, Gavin Ryng-Mayne. In a scene of brutal brilliance, the latter swats off Teddy's bright-eyed, sexually eager schoolgirl daughter as casually as if crushing a fly. As played by Terence Booth and Charlie Mayes, the scene demonstrates the devastation caused by cold-heartedness.

If I prefer *House* to *Garden*, it is because so much is left to our imagination: we can envisage both the emotional havoc taking place in the lower meadow and the sodden awfulness of a summer fete. In *Garden*, we see all this for ourselves. But Ayckbourn also subtly introduces another form of marital destruction: as Barry McCarthy's saintly doctor learns that his wife, beautifully played by Janie Dee, has been having an affair with his best friend, we see the ruinous effect of selfless tolerance.

You have to see both plays to understand Ayckbourn's overall design, and to realise that he is consciously echoing previous plays, such as *Woman in Mind* and *Just Between Ourselves*, while introducing new ideas, such as the disruptive effect of a non-English speaking movie actress, played with glamorous skittishness by Sabine Azema. And only when you see both plays do you appreciate the technical ingenuity by which actors serve two masters simultaneously. Ayckbourn shows not just how social rituals descend into chaos but how women require steel and nerve to transcend the brutalising conventions of middle-class marriage. He is an instinctive feminist and these extraordinary plays, which do something unparalleled in the history of drama, eloquently prove the point.

Ricky Jay and his 52 Assistants
Old Vic, London: 24 June 1999

Talent, Olivier once said, is very plentiful but skill is rather rare. But Ricky Jay, the American sleight-of-hand artist who regularly pops up in David Mamet movies such as *House of Games*, offers us two hours of pure, unadulterated, mesmerising skill: you watch entranced as he proves his own affirmation that playing-cards are "the poetry of magic."

Part of the pleasure is that Ricky Jay is nothing like the average vaudeville entertainer. A portly, brown-suited figure with thinning hair and thick forearms, he faintly resembles Orson Welles, who also practiced theatrical magic, in his mixture of irony and erudition. He doesn't just use a pack of cards to display manual mastery. He gives us the history of trickery and conmanship, invokes legendary illusionists and at one point quotes W.E. Henley's translation of Francois Villon. I don't remember David Nixon doing that.

Inside a mock-Victorian drawing room – the Old Vic stage has been reconfigured with 160 spectators sitting in ten tiered rows – Jay proceeds to dazzle us at close range. He makes aces and queen appear and re-appear at will. He explains the techniques of three-card monty, turns cards into hurled weapons, even piercing the outer skin of a huge water melon, and offers endless variations on thimble-rigging in which coloured balls multiply and move around under copper cups. Is it theatre? You bet it is. In fact, this extraordinary show, which David Mamet has directed, epitomises the two key movements in modern theatre. In one sense, it is deeply illusionist: we are baffled and bemused as a card, on which an audience member has inscribed her name, turns up in a sealed pack inside a suitcase. But it is also anti-illusionist, in a Brechtian sense, in that Jay is consciously giving a performance on which he himself offers a running commentary.

In the case of that particular trick, he permits himself a wry smile as he remarks, with scant regard for truth, that the suitcase has hitherto been closed. In short, Ricky Jay affords a dual pleasure: that of watching a sleight-of-hand genius at work while reminding us that he belongs in the salty tradition of the carnival trickster. Prices at the Old Vic are steep but it is worth raiding your piggy-bank for an awe-inspiring display of expertise.

Mnemonic conceived by Simon McBurney (World Premiere) Riverside Studios, London: 26 November 1999

Memory obsesses modern artists. It is there in Borges's story *Funes. The Memorious*, in Peter Brook's *Je suis un Phénomène* and, on both the personal and the collective level, it is the subject of this dazzling Theatre de Complicite show conceived and directed by Simon McBurney: one that uses the company's kaleidoscopic skills to explore the immediacy and immensity of the past.

The evening starts with McBurney himself, who has the timing of a stand-up comic, discoursing on the nature of memory and reminding us that it is not just an act of retrieval but a creative thing: a point Pinter constantly makes in his plays. Persuading us to don a sleeping-mask, he then asks us to remember specific moments in our recent past. From there he guides us back over the generations to imagine the limitless possibilities of our ancestry and the idea that eventually we are all related.

The point of all this becomes clear in the two interweaving strands that make up this tightly-knit two-hour show. On a personal level, we see a character called Virgil (McBurney again) making telephone contact with his girlfriend Alice (Katrin Cartlidge) who has gone on a trans-European quest in search of her lost father, building up a portrait of him through anecdotal memories. On the archaeological level, the show also pursues the story of the corpse of a Neolithic man discovered in 1991 in a glacier on the Austrian–Italian border. Eventually the two stories converge as if to suggest that our private and historic memories are two sides of the same coin. Some would dispute this. Stephen Poliakoff recently wrote a play arguing that today "we record everything and remember nothing." But this Complicite show is nearer in approach to the work of the German director, Peter Stein, who constantly taps into the idea that we share a collective memory which can be re-created through art. What is impressive about *Mnemonic* is not just the ideas: it is also the deftness and skill with which they are theatrically executed. McBurney's naked body becomes not just the Neolithic iceman but also the solitary Virgil onto whose bare torso is projected a visual memory of his girlfriend. A chair mounted on a table and swathed in white cloth becomes a glacier.

Migration, a constant Complicite theme, also becomes the motif that finally links Alice's Baltic father and the Neolithic man: it is as if the history of Europe over 5,000 years is one of search, quest and upheaval. And the show represents another vital stage in Complicite's artistic quest. They started out doing improvised physical comedy. Latterly, they have tackled classic texts. With this compelling show they display a capacity to explore complex ideas and make them rivetingly theatrical.

Noel Coward was born on 16 December 1899. His centenary prompted this re-evaluation.

30 November 1999

He was a snob, a misogynist, often a blinkered jingoist. But he was also a sexual outsider who defied bourgeois convention, and a passionate moralist. He was, of course, Noel Coward, the centenary of whose birth falls on 16 December. And if any single idea has emerged from this year's swathe of celebratory productions, it is that Coward was a mass of contradictions. The received image is of a cool cosmopolitan sophisticate: the reality is that he was a humble Teddington piano-salesman's son who dreamed of making the world dance to his tune.

Contradiction is the essence of Coward. It is also the theme of one of the last, and best, revivals of the centenary year, Philip Prowse's production of *Cavalcade* at the Glasgow Citizens Theatre. Originally conceived for Drury Lane in 1931, the show is traditionally seen as a patriotic pageant about the first 30 years of the century: a parade of *papier mâché* figures leading to a speech about the need for "dignity and greatness and peace" which Margaret Thatcher unashamedly borrowed for a pre-election party political broadcast in 1979. But Prowse has stripped away much of the spectacle, reduced the running time to 90 minutes and exposed the curious mix of sentiment and savagery that holds the piece together. In particular, he brings out the show's anti-militarism. It is no accident that immediately before *Cavalcade* Coward wrote *Post-Mortem*, a bitterly ironic piece about the pointless slaughter of the First World War. And the fulcrum of *Cavalcade* is an extraordinary scene, anticipating *Oh What A Lovely War*, in which the sexy recruiting songs of 1914 are followed by strange images of death. This is hauntingly rendered as a giant Kitchener poster gives way to an expressionist Grim Reaper while lines of stretcher-bearers carry off the dead to the strains of Roses of Picardy.

Class is another key motif in Prowse's revisionist production. In the past the show has seemed a tribute to the gracious stoicism of its heroine, Jane Marryot, who loses one son to the *Titanic* and another to the Flanders trenches. But, as played by Jennifer Hilary, Jane emerges as a radiantly patronising figure who is jolly nice to the servants until the daughter of one of them threatens to marry her son. Prowse also taps into the anger that bubbles away among the working class: when Jane offers her former domestics a present of a doll, her drunken ex-butler rounds on her with a cry of "don't want any fuckin' charity 'ere'." Coward may not have approved the letter, but he would surely have applauded the spirit.

In short, Prowse has brought out the contradictions inherent in *Cavalcade*. In 1931 it was hailed as a patriotic panorama. Yet, on a personal level, it is largely a story of loss and it ends with the famous number, Twentieth Century Blues, which tells us: "In this strange illusion/ Chaos and confusion/People seem to lose their way." *Cavalcade* is actually about the way the high hopes at the start of the century have turned to senseless slaughter and hectic hedonism. In Prowse's production, as a gaunt Michelle Gomez renders the climactic number with Brechtian ferocity, electronic signs whisk us through the century implying that Coward's play was eerily prophetic.

I'm not sure *Cavalcade* can bear quite that much weight but Prowse has grasped an essential truth: that Coward was an extraordinary amalgam of opposites. He was a ceaseless globetrotter who famously liked to retire to bed early with "something eggy on a tray"' a proselytiser for Bohemianism who worked a relentless 12-hour day, a champion of sexual freedom who believed in fastidious decorum.

This last comes out particularly clearly in Sheridan Morley's excellent revival of *A Song at Twilight* at the Gielgud Theatre. The closeted gay writer, Hugo Latymer, lives in permanent fear of repressive, anti-homosexual laws and of Anglo-Saxon moral prejudice. Yet the play is also a passionate defence of artistic privacy. And only two years before he wrote the play, Coward's Diaries show him recoiling with horror from the concentrated camp of New York's gay colony, Fire Island, which he describes as "macabre, sinister, irritating and somehow tragic."

If Coward approved the repeal of the sexual offences act while disliking gay congregations, he was equally Janus-like in his attitude to women. As both Maria Aitken's Chichester revival of *Easy Virtue* and Philip Franks's National Theatre *Private Lives* showed, Coward championed women who were artistic, progressive and unshackled: Larita in the former play reads Proust's *Sodom and Gomorrah* in the shires while Amanda in the latter displays a, for the times, mannish independence. Yet Coward also reveals a dislike of predatory vamps like Myra in *Hay Fever*, who "uses sex like a shrimping net" and of religious frumps such as Marion Whittaker in *Easy Virtue*.

If this year of Noel has proved anything, it is that he is the most maddeningly elusive dramatist of the century. He was a celebrity-snob who idealised "ordinary" people, an empire loyalist emotionally attached to America, a homosexual writer adept at portraying heterosexual passion. If you can never quite pin him down it is because he retained to the last a subversive, adolescent mischief that loved to upend official attitudes. The one thing you can't do is betray his innate verbal rhythm, as proved by the horrendous West End revival of *Hay Fever* which fell over the Coward celebrations like a damp mackintosh.

But Coward has a way of surviving even the worst productions by virtue of his wit, inborn sense of theatre and a paradoxical nature that enabled him to run with the late Victorian hare while hunting with the contemporary hounds. Born into the last century, he came to epitomise this one and managed to keep a delicate foot in both camps.

Hopes of Renewal:
2000–9

The defining moment of the decade came in May 2000. That was when Peter Boyden, an arts management consultant, published a report making an ironclad case for increased public funding of theatre. Arts Council England rose to the challenge, an extra £25 million was made available by Government and the results were instantly visible. Regional theatres had their biggest boost in decades. That, along with the emergence of directorial talents like Michael Grandage in Sheffield, Rupert Goold in Northampton and Gemma Bodinetz in Liverpool, meant for once we had a truly national theatre. There were hiccups along the way – not least during the economic crisis of 2008 when arts funding hit the buffers – but the nub of the Noughties was that theatres were at last able to plan ahead instead of being caught in a permanent backs-to-the-wall crisis.

The other key moment was also financial: the decision by Nicholas Hytner, who took over from Trevor Nunn as director of the National Theatre in 2003, to launch a £10 ticket scheme supported by Travelex. I once heard Peter Brook in a lecture at the Donmar being asked where the future of theatre lay. Everyone expected a lengthy philosophical disquisition. Brook's answer was surprisingly simple: cheap tickets. Hytner proved that to be true. In the £10 ticket scheme's first year, a staggering 33 per cent of the audience said they were visiting the National Theatre for the first time. When you consider that Hytner, under the banner of NT Live, also initiated the relay of productions to cinemas around Britain and the world, you could argue that he did more than anyone in modern times to make theatre available to everyone.

New money and cheap tickets had a liberating effect, particularly in the dramatic re-emergence of political theatre. At the start of the decade, David Hare wrote about the importance for dramatists of recognising that "the external universe may be richer and more suggestive than the inside of their own heads." Anger about the 2003 Iraq War, the growth of verbatim-drama and the emergence of a new generation of Black and Asian playwrights – including Roy Williams, Kwame Kewi-Armah, Tanika Gupta and Gurpreet Kaur Bhatti – prepared to examine the racism inherent in British society all contributed to the idea of drama as a genuinely public forum. You could see the results in Hare's own work (*Stuff Happens*, *The Permanent Way*, *Gethsemane*, *The Power of Yes*), in the rediscovery of political satire (Justin Butcher's *The Madness of George Dubya*, Alistair Beaton's *Feelgood*); in the slew of documentary plays (including *Guantanamo* and *Afghanistan: The Great Game* at the Tricycle, *Alive From Palestine* at the Royal Court, *Black Watch* in Scotland) that took their inspiration from recent events. In the Noughties the theatre was arguably far more adept than television or film at capturing the spirit of an age in which dreams of a new Jerusalem, as Tony Blair lead Labour from 1997 onwards to three successive election victories, were dissolved in the reality of a Middle East war and a financial crisis.

Our senior dramatists were also on top form during the decade: Michael Frayn with *Democracy*, Tom Stoppard with *Rock 'N' Roll*, Alan Bennett with *The History Boys*, Ronald Harwood with *Taking Sides* and *Collaboration*. Sadly, however, we lost Harold Pinter who began the decade with *Celebration*, went on to win the Nobel Prize for Literature and to give a mesmerising performance in Beckett's *Krapp's Last Tape*. Stephen Evans, Pinter's publisher at Faber, once put to me a daunting question. "Where," he asked, "are the writers under 30 who have made the same impact Harold and John Osborne had made by that age?" On reflection, I think it may have been the wrong question. At that point in time you could no more find a like-for-like replacement for Harold Pinter than, in acting terms, you could for Laurence Olivier. What we saw, instead of a handful of solitary icons, was a healthy diversification of writing talent. Lucy Prebble (*The Sugar Syndrome*, *Enron*), Laura Wade (*Breathing Corpses*), Polly Stenham (*That Face*, *Tusk Tusk*) were in the vanguard of a new generation of women dramatists; Conor McPherson and Martin McPherson reminded us of English drama's historic dependence on Ireland; Jez Butterworth and Mike Bartlett charted, in different ways, the crisis in masculinity. If the decade proved anything, it was that writing talent was abundant and democratically spread.

The Noughties also witnessed the growth of groups who no longer depended on a solo author.

The theatre company Kneehigh progressed from being a Cornish collector's item to popular entertainers with their multimedia production, *Brief Encounter*. Punchdrunk merged live performance with art-installation in shows like *Faustus*, *The Masque of the Red Death* and *It Felt Like a Kiss* which ended with spectators being chased down a darkened corridor by a masked man with a chainsaw. Shunt was another collective, often working in the vaults under London Bridge, which produced shows like *Tropicana* and *Amato Saltone*. But while the young especially were drawn to the Punchdrunk/Shunt style of show, a false schism was created in sections of the media between "text-based" (supposedly for traditionalists) and "physical" theatre (which was hip and cool). For a start, I couldn't think of any great theatre that wasn't based on an alliance between word and image. The danger of a theatre that relied too narrowly on a visceral experience, however momentarily thrilling, was that it would leave no trace on the memory.

Like every decade, the Noughties had its downside. As I saw it, audience behaviour, from mid-show texting to the scrunching of plastic glasses under foot, showed signs of decline. Stock genres such as farces and thrillers, on which dramatists like Joe Orton, Tom Stoppard and Michael Frayn had played elegant variations, became ever rarer. Celebrity casting was not exactly enhanced by the appearance of Madonna in *Up in Arms* and even the frequent non-appearance of Martine McCutcheon in the National Theatre's *My Fair Lady*. But, in general, acting standards were as high as ever. One has only to think of Sinead Cusack in Tom Stoppard's *Rock 'N' Roll*, Noma Dumezweni in Kay Adshead's *A Bogus Woman,* Lindsay Duncan in Kevin Elyot's *Mouth to Mouth* and Mark Rylance in everything from *Jerusalem* to *Boeing Boeing* to realise that, whatever the temporal ups and downs of British theatre, you could always rely on the acting.

Above all, it was a decade that showed a renewed sense of purpose and vigour. New institutions arose such as the National Theatre of Scotland which, under Vicky Featherstone, became a peripatetic marvel with productions like *Black Watch* and *Be Near Me.* A long-established institution such as the Royal Shakespeare Company, under the tutelage of Michael Boyd, reaffirmed its identity with an epic eight-play Shakespeare History cycle that moved from Stratford-on-Avon's Courtyard to London's Roundhouse. But much of the credit for the theatre's renewed sense of assurance can be traced back to the Boyden Report which argued that standstill funding leads to a 4 per cent decline in artistic activity whereas even a small increase produces more work, higher attendances and better value for money. That was the real lesson of the Noughties: that, in the words of Nicholas Hytner, "subsidy works."

2000

The Island by Athol Fugard, John Kani and Winston Ntshona (Revival) Lyttelton, National Theatre, London: 27 January 2000

At a time when British theatre seems scared witless of politics, it is exhilarating to see this play back on a major stage. Created by Athol Fugard, John Kani and Winston Ntshona and first seen 25 years ago at the Royal Court, it has, if anything, gained with time. Apartheid may have crumbled, but the play's celebration of defiance and awareness of the human cost of incarceration remain timeless. Its setting is Robben Island and its subject is imprisonment: the way it both unites and divides, affirms the resisting spirit while punishing the vulnerable body.

John and Winston, the names of the characters as well as the actors, have shared a cell for three years and have become like an asexual Beckettian marriage. At first we see them mimetically shifting sand in a meaningless Sisyphean labour. Back in their cell, having tended each other's wounds, they prepare a scene from Sophocles' *Antigone*: John is bullyingly dominant, Winston fearful of public humiliation. But the crunch comes when John learns that a commutation of his sentence means he will be released in three months while Winston will do life. This arbitrary divorce both releases covert tensions and yet makes possible the performance of Antigone's trial and punishment.

Politics and art miraculously coalesce. Quite obviously, the play is a protest against a brutal system: the horror of the sand-shifting lies in its utter pointlessness. But the play also makes a complex statement about imprisonment. The two men enjoy the testy togetherness of married partners. But John's provisional release is also divisive. When Winston cries: "Your freedom stinks and it's driving me mad" it both expresses Winston's envious rage and questions the meaning of freedom in the South Africa of the 1970s. As in all good political theatre, and as in *Antigone* itself, there is both irony and ambivalence.

The piece is inseparable from its two superb performers and what is astonishing watching Athol Fugard's production, now supervised by Peter Brook, is how the passing years have enriched the molten relationship between Kani and Ntshona. It's not just that the opening scene requires even more Herculean effort. They are so finely tuned to each other's responses that they do seem to be cellmates. This revival could have been an act of cultural piety, but has become a piece of living theatre: it transcends the moment of its creation to express permanent truths about strategies of survival wherever oppression and unjust imprisonment prevail. It also reminds us that the best political theatre is always vibrant, compelling art.

Celebration (World Premiere)/*The Room* (Revival) by Harold Pinter Almeida, London: 24 March 2000

More than 40 years separate these plays: Pinter's latest and his very first which together make up a richly entertaining double bill. Yet, for all their obvious contrasts, I was struck by a curious similarity between the two works: both reveal Pinter's abiding fascination with hermetic, insulated figures who suddenly find their space invaded and their territory threatened.

In *Celebration*, the funniest, feistiest piece Pinter has written in years, the safe haven in question is a smart restaurant where a wedding anniversary is in full, raucous swing. Two married couples, actually brothers and sisters, sit at one banquette: a banker and his wife at another. What Pinter reveals, with a good deal of satirical verve, is the coarse swagger and loutish insensitivity of these walking wallets and their spouses.

But Pinter's play is much more than an obvious attack on the nerdy nouveau riche. Just as in *Party Time* we see a group of smart socialites rejoicing in a "club" which cuts them off from grim reality, so here the diners use the restaurant as a retreat from the outside world: a world in which the two brothers operate as strategy consultants whose job is "enforcing peace." And, as always in Pinter, there is no such thing as a harmless sanctuary: here the threat to an evening of crude conviviality comes from an intrusive waiter who offers increasingly bizarre, name-dropping tales of a grandfather who seems to have known everyone this century.

Behind the play's wild comedy lurks something strange and incalculable which is beautifully caught in Pinter's fast-moving production. The performances too are spot-on with Keith Allen and Andy de la Tour catching the matching vulgarity of the two brothers, Lia Williams combining sexiness and asperity as the banker's trophy wife and Danny Dyer as the far-from-dumb waiter implying a world of eccentric otherness far beyond the comprehension of these self-absorbed diners.

If the archetypal Pinter situation is one of space-invasion, then you see its origins in *The Room*, first performed at Bristol University in 1957. Here the immured heroine, Rose, finds the rooted privacy which she shares with her silent husband successively threatened by her talkative landlord, a pair of married flat-hunters and by a blind Black man called Riley who mysteriously bids her to come home. The milieu may be miles away from that of *Celebration* but in both plays womb-like retreats are opened up and anything "foreign" is seen as a potential menace. Admittedly the symbolism is more heavy-handed than in later, greater Pinter but what is extraordinary about his new production is the intensity of feeling between Lindsay Duncan's panic-stricken Rose and George Harris's monumentally imposing Riley. Pairing the play with *Celebration* also seems an inspired idea.

Richard II by William Shakespeare
The Other Place, Stratford-upon-Avon:
1 April 2000

A great adventure has begun. Over the next year the Royal Shakespeare Company is to stage all eight of Shakespeare's histories in chronological sequence. It kicks off with Steven Pimlott's fiercely intelligent, modern-dress *Richard II* in The Other Place, converted by David Fielding into a space resembling a white-walled squash-court or science lab: a perfect setting for this masterly dissection of kingship.

Modern dress, even when stylised with lots of maroon and grey maxi-coats, creates problems for this most ceremonial of plays: one that is steeped in medieval myth and that shows the notion of the king as God-sanctioned monarch giving way to personal ambition and legalistic statecraft. But Pimlott and his designer, Sue Willmington, pull it off in various ways. They suggest Richard presides over an already divided kingdom: one in which rancorous bullies confront each other in the lists at Coventry, with lethal axes. They make good use of symbolic props, including a long wooden casket which variously becomes throne, vertical mirror and coffin. Above all, with the aid of Simon Kemp's bright, overhead strip-lighting, they give the work a strong European dimension: it becomes a Brechtian analysis of the nature of power.

One could pick holes in the execution: I distrust the modern habit, already seen in *Macbeth* this week at London's BAC, of plucking lines from the fifth act to use as a choric refrain. But the abiding impression is of dazzling clarity. Samuel West's Richard moves from heedless tyrant to Christian martyr with absolute, and absolutist, conviction. Donning crown and ermine when it suits him, West shows the raging wreck that lurks beneath: he lunges at the prophetic John of Gaunt like a berserk thug and, having been likewise ticked off by the Duke of York, promptly makes him Lord Governor.

West also captures Richard's accelerating self-consciousness, wrapping himself in the national flag for the Westminster deposition scene, and mordant irony: his cry to Bolingbroke of "Here, cousin, seize the crown" ripples with taunting ambiguity. I have known more lyrical Richards: what West conveys is the character's progress from Ceausescu to Christ. David Troughton's Bolingbroke is also brilliantly effective: an overweening politician who cloaks driving ambition under a sense of wrong – "I am a subject and I challenge law" – and who swiftly dispatches Richard's followers with a bullet through the brain. But, having staged his takeover, Troughton also captures the hermetic isolation of power, making redundant the decision to end the play with the opening lines of *Henry 1V Part One*. David Killick's dithering York, Christopher Saul's Machiavellian Northumberland and Adam Levy's armed-to-the-teeth, SAS-style Harry Percy lend unflinching support.

Since the Histories will have a variety of directors, this production may not provide a pattern for the future. It does, however, rescue *Richard II* from medieval pageantry and reveal its modern relevance as a study of the way revolution often begets tyranny

Blue/Orange by Joe Penhall (World Premiere) Cottesloe, National Theatre, London: 14 April 2000

Joe Penhall's exuberant new play lifts the curse that has afflicted the National's new writing policy for the past three years. Very much in the manner of Shaw in *The Doctor's Dilemma*, Penhall uses the medical trade as a metaphor for the vanity, self-deception and ostentatious certainty of all professions that work against the common interest.

Penhall's setting is a psychiatric hospital where two doctors engage in a Darwinian battle for survival. The catalyst for their conflict is Christopher, a young Black patient who believes that oranges are blue and that Idi Amin is his father. The senior consultant, Robert, wants him thrust back into the community immediately, partly on principle and partly because of an acute bed-shortage. Bruce, a first-year doctor, argues with equal vehemence that Christopher is on the border between neurotic and psychotic and needs further treatment. What follows is a ferocious contest of wills carried out, literally, over the head of the patient.

Part of Penhall's success lies in keeping one's sympathies constantly shifting. One moment you think Bruce has a protective idealism: the next that Robert has a paternalistic common sense. Gradually it dawns on one, however, that they are both more concerned with confirming their pet theories than with responding to the patient's needs: he becomes the ping-pong ball in their private battle and a means of revealing their covert racism.

But, although there are references to the pros and cons of community care, Penhall is really making the wider Shavian point that all professions are a conspiracy against the laity and eventually become wrapped in hermetic self-regard.

Credibility is sometimes stretched, as when Robert naively swallows the idea that his junior rival is on drugs. But Penhall has the gift of making serious points in a comic manner and of conveying moral indignation without preaching. He also gets the benefit of a finely tuned production by Roger Michell played on a slightly skewed, in-the-round stage in which William Dudley's clinical conference room is gradually reduced to chaos.

Bill Nighy is excellent as the senior consultant whose willowy assurance gives way to bursts of throttled, incoherent rage. But there is equally good work from Andrew Lincoln as his junior whose curative instinct masks a deep careerism and from Chiwetel Ejiofor as the schizophrenic patient who both sees through these warring bullies and yet is poignantly dependent on their help. Sympathy for the victim is perfectly matched by Penhall's stinging satire on the arrogant assurance of professionalism.

4.48 Psychosis by Sarah Kane (World Premiere) Royal Court Theatre Upstairs, London: 30 June 2000

Five-and-a-half years ago Sarah Kane burst upon an astonished world with *Blasted* at the Royal Court's Theatre Upstairs. Now her final play, *4.48 Psychosis,* gets a posthumous production at the same address. What is staggering is the contrast between the two occasions.

Blasted, in which the raw violence of Bosnian civil war erupted into a Leeds hotel room, was greeted when I saw it with a mixture of disbelief and outrage: the homburg-hatted man in front of me stomped out shouting "bring back the censor." At the new play, a sombre, poetic and subjective meditation on suicide, the audience watches in near-silence: lovers clutch each other for comfort, someone quietly weeps, and, at the end, one person incongruously rises to applaud the cast. In just over five short years Sarah Kane moved from disrupter of the peace to dramatic icon.

Judging *4.48 Psychosis* is difficult. How on earth do you award aesthetic points to a 75-minute suicide note? – which is what the play, written shortly before Kane's death, effectively is. Three actors – two women and a man – sit under a vast tilted mirror in Jeremy Herbert's spare, beautiful design and explore the rage, pain, turbulence and self-excavation that leads to suicide. It is not a play in the familiar sense of the word. It is more, in the manner of Kane's penultimate work, *Crave*, a dramatised poem. A piece for voices. But one in which the main voice has been stilled. "After 4.48," runs one prophetic line, "I shall not speak again."

But does the play, which takes us inside Kane's head, have any general application? I cannot speak for others, but what it taught me was the frustration of the potential suicide at the way the rest of the world marches to a different, rational rhythm, and assumes there are cures and answers for a state of raging alienation. "I am deadlocked," says Kane, "by that smooth psychiatric voice of reason which tells me there is an objective reality in which my body and mind are one. But I am not here and never have been." It is the sheer disconnectedness of the suicide that Kane expresses so vividly.

A Tennessee Williams character says that we are all sentenced to solitary confinement inside our own skins. For Kane, a poetic metaphor became a literal truth. And it is her own tragic isolation she so fiercely articulates: "My life is caught in a web of reason spun by a doctor to augment the sane." It is a ruthlessly self-analytical theatrical poem. But within it there is evidence of Kane's gallows humour. At one point she contemplates a conclusive method of suicide: take an overdose, slash one's wrists and then hang oneself. "It couldn't possibly be misconstrued," she wryly says, "as a cry for help. "At other moments Kane seems be taking her sly, posthumous revenge on her critics. "An expressionist nag," she calls herself, which is exactly the phrase used by one reviewer of *Cleansed* but then she adds, in a typical Kane touch, "stalling between two fools."

As a piece of theatre, *4.48 Psychosis* is grave and haunting. James Macdonald directs it with meticulous precision Daniel Evans, Jo McInnes and Madeleine Potter perform it with unsparing honesty. But the play is as much a literary as a theatrical event. Like Sylvia Plath's *Edge*, it is a rare example of the writer recording the act she is about to perform. "The woman is perfected," wrote Plath just before her own suicide. "Her dead body wears the smile of accomplishment." I am not sure if you could quite say that of Sarah Kane: what this play proves is that her death was every bit as uncompromising as her creative life.

The Bogus Woman by Kay Adshead
(World Premiere)
Traverse, Edinburgh: 9 August 2000

I recently suggested that women dramatists tend to take an oblique view of politics. But now along comes a play which demolishes that argument by overtly attacking the abuse of human rights in Britain. It is called *The Bogus Woman*, is written by Kay Adshead and is stunningly performed by Noma Dumezweni at Edinburgh's Traverse Theatre.

Adshead's central character is a journalist and poet who has fled civil strife in Africa where she has seen her father, husband and child killed before her eyes. Once in Britain, however, she suffers the ritual humiliations of the asylum-seeker. At Campsfield Detention Centre she witnesses and endures racial abuse and protests by going on hunger strike. The British authorities make basic mistakes in verifying her credentials. Her case goes through a protracted legal process worthy of *Bleak House*. And, even when she is granted temporary admission, she finds life economically impossible, is driven into homelessness and prostitution and is eventually sent back home to await certain death.

Adshead has researched her play thoroughly and has come up with a terrifying scenario: one that attacks the system of entrusting detention centres to private security firms, of Kafka-esque appeal tribunals and judicial reviews, and, not least, of the weekly £30 food vouchers that barely cover life's basic necessities. My only cavil is that the play pins the entire blame on New Labour which, we are told, "is looking for scalps to hang on the Home Office belt." No mention is made of the rancid xenophobia of the middle-market tabloids or the braying hysteria of the Tories, both of which have helped to create the climate of fear that surrounds the issue of asylum seekers.

But this is a powerful, passionate, committed piece of theatre that, if seen widely enough, might change hearts and minds. If I were Greg Dyke, I would put it straight on BBC TV and invite Jack Straw to respond in the course of a properly focused, rational debate. But, even if that doesn't happen, at least this production, staged by the Red Room and Mama Quillo, shows that theatre still has the capacity to address public issues. It is also brilliantly played by Dumezweni, who switches astonishingly from playing the abused, suffering protagonist to portraying the warders, nurses, lawyers and fellow asylum seekers she encounters on her journey through a land that once stood for tolerance and liberty.

The opening sentence of this review now looks faintly misogynist. It was based, however, on my review of three plays seen at the Traverse immediately before The Bogus Woman. *All three were very good: what they had in common was the confrontation of opposed worlds and a fascination with oblique, unresolved situations. Abi Morgan's* Splendour *showed four women from different cultures thrown together in a city on the brink of civil war. Zinnie Harris's* Further Than The Furthest Thing *was about the disruptive effect on individual lives of a volcanic explosion on a remote Atlantic island. Sue Glover's* Shetland Saga *dealt with the collision between a Shetland community and a group of stranded Bulgarian sailors. I admired all three plays but I noted their tendency to confine political realities to the periphery. Any idea that this was related to gender was instantly rebutted by* The Bogus Woman. *I should also have remembered Sarah Kane's* Blasted.

Is there a Crisis in Black Theatre? An inquiry prompted by an interview with the Tricycle Theatre's director, Nicolas Kent.

18 October 2000

Nicolas Kent, who runs the Tricycle Theatre in north London, has done as much as anyone in British theatre to raise our consciousness of race issues. It was he who presented the most important play of last year – *The Colour of Justice*, a work that dealt with the Stephen Lawrence inquiry. So when I asked Kent whether British theatre is racist, whether there is a prejudice against Black and Asian companies, whether our theatre fails to reflect the cultural diversity of modern Britain, I expected him to be critical. What I did not expect was a wholesale indictment of theatrical racism and a vigorous seminar on the subject.

We were talking in Kent's office 90 minutes before the Tricycle's curtain rose on an intriguing double bill. The plays were Alice Childress's *Wine in the Wilderness* – a 1969 Black American play – and Winsome Pinnock's *Water*, a modern British response to it. When I asked Kent if there is a crisis in Black theatre in Britain, he went off like a rocket.

"Absolutely," he said. "A total crisis. In the past two years alone a number of companies and events have disappeared: Carib, Temba, Double Edge, the Black Theatre Season, the Roundhouse Project. Along with the companies, the regular African-Caribbean audience is also dissolving. But I could go on and on listing the problems. The fact that there is no theatre building run by a Black or Asian director, that there is no Black children's company and that theatre staffs and boards are overwhelmingly white. If you read the Arts Council-commissioned Boyden Report into English Producing Theatres, you discover that only 16 out of 463 board members nationwide are Black. Given that we at the Tricycle have eight of them, Stratford East five and Hampstead two, that must leave one Black board member for the rest of the country."

But hasn't some progress been made? The National Theatre and the Royal Shakespeare Company, for instance, actively pursue a policy of integrated casting that transcends mere tokenism. "That's welcome," says Kent. "But it's not the real issue any more than are the kind of cosmetic schemes dreamed up by the London Arts Board. We don't just need to be told that the RSC is to have a Black Henry VI. What we need is enough money to support Black companies to do Black-generated work. I think we also need to confront our own racism on a personal and institutional level. The press and broadcasting media, for instance, have a built-in racism that is just as pervasive as anything you will find in the theatre."

All the facts support Kent's arguments about the British theatre. Once there were 18 revenue-funded Black and Asian theatre companies, now there are two. All but 80 of the 2,009 staff permanently employed in English theatres are white. And with odd exceptions – such as a season of short plays called Ticket to Write produced by Paines Plough and West Yorkshire Playhouse – contemporary Black and Asian experience goes largely unrecorded.

Yet within all this I discover a strange paradox. While Kent attends to pressing first-night matters, he asks three colleagues to add their perspectives. In defiance of economic logic and social fact, it is their overwhelming faith in the future that hits me between the eyes. Two of them, both Kent protegees, have the advantage of youth. Gemma Emmanuel-Waterton is a trainee administrator who radiates energy the moment she walks into a room. In July 2001 she will be running a Black arts festival called Push, on the South Bank. If there is a crisis in Black theatre, she thinks it's partly because young artists are drawn to the economic security of TV. "Racism," she says, "is my last port of call as an excuse."

Surian Fletcher-Jones, an Asian director, also finds she has acquired enough confidence and contacts at the Tricycle to launch herself into the freelance world. And actor Ray Shell, who spent four years in *Starlight Express* and who is writing a new musical, talks animatedly about the melting-pot mateyness he finds in his part of the East End. None of the three is complacent. Each desperately wants to raise the Black and Asian profile. But each has a fiery positiveness that counterpoints Kent's legitimate sense of crisis.

So too does the Tricycle's double bill. It puts to shame much of the gilded shit that currently passes for entertainment in the West End. Winsome Pinnock's *Water* is a fascinating two-hander about a young Black painter, famed for the raw, blood-and-guts veracity of her work, who turns out under journalistic probing to be not quite what she seems. Like Orson Welles's *F for Fake*, it deals with questionable notions of authenticity in art. Vigorously performed by Cecilia Noble and Gary McDonald, it also suggests that much overhyped Britart is a load of bull and that, in our celebrity-crazed culture, the hoaxer is the ultimate hero. Whereas Pinnock's play is about the commercial value of artistic lies, Alice Childress's *Wine in the Wilderness*, originally written for American television, is about the moral value of personal truth. The setting is a Harlem studio at the time of the 1964 riots where a young artist is painting an iconic triptych exploring Black womanhood. Youthful innocence and mythic nobility have been done. Now he needs an image of messed-up modernity and, to that end, is provided with a brash factory worker named Tomorrow whose flat has just been burned to the ground.

Essentially, this is a variation on the Pygmalion story. Instead of a statue that comes to life we have a funky Harlemite who persuades the painter that real beauty is to be found not in dead myths but in the rich variety of 1960s Black America. Childress sometimes makes her points with the subtlety of a sledgehammer, but the play has a soaringly affirmative conclusion, reminiscent of Arnold Wesker's *Roots*, and yields a stunning central performance from Jenny Jules. A product of the Tricycle's Youth Theatre, she combines an attenuated frame with a spirit as big as Grand Central Station. In her mixture of ebullience and vulnerability, she knocks into several cocked hats the superannuated supermodels and celluloid idols who reduce some theatre critics to pulp. She not only crowns an intricately programmed and richly entertaining evening, but also embodies the perverse paradox of Black theatre. On an institutional level, it is in deep crisis. Individually, however, it brims with talent that adds to the joy of life. The real tragedy would be if that talent were wasted because of our theatre's unconscious racism.

2001

A Raisin in the Sun by Lorraine Hansberry (Revival) Young Vic, London: 5 June 2001

Lorraine Hansberry has her place in the history books. With this play she became, in 1959, the first Black woman, and the youngest American ever, to have her work on Broadway. But, although formally traditional, the play revives superbly both because of its militant passion and truth to lived experience.

Hansberry presents us with a three-generation Black family, the Youngers, living on Chicago's Southside and the action revolves around a $10,000 insurance cheque resulting from the late patriarch's life policy. His feckless chauffeur son, Walter Lee, plans to invest the money in a liquor store. But the dead man's widow, Lena, has other plans: she not only hopes to kick-start her daughter Beneatha's medical career but puts down a deposit on a house in Chicago's white suburbs. But when the white community offers the family money not to move, it is met with a defiance that is sorely tested by Walter Lee's revelation that he has blown the bulk of the insurance payment.

What makes the play so moving is Hansberry's portrait of the Younger family: residually idealistic but never remotely idealised. The matriarchal Lena is a staunch religious conservative who slaps her atheistic daughter across the face. Walter Lee, blending aspects of Miller's Willy Loman and O'Casey's Captain Boyle, is a fantasist who has absorbed the worst aspects of the American dream. Even Beneatha, searching for her identity through her relationship with a young Yoruba intellectual, lapses into a despairing cynicism.

Hansberry paints an unsparing picture of this riven family. But, ultimately, what unites them is an absolute refusal to surrender to white prejudice and pressures. Through intense realism Hansberry turns the family into a resonant metaphor for Black experience. And my only cavil with David Lan's production is that Francis O'Connor's set hardly suggests the poverty in which the Youngers live. But the production is richly cast with fine performances from Novella Nelson as the domineering matriarch, Lennie James as her angry son, Kananu Kirimi as her identity-seeking daughter and Ofo Uhiara as the Nigerian boyfriend. The play is of its time but it transcends its period through incandescent prose and its belief in the right of the socially oppressed to achieve their dreams and live a life of honest dignity.

Alive From Palestine, conceived by George Ibrahim (UK Premiere) Royal Court, London: 30 June 2001

How often do you see a piece of necessary theatre? Pretty rarely. But these "stories under occupation," brought to us by George Ibrahim's Al-Kasaba Theatre from Ramallah as part of the London International Festival of Theatre, fall precisely into that category. We are used to the idea of theatre as a diversion. Here it is fulfilling a more important function of bringing us the news.

News is indeed a dominant element in this remarkable hour-long, late-night production. The stage is piled high with mounds of Palestinian newspapers, from which the seven actors emerge to tell their stories. It is a potent image because it suggests that for all the news reports of the Palestinian intifada, and the 500 deaths that have accompanied it, we have little sense of the reality of daily existence. What these tales offer is an indication of the mordant humour and survival-instinct irony that many Palestinians bring to their occupied lives.

Perhaps the most eye-opening of many sketches and tales is one in which Hussam Abu Eisheh plays a West Bank resident on the phone to his son in London. As he chattily catalogues the family's endless succession of disasters, he keeps saying: "No, no we're fine, don't worry," as if tragedy were now the norm. And the point is reinforced by another sketch in which two lovers meet for a dinner date; they go through the expected rituals of courtship except that their presents to each other consist of rubber bullets and small armaments.

Under the show's satire there is clearly both fierce anger and sadness at the extent to which the abnormal has become the normal for Palestinians. But the stories are also capable of recording naked desperation. One man, tracked by a buzzing helicopter, raises his arms to it, crying, "Let me die as I wish." And there is a potent tale of a boy, reared on fictive American images of violence and regretting the closure of the cinemas under the intifada, awakening to the fact that he is living amid something far more terrifying than movie-location mayhem.

Performed in Arabic with English surtitles and directed and designed by Amir Nizar Zuabi, this show is an astonishing testament to the power of theatre. It shows how, even as a society's infrastructure collapses, people continue to tell each other stories to make sense of their lives. What I also learned was the desperate desire of the Palestinians to be something other than global headlines. As the actors are finally obliterated, they sink once more under a morass of newsprint. But the emergence of their flickering hands through the jumbled-up journals unforgettably asserts their unsuppressed humanity and wish simply to be allowed to live.

Mother Clap's Molly House by Mark Ravenhill
Lyttelton, National Theatre, London:
5 September 2001

Mark Ravenhill clearly likes to have it both ways. In this wonderfully exuberant new musical play, he celebrates Sodom like there's no Gomorrah. But the satirist in him also attacks the commodification of sex and the resultant loss of love. The result is an evening rich in rudery and ambivalence.

The first, undeniably more brilliant half is set in London in 1726: a period when sex and capitalism went hand in hand. We watch intrigued as the widowed, childless Mrs Tull reluctantly inherits her husband's dress-hire shop for whores. Discovering her apprentice, Martin, and some of his night-wandering chums in skirts, she realises there is a bustling subculture that will enable her to fulfil two of her fantasies: to become a surrogate mother and to earn a pretty penny. From there it is but a short step to setting up a molly house or male brothel.

The wit of the first half lies in the way Ravenhill gradually draws us into this world of secret sodomy and entrepreneurial initiative. The scene where Martin and his friend Thomas don dresses and act out sexual games is both touching and funny: clothes not only make the man but release the hidden woman. But Ravenhill also cunningly makes us admire the blossoming of Mrs Tull while questioning the amorality of capitalism as she dubiously announces "That's the beauty of business – it judges no one."

After all this parodic verve and sexual subversiveness, Ravenhill becomes more explicitly moralistic in the second half. The scene shifts to modern London where two Bloomsbury males are staging a gay orgy dutifully preserved by one of the guests on his camcorder. Although the scene is penetrated by echoes of the eighteenth century, Ravenhill makes his points a little too obviously: that innocent games have turned into fetishistic rites and that a one-time celebration of otherness has now led to a world of pink pounds and commercialised sex in which love is a precarious survivor. In the process some of the ribald ecstasy goes out of the play.

But this is still an astonishing work to find at the National Theatre – or anywhere else for that matter – and it shows Ravenhill working on a much broader, bigger canvas than in his previous plays. Nicholas Hytner's inventive production also boasts a fine set by Giles Cadle full of skewwhiff beams and city vistas, lively music by Matthew Scott and a host of good performances. Deborah Findlay's Mrs Tull is a delicious Hogarthian mix of native shrewdness and maternal longing and there is fine support from Paul Ready and Dominic Cooper as the apprentice lovers, Ian Redford as a burly transvestite and Danielle Tilley as a rustic whore. Delicate souls may be offended but there is no doubting the sincerity of Ravenhill's assault on the transformation of sex into a dirty business.

The Seagull by Anton Chekhov
Dundee Rep: 20 October 2001

Dundee Rep, under Hamish Glen, has created something unique in Britain: a permanent company of 14 actors that is now in its third consecutive season. The result is a molten ensemble of the kind you associate with mainland Europe. And the highest tribute I can pay this astonishing Scottish troupe is that it triumphs over the often wilful eccentricities of Lithuanian Rimas Tuminas, who has been imported to direct *The Seagull* in the Tom Stoppard version.

Tuminas and his designer, Adomas Jacovskis, pull off some striking visual effects. The opening scene, in which Konstantin stages his play in Sorin's park, is beautifully mounted. Candles are ritually placed on a downstage log. The spectators enter in a phalanx bearing wooden chairs and sit upstage, allowing us to see their shifting reactions to Konstantin's symbolist work. And, after Arkadina has thoughtlessly ruined it, a rough curtain is drawn across the stage through which we glimpse the resulting chaos.

But Chekhov's special genius is for showing the way drama emerges through the flux of daily life – a point overlooked by Tuminas, whose tendency, in the rest of the production, is to hammer home his points. Instead of being an almost casual act of seduction, Trigorin's lecture to Nina on the mundane nature of the literary life is turned into a manic rant. Trigorin's crucial return at the end of the third act to make an assignation with Nina is also sacrificed to achieve a spectacular exit on a luggage-laden trolley. And Chekhov's astonishing low-key climax, in which Konstantin's suicide is whisperingly revealed, is trumped by the concurrent death of the aged Sorin.

Theatricality rather than reality is the keynote of Tuminas's production, a point symbolised by the constant background music of Latenas Faustas, which varies from fairground jauntiness to pianistic plangency. But, although the production often infuriated me, I concede that Tuminas gets impressive performances from his Scottish cast. Meg Fraser's Masha becomes a pivotal figure reduced to visceral howls of pain by her thwarted love for Konstantin. John Buick's Sorin is also an angry, embittered character whose disappointment with life leads him to give the finger to Sandy Neilson's vainly consoling Dorn. And, from the start, you feel the lurking sexual rivalry between Irene Macdougall's grandstanding Arkadina and Emily Winter's ardent Nina. Something extraordinary is clearly happening in Dundee, even if Tuminas's *Seagull* misses the diurnal materiality that is a vital part of Chekhov's mastery.

No Man's Land by Harold Pinter
Lyttelton, National Theatre, London:
7 December 2001

This is a haunted as well as a haunting play: it is stalked, for those of a certain generation by memories of Gielgud and Richardson in the original 1975 production. But the brilliant thing about Harold Pinter's revival of his own play is that, without banishing the ghosts, it forces us to re-examine what the work is actually about. As Patrick Marber writes in the programme, the play is never fully knowable. But what Pinter's production clearly presents us with is a collision between two different forms of desperation.

Hirst, the wealthy writer, within whose luxurious drawing room the action takes place, is not merely trapped in the present but plagued by inconsolable memories of the past. The tragedy of Spooner, the ageing Chalk Farm pub worker who seeks to rescue him, is that he has no definable past but only a series of self-invented myths. Either way, Pinter implies, we are the victims of our memories. But the play is a poem, not a thesis: the great thing about it is the way it is defined by its performers and here Corin Redgrave and John Wood prove an astonishing match for past interpreters. What is remarkable about Redgrave's Hirst is not merely the contrast between the legless night-drinker and the spruce morning-after figure – Pinter himself caught that in the 1992 Almeida revival – but the intensity of both his rage and compassion. In his cups Redgrave becomes a demonic figure as if trying to lay the ghosts of his remembrance; but he later lends the speech where Hirst urges Spooner to "tender the dead as you would yourself be tendered" a grave and quiet beauty.

If Redgrave's Hirst is forever haunted by the past, Wood's amazing Spooner is constantly seeking to create one. Far more clearly than Gielgud, he shows us that Spooner is the superfluous man trying to find his mission in life: to that end he creates a series of elaborate fantasies. One of them is that he is a poet so that when Wood describes golden versifying evenings at his country house, his eyes glaze over. A born fantasist, Wood's Spooner also enters into other people's dreams: there's a great moment when he stares in astonishment at Hirst's description of their Oxford past before entering enthusiastically into the game. But Wood also beautifully suggests there is something quixotically chivalric about Spooner's final attempt to rescue Hirst from a doomed stasis.

As Hirst's two sexually interlocked servants, Andy de la Tour is a brutally protective Briggs and Danny Dyer a fly, charm-exploiting Foster. Like Eileen Diss's expensively stark design, they add to a rich evening in which Pinter memorably shows how the past, in theatre as in life, is fixed and fluid at the same time.

2002

The York Realist by Peter Gill (World Premiere) Royal Court, London: 9 January 2002

Peter Gill first achieved fame for his theatrical restoration of D.H. Lawrence. And his new play, presented by English Touring Theatre, is like a glowing tribute to the Eastwood exemplar. It has the Lawrentian qualities of emotional intelligence, raw honesty and fascination with the intersection of class and sex.

In outline it sounds like a gay love story. George is a farm labourer who gets involved in an early 1960s production of the York Mystery Plays: John is the shy assistant director who comes to woo him back to rehearsals when he withdraws, ostensibly to look after his widowed mother. The two men's physical and emotional rapport is palpable. But Gill shows, with rigorous honesty, the obstacles that lie in the path of a long-term relationship. Significantly, sexual bigotry is not one of them: even if the play has echoes of Lawrence's *The Daughter-in-Law* it never turns into a battle for possession of George between his mother and lover. What Gill is writing about is the dual stranglehold of class and roots.

For John, a metropolitan careerist, the Yorkshire countryside has an exotic otherness of which he can never fully be a part. Equally George, although he visits London and relishes its early 1960s intellectual fever, is wedded irrevocably to the land. In the end it is he, as much as the anonymous author of the medieval mysteries, who turns out to be the true York realist.

What is startling about the play, given Gill's Welsh origins, is its profound Englishness: it is about the way the English, however hard they try, can never finally escape their origins. But, far from being emotionally conservative, the play is adventurous, witty and fresh. At a time when sexual acrobatics are all the rage, it captures the hesitant growth of love between two men with rare tenderness. It is also funny not least in the almost embarrassed enthusiasm George's family display after their visit to the Mysteries. "It was very Yorkshire, wasn't it," cries George's mother carefully adding: "Not that I mind."

Gill's production has the same spare honesty, very much in a 1960s Royal Court tradition, as his writing and is superlatively played. Lloyd Owen, a fast-rising star, endows George with exactly the right blend of Yorkshire grit and unashamed delight in his sexuality: it is Richard Coyle, as the supposedly sophisticated Londoner, who is the more tentative. And there is exemplary support from Anne Reid as George's mother whose love takes the form of unspoken understanding, from Wendy Nottingham as a quiet chapel mouse who adores George, and from Felix Bell as his amusedly observant nephew. The play comes like a rare blast of reality.

Up For Grabs by David Williamson (UK Premiere) Wyndham's, London: 24 May 2002

They gave Madonna a standing ovation. But, since her performance in David Williamson's comedy is that of a dogged trier lacking in technique or mystery, the gesture is meaningless: what the audience is applauding is not achievement but some hollow concept of celebrity.

Admittedly the play itself is not one of Williamson's best: only last week I attended a reading of his 1977 Australian play, *The Club*, which knocked spots off this for dramatic intensity. But in this story of a ravenous New York art dealer trying to force the bidding for a rare Jackson Pollock up to $20m, he makes some telling points. In a greedy world, he suggests, the broker will do anything to clinch the deal: even, in the case of Madonna's Loren, to strapping on a black dildo to satisfy the anal cravings of a prospective buyer.

Williamson uses the bludgeon rather than the rapier and skimps on narrative detail. When the dotcom millionaires split over the price of the Pollock there is no suggestion that severance would involve teams of lawyers. But Madonna's Loren is the focus of the action and one is left, like Oliver Twist, hungry for more. "I want money so I can own beauty" cries Madonna. But, instead of an implacably driven heroine, one simply finds an amiably smiling girl in silver top and black slacks. The voice is light and, even from row H, not always easily audible. And the hands flail around like those of a traffic cop. When Madonna talks of "the essence of creativity caught for a moment in time" she signals skywards before slamming her fist into her palm. What we don't see, in all this manual activity, is a character of frenzied ambition who undergoes a last-minute repentance.

Madonna is not positively bad: just technically awkward. But, fortunately, she is buttressed by strong supporting players. Sian Thomas, who can get a laugh simply through the flick of an eyelid, is superb as a Courtauld-trained consultant longing to get her revenge on the corporate world. Megan Dodds, as the dotcom entrepreneur who starts by seducing Madonna and ends up falling in love, combines sexiness and solitude. And Michael Lerner blusters effectively as a crude buyer for whom art is a means of appeasing his wife. But the best feature of Laurence Boswell's production is Jeremy Herbert's design: a two-tiered glass box whose lower panels slide sleekly back and forth to indicate shifting locations. The design is elegant, functional and, in its projected imprints of New York, beautiful. It makes up for the non-event of Madonna's performance which, ironically in a play about the excess valuation of art, simply capitalises on her existing fame

The Marriage of Figaro by Caron de Beaumarchais Royal Exchange, Manchester: 29 May 2002

Napoleon famously called Beaumarchais's 1781 comedy "the revolution in action." But even if the play has been virtually obliterated by the Mozart/Da Ponte opera, Helena Kaut-Howson's brilliant revival confirms that it is a masterpiece in its own right, arguably the most subversive comedy ever written.

What we see is a dual contest of wills, both political and sexual. On the one hand there is the battle between the predatory Count Almaviva and his valet Figaro, whose intended bride, Suzanna, is the cherished prize. It is a battle the Count loses at every turn, and here, far more than in the opera, it functions as a criticism of the deference paid to aristocracy. But the play also develops into a contest of gender: both the lecherous Count and the cocky Figaro are in the end outwitted by their respective partners and left craving forgiveness.

The beauty of Kaut-Howson's production, however, is that it allows Beaumarchais's subversion to emerge through laughter. It starts, ominously, with one of the blocks bearing the Count's wigs toppling off a shelf into a waiting basket beneath. But Kaut-Howson allows the comic situations to convey the message. At one point, for instance, Suzanna is desperately trying to communicate to Figaro that the Count has neglected to place a seal on Cherubino's military commission. Kaut-Howson has the actress, the sparkling Nina Sosanya, bark and flap her hands like the aquatic mammal – which is both ridiculously funny and a reminder that Suzanna is as adroit as her partner.

Like all great comedy, Beaumarchais's play has a breathtaking sanity. It demonstrates that accidents of birth, whether of class or of gender, confer no automatic privilege. And, although the play is always seen as proof of French clockwork precision, Kaut-Howson constantly reminds us of its Spanish setting, with Figaro leading the peasants in a flamenco dance to celebrate his wedding.

Johanna Bryant's design, with its transparent glass doors in the Countess's bedroom and its suspended rockery, also allows us to understand – far more clearly than in most opera productions – precisely who is deceiving whom.

Robert Cogo-Fawcett and Braham Murray have come up with a wittily condensed translation; it topically reminds us that Figaro, in one of his multiple guises, was a writer banned by Mohammedan mullahs. Kulvinder Ghir lends Figaro exactly the right mix of bounce and vulnerability. And there is first-rate work from Simon Robson as the haughtily foolish Almaviva, Emma Cunningham as the neglected but easily aroused Countess and Samuel Barnett as a cheeky, sexually omnivorous Cherubino. Aside from the fact that the concluding lyrics are barely comprehensible, this is a perfect revival of a comedy that helped to change history.

Frozen by Bryony Lavery (Revival) Cottesloe, National Theatre, London: 5 July 2002

Bryony Lavery's remarkable play, first seen four years ago at Birmingham Rep, tackles a notoriously treacherous subject: our attitudes to crime and punishment, in particular to the treatment of child-abusing serial killers. But it is a measure of her sensitivity that she manages to overcome her heroine's and, arguably, our own instinctive hatred.

Lavery introduces her three characters through the form of interwoven monologue. Nancy is the grieving mother who slowly and painfully comes to terms with the disappearance and murder of her 10-year-old daughter. Ralph is the killer who, we eventually learn, has actually abducted seven young girls. And Agnetha is the criminal psychologist who comes to England to lecture on the subject of serial killers and to make a detailed study of the imprisoned Ralph.

What is striking is the dramatic use Lavery makes of her central metaphor. Agnetha, who views serial killing as a form of illness rather than of evil, talks of "the frozen arctic sea that is the criminal brain." Nancy spends much of her time in a state of frozen hate until, partly under the influence of her surviving daughter, she learns to embrace life and forgive her child's killer. And even the psychologist, haunted by the death of her professional partner, seems to exist in a condition of chilly clinical exactitude.

The force of Lavery's play, however, lies in its ability to change hearts and minds. It never mitigates the horror of child-killing and shares our instinctive revulsion at the act itself. But it makes us understand Agnetha's argument that it is physical damage to the brain, rather than inborn evil, that prompts serial murder. And the play leads to an extraordinary scene in which Nancy confronts Ralph in his cell and offers him a forgiveness far more fatal than a cold-blooded revenge.

I still think there are contradictions within Lavery's argument. On one level she is out to prove the predictable banality of the killer, yet Agnetha describes Ralph as "mesmerising like a rattlesnake." And, although she shows Ralph as calculating, Lavery brushes aside the idea of moral responsibility. But in a world filled with tabloid hysteria, her play comes across as a draught of sanity.

Frozen is also flawlessly acted in Bill Alexander's austere production. Anita Dobson brilliantly charts Nancy's progress from emptiness to thawed humanity. Tom Georgeson no less powerfully shows Ralph to be a damaged figure grappling with the alien concept of remorse. And Josie Lawrence conveys the sadness that underlies the detachment of the psychologist. This is a play that genuinely enlarges one's understanding.

The Coast of Utopia by Tom Stoppard
Olivier, National Theatre, London:
5 August 2002

As you might expect, Tom Stoppard's *The Coast of Utopia* is a bundle of contradictions. Comprising three three-hour plays, it is heroically ambitious and wildly uneven. It opens up the subject of revolution while being politically partial. And it contains passages of breathtaking beauty and surprising ordinariness. But I wouldn't have missed it for worlds and at its heart it contains a fascinating lesson about the nature of drama.

Each play in the trilogy, dealing with nineteenth-century Russian revolutionaries, has its own style. *Voyage*, the first and best, focuses on the anarchic Bakunin and the critic Belinsky and seems like a tonic combination of Gorki and Chekhov. *Shipwreck*, the least satisfying, deals with the impact of the 1848 French Revolution on a group of nomadic intellectuals, including the libertarian socialist Alexander Herzen and the Westernised Turgenev. *Salvage*, the final play, is set mainly in London between 1853 and 1865 and offers a Dickensian portrait of the fractious emigre community.

Like Isaiah Berlin in *Russian Thinkers*, Stoppard leaves you in no doubt that Herzen is his hero. According to Berlin, Herzen believed that any dedication to an abstract ideal leads to victimisation and human sacrifice. So Stoppard presents Herzen as a man who rejects romantic anarchy in favour of practical reform and the emancipation of the serfs. Even when that turns out to be a disappointment, he retains his belief in achievable ends: "The labourer's wage, the pleasure in the work done, the summer lightning of personal happiness."

Stoppard loads the dice in favour of Herzen, beautifully played by Stephen Dillane, but the fact is that his rationalist moderation is dramatically unexciting. The great paradox is that Stoppard's trilogy comes most alive when dealing with characters he intellectually disowns, in particular

Bakunin. Capriciously switching his allegiance from one German philosopher to another, cadging off all his friends and both defying and living off his estate-owning father, Bakunin is a rootless anarchist who believes in the "abolition of the state by the liberated workers." Stoppard condemns his ideas, but Bakunin, magnificently played by Douglas Henshall, takes over the trilogy as surely as Falstaff dominates Shakespeare's *Henry IV*.

The moral is that dramatic energy is more important than historical correctness, which makes me regret all the more that Stoppard marginalises the most visionary of all the revolutionary exiles, Karl Marx. But it seems harsh to criticise Stoppard for what he has left out when he has put so much in. In particular, he dramatises the capacity for change so that Will Keen's brilliantly feverish Belinsky begins by arguing in the 1830s that Russia has no literature and ends by claiming that it carries too many burdens. Stoppard also conveys the ambivalent role of women in revolutionary circles with Eve Best, who transforms herself from one of Bakunin's sexually innocent sisters to Herzen's free-loving wife and eventually the strict governess to his children.

Stoppard's vision is expertly realised in Trevor Nunn's production, apart from a descent into *Les Mis*-style flag-waving in 1848, and in William Dudley's projections. The stage is cleared for epic and intimate events, while in the background we see revolving vistas of everything from pine-filled Russian estates to an ice-covered Richmond Park. In the end Stoppard argues, with excessive hindsight, that Herzen was right and the romantic utopians were wrong. But revolutionary fervour has its own unstoppable dramatic momentum, and it is their very wrongness that gives the trilogy its theatrical life.

Tribute to director, Joan Littlewood: born 6 October 1914, died 20 September 2002.

25 September, 2002

Why can't we cope with genius? Joan Littlewood, who died this week, and Peter Brook were the two greatest theatre directors to emerge in postwar Britain. Yet both ended up in exile as victims of the British indifference to pioneering visionaries. Brook, unable to fund a theatrical research centre at home, moved to Paris in 1972 where he thrives to this day. Littlewood, defeated by the need to sustain Theatre Workshop through West End transfers and by public rejection of her plans for a Fun Palace, retreated in 1976 to the French countryside from which she rarely emerged.

Littlewood's "crime," in officialdom's eyes, was that she was always two steps ahead of the game. She was a European, absorbing Stanislavsky, Brecht and the movement techniques of Laban, at a time when British theatre was profoundly insular. She believed in releasing inherent talent long before "access" and "community" became buzzwords. And she demonstrated theatre's ability to instruct delightfully, long before "political drama" turned into an established genre. It is worth recalling that Theatre Workshop toured postwar Britain with a piece called *Uranium 235* that sought to explain the history of atomic energy: it even had Niels Bohr and Max Planck elucidating quantum theory in the guise of a couple of knockabout comics.

The real scandal of Littlewood's story, however, is that her triumphs were achieved in the teeth of official hostility. When Theatre Workshop, then based in Stratford East but still unsubsidised, was asked to represent Britain at the Paris International Festival in 1955, the company was so poor they had to transport the set for *Volpone* as individual hand luggage: after their spectacular Paris triumph, the French had to lend them the money to get home. And as late as 1972 the Arts Council was still haggling over whether to give Littlewood's company a grant of £41,000.

Her career proves that it doesn't pay to be an artist in a world run by bureaucrats. But the miracle is how much she achieved in spite of opposition. And, in all the tributes to her, too little attention has been paid to an innate political radicalism that has all but disappeared from our stages. A classic case was her production of Brendan Behan's *The Quare Fellow* in 1956: set in a Dublin prison on the eve of an execution, the play remarkably combined gallows humour with a Swiftian moral rage at the barbarity of ritualised hanging. Despite the play's Irish setting, there was no mistaking its relevance to our own society, where capital punishment remained on the statute book thanks to a mixture of political cowardice and public apathy.

But if any one show demonstrated Littlewood's ability to change hearts and minds, it was *Oh What A Lovely War* in 1963. Whole generations have now grown up persuaded of the criminal futility of the military conduct of the First World War in which, as Lloyd George said at the time, soldiers were "driven to slaughter like cattle." But in 1963, in spite of books like Robert Graves' *Goodbye To All That* or Leon Wolff's *In Flanders Field*, it was still not a universally held truth. Through its aesthetically brilliant mix of musical nostalgia and brutal fact, Littlewood's show did more to change public perceptions than any work of literature.

That is Littlewood's real legacy: the ability to express political ideas in a popular form. And shows like *Hang Down Your Head And Die* (an anti-capital punishment revue), Peter Nichols' *Poppy* and the plays of John McGrath were all beneficiaries of the Littlewood style. But, when you look around British theatre today, it is hard to find anyone left who has that gift for marrying radical content and popular form. Good political plays occasionally still get written and Kilburn's Tricycle Theatre has an excellent record in staging docu-drama such as *The Colour of Justice*. Meanwhile musicals, lulling us into a state of benign acceptance, continue to proliferate. But where is the artist who today combines a political instinct with the popular touch?

Even if one emerged, I wouldn't give much for his or her chances. For we still prefer institutions to individuals and fail to nourish odd, unclassifiable talent. Declan Donnellan and Nick Ormerod may be working on the Stratford Academy's *King Lear*, but their company, Cheek by Jowl, has disappeared and they are far more honoured abroad than at home. Ditto Simon McBurney and Theatre de Complicité. Stephen Daldry is directing a Caryl Churchill play at the Royal Court but is another maverick talent without a permanent base. And the last time I spoke to Jonathan Kent, at the end of his triumphant tenure at the Almeida with Ian McDiarmid, he was busily commuting between new projects in Tokyo and New York. We talk of the brain drain in science and industry. But we have still myopically failed to learn the crucial lesson of Littlewood and Brook: that we need to back visionary individuals as much as bricks and mortar if we are not to end up with a totally compliant, conformist, bureaucratic culture.

A Number by Caryl Churchill (World Premiere) Royal Court, London: 27 September 2002

Caryl Churchill never stands still. After the dystopian nightmare of *Far Away*, she now comes up with a challenging form of moral inquiry. And the key question she asks in this play is from what the essential core of self derives: from nature or nurture, genetic inheritance or environmental circumstance?

To precis the plot is even more distorting than usual since Churchill works in non-linear fashion. But one can say that there are five scenes in which a father, Salter, confronts three of his adult sons. Bernard One is wild, violent, menacing and was taken into care at the age of four two years after his mother's death. From the cells of this child a doctor has created Bernard Two who is the physical match but psychological antithesis of his "brother." To Salter's horror, however, this experiment has led to a series of cloned sons one of whom he apprehensively meets.

Churchill is not, however, offering us a debate on the ethics of cloning. What she does, in a series of fraught, emotional encounters, is use the scientific possibility to address basic human questions: above all, what the source is of that mysterious thing we call "personality." We are left to deduce whether Bernard One's disturbance can be traced to his depressive mother, to Salter's neglect or to the fact of his being institutionalised. And, if Bernard Two has turned out as Abel to his brother's Cain, is it because he was brought up in a marginally more stable environment?

The play poses endless questions; and, if it is difficult to come to any conclusions, it is because of the elliptical nature of Churchill's hour-long form. Clearly the key figure is Salter, and we deduce, from one son's memory of his failure to respond to a cry in the night, that he was a negligent father. We also assume, from his desire to perpetuate himself and his determination to sue the doctors, that Salter is greedy. But, although the play is in part an attack on patriarchy, it doesn't supply enough hard information to resolve the issue of whether character is determined by genetic or social factors. What is indisputable, however, is that it makes an engrossing spectacle. Staged with exemplary clarity by Stephen Daldry on Ian MacNeil's rectangular platform, it yields two fine performances. Michael Gambon's Salter, by turns explosively angry and wearily remorseful, is a great perplexed bull of a man trying to discover where he went wrong; and nothing is more touching than the way Gambon nervously dons a tie and gazes into vacancy as he prepares to meet his final offspring. Daniel Craig, by the simplest gestures, also brilliantly establishes the key differences between the physically identical sons. But the success of a disturbing evening lies in Churchill's ability to raise big moral issues through the interstices of close human encounters.

2003

Iphigenia by Edna O'Brien (World Premiere) Crucible, Sheffield: 13 February 2003

Edna O'Brien has taken the knife to Euripides's *Iphigenia in Aulis* but with infinitely happier results than in Agamemnon's sacrifice of his daughter. Though one may quibble at some of O'Brien's choices in this free adaptation, she gives force and clarity to a notoriously corrupt text, and rescues the ending from bathos.

The narrative outline remains much the same as in Euripides: Agamemnon is instructed to sacrifice his daughter for the sake of the Greek expedition to Troy. But O'Brien builds up both the cosmic and domestic pressure on the hero. She reminds us, through the interpolated figure of a Witch, of the divine injunction laid upon Agamemnon, and reinforces the back story of the curse on the house of Atreus. But she also enormously strengthens the figure of Iphigenia, whom we first see as a pillow-fighting teenager experiencing her first period and who later, at Aulis, movingly reminds her father of their former intimacy.

The effect of all this is not strictly Euripidean: his is a more political play about the way mob rule and manipulative power-mongers drive Achilles, threatened by the entire army for defending Iphigenia, to accept a war-initiating sacrifice. What O'Brien gives us is a stark, traditional tragedy in which fate intersects with human flaws. Her Agamemnon is both divinely doomed and a moral hypocrite who combines protestations of paternal love with dalliance with a Greek war widow. But O'Brien's most radical change is to the climax where, in place of a *deus ex machina*, the death of Iphigenia ushers in a blood-soaked cycle of revenge.

You could argue with some of O'Brien's alterations: Achilles loses whole speeches showing him mired in self-regard. But what impresses is the swift narrative drive of this 75-minute version and the vigour and irony of O'Brien's language. "It's out of my hands," says Agamemnon at one point, before realising that his daughter's fate lies literally in his hands. And when he cries, "She shall rest upon the cenotaph," that last word unerringly drives home his rhetorical inflation of an ugly deed.

Played on a virtually bare stage against Hayden Griffin's honeycombed back wall, Anna Mackmin's production matches the directness of O'Brien's text. Lloyd Owen, his voice cracking as he calls himself "a broken king," also successfully brings out both the helplessness and the hubris of Agamemnon. Strong support too from Susan Brown as a vehement Clytemnestra, who ends surrounded in a pool of prophetic blood and from Lisa Dillon who, in her stage debut, lends Iphigenia a touching filial trust. Eight young Sheffield women also rescue the chorus from the usual deadly sing-song in a first-rate production that may not be *echt* Euripides but that is very good Edna.

Henry V by William Shakespeare
Olivier, National Theatre, London:
14 May 2003

Jingoistic celebration or anti-war play? The perennial fascination of Shakespeare's play is that it has elements of both. But while I applaud the wit, irony and pacifist leanings of Nicholas Hytner's new modern-dress production, theatrically I found myself wishing it was a bit more emotionally equivocal.

Hytner's intentions are clear from the start: to undercut the theatrical glamour surrounding war. William Gaunt's pragmatic Archbishop of Canterbury has prepared fat dossiers supporting Henry's dubious claim to the French throne.

No sooner has Penny Downie's cardiganed Chorus told us "Now all the youth of England are on fire" than we cut to the pub where Nym zaps TV channels preferring the snooker-channels to the king's bellicose warmongering. And, when we get to France, Henry's cry of "Once more unto the breach, dear friends" is met with a universal groan from his battered army.

What is impressive is the consistency with which Hytner follows through his satiric approach, clearly shaped by our response to the Bush–Blair invasion of Iraq; and at no point does he let Henry off the hook. The embedded TV journalists dutifully fail to record the king's more savage threats to the citizens of Harfleur. Henry himself shoots his old mate, Bardolph, at point-blank range for his church-robbing. Most tellingly of all when Henry gives the infamous order, "Then every man kill his prisoners," the soldiers mutinously refuse until that arch-disciplinarian, Fluellen, comes along and does the job for them.

Without, however, wishing for patriotic drum-beating, I wish Hytner's production contained more contradiction. Adrian Lester is a fine actor but, aside from a single moment of shattered, post-Harfleur relief, he is scarcely ever allowed to give us a hint of the king's residual humanity. You feel, if it weren't for the intervention of his uncle, he would wreak terrible revenge on the common soldier who tells him a few plain truths the night before Agincourt.

Of the production's wit and intelligence, there is no doubt. The French court, led by Ian Hogg's melancholic king, sit watching Henry's sur-titled rhetoric on their TV screens. You also notice how Lester's Henry only invokes God when it suits his purpose. And Peter Blythe's excellent Exeter glances impatiently at his watch when Burgundy describes the devastating impact of war on the French countryside. Tim Hatley's partitioned wall of a set also opens up to allow exciting use of the Olivier's epic space. With its klieg lights and its scepticism, this is absolutely a *Henry V* for our post-Iraq age. All I miss is the moral ambivalence that I suspect was part of Shakespeare's original intention.

Fallout by Roy Williams
Royal Court, London: 19 June 2003

Few writers are better than Roy Williams at exploring the contradictions of our multicultural society. *Lift Off* showed how White kids imitate their Black counterparts. And his latest play dazzlingly overturns expectation by showing how, in a murder investigation, it is the Black rather than the White cop who indulges in disastrous racist stereotyping.

The physical space itself has also been overturned. On top of the Royal Court stalls, the designer, Ultz, has created a stage resembling a wire-meshed basketball court. This becomes the arena for a police probe into the killing of Kwame, a bookish Black teenager bound for university. All the evidence points to a guy called Emile, who hangs out with a gang of local tearaways. But while Matt, the White cop, is prepared to proceed patiently, his Black sidekick, Joe, cuts corners by over-identifying with the dead boy.

What Williams pins down brilliantly is the corrosive envy that pervades a culture of limited opportunities. Kwame, we deduce, has been killed because he wanted to escape from the herd mentality of bleak housing estates. And this has repercussions at police level. Having likewise lifted himself out of the rut, Joe cannot forgive the brutal ethos of the street gangs. From this Williams creates scenes of biting irony in which Joe yearns for "the old school of police" while his White colleague is imbued with a post-McPherson, liberal even-handedness. Williams also shows how sex complicates the issue. Much of the action revolves around the fatal attractions of Shanice, played with astonishing poise by Ony Uhiara, who runs the local cafe. She is a well-intentioned girl who sympathised with the dead Kwame's desire to escape. But, as Emile's girlfriend, she shows loyalty to the gang and is even prepared to intimidate the teacher who had her kicked out of school for theft. In Williams's graphically portrayed world, nothing is ever simple.

My only cavil about a thrillingly staged show is that the opening scene is played for violence rather than clarity, so we miss some crucial information. Otherwise Ian Rickson's production does vivid justice to the play's moral contradictions and its visceral impact. And there is a string of good performances, from Lennie James as the self-destructive Joe, Daniel Ryan as his strenuously fair-minded colleague, Marcel McCalla as the deeply insecure Emile and Michael Obiora as the strutting gang leader. But what is really impressive is Williams's capacity for telling the honest truth and for exposing the divisions within what we misleadingly term "the Black community."

The Elephant Vanishes by Simon McBurney (World Premiere) Barbican, London: 30 June 2003

Simon McBurney has shown a genius for animating European literary texts, and now, in a co-production between Complicité and Tokyo's Setagaya public theatre, he tackles the short stories of Haruki Murakami. The result is an astonishing piece of theatre in which communal storytelling effortlessly blends with hi-tech wizardry.

McBurney has woven together three stories, all dealing with social alienation. In the title piece, a PR man for kitchen equipment becomes obsessed by the disappearance of an old elephant from an abandoned zoo. In *The Second Bakery Attack*, an overwhelmingly hungry couple launch a dawn shotgun raid on a Tokyo burger bar. And in *Sleep*, a dentist's wife rebels against her mechanically organised life through prolonged wakefulness during which she reads *Anna Karenina*.

All three stories are about people whose private world is at odds with the feverish efficiency of urban Tokyo and, aided by designer Michael Levine, McBurney creates a sense of a city in perpetual motion. Video screens whizz across the stage. Projected images evoke cars and trains in ecstasies of permanent transport. Even rest, fitfully snatched, is taken on vertical beds over which the sleeper's other self hovers like a restless angel.

McBurney captures precisely the lonely oddity of individual lives that characterises Murakami's work. In the first story, the hero methodically reads his morning paper before coming across the story of the vanishing elephant: the strangeness of it all is enhanced by the magnified sound of him crunching on a dry biscuit. And there is a wild comedy about the dawn hamburger-heist, which derives from the husband's memory of once raiding a bakery: as he relives it, we see the solitary baker kneading dough in the symbolic shape of a pillow, forcing his attackers to listen to Wagner in exchange for bread.

McBurney underscores the social protest in Murakami's surreal stories and their intuitive sympathy with women. If the heroine of *Sleep* experiences 17 wakeful nights, it is in rebellion against domestic servitude, and the fact that she is represented by four female performers implies that this a universal condition. And, while the PR man is a sympathetic oddball, he also talks of the kitchen as a housewife's workplace, study and living-room. In the show's haunting final image he celebrates the idea of unity of function in the perfect kitchen. By a fine irony, McBurney's achievement in this brilliant show is to have embodied the unifying theme of Murakami's imaginative world: where individuals are at permanent odds with their external, daily selves.

Iain Duncan Smith's Leader's Speech at the Conservative Party Conference. A political sketch.

10 October, 2003

"I have a go lady, don't I, I have a go?" So cries Archie Rice, the clapped-out comic hero of John Osborne's *The Entertainer*. Well Iain Duncan Smith at Blackpool yesterday certainly had a go. But, watching him on television, I felt I was not only witnessing the grisly reduction of conference speeches to pier-end politics but the living reincarnation of Mrs Rice's favourite boy.

The parallels are uncanny. Like Archie, Duncan Smith was fronting a bankrupt show and living in fear of menacing figures waiting in the wings: with Archie it was the taxman and with IDS it was 25 Tory MPs. While Archie camply mocks the conductor's sexuality ("You think I'm like that, don't you? Well I'm not. But HE is"), IDS used Tony Blair and Charles Kennedy as his silent stooges even invoking the latter's love of a tipple. And just as Archie cynically pushes all the right patriotic buttons, so too did the Europhobic Duncan Smith. "Good old England, you're my cup of tea" was actually sung by Archie but yesterday could have come straight from the visibly parched lips of IDS.

The key difference is that where Osborne's Archie was an old pro, Iain Duncan Smith looks like a nervous graduate of a school for trainee comics in Godalming. He's been taught all the tricks but he doesn't quite know how to use them. At one point he used the old panto device of direct address to the audience. "Did you see Tony Blair's performance last week?" he chirpily inquired. Getting zilch response from an audience, he then turned nervously aggressive. "Well, did you?" he bullyingly repeated. As Orson Welles once said, you can do many things to an audience but the one thing you can't do is piss on them.

Not that there were many other signs of Duncan Smith pissing on the Tory faithful; or even the somewhat larger collection of the Tory faithless. He was basically out to tickle their prejudices. But, as any comic will tell you, the key to success lies in timing and structure. Duncan Smith's delivery, however, is so painfully slow that you get the impression the cue cards are being written even as he speaks. And, since he has clearly modelled himself on the Jack Benny slow burn, I think he should remember Benny's limp-wristed response to a wildly applauding Palladium audience's premature ejaculation: "I swear I'm not that good."

Structure is Iain Duncan Smith's other problem. All comics will tell you that you have to surf on the existing laughs and then build to a big finish. But there's something wrong with a stand-up routine – which is what this basically was – that gets 17 standing ovations and that contains more false climaxes than *Oh! Calcutta*! Even the rhetorical conclusion, in which IDS endlessly repeated the word "anger," lacked punch partly because the voice was giving way and partly because of the violent change of tone: you can't be Max Miller one moment and Winston Churchill the next.

I leave it to others to analyse the content of Duncan Smith's speech. But what depressed me was the assumption that all politics is now a branch of showbiz. Iain Duncan Smith gave us a performance rather than policies, one-liners rather than joined-up ideas and, in one give-way moment after impersonating Tony Blair, cried: "Watch out, Rory Bremner – but not just yet." So now we know: the party leaders are taking their cue from the impressionists. But, although Iain Duncan Smith touched the G-spot of the Blackpool audience, I was reminded of Archie Rice's prophetic cry as he foresaw the end of the music halls and stand-alone British imperialism: "Don't clap too hard, we're all in a very old building."

The Sugar Syndrome by Lucy Prebble (World Premiere)
Royal Court Theatre Upstairs: 21 October 2003

This first play by 22-year old Lucy Prebble has many of the virtues – and some of the faults – you expect in early work. It tackles tricky subjects, such as paedophilia and teenage psychological disorders, with unselfconscious candour: at the same time, having outlawed instant moral judgement, Prebble can't quite determine what to put in its place.

Like Patrick Marber in *Closer*, Prebble shows how online chatrooms can easily lead to crossed wires. The screwed-up, sexually knowing 17-year-old Dani (short for Danielle) meets the lonely 38-year-old Tim, who is under the impression he has been in intimate internet conversation with a young boy. Dani, however, discovers in Tim a wounded soulmate to whom she can relate far more easily than her scatty middle-class mum or the geeky guy with whom she has occasional sex: she even optimistically believes she can help the tormented Tim in his guilt-ridden struggles with paedophilia.

Prebble writes honestly and well, in a manner reminiscent of Shelagh Delaney in *A Taste of Honey*, about the attraction of outsiderish opposites: the plausibility of the central relationship is confirmed by Dani's teenage mockery of Tim's "dad-rock" and his despair at her rejection of classical literature. But, although Dani reassures Tim that she belongs to a generation that "doesn't judge anything anyone does, only how it's reported," she is sickened when she sees the sadistically pornographic images on his laptop. You are left unsure whether Prebble is telling us that Dani is not as cool as she seems, that Tim is not as reformed as he would wish, or that, in the end, all actions have to be viewed in a defined moral context.

Prebble's purpose may be unclear but she has an instinctive playwright's gift for grabbing your attention and compelling sympathy for damaged people. And all four actors in Marianne Elliott's deft production have a fine neurotic intensity. Stephanie Leonidas's emotional fragility as the bulimic Dani finds its echo in the defensive irony of Andrew Woodall as the traumatised Tim. And both Kate Duchene as Dani's abandoned mum and Will Ash as her anorak boyfriend exude a strange solitariness as if that, in Prebble's eyes, was the natural human condition. A profoundly promising first play.

How to cut the costs of Shakespeare production.

11 November 2003

So the RSC is looking for "imaginative ways to cut costs on productions to guarantee its future." The answer is clear: simplify Shakespeare by eliminating redundant characters and expensive sets and costumes. Turn the proudly defiant RSC into the Drastically Reduced Shakespeare Company!

They could start with all those needlessly duplicated characters. Instead of Falstaff being harried by two bourgeois housewives why not simply *The Merry Wife of Windsor*? Or how about *The One Gentleman of Verona*, thereby halving the costs of a little-known early comedy at a stroke? They could also cut down those crowds that clutter up the Roman plays. Instead of *Coriolanus* being banished by an angry mob, why not just ask the local butcher if he's free on a Wednesday and could bring along his meat cleaver. Come to think of it, that has already been tried.

But the problem with Shakespeare is that he loved exotic foreign locations that often require elaborate sets. Bring the plays home to England and you can instantly cut costs. I see a great future for *The Merchant of Little Venice*, dealing with usury in the immediate purlieus of Maida Vale. All the decadent luxury of ancient Athens would also become redundant if Shakespeare's masterly study in misanthropy became *Timon of Accrington*. And the problematic central scenes in *Julius Caesar* would be simplified if some funny things happened on the way to the Wythenshawe Forum, with local shoppers standing in for the revolting supers.

Out, also, could go all those expensive effects. Juliet could have a window-box instead of a balcony. Antigonus in *The Winter's Tale*, instead of exiting pursued by a bear, could be chased off by the theatre cat. The gale-force storm in *The Tempest* could be replaced by a mild breeze. And Pericles, instead of journeying round the Med, could take a day-trip to the Isle of Man. There's no limit to the possible economies. Cheapest of all would be to never stage the plays at all, thus doing away with the profligate Stratfordian for good. I've even got a cut-price title for the RSC's final show: *All's Well That Ends*.

Lear's Daughters by Elaine Feinstein (Revival)
Soho Theatre, London: 20 November 2003

Back in 1987 the Women's Theatre Group and Elaine Feinstein created this 90-minute prequel to *King Lear* charting the history of a dysfunctional family. As a text, it now looks decidedly shaky. What gives it resonance is David K.S. Tse's highly imaginative production for Yellow Earth theatre and the casting of British-Chinese actresses.

Lear is here a bruising, abusing patriarch desperate for a son. His wife is driven into madness and an early grave. And his daughters are all screwed up. Goneril, the detested eldest, is a frustrated painter forced to assume state responsibility on her mother's death. Regan, who has a talent for carving, is the neglected piggy-in-the-middle. And Cordelia, the youngest, is forced to play daddy's darling even doing Salome-like dances for her intemperate father. Is it any wonder they had problems in later life?

But, although the play has a fairy tale fascination, it seeks to apply simplistic Freudian solutions to Shakespeare's play. You can't "explain" Goneril and Regan's evil by suggesting that the former was a victim of parental abuse and that the latter had to abort a child before marrying Cornwall. Even if the text looks dated, Tse creates a magical world on stage in which an eldritch fable exists in a world of hi-tech sophistication. Sigyn Stenqvist's design not only gives us a video-throne but shows us Lear's daughters entrapped in quilted circular seats. The actresses also bring to the story their own understanding of a patriarchal society: Liz Sutherland's demure, doll-like Cordelia, Liana Gould's angry, unloved Goneril and Bronwyn Mei Lim's resentfully outsiderish Regan are all first-rate. Antonia Kemi Coker as a sexually ambivalent Fool and Josephine Welcome as a protective Nanny also show how to practice the politics of survival in a brutal tyranny. It's a lovely production but the play is as much of its time as Nahum Tate's sentimental seventeenth-century rewrite.

2004

The Goat, or Who Is Sylvia? by Edward Albee (UK Premiere)
Almeida, London: 4 February 2004

Tragedy, we are often told, is dead: an impossibility in an age that believes all problems are socially remediable. But Edward Albee has boldly defied convention by writing an *Oedipus Rex* for the affluent society that, despite the inferiority of Anthony Page's production to the Broadway original, leaves one emotionally shattered.

In true Aristotelian fashion, Albee presents us with a hero at the height of his powers. Martin is a world-famous, 50-year-old architect chosen to design a $27bn dream city in the American Midwest. He is even, as the play starts, about to be interviewed by his old friend, Ross, for a TV show called *People Who Matter*. There is only one problem: Martin reveals to Ross that he is helplessly, obsessively and physically in love with a goat called Sylvia.

Albee insists, rightly, that bestiality is the occasion rather than the subject of his play. He is not simply smashing old taboos or writing a hippy, dippy hymn to animal-oriented sex, like Rochelle Owens in her 1965 play *Futz*. Instead, he is asking, provocatively, whether love has proscribed boundaries and, if so, who sets them. More immediately he is showing the tragic downfall of a divided individual and the destruction of his marriage to the understandably uncomprehending Stevie.

Admittedly Albee raises big questions which he cannot answer in the compass of a 90-minute play. As in all his best work, from *Who's Afraid of Virginia Woolf?* onwards, Albee implies there is a malaise affecting American society; but he never exactly defines the source of the unhappiness motivating Martin and the fellow-sufferers he meets at a therapy session. If bestiality is also a metaphor for other forms of socially condemned sex, such as incest or paedophilia, Albee never pursues the important question aired by Ross: isn't it the lack of consensuality that raises our moral hackles?

But what Albee communicates powerfully is Martin's mix of incommunicable passion and verbal pedantry. He is in a world where there are no rules and where he is tormented by a love of an unimaginable kind. At the same time, like all Albee's characters, he has a grammarian's obsession with language. He is deeply pained when Ross scathingly refers to "the goat who you're fucking." "Don't say that," he fervently replies. "It's whom." It gets a laugh, while reminding us that Martin is thrashing around in a moral no-man's-land.

Jonathan Pryce superbly conveys Martin's frenetic isolation. From the start he seems like a man in a nightmare. His long, stick-insect fingers are forever caressing his body or describing neurotic patterns in the air. His eyes have a hunted look. Even his verbal nit-picking seems like a defence against unhappiness. But, astonishingly, Pryce enlists our sympathy when he describes his *tendresse* for Sylvia. And he even acquires a genuine moral rage when Martin asks, after Ross has recoiled in disgust at the idea of parental sexual arousal, "Is there anything anyone does not get off on, whether we admit it or not?"

If Page's production, as a whole, is less effective than the Broadway prototype, it is because it seems curiously deracinated. In New York you could almost smell the Park Avenue affluence of Martin and Stevie's world, which made its destruction all the more poignant. Here, everyone is drably costumed and even Hildegard Bechtler's split-level set, for all its chic Afro-art, seems oddly sterile. Kate Fahy's Stevie also comes across as a shrill scold rather than a woman whose genuine love for her husband has been savagely overturned. Matthew Marsh as the bluntly disbelieving best friend and Eddie Redmayne as Martin's gay, emotionally fraught son are more in tune with Albee's rhythms. And by the end one is emotionally drained.

It is partly because Albee follows an ancient rule of tragedy defined by Boethius as "a story of prosperity that endeth in wretchedness." But it is also because Albee has shocked us out of our familiar complacency. He has shown that passion is something that can neither be controlled, ordained nor directed to socially acceptable ends. He has also demonstrated that the victim of a condemned passion is like a traveller in a foreign country who cannot speak the language. And what I shall long remember from this production is Pryce's pain and bewilderment as he tries to express the tragically inexpressible.

When Harry Met Sally. Adapted by Marcy Kahan from a Nora Ephron movie (UK Premiere) Theatre Royal Haymarket, London: 23 February 2004

Is theatre slowly turning into live cinema? After the West End run of *The Graduate*, we now have this equally tame theatricalisation of Nora Ephron's

1989 Hollywood romantic comedy. Doubtless even now someone is beavering away in a back room on an idea to outdo them all: *Citizen Kane – The Play.*

If this particular script, adapted by Marcy Kahan, makes for a dull play, there are several reasons. One is that Harry's idea that friendship between hetero couples is a near impossibility comes as no surprise to theatregoers. Dr Astrov says exactly the same thing in *Uncle Vanya.* More importantly, the theatre demands robuster language, saltier exchanges, more extreme situations than the contemporary cinema provides: compare this script with David Mamet's *Sexual Perversity in Chicago* or Patrick Marber's *Closer* and you realise how far behind the cinema lags when it comes to exploring modern sexual mores.

I was also struck by the lack of texture in the writing. What do we actually learn about Harry and Sally other than that he's a corporate lawyer and she's some kind of journalist? At no point do their jobs, careers or family obligations (do they have parents or were they virgin births?) impinge on their endless yackety-yak about relationships. The best thing about a pointless evening is Alyson Hannigan who lends Sally a bright-eyed perkiness that makes the sexual dilatoriness of Luke Perry's under-cooked Harry even more inexplicable than it is already. Loveday Ingram's direction, with its use of filmed inserts, has a certain cool chic but two hours is a long time to spend in a theatre just for a fake orgasm.

Endgame by Samuel Beckett (Revival)
Albery, London: 11 March 2004

A tatty, threadbare curtain rises to the accompaniment of a circus drum-roll. Clearly Matthew Warchus sees Beckett's play as an apocalyptic vaudeville and, given the presence of a virtuosic duo like Michael Gambon and Lee Evans, this makes sense. It also overcomes the faint *Endgame*-fatigue resulting from the play's third London revival in eight years.

Cyril Connolly pointed out that while *Waiting For Godot* is a fresh assault on a universal problem, *Endgame* " is the statement of a private one." By that he meant that it not only reflects Beckett's vision of life as a meaningless farce: the fractious dependence of the blind master, Hamm, on his oppressed servant, Clov, may also be a re-enactment of the Joyce–Beckett relationship currently depicted in *Calico.* But, while *Endgame* meant a lot to Beckett, I increasingly wonder how much it means to the rest of us, especially if we don't share his view of the unalterable absurdity of existence.

My doubts were largely quelled by the heightened theatricality of Warchus's production. Centre stage sits Gambon's magnificent Hamm, which evokes multiple images: a screaming Bacon Pope, a dying Prospero, a decaying Irish landlord. With a voice oscillating between organ-like thunder and strangled quietness, Gambon brings out Hamm's terminal desperation. When he cries "If I could drag myself down to the sea!" it is like one vainly clutching at salvation. But the dominant impression is of Hamm as a frustrated creator tortured by art's inability to counter life's pointlessness.

Gambon's moulting majesty is perfectly offset by the comic cluelessness of Evans's Clov. Scuttling about in his crumpled long johns, he looks like a scrawny Dickensian potboy as drawn by Cruikshank. Evans also highlights Clov's gift for mislaying ladders and telescopes, as if he is at the endless mercy of material objects. He is the permanent Fool to Gambon's raddled Lear, yet in his refusal to kiss his master reminds us that even the dispossessed have their dignity.

With Geoffrey Hutchings's Nagg and Liz Smith's Nell popping up from their dustbins like incarcerated clowns, everything reminds us of Beckett's theatricality. Yet, while we are royally diverted, I found myself for once questioning the universality of Beckett's despairing vision.

Festen. Adapted by David Eldridge from the Thomas Vinterberg movie (World Premiere) Almeida, London: 27 March 2004

Extraordinary how responsive *Festen* is to different interpretations. Thomas Vinterberg's original 1998 Dogme film had the feel of docu-drama. A recent Polish stage version turned the story into doom-laden Shakespearean tragedy. Now David Eldridge's adaptation heightens the work's element of black comedy.

The subject of childhood sexual abuse is obviously no laughing matter; and we are suitably appalled as a Danish patriarch is accused by his son, at a 60th birthday party, of raping him and his late sister. But both Rufus Norris's production and Eldridge's text show there is something grotesque about the guests' reaction. The accusation is greeted with awkward silence. A guest remarks that the revelations are not helping his depression.

The brilliance of this version lies in the tension between the decorousness of the occasion and the dire nature of the revelations; and the horror is even more acute because of the heightened absurdity. Jane Asher, impeccable as the patriarch's grimly smiling wife, pays tribute to her "wonderful granddaughter" only to swat her away like a fly. And one watches with incredulity as Robert Pugh, the disgraced father, turns up the next morning to tell his son, Christian, "well fought, my boy."

But the beauty of Norris's production is that it implies familial disintegration from the outset. The first sound we hear is that of a child's unnerving laughter. Jonny Lee Miller's excellent Christian is initially seen in brooding solitude like a man tense with expectation. Above all, Norris reminds us this is a work about social hypocrisy. It offers us a formal celebration in which no one stands up to speak without first tapping their glass: what it uncovers is a world of paternal abuse, wifely complicity and racism. Admirably designed by Ian MacNeil and flawlessly acted, it suggests not merely that there is something rotten in the state of Denmark but that pomp and ceremony are universally a mask for guilt.

Sing Yer Heart Out for the Lads by Roy Williams (Revival) Cottesloe, National Theatre, London: 3 May 2004

I noticed members of the audience shaking hands with the cast at the end of Roy Williams's excoriating attack on British racism – a sign of the extent to which the work, first seen in the Lyttelton Loft two years ago, has become a major public event in its move to the Cottesloe. The play has been redirected, largely recast and totally redesigned, and it has brilliantly expanded to fill the space.

Williams's choice of setting is particularly canny: a south London pub on the October day in 2000 when England played Germany in a World Cup qualifier. As the pub's own football team arrives to watch the match, Williams shows how generalised xenophobia conceals a more specific racism. Barry, the team's star Black striker, may have a Union Jack tattooed on his bum and chant "Inger-land" along with the rest, but we soon realise that he is a barely tolerated outsider; when the publican's son is relieved of his mobile phone by a Black chum, the racial divide is violently exposed.

I criticised the play originally for dealing more in symptoms than causes. On a second viewing, however, what strikes me is how sharply Williams delineates the different faces of British racism. There is the apocalyptic nostalgia of the old White supremacists, forever harking back to Enoch Powell's "rivers of blood" speech. There is the inarticulate animalism of a figure like the team captain, Lawrie, bred in ignorance. And, most dangerously, there is the skin-deep liberalism of Lawrie's brother, a policeman, and the female publican whose anti-racism is punctured by personal experience.

Williams captures especially well the dilemma of figures like Barry and his ex-soldier brother, Mark, who are damned if they proclaim their Britishness and damned if they don't. In Paul Miller's expansive production, these roles are vividly played by Ashley Walters and Ray Fearon, and there is frighteningly good support from Jake Nightingale as an ugly thug, Paul Moriarty as a bookish fascist and Gawn Grainger as the publican's miserabilist father. Hayden Griffin's set cunningly ensures that part of the audience is seated within the pub, and it was clear from the first-night reaction how many spectators recognised the chilling authenticity of Williams's portrait of the maggot within the culture.

Guantanamo compiled by Victoria Brittain and Gillian Slovo (World Premiere) Tricycle, London: 25 May 2004

The Tricycle is now firmly established as the home of documentary drama. And even if this latest example, compiled from spoken evidence by Victoria Brittain and Gillian Slovo, deals with the familiar horrors of Guantánamo Bay, it still has the power to shock: in particular, it reminds us that the release of five British detainees in no way diminishes American abuse of international law.

Brittain and Slovo move outward from specific cases to general principles: they start, with three intercut monologues describing how specific individuals ended up in a legal black hole. One is by a recently freed Mancunian detainee, Jamal al-Harith, who moved from being a prisoner of the Taliban to terrorist suspect. We also hear from the father of the still-imprisoned Moazzam Begg, who describes how his son was building hand pumps for deprived Afghans when he was arrested. And the entrepreneurial Wahab-al-Rawi recounts how his brother, Bisher, was arrested in The Gambia before being taken to Cuba via the US airbase at Bagram, Afghanistan.

In each case the impression is of people picked up on the flimsiest of suspicions. But the real power of Brittain and Slovo's piece lies in its ability to question the very basis of what is happening in Guantánamo Bay. Clive Stafford-Smith, who runs an American legal charity, describes the Cuban prison as "a massive diversion." A defence counsel at the military commissions says: "It's not a justice system, it's a political system." And Lord Steyn talks of the "utter lawlessness" of Guantánamo Bay.

But what can a piece of theatre contribute to a well-documented issue? In this case, what it does is both localise it and universalise it. It sharpens our awareness of specific cases and reminds us that, while all democracies have a right to defend themselves, they have to operate within an accepted judicial code. The production by Nicolas Kent and Sacha Wares scrupulously maintains this balance between the local and the general. There are also impressive performances from Patrick Robinson as a released detainee, Paul Bhattacharjee as the still-confined, rapidly deteriorating Moazzam Begg, and Badi Uzzaman as his distraught father. But, without raising its voice, the show leaves you shocked at the violations of justice committed in the name of freedom.

Stuff Happens by David Hare
Olivier, National Theatre, London:
11 September 2004

David Hare's *Stuff Happens* has already become a chewed-over public event. But, after attending its Olivier press night, it also strikes me as a very good, totally compelling play: one that may not contain a vast amount of new information but that traces the origins of the Iraq war, puts it in perspective and at the same time astutely analyses the American body politic.

Political theatre comes in all shapes and sizes: satirical, fictional, documentary and agitational. But Hare claims, with some justice, to be writing a history: one that traces a dramatic sequence of events through characters and issues. We know, on the whole, when characters are speaking verbatim. We also deduce, as in a Bush–Blair encounter on a Texas ranch, when Hare is extrapolating from the known facts. We also can work out for ourselves when Hare is deploying dramatic licence.

This last point is crucial because Hare avoids the trap of agitprop. Hare, in fact, constantly creates a form of internal dialectic. The play ruthlessly exposes the dubious premises on which the war was fought. At the same time, it questions our complacency by reminding us of the pro-war arguments. A New Labour politician – possibly not a million miles from Ann Clwyd – admits that the supposed weapons turned out not to exist and that a military victory was compromised by sloppy Pentagon planning for peace. "At the same time," she argues, "a dictator was removed."

Hare's other key means of creating conflict is to view Colin Powell as a stern realist in a Bush war cabinet made up of deluded fantasists. In a big showdown with Bush, based on documented facts, Powell passionately presses the case for treating war as a last resort after diplomacy has been exhausted. In the play's best line, he points out the hypocrisy of American attitudes. "People keep asking," he says of Saddam, "how do we know he's got weapons of mass destruction? How do we know? Because we've still got the receipts."

In Hare's terms, and in Joe Morton's performance, Powell emerges as a tragic figure: the one key player in the administration who sees the folly of invasion but who, in a climactic encounter with Bush, bites the bullet and goes along with the Cheney–Rumsfeld line. Hare never explains what leads to Powell's capitulation, but he leaves you in no doubt that it was a form of self-betrayal.

The great surprise of the show, however, is the way performance leads to reassessment of character. Bush, in many British eyes, is seen as some kind of holy fool or worse. But, through Hare's writing and Alex Jennings's performance, he emerges as a wily and skilful manipulator who plays the role of a bumbling pseudo-Texan but constantly achieves his desired ends. Jennings, with his wire-drawn upper lip and tentative gestures, has caught the Bush mannerisms exactly: more significantly, he suggests Bush is the most adroit politician on stage.

By contrast, Tony Blair is seen satirically: the hints of a moral crusader are there, but in Nicholas Farrell's performance, he emerges largely as a demented egoist obsessed by his own political standing. There may be some truth in this, but the play would be stronger if Hare admitted that Blair may have been propelled by idealistic motives. However, the pleasure lies in seeing recent history, in which we all have a stake, enacted on Britain's most prominent public stage. Nicholas Hytner's production is also elegant and unfussy, with the cast seated on stage throughout and emerging, as required, to enact their part in the drama. And, in a vast cast, there are standout performances from Desmond Barrit as an ideologically-driven Cheney, Dermot Crowley as an assertive Rumsfeld, and Adjoa Andoh as an ice-cold Condoleezza Rice.

No play about Iraq can tell the whole story; and I was surprised by Hare's omission of the crucial role played by the military, especially General Tommy Franks, who gave the war its own unstoppable momentum. But Hare's play offers a probing guide to the Iraq war and shows how the whole mess was based on a disastrous, unproven link between Saddam Hussein and al-Qaida. One comes out enriched and better informed.

Ten Rules For Theatregoers.

22 Sep 2004

Kevin Spacey has warned audiences for the Old Vic that, if they cannot turn off their mobile phones or insist on rustling sweet papers, they should stay away. Here is my own list of Ten Commandments for theatre-going. Do not:

1   Text-message friends, relations and colleagues and then, like my neighbour at the recent Old Vic *Hamlet*, look angrily indignant when asked to desist.

2   Wait till the play's tensest moment to cough or expectorate, thus confirming James Agate's point that "in England nobody goes to the theatre unless he or she has bronchitis."

3   Pass audible comments on the performance in progress, like the lady at *Side by Side by Sondheim* who, staring fixedly at David Kernan, announced to her neighbour: "I see turn-ups are coming back." Or, worse still, the spectator at *Macbeth* who loudly proclaimed: "Something very similar happened to Monica."

4   Ransack your briefcase or handbag and empty its entire contents on the floor in search of the missing tissue that invariably lies at the bottom.

5 Snog, canoodle or have oral sex with your partner in a stage-box, as happened in *Jolson – The Musical* at the Victoria Palace, thus riveting the attention of not only the entire audience but also everyone in the cast.

6 Ostentatiously read the programme or even the play-text while some unparalleled *coup de théatre* is taking place on stage or some vital piece of plot information is being relayed.

7 Laugh hysterically at the most mundane piece of comic business to prove that you too are a paid-up member of the acting profession.

8 Noisily swig from a water bottle as if the mere act of watching a play were likely to cause you to expire from premature dehydration.

9 Turn to your partner at the delivery of every other line as if to advertise to the world that you are in love, on honeymoon or incapable of solitary enjoyment.

10 Die in the middle of a performance. Please, have the decency to wait until the interval.

Don Carlos by **Friedrich Schiller**
Crucible, Sheffield: 4 October 2004

Seventeen years ago Michael Grandage played the title role in Schiller's romantic tragedy in a thrilling revival by Nicholas Hytner at Manchester's Royal Exchange. Now, for his final Crucible production, Grandage directs an equally exciting version that would do honour to any of our big national stages.

At the heart of Schiller's play, written two years before the French Revolution, lies a confrontation between absolutism and liberty. Philip II of Spain stands for iron rule. Against him, the Marquis of Posa, championing Spain's oppressed subjects, voices Rousseau-esque ideals of freedom. Caught between them is Philip's son, Don Carlos, fatally in love with his Valois stepmother but also seduced by Posa's visionary dream. If the play sometimes buckles under its mix of passion, politics and melodramatic plotting, it vividly expresses the young Schiller's own yearning for liberty.

The triumph of Grandage's production and Christopher Oram's design lies in their visualisation of Schiller's ideas. A swinging thurible, a prison-like court with high, barred windows, even the menacing hiss of the ladies-in-waiting's fans all tell us that we are in a world of religious and political tyranny: a point underlined by Mike Poulton's translation where Philip announces "The instrument God places in my hand is terror." But Grandage also captures the subversive eruption of feeling in this crepuscular hell: at one point Richard Coyle's neurotic Don Carlos beats against the court doors like a trapped animal and his simultaneous passion for Posa and the queen implies a state of Hamlet-esque sexual confusion.

Madness is never far below the surface in this production. Derek Jacobi's magnificent Philip II starts as a figure of cold intransigence, dismissing his kneeling son "Spare us this playhouse pathos"; but Jacobi impressively gains our sympathy as he reveals the king's Lear-like fear of insanity. Claire Price also turns the queen into a vigorously angry exile trapped in a world of rigid etiquette. If Elliot Cowan could do more to persuade us of Posa's political fervour, there is superb support from Charlotte Randle as the lovestruck Princess Eboli and from Ian Hogg and Michael Hadley as a pair of insidious plotters.

The production marks another stage in the British theatre's absorption of Schiller – unsurprisingly since his work is full of Shakespearean echoes, shows the intersection of private and public passion and captures the timeless rebelliousness of youth.

2005

Professor Bernhardi by Arthur Schnitzler
Arcola, London: 2 April 2005

Vienna, 1900. The words conjure up an image of sex, sophistication and Strauss polkas. But Mark Rosenblatt's rediscovery of this astonishing Schnitzler play – written in 1912 – for the Last Waltz season, reminds us of the worm inside the apple. For Schnitzler's theme is nothing less than the anti-Semitism that corroded Viennese society and was to shape the century.

Schnitzler's eponymous hero runs a private teaching hospital. In the first act he refuses a Catholic priest admission to an ailing female patient. His reasons are strictly medical, as the girl is in a drug-induced euphoria, but, when she dies without receiving the last rites, Bernhardi becomes the victim of a political witch-hunt. He is accused of "religious agitation," arraigned in court and driven out by the anti-Jewish faction in his own hospital.

What makes the play thrilling is that Schnitzler exposes the poisonous nature of Viennese racism without exculpating his hero. You sense the virulent factionalism from the first scene when one of Bernhardi's diagnostic successes is greeted by his deputy with a murmur of: "Great celebrations in Israel, hmmn?" And Vienna's economic tensions are exemplified by the fact that 85 per cent of the patients are Catholic yet the same amount of funding comes from the Jewish community.

But, while the victimised Bernhardi is dubbed in the press "the Dreyfus of the hospitals," Schnitzler shrewdly refuses to sanctify him. Bernhardi's crime is that, as he tells an opportunistic minister, "I don't care about politics." And Schnitzler's point is that political innocence is no defence in a society as divided as turn-of-the-century Vienna. Christopher Godwin hits the right note as Bernhardi by conveying both the doctor's fundamental decency and naive belief in the unassailability of truth.

Strong support comes from Dale Rapley as a vehemently anti-Semitic doctor, Deka Walmsley as an urbane civil servant and John Stahl as both a coat-turning minister and a passionately liberal optometrist. And even if Samuel Adamson's version occasionally lapses into the anachronistic vernacular, as in the minister's cry of "Fuck politics!" Rosenblatt's production

not only brims with energy but reminds us of Schnitzler's ability to turn
social observation into prophetic insight.

*Normally the process of rewriting the classics leaves me uneasy but in 2019
Robert Icke did a brilliant update of Schnitzler's play, entitled* The Doctor,
*at the Almeida. Juliet Stevenson as the protagonist was one of a series of
gender-switches in a production that raised contemporary questions about
religion, race, class and medical ethics without damaging the fabric of the
original play.*

Mammals by Amelia Bullmore
(World Premiere)
Bush Theatre, London: 11 April 2005

Sometimes the sheer brio of the writing and performing makes up for the
familiarity of the subject: such is the case with Amelia Bullmore's first play
which is an invigorating kitchen comedy about the perils of monogamy.
After a bout of semi-abstract, doom-laden plays, it is refreshing to find one
that has a proximity to recognisable life.

Bullmore starts by showing a harassed mum, Jane, coping with two
demanding children: what makes it funny is that the kids are played by
stamping, shouting, rampaging adults. Jane's world is blown apart when her
husband, Kev, returns from one of his business trips as a building safety
inspector to announce that he's smitten with a member of his team. And
right in the midst of domestic crisis, in comes Kev's oldest chum, Phil, a
bachelor Scot whose relationship with a doolally handbag designer, Lorna,
seems to possess the jazzy fervour hard to sustain in a 12-year-old marriage.

We have been here before but Bullmore refreshes a stock situation by her
sharp eye and ear for the oddities of human behaviour. Jane is not just a
boxed-in mum but a woman driven to hit her kids out of desperation. Lorna
is a beautifully observed study in glamorous narcissism who, in describing
an unrequited love affair, announces "I lived off apples for a year." And the
kids, forever asking embarrassing questions about mortality and hairy
fannies, are hilariously inquisitive.

The play suffers from a clumsily contrived ending but Bullmore writes
with clinical accuracy about the conflict between marriage and our
mammalian urges. And, having just directed Laura Wade's stylised study of
confinement in *Breathing Corpses*, Anna Mackmin shows she is equally at
home with domestic realism. She even retains from the previous show
Niamh Cusack whose Jane has a devastated anguish that cuts through the
comedy.

Nancy Carroll wittily plays Lorna like a sexy anglepoise lamp while
Daniel Ryan as the errant Kev and Mark Bonnar as the free-floating Phil are

very good as the floundering males. But it is Helena Lymberry and Jane Hazelgrove who all but steal the show as the two kids who want kisses and cuddles on demand but who regard the house as the territory in which the adults just happen to live. As a report from the front line of the domestic battleground, Bullmore's play bulges with promise.

Is the fashion for the 90-minute play suffocating dramatists?

16 April 2005

How long, ideally, is a play? The question is palpably absurd. How long is a piece of string? Samuel Beckett's *Breath* lasts 40 seconds; Eugene O'Neill's *Mourning Becomes Electra* runs four-and-a-half hours. Form, as in architecture, follows function. But, while I've no wish to lay down laws, I find myself increasingly disturbed by the fashionable tyranny of the 90-minute play. It is everywhere; and I believe it is crippling ambition, ironing out contradiction, and effectively de-politicising drama.

What are the reasons for the 90-minute rule? I suspect there are several. Social customs are changing and, in a busy restaurant culture, 90 minutes is the ideal prelude to a night out: after *Art* or *Oleanna* you ate and argued about the show. Audiences, trained on TV advertising, are also quick to absorb information and no longer need lengthy exposition. There is also the visible influence of the "Edinburgh factor": the bustling hypermarket of the Fringe, where people rush from show to show and anything much over an hour is regarded as an impertinent incursion into one's time.

On the plus side, modern drama has in many cases proved the power of brevity. Beckett's *Footfalls* uses the hypnotic image of a woman's solitary pacing to externalise her inner anguish. Harold Pinter's *Ashes to Ashes* shows how a drawing room confrontation can open up to admit the Holocaust. Caryl Churchill's *A Number* brilliantly explored, in one hour, not only the anguish of parent–child relationships but the defining marks of human identity. But it is worth remarking that Beckett, Pinter and Churchill all began by writing conventionally structured plays and only gradually mastered the technique of creating images that distil a wealth of human experience.

Only a fool would deny dramatists the right to choose the appropriate form. But what worries me is the way relatively young writers are settling into the 90-minute groove: a form midway between pure Beckettian cystallisation of an idea and the once-familiar two-act structure. And while much may be gained – not least for critics up against a deadline – something vital is being lost: the ability to explore the ramifications of a situation or the inconsistencies of human character. The symptoms are everywhere; but it is particularly striking that the Royal Court, still the epicentre of new writing, has offered us a succession of interval-free plays over the past six months.

One result is that you get cut-to-the-chase crisis without social analysis. Joe Penhall, as we know from *Some Voices* and *Blue/ Orange*, is a talented writer. But his latest piece, *Dumb Show*, dealt with the process of celebrity entrapment by tabloid journalists without exploring the wider issues. Who creates the ethos that makes such entrapment possible? Is it an editorial vendetta? Is it a by-product of the circulation war? Or does it spring from some public need to see our secular idols mocked and humiliated? I ended up the none the wiser; and that was because Penhall, in his 90 minutes, had no room to range beyond an examination of a sleazy journalistic device.

The new compressionism can also leave too much unsaid. Kevin Elyot's 70-minute Royal Court play, *Forty Winks*, was both fascinating and cryptic. You could understand Elyot's theme: the destructiveness of erotic obsession. But, in exploring his peripatetic hero's lifelong preoccupation with his first love, Elyot reduced the other characters to unexplained ciphers: the neurotic love-object, her brutal husband, her narcoleptic daughter. No one is asking for easy resolutions: incompleteness, as Dilys Powell wrote many years ago of Antonioni's *L'Avventura*, is often part of a work of art's mystery. But Elyot's abbreviated form left the audience not merely to join up the dots but to find where they were located.

Perhaps the gravest charge against the new playella is that it fails to allow room for debate, discussion, dialectic. No one could accuse April De Angelis, a genuinely inventive socialist feminist, of a lack of ideas in her latest play, *Wild East*. It positively bulged with issues: corporate responsibility, economic imperialism, environmental rape, gender politics and many more. But the 80-minute length and the job-interview format meant that attitudes were struck without any counter-propositions being offered. And, having accused big companies of manipulating individuals, De Angelis proceeded to do precisely that with her own characters.

None of these plays was empty or dull; but in each case I felt the dramatist was constricted by his or her chosen form. And, although I've singled out the Royal Court, I could make the same charges against other venues. Recently, for instance, I saw a promising play, Gerald Murphy's *Take Me Away* at the Bush, about the breakdown of a dysfunctional Irish family. At Edinburgh it had been extravagantly praised. But yet again I felt Murphy had failed to address the really hard question: what is it about the supposedly thriving Celtic Tiger that produces so much misery? In the 1920s Sean O'Casey plotted the connection between poverty and tragedy, so why today has today's Irish boom led to noisy desperation?

I am not asking for a standard structure or a return to the days of the two-interval play. But what I miss is the polyphonic richness of which drama is capable, or the complexities of character revealed by an unfolding narrative. One reason why people are flocking to *Don Carlos* is that it provides exactly the kind of stimulus so much modern drama lacks: exploration of ideas through character, examination of the manifold selves that make up individuals, the thrilling collision of private and public worlds.

You can't, of course, simply re-create old forms: as Alain Robbe-Grillet shrewdly pointed out, *Hamlet* would not be a masterpiece if it were written today since we do not live in the age of the five-act tragedy. But the new, slavish obeisance to the 90-minute rule stems, I suspect, from a mixture of fashion and ignorance; in particular, a shocking unawareness of even the recent past when drama moved beyond a single situation or point of crisis to examine causes as well as effects. To put it bluntly, perhaps our own practitioners should simply read more plays. Whatever the remedy, I am getting impatient with these dramatic driblets that offer ideas for plays rather than plays of ideas. Too many of our best playwrights are being inhibited by their surrender to a modish, audience-friendly form.

Needless to say, my piece infuriated many people. The dramatist David Eldridge wrote a 2,000-word riposte in The Guardian *in which he accused me of a backward-looking agenda. He also made some practical points. "Instead of clobbering playwrights," he wrote, "Billington ought to look for the real reason behind the current lack of variety in length. It is this: consistently over the past 20 years, as theatres have cut costs, writers have been forced to think of making plays that require fewer actors to perform them." I acknowledge that. But it is intriguing that a counter-movement to the 90-minute play has developed over time. Richard Bean led a number of dramatists in creating "the Monsterists" demanding more resources for new plays. Nicholas Hytner at the National, Michael Boyd at the RSC and Ian Rickson at the Royal Court encouraged writers to create for a big company of actors. Today we still have 90-minute plays but there is a growing appetite for the expansive, the epic and the inordinate.*

Elmina's Kitchen by Kwame Kwei-Armah (Revival) Garrick Theatre, London: 27 April 2005

Things are moving. Kwame Kwei-Armah's National Theatre hit has at last made it into the West End to be followed later this summer by Stratford East's *The Big Life*. But, while it's cheering to find Black theatre taking centre stage, Kwei-Armah's lively, dialogue-rich play eventually lapses into melodrama: it's good, gutsy stuff but less thoughtful than his follow-up play, *Fix Up*.

The author himself plays, with quiet charisma, an ex-boxer called Deli who runs a dingy West Indian takeaway in Hackney and faces a multitude of problems. His 19-year-old son, Ashley, spurns education and falls into the clutches of a protection-racket boss. Deli's parasitic dad, who abandoned him as a kid, turns up and wrecks his son's relationship with a feisty waitress. And, as if this were not enough, Deli's brother is released from the slammer but never makes it as far as the Hackney caff.

In attempting to cram in the generation war, local gun-culture and the battle between books and booming consumerism, Kwei-Armah over-stretches his crowded plot; and he resolves it with a not wholly convincing father–son showdown. But what he does have is a fantastic ear for dialogue and an eye for the spectacle of old men behaving badly. There's something authentically creepy about the sight of Deli's dad coming on to his son's would-be girlfriend. And the dad's chum, Baygee, is a richly funny character who, hearing of a planned fast-food joint, announces: "If you ask me, West Indian and fast is a contradiction in terms."

Angus Jackson's production can't solve all the plot problems but adorns the action with vibrant live music and gets excellent performances all round. Don Warrington and Oscar James are superb as the old men forever harking back to some paradisal era of licensed promiscuity. Dona Croll is both sharp-tongued and sympathetic as the bookish, sparky waitress. And Michael Obiora as Deli's brashly materialistic son finds a chilling surrogate father in Shaun Parkes' racketeering mentor.

In many ways, it's a highly traditional play echoing Odets' social-issue dramas of the American 1930s. But the occasion matters more than the play. To find a culturally diverse West End audience cheering on a play that at least vividly addresses the maelstrom of modern Hackney life is to give one hope for the theatrical future.

Talking to Terrorists. A verbatim piece created by Robin Soans (World Premiere) Oxford Playhouse: 28 April 2005

Verbatim theatre is not just living journalism. If it is to succeed, it has to have the shape and rhythm of art. That was true of the Tricycle's *Bloody Sunday* and *The Colour of Justice*. And at its best its also true of this extraordinary kaleidoscopic collage created by Robin Soans and co-produced by Out of Joint and the Royal Court.

The whole show is based on the testimony of those who have had experience of terrorism. And there is a moment in the second half when it juxtaposes the words of perpetrator and victim with a directness that would be hard to achieve in fiction. At a desk sits the ex-IRA man responsible for the Brighton bombing of 20 years ago. A few feet away stands a Tory landowner who was in the hotel on the night of the explosion. And their intersecting recollections produce remarkable theatre. The bomber explains, with mathematical precision, how he took a room in the Brighton hotel and set the timer to explode during the Tory conference. "Of course I regret the suffering I caused," he says, "but circumstances made our actions inevitable." The female survivor who was staying in the hotel then describes the shock of the explosion, the astonishing lack of panic as people exited through the debris, and the strange air of almost wartime stoicism. The moment provides not just a tonal contrast. It pinpoints the divergence of outlook and attitude between bomber and victim in a way that is unique to theatre. It is played by Lloyd Hutchinson and June Watson at just the right unhysterical pitch.

What Soans's script does for much of the evening, however, is offer insights into terrorism and explain its multiple causes. A psychologist, smoothly played by Christopher Ettridge, is particularly enlightening in defining its origins. He pins down the need for an organising guru who eventually retreats into the background. He talks of the importance of recruiting adolescents who crave status, who like to feel they are shaping history and who have "a strong illusion of immortality." What is terrifying is that he explains how relatively easy it would be to organise such a group for such a limited, local cause as blowing up four-wheel drives in Chelsea.

The inherent danger in a show like this is that it romanticises terrorism. But it strenuously avoids this by showing how torture and oppression often create their own violent antidote, using Uganda and Kurdistan as potent examples. It never lets us forget that terrorist acts punish the innocent as well as the guilty. One of the most moving testimonies comes from an envoy, clearly Terry Waite, who found that attempted negotiation turned him into a Lebanese captive. There is even a wild humour about his revelation that, pleading for something to read while incarcerated, he was offered *Great Escapes* by Eric Williams.

Soans's script strives hard to balance cause and effect. But it would be faux-naif to pretend that it doesn't have a political agenda. If any theme runs through the show, it is that terrorism can never be countered by retaliatory force alone. It also touches on current concerns by including testimony from the former British ambassador to Uzbekistan: the man who was recalled after revealing that CIA intelligence about armed Islamic units roaming the mountains above Samarkand was patently untrue. What the show doesn't say is that his outrage at British faith in false intelligence has led him to stand as an independent candidate in Blackburn.

But the eternal question raised by factual theatre like this is whether it does anything fictional theatre can't. Watching Max Stafford-Clark's calculatedly low-key production, I would say it does. It sheds light on a dark subject. It forces us to think about what actually constitutes "terrorism." It shows that people acquire a strange eloquence when talking about subjects close to their hearts.

It is not the only form of theatre. But this show, staged very simply against Jonathan Fensom's set of graffiti-strewn concrete blocks, is aesthetically satisfying and well acted by an eight-strong cast including Jonathan Cullen, Alexander Hanson and Catherine Russell. Just occasionally I could have done with more instant identification of who the speakers actually were. But this is a quibble in an evening that takes a subject surrounded by fear and panic and offers progressive enlightenment. At its highest point, as in the contrapuntal recollections of the Brighton bombing, it also proves that edited memories can achieve the potency of art.

Death of a Salesman by Arthur Miller
Lyric Theatre, London: 18 May 2005

It has taken six years for Robert Falls' production of Arthur Miller's masterpiece to reach us from Chicago. But it was worth the wait, since this is as fine a rendering of the play as one could hope for; one that realises that the key to the play lies in the word "dream."

Willy Loman, Miller's archetypal salesman-hero, is accurately described as "a man who lives in his dreams"; and it is that inability to confront the reality about himself, his son Biff and his society that makes him a tragic figure. But Falls recognises that the whole play is structured with the fluidity of a dream. In the opening moment, when Willy unexpectedly returns home from a trip to New England, his wife's anxious voice seems to be resonating in his head. And, as Mark Wendland's ingenious designs whirl round on a dual revolve, Willy's past and present merge in a nightmarish kaleidoscope.

But Miller's play is also a critique of the debased American dream and the substitution of salesmanship for the old ideals of hard work and courage. Willy tries to commodify his own personality; and, in that sense, the key scene in the play is the one where he confronts his young boss, Howard, who is more interested in his new tape recorder than in Willy. When Willy cries, "You can't eat the orange and throw the peel away," you realise he is wrong: that is what happens in any business system that depends on salesmanship.

The strength of Falls' production also lies in its casting. And Brian Dennehy plays Willy superbly as a man who has lived all his life on a level of fantasy. Dennehy is a man of titanic proportions; but what he brings out wonderfully is the contrast between the agonised, ageing Willy, forever beating his temple with his right hand, and the younger self who believed that he could smile, josh and kid his way to success. You can play Willy as a little man with big ideas; but what Dennehy gives us is a physical giant facing up to his own vulnerability.

Clare Higgins also highlights the hidden strength of Willy's wife, Linda, vehemently thumping the table when telling us that "attention must be paid." And there is impeccable support from Douglas Henshall as a neurotically insecure Biff who finally cuts through the miasma of deceit, from Howard Witt as Willy's shrewdly kind neighbour and from Jonathan Aris as the neighbour's nerdy son who finally makes good. In the year of Miller's death, it is good to be reminded what a great playwright he was and why this of all his plays epitomises the hollowness behind America's eternal optimism.

Blackbird by David Harrower
(World Premiere)
King's Theatre, Edinburgh: 17 August 2005

Over the years the Edinburgh International Festival has not had much luck with new plays. The curse has, however, been lifted with David Harrower's *Blackbird*: a riveting study in sexual obsession that leaves one both shaken and stirred.

It deals with a confrontation between 28-year-old Una and 56-year-old Ray in a debris-filled factory recreation room. Fifteen years ago they had a relationship for which Ray was sent down. Now Una has come in search of him. The shock lies in discovering that Una is not after revenge but some sort of closure to a relationship that ended tantalisingly in a Tynemouth hotel when Ray went out for a packet of cigarettes and never returned.

Harrower doesn't exculpate Ray but he asks difficult questions. Can one separate love from paedophilia? Is consensual sex possible with a minor? Should we recognise that children now reach sexual maturity much earlier? Harrower can't provide all the answers. He also never makes clear how much Una's adult life has been ruined by her early experiences. He does, however, suggest that there may be a strange affinity, tantamount to love, between people of different generations and that adult guilt and childhood innocence should never be automatically assumed. If the piece shocks and disturbs, it is partly because of the visceral force of Peter Stein's masterly production. Jodhi May is perhaps a little too patently the sexual aggressor but brilliantly re-enacts the nightmare moment of her desertion. Roger Allam is extraordinary in suggesting the shame, fear and lingering desire of a middle-aged man who has earnestly tried to reinvent himself. Ferdinand Wogerbauer's set, with its Perspex window through which passing factory-hands intrusively peer, reminds us of our own voyeuristic fascination with transgressive sex. I can't believe Harrower's harrowing play will disappear after only nine Edinburgh performances.

The Wild Duck by Henrik Ibsen
Donmar Warehouse: 14 December 2005

Michael Grandage is quite an ironist. Just in time for Christmas he brings us one of the greatest attacks on goodwill ever penned. But the pleasure of seeing Ibsen's 1885 masterpiece, in its first London showing for 15 years, lies in relishing its blend of faultless technique and thematic timelessness.

David Eldridge's version brings out Ibsen's permanent relevance without any textual coarsening. We watch enthralled as the idealistic Gregers Werle intervenes in the happy home life of Hjalmar Ekdal in an attempt to reveal its shaky moral foundations: in particular the family's economic dependence on Werle senior who may well be the father of Hjalmar's child. As Gregers wreaks his well-intentioned havoc, we are told he is afflicted by "a fever called 'I am always right'"; and it doesn't take much imagination to see that the fever is still flourishing in Blairite Britain.

But Ibsen's genius lay in creating men, not monsters: as Shaw said, while watching the play "you are getting deeper and deeper into your own life all the time." The photographer Hjalmar, in his idle fantasies and domestic dependence, induces moments of painful recognition. And even Gregers, although he is an agent of destruction, is no simple villain but a victim of heredity and a man who believes in what he calls "the claims of the ideal."

All this comes across strongly in Grandage's flawless production which acknowledges Ibsen's poetic symbolism while maintaining a sense of daily reality. Ben Daniels's Gregers is no bulging-eyed fanatic but a man who exudes a quiet, low-keyed certainty. He prowls round Hjalmar's airy Nordic studio, nicely realised in Vicki Mortimer's design, like a sympathetic detective looking for clues. He even exudes a kindly avuncularity towards the 14-year-old Hedvig which makes it all the more shocking when he tells everyone that they are living in "a poisonous swamp."

Paul Hilton also scrupulously follows Ibsen's injunction to play Hjalmar without any trace of parody. Hilton has a haggard, negligent charm that explains the affection Hjalmar induces: at the same time he brings out the character's fatal weakness as he prepares to abandon hearth and home. And there is superb support all round: from Sinead Matthews who has all of Hedvig's carefully articulated youthful curiosity, from Peter Eyre who captures her grandfather's dilapidated grandeur, from Michelle Fairley who reveals Gina Ekdal's compassionate resilience and from Nicholas Le Prevost as a drunken doctor who is Ibsen's voice of sanity. Alongside *Pillars of The Community*, currently at the National, it is an evening that explains why Ibsen is the greatest dramatist after Shakespeare.

2006

Nights at the Circus. Adapted by Tom Morris and Emma Rice from the novel by Angela Carter (World Premiere) Lyric Hammersmith, London: 27 January 2006

Angela Carter's famous novel is both a lure and a trap for the stage adapter: it hymns live performance while also being a rich-textured, postmodernist fantasy. But this freewheeling version by Tom Morris and Emma Rice, directed by the latter, is a joyous affair that captures astonishingly well Carter's celebration of the possibilities of freedom.

The setting is 1899 and, as in the book, we see an angel-winged, music-hall aerialist known as Fevvers being interviewed by a cynical journalist, Jack Walser, who hopes to expose her as a fraud. But as Fevvers tells her story of her brothel education and experiments in flight, Walser's scepticism turns to enchantment. In pursuit of her, he joins a circus where he turns clown and undergoes endless humiliations to pierce the heart of this Cockney Venus.

While inevitably filleting Carter's book, Rice and Morris stay true to its intentions. Fevvers herself is both a richly vulgar reality and a symbol of feminine possibility as she is told: "You are the pure child of the century, the new age in which no woman will be bound to the ground." But on stage it also becomes a story about the demolition of Walser's detachment: as he dons a clownish chicken-head, I was reminded of Emil Jannings in *The Blue Angel*, who undergoes similar indignities in his pursuit of Marlene Dietrich. The big difference is that in Carter's version Walser discovers his freedom through his infatuation with Fevvers.

But the pleasure of Rice's production lies in its overflowing theatricality. Natalia Tena's Fevvers begins as a voluptuously decorative, music-hall icon singing "I'm Only A Bird In A Gilded Cage." By the end she has escaped her entrapment and swings vertiginously through the air with Gisli Orn

Gardarsson's similarly liberated Walser, here dubbed the "Nordic adventurer" in deference to the actor's Icelandic origin. Eschewing sentimentality, the production also brings out the cruelty that is part of the metaphorical circus world. Ed Woodall's fearsome chief clown beats Amanda Lawrence as his bruised female partner and, in one extraordinary number, lyrically hymns his serial abuse. We are reminded of the danger of circus life as the female animal-tamer goes into the ring, here skilfully evoked through a circle of flame-filled buckets, with menacing tigers.

Admittedly John Bayley once wrote of Carter that "whatever spirited arabesques and feats of descriptive imagination she performs she comes to rest in the right ideological position." But the virtue of this production is that underplays political correctness to become a celebration of human, not simply female, freedom. And Stu Barker's haunting music and the ceaselessly versatile cast of six highlight the mythic ideal that liberty can only be achieved after one has undergone ritual tests and trials. I am wary of novel adaptations, but this one gives Carter's book abundant theatrical life.

Resurrection Blues by Arthur Miller
(UK Premiere)
Old Vic, London: 3 March 2006

I feel sorry for Arthur Miller. When I saw his penultimate play in Minneapolis four years ago, it struck me as a sparky, neo-Shavian satire both on the commercialism of the modern age and its credulity. But it's almost impossible to judge the play fairly on the basis of the clumsily inept, poorly acted production that Robert Altman has devised at the Old Vic.

Miller's play is clearly intended as a moral fable. It starts from the premise that a charismatic revolutionary, venerated as the risen Christ, has appeared in a Latin American republic. To the country's corrupt military ruler, who sells exclusive TV rights to his crucifixion, the holy guerrilla is a source of profit. To the American ad agency that negotiates the deal, he is a means of selling their products. But to his loyal followers, the unseen saviour is a way of preventing further persecution. It may not be the subtlest of satires but it squarely hits its chosen targets. In a country where the execution of the Oklahoma bomber was accompanied by bids to carry the event live on the internet, Miller's attack on the American commercialisation of death is apt.

His argument that greed, rapacity and fantasy increasingly govern our civilisation is also hard to gainsay. But Miller also suggests that, in a world of obscene inequalities, the have-nots are driven to elevate revolutionaries into spiritual leaders. Sadly Miller's ideas are given little chance to emerge in Altman's production which sacrifices language and thought to spurious atmosphere. Overlapping dialogue and semi-audibility may have a valid place in Altman's movies but they prove fatal in a text-driven play.

When, for instance, the military dictator's cousin announces "I will not superimpose American mores on a dignified foreign people," the line got loud guffaws in Minneapolis: as delivered by James Fox, who looks like an English country gent who has wandered into the wrong play, the sentiment falls flat as a Shrove Tuesday pancake. But the gravest piece of miscasting is Maximilian Schell as the military dictator. One's worst fears were aroused when, in his first scene, Schell bungled simple actions like replacing a telephone on its stand or firing a pistol. But Schell barks his lines, chops up sentences into meaningless phrases and generally behaves as if he were playing a comic general in a Mel Brooks movie. Miller's character should exude danger and menace; but, lacking a firm director, Schell gives a performance straight out of *The Producers*. Apparently given their heads, the actors collectively lose them. Jane Adams as a guilt-stricken TV director constantly uses sagging knees to indicate moral collapse. Neve Campbell falls back on manual semaphoring as a suicide-prone acolyte of the revolutionary leader. Almost the only actor to give a coherent performance is Peter McDonald as another hippy disciple who makes the most of the revelation that the leader is trisexual in his love of men, women and vegetation.

What saddens me is that Miller's play has not been given a fair chance. It may not be *The Crucible*. But when Miller argues that we live increasingly in a world of debased fiction he is making a serious point; and his assertion that the Vietnam war was set off by an imagined attack on an American warship in the Gulf of Tonkin obviously has chilling relevance to the public pretexts for invading Iraq. Points like this get lost, however, in a production that creates no coherent world on stage and that sacrifices ideas to momentary effects. Altman is a wonderful movie-director and a humane man; but, on this evidence, he has little respect for writers or the intentions behind Miller's satiric tale.

The Clean House by Sarah Ruhl (UK Premiere) Crucible Studio, Sheffield: 22 March 2006

Who cleans up after whom? That was the starting point for this unusual comedy by Sarah Ruhl; and it's a good question, because it raises all kinds of issues about class, gender, psychology and politics. But a play that starts as wittily as a Jules Feiffer cartoon drifts towards the end into cosmic wooziness.

Ruhl's talent, I suspect, is for social observation; her play kicks off with sharp, thumbnail sketches of domesticity. Lane, a high-powered doctor, claims she didn't go to medical school in order to clean her own house. However, her hired hand, Matilde, is a young Brazilian comic less interested in cleaning pans than in scouring the world in search of the perfect joke. So

Lane's sister, Virginia, who regards dust as an affront and whose day goes dead at 3.12 after she has done her own house, surreptitiously takes over Matilde's role.

All this is good clean fun that shows how domestic order offers a clue to character: Lane needs it, but hires others to create it; while her sister compensates for the emptiness of her own life by turning housework into a religious ritual. Selina Cadell's Virginia is a joy to watch as she immaculately folds every piece of linen, talks rhapsodically of the way her curtains sing to the ottoman, and recalls her testiness on examining Greek ruins and thinking "Why doesn't someone just sweep them up?

But a play is more than a series of apercus. It also needs a plot; and this is where Ruhl goes off the rails. She shows Lane's life being disrupted when her surgeon husband falls in love with a 67-year-old patient in the course of a mastectomy. This leads to wry jokes in which the lovers justify their selfishness by reference to an ancient Jewish law which legitimises absconding with your soulmate. Having begun like a Woody Allen comedy, Ruhl's play turns into a whimsical piece about the search for sisterly solidarity and cosmic laughter in the face of death.

Still, Samuel West as director has certainly attracted an ace cast. Patricia Hodge captures exactly Lane's brisk supercharged capability and gradual emotional disintegration. Selina Cadell is plausibly her sister, while Rebecca Santos as the Brazilian maid makes one laugh even when telling jokes in Portuguese. And luxury casting gives us Robert East as Lane's self-righteous husband, and Eleanor Bron as the slowly expiring cancer victim. You can't fault the acting. But I still prefer Ruhl when she caustically observes our domestic foibles rather than theorises about laughter as a cleansing global force.

Rock 'N' Roll by Tom Stoppard
(World Premiere)
Royal Court, London: 15 June 2006

Tom Stoppard's astonishing new play is, amongst many other things, a hymn to Pan. It starts in a Cambridge garden in 1968 with a piper playing the Syd Barrett song, Golden Hair. It ends in Prague in 1990 with film of a Rolling Stones concert led by Mick Jagger, who was in the Royal Court first-night audience. And, although Stoppard's play deals with Marxism, materialism and Sapphic poetry, it is above all a celebration of the pagan spirit embodied by rock 'n' roll.

In plot terms, Stoppard deals with the contrasting fortunes of two worlds: that of Czech freedom-fighters and Cambridge Marxists. The former are represented by Jan: an exiled Czech who returns to Prague in 1968, at the time of the Soviet takeover, and who, although primarily a rock-loving non-combatant, finds himself inexorably drawn into dissidence and Charter 77. Meanwhile the Cambridge left is powerfully embodied by Max: an unrepentant Marxist don, as old as the October Revolution, who is still drawn to "this beautiful idea."

What is fascinating about the play is that there are no easy victories. Jan is no heroic martyr, but an observer more drawn to the subversive band, the Plastic People of the Universe, than to protest-movements: it is only the steady erosion of Czech freedom that turns him into a dissident. As for the fervently ideological Max, Stoppard treats his convictions seriously and allows him to score strong debating-points: he is, in fact, the first sympathetic Marxist I can recall in all Stoppard's work.

In presenting two worlds, Stoppard also suggests that, while the Czechs have fought strenuously for their freedoms, we are allowing ours to slip from our grasp. In a crucial second-act dinner-party scene, Stoppard brings together Max, Jan and various representatives of two different cultures. But it is Lenka, an expatriate Czech don who seems to voice his sentiments when she urges Jan not to return, saying "This place has lost its nerve. They put something in the water since you were here. It's a democracy of obedience."

But although Stoppard takes a pessimistic view of an England that seems to have lost any sustaining faith or principles, his play paradoxically finds hope in the liberating spirit of rock 'n' roll. Each scene is punctuated by the sounds of legendary groups including the Stones, Pink Floyd and the Grateful Dead. Even though he acknowledges that they have given way to the blander effusions of today, he constantly uses music as a symbol of pagan ecstasy.

All this is clearly articulated in Trevor Nunn's excellent production, in which the scenes are spliced with exultant rock. And the other great virtue of the production is that it allows ample scope for each intellectual viewpoint. Brian Cox exudes massive power as the Marxist Max who goes on fighting to the end even after the loss of his wife and his political faith. Rufus Sewell as Jan charts immaculately the character's gradations from passive observer to disgraced dissident and shows him emerging on the other side. And Sinead Cusack, doubling as Max's cancer-stricken wife and grown-up daughter, and Peter Sullivan as a Havel-like Czech protester turn in equally strong performances. But the remarkable thing about the play is that it touches on so many themes, registers its lament at the erosion of freedom in our society and yet leaves you cheered by its wit, buoyancy and belief in the human spirit.

Frost/Nixon by Peter Morgan (World Premiere) Donmar Warehouse, London: 22 August 2006

Peter Morgan is clearly hypnotised by power. Having explored the Blair–Brown relationship in *The Deal*, he now turns his attention to David Frost's

1977 TV interviews with Richard Nixon. The result, even if it induces a dubious sympathy for the fallen president, is a gripping study of the politics of the media.

In Morgan's hands, the Californian showdown between the protagonists takes on the aura of a boxing bout. On the left, you have the supposedly lightweight English TV talk-show host: on the right, the veteran occupant of the seats of power. Each man also has his seconds: in Frost's case a positive army of them led by a liberal academic, Jim Reston, while Nixon is supported by a tough military slugger. And, as in all good fight stories, the challenger loses the opening rounds only to deliver a final knockout punch by getting Nixon to confess to his Watergate sins.

But the real fascination of Morgan's play lies in its suggestion that, behind the contest, there was a symbiotic link between Frost and Nixon. Frost, having lost his American and Australian shows, desperately needed the interviews to restore his dwindling fortunes; Nixon, for his part, craved public redemption. And Morgan pushes the parallels further by having Nixon make a phone call to Frost suggesting they are both insecure men seeking vindictive triumph over their enemies. It's a risky device which comes off only because Morgan leaves you in doubt as to whether it's a shared fantasy.

My only cavil is that almost too much stress is placed on Nixon's vulnerability: not enough on his real crime, which was a South-East Asian policy which resulted in a million Indo-Chinese deaths. But, as a study of two men in a camera combat, the play rivets the attention and is directed with fierce lucidity by Michael Grandage. Christopher Oram's design, by placing an enlarged TV screen above the interview, yields devastating close-ups of Nixon's crumbling confession.

The magnificent central performances offer an intriguing contrast. Michael Sheen exactly captures Frost's verbal tics and mannerisms while suggesting a nervousness behind the breezy self-assurance: there's a moment when he almost puts a hand on Nixon's shoulder before hastily withdrawing it. Meanwhile Frank Langella, although not looking much like Nixon, by sheer acting convinces you this is a desperately solitary man aching for the activity of power. By the end, I felt I had not only got a glimpse into the characters of the two men, but also became nostalgic for an era when television itself had a theatrical weight and power it has since sadly lost

A Moon for the Misbegotten by Eugene O'Neill
Old Vic, London: 27 September 2006

Eugene O'Neill's *The Iceman Cometh* first drew Kevin Spacey to the Old Vic. Now another late O'Neill, again superbly directed by Howard Davies, proves the highlight of the Spacey regime to date. With the exception of

Richard II, this theatre has lately roamed the foothills of drama; now at last it seems to be aiming for the peaks.

O'Neill's play is deceptive. The setting is a broken-down farm in rural Connecticut in 1923 and we seem to be in for a folksy mortgage melodrama. Cussed old Phil Hogan, an Irish-American tenant farmer, is apparently concerned that the property will be sold from under him. Deserted by his three sons, he is helplessly dependent on his daughter, Josie, who poses as a rustic trollop. The only hope of saving the land it seems is for Josie to trick their drunken landlord, Jim Tyrone, into her bed.

But this is only the shell of a scorching play about the eternal American theme of reality and illusion. It is in the third act, when the onion layers of pretence are finally peeled off, that we get to the play's core. Josie and Jim, we realise, are two "misbegotten" people who in the moonlight are forced to confront the truth. While Josie is a desolate virgin aching with love for Jim, he is hiding a profound sense of guilt under the guise of a heartless city slicker. And even if there is no hope of a permanent union, they achieve a moment of transcendent self-realisation.

This scene, which justifies the whole play, is breathtaking. Eve Best makes no pretence at being the ungainly, 180lb figure O'Neill describes in his stage directions. Instead, her Josie is a hard-working rustic slave who has grown used to hiding her feelings and who deflects every compliment with a shy, nervous laugh. It is a beautiful performance, about the pain of living a constant lie, perfectly matched by Spacey's Jim. Above all, Spacey reminds you that Tyrone is a one-time actor who masks his self-loathing under the carapace of the constant drinker. Spacey grasps each glass of bourbon like a drowning man and even flinches when offered water. But the brilliance of his performance is its suggestion that even this is a public act designed to hide the remorse he feels over his shameful behaviour when accompanying his mother's funeral coffin. Watching Best and Spacey together is like seeing two desperate people stripping their souls naked. Bob Crowley's ramshackle rural set and Colm Meaney's self-deceptive Hogan lend weight to a production that offers that rarest of theatrical treats: an evening of raw, powerful emotion.

Krapp's Last Tape by Samuel Beckett
Royal Court Theatre Upstairs,
London: 16 Oct 2006

It is easier to get a cup final ticket than one for Harold Pinter's performance. But, although the event has stimulated its own extra-theatrical curiosity, the fact is that Pinter not only gets through it well but also offers the harshest, least sentimental reading of Beckett's play I can recall.

Beckett's abiding image is of a 69-year-old man hunched over a tape recorder listening to his recollections of 30 years ago. But, where Beckett's text offers lots of scuttling around and by-play with bananas, Pinter sits behind a desk in a motorised wheelchair. The dominant impression is of total entrapment. And the sense of Krapp as a marooned soul is intensified by the crepuscular gloom of Paule Constable's lighting and the gaunt vacancy of Hildegard Bechtler's set, in which only a dusty, manuscript-filled cupboard is easily visible.

This, in Ian Rickson's meticulous production, is a play that offers scant consolation. It begins with Pinter staring out front in prolonged silence. Having found the one tape he wants, he sweeps the rest to the floor in angry exasperation. And, even when he listens to his memories of a night on a lake with a young woman, there is little sense of lost happiness. I have seen other Krapps who have cradled or clutched the tape recorder at this point: the most Pinter offers is a sardonic cackle.

This not only plays to Pinter's strengths. It also seems true to Beckett's text: the ageing Krapp recalls his younger self as "drowned in dreams and burning to be gone." But the bitter irony, which Pinter skilfully heightens, is that Krapp is now terrified of the extinction he once craved. At two precise moments, Pinter looks anxiously over his left shoulder into the darkness as if he felt death's presence in the room. This is the moment that will linger longest in the memory. It is impossible to dissociate Pinter's own recent encounters with mortality from that of the character. But this is a performance, not an exercise in self-revelation. And what is striking is the accommodating nature of Beckett's text. One of the most famous of all Krapps, the German actor Martin Held, implied the character's earlier vitality. Pinter, however, brings out the black nihilism of a Krapp for whom the planet is simply "this old muckball." And the final irony of an unsparingly honest performance is that, even when Krapp talks of "the fire in me now," it is followed by a long, agonised silence as a death-bell distantly tolls.

2007

The Seagull by Anton Chekhov
Royal Court, London: 26 January 2007

Ian Rickson ends his tenure at the Royal Court with a familiar masterpiece. But, while some might think it a conservative choice, it is an unusually apt one since Chekhov's play deals obsessively with new writing. And, after the recent travesty at the National, it is heartening to find a richly textured production that respect its author's intentions.

Christopher Hampton's new version is also sharp, fresh and comic. Masha ruefully tells Trigorin "once I'm married there'll be no time left for love" and, after Madam Arkadina has rescued her writer-lover from Nina's clutches, she boldly announces to his face "Got him!" But, if one timely theme leaps out of Hampton's version, it is the hollowness of celebrity. As the actress Nina tells Konstantin in the final act "in our work what's important isn't fame or glamour, it's the ability to endure." The irony is that this is one gift Konstantin doesn't possess.

Significantly, one of the delights of Rickson's production is that it is not necessarily the most famous names that come off best. Katherine Parkinson's brilliant Masha signals her hopeless passion for Konstantin from the start. Pearce Quigley's bumbling, awkward schoolteacher reveals his own role in this daisy-chain of unrequited love by ardently tracing Masha's every move. And both Peter Wight as the unfulfilled Sorin and Paul Jesson as his stage-struck estate manager have the emotional and physical weight one associates with the Moscow Art Theatre in its heyday.

This is not to diminish the key players. Kristin Scott-Thomas is a very good Arkadina: less the familiar egotistic monster than a woman who theatricalises every emotion so that when she hails the defecting Trigorin as "my wonderful, magnificent man" she ensures the whole estate can hear. Mackenzie Crook's lean, hungry Konstantin also captures the character's vital change from aspiring mould-breaker to self-acknowledged literary failure.

Admittedly Carey Mulligan doesn't fully convey Nina's ravening ambition and, although Chiwetel Ejiofor is a perfectly decent Trigorin, he seems almost too charismatic and assured. But this is a fine production that brings out Chekhov's obsession with misdirected passion and the vanity of fame and ensures Rickson leaves the Court on a high note.

Black Watch by Gregory Burke (Revival)
Harlaw Academy, Aberdeen: 4 April, 2007

After winning every award going at last year's Edinburgh Fringe festival, Gregory Burke's play is now on the road, where it faces a far stiffer test. But it was moving to see a Monday night audience in an Aberdeen school gym rise to John Tiffany's National Theatre of Scotland production as if they were honouring a piece of their own history.

Burke's play is not instantly easy to absorb. Many of the words fly up into the school roof. The accents, to my English ears, are sometimes impenetrable. And, in a play based on interviews with Black Watch squaddies recently returned from two tours of duty in Iraq, Burke's own position is somewhat equivocal. He vividly records the disillusion of soldiers left "pissing about in the desert" in a foreign policy disaster. He also charts the sense of political betrayal felt by a regiment on the verge of amalgamation. But Burke's ambivalent admiration for male camaraderie and the "golden thread" of military history leaves certain questions unexamined, in particular the Black Watch's own record as an instrument of colonial oppression.

Whatever the gaps in the writing, Tiffany's production is an exhilarating blend of words, music, movement and mime in the great populist tradition of Joan Littlewood and John McGrath. Tiffany stages the writer's poolroom interviews with the squaddies brilliantly, suggesting a growing gulf between the two parties, as if the dramatist himself were somehow on trial. He also, in one remarkable scene, captures exactly the Scottish soldiers' mixture of professional awe and moral revulsion as they watch a massive American aerial bombardment in Iraq. And the physical movement by Frantic Assembly's Steve Hoggett is both pointed and precise: at the end, as the soldiers parade to the sound of bagpipes and drums, we gradually see the formations disintegrate as if we are witnessing not just the demise of a regiment, but of a whole way of life.

Though it's an ensemble piece, two performances stand out. Brian Ferguson catches perfectly the growing despair of a young soldier who, after seeing his colleagues killed by suicide bombers, questions what he and the regiment are doing in Iraq. And Peter Forbes is equally good as the Black Watch officer who has to express to his men a conviction in the validity of their mission which he patently does not believe. The climactic encounter between these two is the high point of a show that has, justly, become a landmark in modern Scottish theatre.

King Lear by William Shakespeare
Courtyard Theatre, Stratford-upon-Avon:
1 June 2007

It is no exaggeration to say this *King Lear* is long-awaited. Critics, in fact, have waited impatiently for nine weeks to glimpse a production that has been playing to a paying public. But, however absurd the delay, I can report that Ian McKellen is a majestic, moving Lear and that Trevor Nunn's production, while nothing like as radical as Brook's or Hytner's, is largely satisfying.

It begins thrillingly. We are in a late-nineteenth-century world evoked by Christopher Oram's design of a curving, elliptical, heavy-curtained theatrical balcony. To a thunderous peal of organ music, McKellen's gold-robed Lear enters between lines of courtiers to bestow honours upon his beloved Cordelia. All this, in its reminiscence of *Ivan the Terrible*, is pure Eisenstein; what it tells us, before a word is spoken, is that Lear occupies a kingdom steeped in elaborate, meaningless ritual.

The idea is continued wittily in the first scene. The division of the realm is clearly a staged event, in which McKellen reads a prepared speech announcing he will "unburdened crawl towards death" with a wry chuckle: obviously, he intends the exact opposite. Goneril and Regan also deliver their pronouncements of love from a lectern. But it is Cordelia who cuts through the pageantry with a refusal to play the game that unwittingly provokes the entire tragedy.

What follows is a stripping away, in every sense, of public ceremony to reach the square root of humanity. In McKellen's case, I was reminded of his early triumph as Richard II. That was a young king encased in ritual who had to learn about human suffering; his Lear is an old king who has to undergo a similar moral journey in which he acquires sanity via madness. And what makes McKellen so moving is his awareness of the path he has to undertake. His simple statement of "I did her wrong" pricks one's tears because of Lear's premonition of the pain that is his due.

Some may be shocked that McKellen's remorseless journey to the centre of his self leads him, at one point, to strip to the buff. But the gesture seems entirely logical. McKellen has just been staring at an almost naked Poor Tom as if he were a scientific specimen before declaring: "Unaccommodated man is no more but such a poor, bare forked animal as thou art." This is Lear's moment of revelation in which he sees the truth as to what lies behind the carapace of costume. And, by his own disrobing, Lear acknowledges he is a member of the human race. Only those with dirty minds will be dismayed by McKellen's nudity.

What is most striking about his Lear, in its pilgrim's progress, is its curiosity. McKellen's Lear is a man always asking questions. The big conundrum, which he delivers with racking slowness, is: "Is there any cause in nature that makes these hard hearts?" It is his uncertainty as to the answer that touches one's own heart. Even to the last, McKellen is a probing, questioning figure staring quizzically at Kent and asking: "Who are you?" By the end, you feel this is a Lear who has somehow undergone a rigorous moral education.

If I miss anything in Nunn's well-ordered production, it is the dizzying, vertiginous senselessness that pervaded Hytner's 1990 version with John Wood. The Courtyard, for all its supposed intimacy, also thrusts much of the action upstage so that the actors often seem distant even from the front stalls. But Frances Barber, whose knee accident prompted the first night's postponement, gives us a good, uncomplicated Goneril who is easily the harshest of the three sisters: one notices how she prevents Monica Dolan's Regan from expressing her fellowship with the distressed Lear. Romola Garai also allows us to glimpse Cordelia's spontaneous virtue.

I felt neutral about Sylvester McCoy's Fool: a spoon-playing old joker in a tasselled toque who missed some of the character's piercing veracity. And Philip Winchester's Edmund could have used a bit more villainous buoyancy. But there is solid support from William Gaunt's Gloucester, Jonathan Hyde's Kent and Julian Harries' Albany, who all demonstrate that goodness can exist, even in an anarchic world. And, if any theme emerges from Nunn's production, it is not just the vanity of ceremony but the need for human endurance. But it is for McKellen, and his triumphant progress towards a kind of enlightenment, that I shall really remember the occasion.

Macbeth by William Shakespeare
Minerva Studio, Chichester: 4 June 2007

Rupert Goold is the intemperately exciting young director who gave us a sensational *Tempest* last year at Stratford. Now, reunited with Patrick Stewart, he has come up with an equally astonishing *Macbeth*: one that is fiercely conceptual, in its evocations of both Soviet tyranny and gothic horror but one that is also spoken with crystalline clarity and that keeps the spectators on the edges of their seats.

Anthony Ward's white-walled, underground setting suggests a mixture of abattoir, kitchen and military hospital. Its prime feature is an iron-gated lift in which characters either descend to, or flee from, the Macbeths' subterranean hell. As Macbeth achieves power through a military coup, we see projections of massed troops marching through what looks like Red Square. Meanwhile, Banquo's murder is accomplished by sinister figures on a night train to nowhere, evoked by a few chairs and Adam Cork's eerie sound design. Other directors, such as Max Stafford-Clark and Greg Doran, have highlighted the militaristic nature of Macbeth's regime. Goold pushes it further by suggesting that Macbeth emerges from a dictatorship in which Duncan is accompanied by goose-stepping troops.

Patrick Stewart, without minimising Macbeth's evil, excellently highlights the paranoia that accompanies power. He eyes Banquo nervously from the start. Even when dressing for dinner with his wife, he seems haunted by fear. And Stewart never lets us forget that Macbeth, uniquely among Shakespeare's villains, is morbidly aware of what he has sacrificed: like Olivier, Stewart allows his voice to soar when describing the "troops of friends" he knows he will never enjoy.

The potential danger of Goold's approach is that it reinforces Malcolm's description of the Macbeths as "this dead butcher and his fiend-like queen." But Goold shows that tyranny, however insecure, is still based on slaughter. The idea is brilliantly underlined when Kate Fleetwood's terrifying Lady Macbeth seeks to cleanse her hands under a kitchen tap that runs blood-red water. Goold takes other justifiable liberties, so that Michael Feast's Macduff turns up at the Macbeths' house-party with his family only to bundle them away after the murder. And the England scene is wittily staged, with Scott Handy's Malcolm discovered attending a musical soiree that contrasts strongly with the Macbeths' own brutal banquet barn dance. But that is typical of a production which, by its imaginative inventiveness, makes you experience the play anew.

The Crisis in West End Theatre.

2 August 2007

We have cried wolf once too often. Over the years, whenever a handful of commercial theatres has been closed, newspapers have prophesied gloom and doom. This, we are told, is the end of West End civilisation as we know it. But today the crisis is real. Never in my lifetime has London's West End theatre looked so narrow in its range of choices or so out of touch with contemporary reality. And it is high time the crisis was confronted and a debate launched about what we expect of commercial theatre.

"What crisis?" some may ask. The Society of London Theatre last year announced record attendances of more than 12 million visitors. They also pointed to the West End's contribution to the wider economy: the commercial theatre regularly generates more than £200m in tax and produces an estimated £400m of ancillary spending on restaurants, bars and transport. Stroll around the West End any evening and the place seems to be seething with visitors, many of them heading towards a theatre. But numbers alone cannot disguise the truth: that the West End lacks any dynamic creative initiative and is living on borrowed time, in that many of its buildings are barely fit for purpose.

Look, for a start, at what is actually on offer. At this moment, there are 26 musicals in the West End but only seven straight plays and three comedies. "The drama's laws, the drama's patrons give," said Dr Johnson, and it would be absurd to deny the public hunger for tune-and-toe shows that offer fantasy and escape. Economic factors also shape public taste: if people are paying up to £50 for a West End stall, at least with a musical they feel they are getting visible value for money in terms of sets, costumes and number of people on stage. I have nothing against musicals. Doubts only begin to arise when you examine the provenance of the shows currently playing.

Of the 26 musicals now showing, 12 derive either from films or TV programmes or are compilation shows drawn from back catalogues. That leaves 14 shows that might loosely be described as "original," even if many of them are adapted from novels. And of those 14, only four hail from the current decade: *Wicked* (closely based on *The Wizard of Oz*), *The Drowsy Chaperone* (due to close after mysteriously ecstatic notices), *Avenue* Q (a lightweight American import) and *The Lord of the Rings*. In defiance of my critical colleagues, I happened to like the last. But the melancholy truth is that the musical as a living creative force seems to be in decline. In Britain we have seen no popular, native commercial composer emerge since Andrew Lloyd Webber in the early 1970s: even A.R. Rahman, chiefly responsible for *Bombay Dreams* and *The Lord of the Rings*, has been dubbed by *Time* magazine the "Mozart of Madras." A genre that in Britain once produced estimable figures such as Ivor Novello, Lionel Bart, Sandy Wilson, Julian Slade and David Heneker is now heavily dependent on a single composer who, at the age of 59, cannot be expected to last for ever.

Also, I wouldn't say the list of musicals opening late this year or early next sound like models of innovation: *Desperately Seeking Susan*, enhanced by the greatest hits of Blondie, is yet another movie-based musical, while *Jersey Boys* tells the story of Frankie Valli and the Four Seasons. And does the pulse race any faster at the prospect of a second musical version of *Gone With The Wind*?

But, if the West End musical relies parasitically on American imports, the straight play as a commercial proposition seems to be in an even more parlous state. When I started as a critic in 1971, I lamented the fact that virtually all the best plays in the West End stemmed from the subsidised sector: they included John Osborne's *West of Suez*, Peter Nichols' *Forget-Me-Not-Lane*, Alan Ayckbourn's *How the Other Half Loves* and Christopher Hampton's *The Philanthropist*.

From today's vantage point, however, that seems to have been a time of enviable riches. Of the seven straight plays in the West End today, five are thrillers ranging from *The Mousetrap* to *The Last Confession*. The other two are *Elling*, adapted from a cult Norwegian movie, and David Storey's

In Celebration, which is a revival of a fine 1969 Royal Court play. But, however good these two are, their commercial viability clearly rests on the presence, respectively, of John Simm and Orlando Bloom. What we have in London is a clear and potentially damaging trend. The audience for plays basically goes to subsidised theatres. They will only pay West End prices if offered a bona fide star. The most one can say is that there is still a market for comedy as shown by the success of *Boeing Boeing*, *The 39 Steps* and The Reduced Shakespeare Company.

At the risk of sounding like a critical Thersites, I would add that the fabric of the bricks and mortar also raises cause for alarm. Cameron Mackintosh is the prime example of a West End theatre-owner who has taken serious steps to improve his properties and plough his profits back into the buildings. Under his stewardship, the Prince of Wales and the Prince Edward have been magnificently restored, and the Novello has acquired something of its pristine splendour. The Theatre Royal Haymarket is also a delight to enter. But too many West End theatres are crumbling, decaying edifices. In 2003, the Theatres Trust produced a report confirming that 60 per cent of West End theatres had seats from which the stage was not fully visible, and that 48 per cent had inadequate foyers and bars. They estimated that at least £250m would have to be spent over the next 15 years to make the theatres safe, usable and attractive. But where is the money to come from? There is a clear case for rewriting Lottery rules to enable public funds to be spent on modernising our theatres. Otherwise, visitors to London for the 2012 Olympics will be confronted by a bizarre mixture of spanking new sports stadia and theatrical slums.

But what can be done to improve the West End artistically as well as structurally? The most urgent need is for dynamic young producers to succeed the senior generation of Michael Codron, Robert Fox, Bill Kenwright and Thelma Holt. Only two have made their mark in recent years: the admirable Sonia Friedman and Matthew Byam Shaw. The latter was the beneficiary of a bursary called Stage One, in which money from the Theatre Investment Fund is used to kick-start individual careers. I sit on its selection panel, and twice a year we meet to interview a dozen young hopefuls. It is an intriguing process and a valuable scheme. But what strikes me, and some of the other panellists, is the relative scarcity of applicants who think in broad commercial terms: reared in the ethos of Fringe theatre, they largely come armed with small-scale projects.

My belief is that the really imaginative producers of today are to be found not in the commercial sector but among the directors of subsidised theatres. People like Nicholas Hytner at the National, Michael Grandage at the Donmar, Dominic Cooke at the Royal Court, Vicky Featherstone at the National Theatre of Scotland, Jonathan Church at Chichester and Gemma Bodinetz and Deborah Aydon at Liverpool are the real Diaghilevs of modern British theatre. They may be partially protected by subsidy but they still have to think in terms of filling theatres and of devising a dozen or more productions a year that will combine quality with audience appeal. Without wishing to denude the non-profit sector of its talent, it seems vital that the commercial theatre benefits from the wisdom and shared experience of people with a proven track record.

To some extent, it happens already with subsidised transfers. Rupert Goold's *Macbeth* and the Jonathan Church-Philip Franks *Nicholas Nickleby* are scheduled to move from Chichester into the Gielgud Theatre this autumn. Mackintosh's theatres also have a tie-in with the RSC. And it would be madness if Peter Hall's revelatory production of *Pygmalion* at Bath, which captures both the pain and the ecstasy of Shaw's original play, did not move into the West End.

Jonathan Kent's impending season at the Haymarket is clearly an attempt to capitalise on his experience at the Almeida. And, although I've urged it before, I repeat that this should be a working model for the future. Why not give Richard Eyre or Stephen Daldry the freedom to create a West End company? Or why not turn over a West End venue to Emma Rice's Kneehigh troupe for a year in order to woo the audience for visual theatre?

What the West End needs is a radical makeover, even a minor revolution, in the interests of both quality and variety. I'd like to see Sunday openings, Lottery money for the rotting fabric, more imaginative use of the buildings themselves: in particular, pre-show talks, jazz and poetry recitals, stand-up comics in the dead hours before the 7.30 pm opening. If the commercial theatre can't beat the subsidised sector, it should, in effect, join it: not only by adopting its practices but by employing its personnel. In the old days, the West End theatre relied on actor-managers to give it body and substance. Now what it needs are director-managers, or even dramatist-impresarios, of proven vision. Otherwise it is destined to become little more than a gaudy musical fairground based on sinking land and of scant relevance to the art of theatre or to life.

This was one of my periodic jeremiads about the state of West End theatre. But my fears about the fabric of the buildings themselves was not unjustified. In 2013 part of the ceiling of the Apollo Theatre collapsed during a performance of The Curious Incident Of The Dog In The Night-Time *leaving 58 people hospitalised. A less serious event occurred at the Piccadilly Theatre in 2019 during* Death of a Salesman *when four people were taken to hospital because of collapsing plasterboard. Enlightened theatre owners are aware of the problem. Cameron Mackintosh has invested £200 million in his eight West End theatres and Andrew Lloyd Webber £100 million in his six properties. But, aside from the buildings themselves, the question remains as to whether the West End is a genuinely creative force or a shop-window for transfers from the subsidised sector and Broadway.*

Noughts and Crosses. Adapted by Dominic Cooke from the novel by Malorie Blackman (World Premiere) Civic Hall, Stratford-upon-Avon: 7 December 2007

I haven't read the Malorie Blackman novel which Dominic Cooke has adapted and directed for the RSC; and, for once, I was grateful for my innocence. I found myself caught up in the narrative twists of this absorbing political allegory which posits a society in which a White underclass, the Noughts, is pitted against a ruling Black majority, the Crosses.

The role-reversal, especially in the first half, pays off handsomely. We watch the growing friendship, across the race and class divide, between 16-year-old Callum and 14-year-old Sephy, whose father happens to be deputy prime minister. And, as the relationship matures, each pays a heavy price. Sephy is tormented by her schoolmates for consorting with the "Blankers," as they are damningly known, "who smell funny and eat weird food." Callum discovers that his father and brother are part of a liberation militia whose aim is to commit terrorist acts on the opposing "Daggers."

All this is worked out with considerable skill and enlivening detail. The script also brings out the contradictions inherent in this kind of two-tier society: Callum's father is both delighted that his son has been accepted as a token Nought at a school for high-achieving Crosses and, at the same time, endorses the overthrow of the system. And the story has all kinds of resonances: one thinks of apartheid South Africa, sectarian Northern Ireland and, when a supermarket bomb kills innocent victims, of events in our own backyard.

The tension slackened only when the story got closer to the obvious source of *Romeo and Juliet*: there is a moment here when Callum and Sephy's planned escape is aborted by a stroke of bad luck, exactly as in Shakespeare's tragedy. The play also depends too much on the idea of a unified Black community: a myth lately subverted by dramatists such as Roy Williams and Kwame Kwei-Armah.

But my qualms were stilled by the visceral excitement of Cooke's production. Christopher Shutt's sound score is also full of ominously reverberant echoes which prepare us for the big explosion. And the acting is uniformly impressive. Richard Madden as Callum and Ony Uhiara as Sephy express the poignancy of doomed love. Tyrone Huggins as a pair of ruling-class authority figures, Jo Martin as Sephy's mother and Michelle Butterly as Callum's mum also display real emotional weight. Clearly, the play doesn't offer a realistic picture of modern Britain but still expresses disturbing truths about a society in which worth and status are determined by racial origins.

2008

Tribute to actor Paul Scofield: born 21 January 1922, died 19 March 2008.

21 March, 2008

"Acting," David Hare once said to me, "is a judgment of character." That was amply borne out by Paul Scofield, who has just died at the age of 86. Scofield had a moral integrity and quiet authority that shone through everything he did. Even his choice of roles was exemplary: many actors trade fame for money, but I can't think of a single meretricious piece of work Scofield ever did.

A few years back I had the pleasure of presenting Scofield with a lifetime achievement award on behalf of the Critics' Circle; and I remember saying at the time that I felt I'd measured out my life in Scofield performances. As an eight-year-old, I'd been taken on my first visit to Stratford to see him play Shakespeare's Troilus. As a 20-year-old student, I'd seen the first performance, at the Oxford New, of *A Man For All Seasons*; I recall his modesty when pushed into taking a solo curtain-call by his fellow actors. And, while working in a regional rep, I'd made the pilgrimage to London to see his famous Lear. It was astonishing to think Scofield was only 40 when he took the role, revealing a man in whom flinty autocracy gave way to tragic vulnerability.

Everything Scofield did was touched by distinction. But, although he conquered the peaks of Hamlet, Lear and Othello, he also illuminated modern plays. He was extraordinary as a camp, silvery hairdresser in Charles Dyer's *Staircase*. As the self-hating writer-hero of John Osborne's *The Hotel in Amsterdam* he exuded a waspish melancholy. And he was the original Salieri in Peter Shaffer's *Amadeus* at the National: a flickering romantic presence savouring the acclaim of the court while being corroded by envy of Mozart's genius.

I never saw Scofield give a flashy, showy, unfelt performance; and his mixture of gravity and mischief transferred easily from stage to screen, as shown in his Oscar-winning performance as Sir Thomas More. In his rigorous focus on the work in hand, his determination to protect his privacy and his mixture of classic and contemporary work, he was a reminder of an all but vanished age when actors preserved their sense of mystery. If Scofield revealed himself, it was through his work; and what we saw was a figure of rich humanity, wide-ranging compassion and unflinching integrity.

Gone With The Wind. Book, Music and Lyrics by Margaret Martin (World Premiere) New London Theatre, London: 23 April 2008

Does no one ever learn from the past? An earlier musical of Margaret Mitchell's mammoth novel, having been seen in Tokyo and London, eventually burned out in Atlanta. Undeterred, theatrical tyro Margaret Martin has written book, music and lyrics for this new version which Trevor Nunn directs; and the result feels like a hectic, strip-cartoon account of a dated pop classic.

The problem is structural: how do you cram a 1,000-page novel into three-and-a-half hours of stage time? The answer is "with great difficulty." Starting in 1861, the show bustles through 12 years of Scarlett O'Hara's life and American Civil War history with such speed that nothing much registers. At one point, in order to spite her adored Ashley Wilkes, Scarlett marries, is widowed and gives birth to her first child in the space of 40 seconds.

The other key problem is political. Commendably the show seeks to avoid turning into a nostalgic paean, as the Selznick movie does, to old southern values. Far and away the best moment comes when Mammy, Prissy and all the Black slaves who have kept plantation life going join forces to sing "all men fight for freedom from the moment of their birth."

This, you realise, is where the real drama lies. Confronted by a movement of history, the story of the wilful Scarlett, of her eventual marriage to the profiteering Rhett Butler and of her long-burning flame for the dithering Ashley seems small beer. Deep down, I suspect, the show's creator knows this. But she is shackled by the dead conventions of a novel which deploys history as a colourful backdrop to private emotion. What I crave is less a repeat of *Gone With The Wind* than a complete reversal of it: one that tells the whole story from the slaves' viewpoint and stresses the fact that large numbers ran away to join the Union armies.

Nunn's production makes tentative steps in this direction by, as in *Nicholas Nickleby*, splitting the narrative amongst various voices, including the Black characters. But, like Martin, he is tethered to his source and forced to follow the tedious ups and downs of the privileged White southerners. To those who see Scarlett as a feminist role model, I can only say that heartless opportunism and emotional blindness don't strike me as the most attractive qualities; but Jill Paice does an excellent job of reconciling us to one of literature's least beguiling protagonists.

Darius Danesh also endows the morally dubious Rhett Butler with a graceful virility and residual guilt. But the most engaging performances come from Natasha Yvette Williams as the stoically enduring Mammy and from Jina Burrows as the flighty Prissy, both obliged to serve the self-regarding Scarlett. The rest of the vast cast spend much of the evening hurtling round the balconies of John Napier's circumambient, Nickleby-style set, substituting energy for detailed exploration of character. But there is something extravagantly pointless about the whole enterprise. Why revive a novel that, for all the liberal exertions of Martin and Nunn, obstinately views history through the wrong end of a telescope?

The English Game by Richard Bean
(World Premiere)
Yvonne Arnaud, Guildford: 14 May 2008

Many writers, from Neville Cardus to C.L.R. James, have seen cricket as a national metaphor. Richard Bean is the first dramatist to construct a state-of-England play out of a cricket match. And, even if its omission of women obviously limits its application, Bean's play is both wildly entertaining and strangely moving in the manner of David Storey's *The Contractor*.

The setting is the edge of a London park where The Nightwatchmen have come to play their weekly game of recreational cricket. Like most such teams, they are made up of odd bods united only by their sporting obsession. Their nominal captain, Will, is an old crock, whose air of benign liberalism turns out to be misleading. The match skipper, meanwhile, is a mixed-up journo with a disintegrating marriage. And the motley team includes a joke-spinning rock legend, a gay Hindu, an Oxbridge actor, a doctor, a plumber and a British Council desk-wallah who happens to be Black. The one newcomer is a mouthy Telecoms worker who idolises Enoch Powell.

Far from being a rigged assembly, this is a fair representation of weekend cricket teams. And what Bean brings out beautifully is the way cricket, while briefly unifying a disparate group, can no longer disguise the fractious nature of modern England. We get caught up in the off-stage game, willing The Nightwatchmen to win. Yet Bean suggests that any pretence of national cohesiveness is breaking down along with the spirit of cricket itself. The key fissure occurs between Will, a media pundit with strenuous views on Islam, and Theo, the doctor and lay preacher, who embodies a rapidly vanishing native tolerance. England, implies Bean, is a country riven by an attitudinal divide that not even cricket can heal.

You do not have to be a cricket nut – as I am – to relish the play. And Sean Holmes, in this touring Headlong production, captures exactly the rhythms of an English summer day, in which a patch of green is filled with hectic activity and then quietly empties. As in cricket, a team effort also allows individuals to shine (which may be why the game is so adored by actors): Robert East as the deceptive Will, Howard Ward as the good doctor, Fred Ridgeway as the bumptious intruder and Tony Bell as the unhappy hack score all round the wicket. There have been good plays about cricket before, such as Richard Harris's *Outside Edge* and Alan Ayckbourn's *Time and Time Again*, but none that told us so much about our splintering land.

The Pitmen Painters by Lee Hall
(World Premiere)
Cottesloe, National Theatre, London:
22 May 2008

Lee Hall's remarkable play, imported from Live Theatre Newcastle, hits a number of targets dead centre. At its most basic, it offers a funny, richly informative account of the growth of a group of Ashington miners into formidable painters in the years from 1934 to 1947. But Hall also provides a fascinating debate about art and socialism of a kind we haven't heard in the British theatre since Wesker's *Roots* half a century ago.

Inspired by a book by William Feaver, Hall starts from the known facts. He shows a band of pitmen coming together for an Art Appreciation Class. Their tutor, Robert Lyon, realises there is little point in showing slides of the High Renaissance to men who have barely set foot inside a gallery. So he sets them to work: first on linocuts, and then on paintings reflecting their communal culture. This leads not only to fierce critical arguments, it produces a body of work that attracts the attention first of a local shipping heiress, then of regional galleries, and eventually the art establishment.

Hall tells his story with wit and imagination. He shows that under the collective endeavour there is a group of querulous individuals ranging from a Marxist hardliner to a pettifogging WEA official. Hall also punctures easy sentiment. When Lyon suggests we are all artists, one of the group puts the case for specialist gifts, saying: "You wouldn't want just anybody filling your teeth in." While resurrecting a half-forgotten movement, Hall also widens the debate. It is no accident the play ends on the eve of nationalisation.

And Hall's larger point is that art by itself cannot change the world: this has to come from political initiatives which will produce a fairer society.

Breathtaking in its scope, the play is sometimes harsh on the few non working-class characters: Lyon himself, who moved on to become an Edinburgh professor, is seen as a careerist using the Ashington achievement to advance his academic status. But this is a minor flaw in a generous-spirited play which, like *Billy Elliot*, argues that artistic skill is not the exclusive prerogative of the privileged.

Max Roberts's fine production contains a whole set of sharply individualised performances: Christopher Connel as a shining talent who resists the lure of private patronage, Deka Walmsley as the uptight local official, Michael Hodgson as the devout Marxist, and Ian Kelly as the inspirational but ultimately defecting Lyon are exemplary. But the final achievement is that of Hall, who has produced a play that is both a riveting social document and an invigorating political war-cry.

Her Naked Skin by Rebecca Lenkiewicz (World Premiere) Olivier, National Theatre, London: 2 August 2008

It is shocking to think that Rebecca Lenkiewicz's play is the first full-length work by a woman to be seen on the Olivier stage. But Lenkiewicz makes up for lost time by exploring the hunger for political and personal emancipation that fuelled the suffragette movement in 1913; and, though one can niggle about this and that, her play colonises this daunting space with bravura confidence.

Lenkiewicz's method is to start with a wide-angled shot and then gradually focus on intimate relationships. Film footage of Emily Davison's sacrificial gesture at the 1913 Derby is followed by a sketch of male political intransigence over female suffrage. But Lenkiewicz's real concern is to show how female militancy transcended class and sexual convention. Lady Celia Cain, trapped in a loveless marriage, is erotically drawn to Eve, a young suffragette machinist. Passion and politics coalesce as they pursue an intense affair, but the question Lenkiewicz obliquely raises is whether liberation is more easily achieved from a position of social privilege.

It is a question I wish she had articulated more clearly: she is so keen to celebrate Lady Celia's escape from her own Ibsenite doll's house that she downplays the extent to which she simultaneously exploits her working-class lover. But Lenkiewicz's power lies in her ability to recapture the triumphs and tribulations of a historic movement. She shows in graphic detail the daily humiliations the suffragettes endured in Holloway prison. And, in one of the most horrifying scenes on the London stage, she shows how the mutinous Eve is forcibly fed with the aid of a rubber tube attached to her nostrils. But, while one's gorge rises, the play's overall gesture is one of tribute to the tenacity of these tough campaigners.

The play is also excitingly staged. Rob Howell has created a magnificent design in which a series of interlocking steel frames constantly reform to remind us of the entrapment experienced by Edwardian women. The set is matched by the propulsive urgency of Howard Davies's production, which moves easily between the intimate and the epic, and the acting is faultless. Lesley Manville brilliantly conveys the inherent contradictions of Lady Celia, whose vision of sexual and political freedom is compromised by her attachment to the benefits of her class. Jemima Rooper lends her lover the right surly sensuality, and, in the supporting performance of the year, Susan Engel sweeps all before her as a silver-haired militant buoyed up by a vision of the future. But that symbolises Lenkiewicz's play, which plants a defiant feminist flag on the Olivier stage.

Hamlet by William Shakespeare
Courtyard, Stratford-upon-Avon:
6 August 2008

It's a sign of our star-crazy culture that there has been months of speculation about David Tennant's Hamlet. The big news from Stratford is that Gregory Doran's production is one of the most richly textured, best-acted versions of the play we have seen in years. And Tennant, as anyone familiar with his earlier work with the RSC would expect, has no difficulty in making the transition from the BBC's Time Lord to a man who could be bounded in a nutshell and count himself a king of infinite space. He is a fine Hamlet whose virtues, and occasional vices, are inseparable from the production itself.

Doran's production gets off, literally, to a riveting start: the first thing we hear is the sound of hammering and drilling as Denmark's night-working Nibelungen prepare the country for war. And our first glimpse of the chandeliered, mirrored, modern-dress court gives us an instant clue to Hamlet's alienation. Patrick Stewart's superb Claudius insultingly addresses Laertes' problems before those of Hamlet. And, urging Hamlet not to return to university, Stewart has to be publicly reminded that Wittenberg is the place in question. Immediately we sense Claudius's hostile suspicion towards, and cold contempt for, his moody nephew.

Tennant's performance, in short, emerges from a detailed framework. And there is a tremendous shock in seeing how the lean, dark-suited figure of the opening scene dissolves into grief the second he is left alone:

instead of rattling off "O that this too too sullied flesh would melt," Tennant gives the impression that the words have to be wrung from his prostrate frame. Paradoxically, his Hamlet is quickened back to life only by the Ghost; and the overwhelming impression is of a man who, in putting on an "antic disposition," reveals his true, nervously excitable, mercurial self.

This is a Hamlet of quicksilver intelligence, mimetic vigour and wild humour: one of the funniest I've ever seen. He parodies everyone he talks to, from the prattling Polonius to the verbally ornate Osric. After the play scene, he careers around the court sporting a crown at a tipsy angle. Yet, under the mad capriciousness, Tennant implies a filial rage and impetuous danger: the first half ends with Tennant poised with a dagger over the praying Claudius, crying: "And now I'll do it." Newcomers to the play might well believe he will.

Tennant is an active, athletic, immensely engaging Hamlet. If there is any quality I miss, it is the character's philosophical nature, and here he is not helped by the production. Following the First Quarto, Doran places "To be or not to be" before rather than after the arrival of the players: perfectly logical, except that there is something magnificently wayward about the Folio sequence in which Hamlet, having decided to test Claudius's guilt, launches into an unexpected meditation on human existence. Unforgivably, Doran also cuts the lines where Hamlet says to Horatio, "Since no man knows of aught he leaves, what is't to leave betimes? Let be." Thus Tennant loses some of the most beautiful lines in all literature about acceptance of one's fate.

But this is an exciting performance that in no way overshadows those around it. Stewart's Claudius is a supremely composed, calculating killer: at the end of the play scene, instead of indulging in the usual hysterical panic, he simply strides over to Hamlet and pityingly shakes his head as if to say "you've blown it now." Oliver Ford Davies's brilliant Polonius is both a sycophantic politician and a comic pedant who feels the need to define and qualify every word he says: a quality he, oddly enough, shares with Hamlet. And I can scarcely remember a better Ophelia than that of Mariah Gale, whose mad-scenes carry a potent sense of danger, and whose skin is as badly scarred by the flowers she has gathered, as her divided mind is by emotional turmoil.

That is typical of a production that bursts with inventive detail. I love the idea that Edward Bennett's Laertes, having lectured Ophelia about her chastity, is shown to have a packet of condoms in his luggage. And the sense that this is a play about, among much else, ruptured families is confirmed when Stewart as the Ghost of Hamlet's father seeks, in the closet scene, tenderly to console Penny Downie's plausibly desolate Gertrude. Audiences may flock to this production to see the transmogrification of Dr Who into a wild and witty Hamlet. What they will discover is a rich realisation of the greatest of poetic tragedies.

Breaking the Rules. Leading Article on Harold Pinter: born 10 October 1930, died 24 December 2008.

27 December 2008

"I don't think Harold," Antonia Fraser once said, "would accept anything, except the laws of cricket, without question." And that remark by his second wife, and a distinguished historian in her own right, gets as close as anything to explaining Harold Pinter. Whether in art, politics or religion, Pinter was a born nay-sayer who examined all received truths with a rigorous scepticism. That quality that made him both a great dramatist and a combative polemicist; and in many ways it accounts for the glowing worldwide tributes that have greeted the news of his death. In an age of intellectual conformity such independent spirits as Pinter are rare.

In drama, Pinter detonated existing precepts. He emerged at a time, in the late 1950s, when the ground rules were already starting to change thanks to the pioneering work of Samuel Beckett. But it was Pinter, more than Beckett, who put postwar existential uncertainty into a domestic context. And it was Pinter who, from *The Room* and *The Birthday Party* onwards, demolished the idea of the omniscient author. What is the source of Rose's fear in the first play? Where is Stanley being taken at the end of the second? As Pinter constantly insisted, he knew no more than we did. He did not say this to tantalise or mystify. He was speaking the absolute truth. And part of his achievement was to empower the spectator and to give audiences an active and crucial role in determining a play's meaning.

Pinter's other lasting legacy was to redefine theatrical poetry. For Shakespeare and the Elizabethans, poetry was a natural form of dramatic expression. But, for all their many admirable qualities, Christopher Fry and T.S. Eliot had used verse-drama as an often ornate or encoded way of saying something that could more simply be said in prose. Pinter, through his attentive and sophisticated ear, grasped an essential point: that the non sequiturs and repetitions of everyday speech, if carefully orchestrated, contain their own vernacular poetry. Even the famous Pinter pause was not an arbitrary hiatus but a means of escalating tension.

Pinter was a radical innovator in theatre; but less attention has been paid to his pioneering work on screen. His hour-long 1963 TV play, *The Lover*, caused consternation in the home counties by its suggestion that many a suburban marriage was sustained by fetishistic role-playing. In the cinema, Pinter also explored the fluidity of time in new and often startling ways. In that respect, his most daring work was his script for *The Go-Between*, which jettisoned the strict chronology of L.P. Hartley's novel and eliminated hard-and-fast distinctions between past and present. It dismayed the front-office but it made for a great film.

Pinter's rule-breaking caused most controversy in the public affairs arena. Even his most fervent admirers found it difficult to endorse his support for the International Committee to Defend Slobodan Milosevic; but that was based on a sincere belief that NATO's aerial bombardment of Serbia was morally unjustified and gave Milosevic the excuse to escalate attacks on the Kosovan Albanians. More often than not, however, Pinter was ahead of the game. By the time of his Nobel lecture in 2005, a large swathe of British public opinion supported his contention that the invasion of Iraq was a bandit act "demonstrating absolute contempt for the concept of international law."

Pinter's role in art and politics was always to be a pathfinder; which is partly why his plays were nearly always better received in revival rather than on first appearance. But he was fortunate to live long enough to see his work enter the theatrical canon. And, although no one can second-guess posterity, it is a fair bet to say that his plays will endure as long as audiences savour linguistic precision and accept Pinter's basic premise: that nothing in life, except the laws of cricket, can be seen as fixed, absolute or certain.

Tribute to Harold Pinter.

27 December 2008

I first met Harold Pinter in the early 1970s, when I sat on a sunlit lawn at Shepperton studios interviewing him about Peter Hall's film of *The Homecoming*. That went well enough, and Harold even told me that the famous "Pinter pause" owed a lot to the American comedian Jack Benny, whom he had seen at the Palladium in the 1950s.

There was a distinct froideur after my review of his play *Betrayal* at the National Theatre in 1978. As I wince to recall, I wrote that Pinter "has betrayed his immense talent by serving up this kind of high-class soap opera." A few months later the play won the top prize at the Society of London Theatre awards. In his acceptance speech, Pinter unveiled his dentist's smile and said: "I must be the most surprised person in the room, with the possible exception of . . . (long pause) . . . Michael Billington." A thousand heads turned towards me as I slumped into my seat.

It took a while to get over that. I remember a ludicrous occasion when Pinter and I found ourselves standing in parallel entry queues one summer at JFK airport. As the lines gradually diminished, we ignored each other and maintained an immaculate, frosty silence. The thaw only set in when I interviewed him for a book I was writing on Peggy Ashcroft. He was not only helpful, he gave me a copy of his play, *One for the Road*, inscribing it: "You didn't like it much but what the hell?"

The real breakthrough came in 1990 when I presented a four-hour programme on BBC Radio 3 celebrating his 60th birthday and charting not just his theatrical career but his passion for poetry, politics and cricket. In 1992, out of the blue, came an invitation from Robert McCrum, chief executive at Faber, suggesting I meet with him and Harold to discuss my writing a short book on Pinter's politics. At some point over lunch Pinter turned to me and said: "Of course, you can talk to anyone you like about my life." I realised, to my astonishment, that I was being given the green light to write a full-scale biography.

That led to four years of research and writing that taught me a lot about Harold Pinter. But what exactly did I learn? Most obviously, that his plays were almost invariably triggered by some memory or incident from his past. I also learned that Pinter's politics were the product of a rage against any form of injustice, partly the result of his postwar Hackney youth, in which he and his friends were appalled by the licence given to anti-Semitic organisations. If any later episode fuelled that anger, it was the American government's proven involvement in the 1973 overthrow of President Salvador Allende. I realised that Pinter's politics were driven by a deep-seated moral disgust at the way Western states not only manipulated language but often undermined the concepts of "freedom" and "democracy" to which they claimed exclusive entitlement.

But Harold's anger was balanced by a rare appetite for life and an exceptional generosity to those he trusted. I saw that in myriad ways, large and small. He couldn't have been more generous in giving me access to his life, his manuscripts, even his study: at one point, we played Box and Cox as I worked there in the afternoons and he in the mornings. Sometimes his help was purely practical. A few years back, when I was required to have an endoscopy, I asked Pinter's advice as to whether I should have an anaesthetic, since the hospital implied that real men didn't. "Don't be so bloody silly," said Harold, "of course you do with that tube stuck down your throat."

Pinter was, even more than most of us, a man of contradictions: his fierce concern for language was balanced by an equally warm regard for individuals. His friend Michael Colgan, who runs the Dublin Gate Theatre, tells a great story of recently going out for drinks with Pinter in a posh Dublin hotel. As they placed their drinks order with an over-enthusiastic waitress, she cooed at them, "No problem, no problem." Pinter looked at her levelly and announced: "I wasn't anticipating one." A reminder that you don't waste words in Pinter's presence.

If that sounds harsh, I can only recount an amazing experience I had two months ago when I directed Pinter's *Party Time*, *Celebration* and a staged version of his Nobel lecture with drama students at LAMDA (the

London Academy of Music and Dramatic Art). Pinter had promised to come to the final performance and, on a cold autumn Saturday, he and his wife, Antonia, duly turned up. Not only that. As the cast gestured towards him at curtain-call, he struggled to his feet with great difficulty, shook them individually by the hand and made an impromptu speech expressing his admiration for their performance. It was something neither they, nor I, will ever forget.

Only later, when we had supper, did I realise just how desperately ill he was and what it had cost him, physically, to attend the performance. It was almost the last time I saw him and it reinforced something I had long known: that Pinter wasn't simply the finest dramatist of his generation, he was a man with a great heart.

2009

Be Near Me. Adapted by Ian McDiarmid from a novel by Andrew O'Hagan
Palace, Kilmarnock: 20 January 2009

"This," I was told, "is the most excitement Kilmarnock has seen since William Wallace marched through the town." My source was referring to the National Theatre of Scotland's premiere of Ian McDiarmid's version of Andrew O'Hagan's fine novel. It was certainly a big do, attended by local worthies and Scottish celebs. But what struck me was a strange synchronicity between the play and the place that can never quite be recaptured when the show moves to London's Donmar or goes on a UK tour.

The subject is the crisis that afflicts a Catholic priest when he takes over a small Ayrshire coastal parish. Father David Anderton, a posh, Oxford-educated Anglo-Scot, understandably feels alienated from the local, predominantly Protestant community. Lacking real friends, aside from his housekeeper, he turns for solace to two teenage tearaways, Mark and Lisa. It is his fondness for Mark, climaxing in a furtive kiss during a drunken carousal, that is Anderton's undoing.

This is a serious play for serious people. It raises any number of issues, from the violent prejudices of small communities to the sexual provocation offered by modern teenagers. It even, in a noisy dinner-party scene, explores the dangers of applying religious concepts of good and evil to foreign policy. However, though McDiarmid has been faithful to O'Hagan's book, he can't quite capture the thing that matters most: the idea that Anderton's actions are rooted in old memories and explicable only in terms of personal loss. Whereas the novel moves fluidly between past and present, the play takes place exclusively in the here and now.

In compensation, John Tiffany's production makes brilliantly manifest one of the book's background themes: the violent sectarian passions of Ayrshire life. Keeping the actors on stage throughout, Tiffany has them periodically burst into IRA and Orange anthems, thus lending Anderton's personal crisis a strong political dimension.

McDiarmid plays the damaged priest with exactly the right mix of feyness, folly and vulnerability. He makes you understand why the man would get up the noses of local bigots, yet allows you to sympathise with his enslavement to the past. It's a compassionate performance loyally supported by Blythe Duff as the tart-tongued housekeeper, Colette O'Neil as Anderton's mother, and Richard Madden and Helen Mallon as the reckless kids.

I only grasped the play's enduring relevance when I was whisked back to my hotel by a voluble cabbie. Complaining about the town's youth-driven social problems, he advocated a radically simple solution: "Bring back the birch." Clearly, the spirit of intolerance lives on even in lovely Kilmarnock.

Death and the King's Horseman by Wole Soyinka (Revival) Olivier, National Theatre, London: 9 April, 2009

Wole Soyinka is adamant that his great, neglected 1975 play cannot be reduced to a study of "the clash of cultures." I see what he means. This rich turbulent piece, which starts as folk comedy and ends as Greek tragedy, takes on board an abundance of ideas: identity, tradition, the passage from life to death. It says much for Rufus Norris's liberating production that these themes emerge with tumultuous force.

Although set in what is now Nigeria during the Second World War Soyinka's play is based on an incident that took place in the Yoruba town of Oyo in 1946. What we see is the king's horseman, Elesin, preparing to follow the ancient custom of committing ritual suicide after his master's death. But the event is the cause of celebration with the swaggering Elesin impregnating a young bride on the eve of his extinction. All this is anathema to the British district officer, Pilkings, who decides to intervene. Against the wishes of Elesin's eldest son, returned from studying medicine in London, Pilkings places the horseman under arrest with disastrous consequences.

In one sense, the play is a timely warning against the perils of "humanitarian intervention": in a key passage Olunde, the horseman's son, tells Pilkings' wife: "You have no respect for what you do not understand." But Soyinka's play is as much philosophical as political. Through the character of Olunde, it raises the dilemma of being caught in the crossfire between rival traditions. Even more disturbingly, Soyinka asks us to look beyond our rational distrust of ceremonial suicide.

This is tough stuff for a materialist British audience to take on board. But, in a stroke of radical daring, Norris makes it easier by presenting the play with an all-Black cast that "Whites" up to play the colonialists. This is a classic piece of Brechtian alienation that forces us to examine the issues at stake. It also yields moments of startling comedy. To see Lucian Msamati and Jenny Jules as the Pilkings posing as upper-class imperialists is initially as hilarious as watching a group of Yoruba women mimicking the British habit of crossing and uncrossing their legs.

Norris's production, with the aid of Katrina Lindsay's spectacular design, moves assuredly from the teeming world of a raffia-filled market to the play's elemental conclusion. There are sterling performances from Nonso Anonzie as the horseman, Kobna Holdbrook-Smith as his son and Claire Benedict as the market leader. One emerges dazzled but also disturbed by Soyinka's ideas: in particular, the unfashionable notion that death can be seen as a triumphant entrance rather than a tragic exit.

The Arts in the 1980s: reflections on a decade dominated by Margaret Thatcher.

11 April 2009

Was the 1980s an unacknowledged golden age? In theatrical terms, absolutely not. Talent, of course, can never be entirely suppressed. Opposition to the Thatcherite ethos eventually formed. And a handful of new initiatives prospered. But the theatrical narrative of the 1980s consisted of the triumph of the unthreatening, hi-tech popular musical over the quirky, questioning individual playwright. Subplots were provided by the shift in power from subsidy to commercial sponsorship and from the artist to the executive director. Even today, theatre, like so many features of public life including the BBC, is still suffering from the 1980s assault on fundamental principles.

Admittedly, the attack on inherited institutions – which, in theatrical terms, meant the triumvirate of the National, RSC and Royal Court – may have encouraged the emergence of rival groups. In 1981, Declan Donnellan and Nick Ormerod created Cheek by Jowl based on visual simplicity and eclectic internationalism: its repertoire embraced Racine, Corneille, Ostrovsky and Calderon. In 1983, a group of graduates of Jacques Lecoq's Parisian mime school joined forces to create Theatre de Complicite (now Complicite), which soon moved from anarchic comedy to reinterpretation of the classics. And in 1987 a charismatic actor-manager, Kenneth Branagh, along with David Parfitt, created the Renaissance Theatre Company to take Shakespeare to the people. All did vital work without radically changing the landscape. Cheek by Jowl and Complicite still survive, but are as much honoured abroad as at home, while Branagh now pursues a thriving individual career.

Alongside new companies, you can also point to a small number of plays that effectively challenged the prevailing values: Caryl Churchill's

Top Girls (1982) and *Serious Money* (1987); David Hare and Howard Brenton's *Pravda* (1985) and Hare's own *The Secret Rapture* (1988); Jim Cartwright's *Road* (1986). But, arguably, the most effective of all the guerrilla attacks on the dominant ethos was Alan Ayckbourn's *A Small Family Business* (1987), which speared the essential contradiction of Thatcherism: the collision between the elevation of traditional family values with the sanctification of individual greed.

But, despite random successes, it would be silly to get starry-eyed about the 1980s or take a revisionist historical line. The cultural tone was set by the arts minister Richard Luce, who declared that many in the arts world had "yet to be weaned away from the welfare-state mentality" and that "the only test of our ability to succeed is whether we can attract enough customers." The role model, much admired by Thatcher, was the commercial musical, which ticked all the right boxes. It was popular, profitable, capable of generating international franchises and, above all, conservative in outlook. "When," as playwright Nick Dear once asked, "did you hear a musical with surprising opinions?" And the shows that defined the decade were *Cats* (1981), *Starlight Express* (1984), *Les Miserables* (1985) and *The Phantom of the Opera* (1986).

To point out that the musical was Thatcherism in action is neither snobbish nor elitist. The shows mentioned have given many people a lot of harmless pleasure. But, artistically, they led the musical down a technically ingenious and increasingly expensive cul-de-sac. They also supplanted new plays and classic revivals at the centre of our theatrical culture. The long fight-back has begun but, even now, there is a prevailing media assumption that a hyped-up West End extravaganza such as *Priscilla, Queen of the Desert* is somehow more "important" than, say, a new Royal Court play by Polly Stenham; that in itself is a direct legacy of a decade in which "bums on seats" became a more significant criterion of judgement than "ideas in heads."

The Great Game: Afghanistan. A multi-authored work by 12 different writers (World Premiere) Tricycle, London: 25 April 2009

If there were any doubt about the Tricycle's status as Britain's foremost political theatre, it is silenced by this mind-blowing achievement. Nicolas Kent and his team have commissioned 12 half-hour plays which make up *The Great Game* and which cover Afghan history from 1842 to the present. Over the next few weeks they will be accompanied by films, exhibitions and discussions. And, having seen the dozen core dramas, which can be viewed either on a single day or separate evenings, two things strike me.

One is that they fulfil a basic function of art by instructing delightfully. The other is that, rather than pursuing an editorial line, they give us the information to allow us to make up our own minds about Afghanistan's future.

What is fascinating is how certain themes echo through the plays. In Stephen Jeffreys' deeply moving *Bugles At The Gates of Jalalabad*, which kicks off proceedings, we are reminded of the unwinnable nature of Afghan wars. As Rick Warden's Hendrick, one of four beleaguered buglers stranded after the British army's massive defeat at Kabul in 1842, remarks: "This country is a deathtrap for foreign armies." And that idea recurs in David Edgar's equally fine *Black Tulips*, which shows how the Soviet troops who occupied the country from 1979 to 1989 learned the same bitter lesson: "the Afghan people have never accepted occupation by foreigners with guns."

But Afghan intransigence has never prevented outsiders seeking to impose their own concept of order. The tragic irony of this is best shown in my own favourite among the plays: Ron Hutchinson's *Durand's Line*. In this we see Michael Cochrane as the British diplomat Mortimer Durand, locking horns with Paul Bhattacharjee's ruling emir in 1893. Durand naively believes that maps define nations and that, by creating fixed borders, the Russians can be kept at bay. In return the Afghans will enjoy a monopoly of the opium trade. It is a defining historical moment and a symbol of the endless desire for intervention. And that play is neatly juxtaposed with Amit Gupta's *Campaign*, which wittily shows a modern Foreign Office politician pushing, with equal simplicity, the dream of turning Afghanistan into a secular liberal democracy.

What becomes clear throughout the plays is that Afghanistan's tragedy stems as much from geography as history. And the failure of America, especially, to grasp local realities emerges time and again. In J.T. Rogers' brilliant *Blood and Gifts*, an undercover American emissary supplies an anti-Soviet 1980s warlord with arms only to learn too late that he has been aiding the Islamist cause. A similar point is made, more diffusely, in Ben Ockrent's *Honey*, which implies that American failure to read the situation led to the collapse of Kabul to the Taliban in 1996 and ultimately to the horrors of 9/11.

These plays, however, are not simply an attack on blundering Western incomprehension. They also demonstrate the horrors of Taliban rule. In Colin Teevan's chilling *The Lion of Kabul*, Lolita Chakrabarti's UN representative impotently confronts a rigidly inflexible Taliban ruler, and in David Greig's *Miniskirts of Kabul* we are reminded of the horrific death of the pro-communist President Najibullah at the hands of the fundamentalists. Almost the only play that sounds a note of hope is Abi Morgan's *The Night is Darkest Before the Dawn*, set in the Kandahar countryside in 2002, which suggests that education and female enfranchisement will counter years of oppression.

The big question is what happens next. *The Great Game*, jointly directed by Nicolas Kent and Indhu Rubasingham assisted by Rachel Grunwald, offers no solutions. But it gives us an historical context in which to discuss the issues.

In the final play by Simon Stephens, *Canopy of Stars*, we are reminded of the impossibly difficult choices that lie ahead. Tom McKay as a British sergeant returning from Helmand province is confronted by Jemima Rooper as his angry wife begging him not to go back: "You are changing nothing," she tells him. To which he replies with a story about a 10-year-old girl at Delaram whose eyes were sprayed with acid for the simple offence of going to school. And that, in a way sums up the virtue of *The Great Game*. It reminds us of all the past blunders in Afghanistan. At the same time, it does not spare us examples of present-day Taliban cruelty.

It is up to each individual to decide whether they feel NATO forces should stay or go. But these plays give us the chance to make an informed judgement. And I can only salute the entire cast, including Ramon Tikaram, Vincent Ebrahim, Daniel Betts and Jemma Redgrave, and the design of Pamela Howard and Miriam Nabarro. Something remarkable is happening at the Tricycle, where Afghan history and culture are being made manifest in a uniquely challenging, theatrically exciting way.

The Contingency Plan by Steve Waters (World Premiere) Bush Theatre, London: 8 May 2009

We have waited a long time for a play that dealt comprehensively with climate change. Steve Waters has generously provided two, *On The Beach* and *Resilience*; they can be viewed independently, but only make total sense when seen as a pair. Their virtue is that they not only act as an urgent wake-up call, but they present the issues in compelling human terms.

On The Beach is, at heart, a father–son drama. Will Paxton, a glaciologist, returns to his Norfolk family home from Antarctica convinced the polar melt will cause catastrophically swollen sea-levels. He confronts his father who 34 years previously reached similar conclusions, was ignored by Government, and has retreated into hermetic obduracy. Will, however, is determined to be heard; in *Resilience* we see him, aided by his civil servant lover, putting his case to Whitehall ministers in a future Cameron government. He finds himself the victim of departmental rivalries and cautious advisers; and, when action is finally taken, it is too late to avert a national crisis.

Avoiding preachiness, Waters presents his arguments through action. And he is at his best in the first act of *Resilience* which, for sheer emotional intensity, has no rival on the London stage. Following a Shavian pattern, Waters presents us with a passionate dialectic between two men, who each believes he is right. The setting is the office of the new climate change minister. On one hand we have the resident adviser, played with superbly emphatic vigour by Robin Soans, who argues for methodical mitigation of the effects of rising sea-levels. Against him stands Will, played with fine escalating desperation by Geoffrey Streatfeild, who puts the case for immediate action including more sea defences and readiness for evacuation of all coastal settlements. It is a ding-dong battle invested with mounting ferocity.

Waters' other great asset is that he makes you interested in the people involved. In the first play there is real pathos in the portrait of Will's father, given a masterly performance by Soans, who rejects the loving concern of Susan Brown as his wife and waits for the sea to engulf them in confirmation of his theories. And in the second play the new minister, played with Old Etonian chumminess by David Bark-Jones, is horribly credible in his wilful blindness to reality and his belief there is something almost festive about a national crisis. Despite a good performance from Stephanie Street as an ambitious civil servant, the love interest is rather patchily explored. And, although the plays are well directed by Michael Longhurst and Tamara Harvey respectively, the second has too many false climaxes for its own good. But the flaws pale beside Waters' massive achievement which is to have made the most important issue of our times into engrossing theatre.

Jerusalem by Jez Butterworth (World Premiere) Royal Court, London: 17 July 2009

Jez Butterworth's last play, *Parlour Song*, transported us to a housing estate on the edge of a dark forest. Now he takes us into the woods for a bucolic frolic depicting the disappearance of a pagan, primitive culture. Even if there is a touch of romantic nostalgia to Butterworth's portrait of deep England, his play justifies its three-hours-plus length and contains a star role momentously played by Mark Rylance.

Butterworth's dominant character is Johnny "Rooster" Byron: a mixture of Pied Piper, Romany roustabout and Wiltshire Falstaff. A former daredevil, he now lives in a woody trailer from which he dispenses booze, drugs and fantastic fables to a gang of admiring onlookers. But on the day of the local fair, which also happens to be St George's Day, he faces eviction for unauthorised encampment. With a new estate about to be built in the area, there is no room for a charismatic anarchist, disturber of the peace and wild man of the woods like Johnny Byron. He is such a rich creation that you feel that the author himself has been seduced by him. Defending the fact that 15-year-old kids attend his druggy rave-ups, Johnny declares "half of them are safer here than they are at home." Since the only representatives of supposed normality we see are an abusive stepfather, a morris-dancing

publican and a pair of council officials, the dice are heavily loaded in
Johnny's favour. Where the play works best is in its reminder that magnetic
spellbinders like Johnny are often profound solitaries who depend on an
unreliable audience. One of the hero's tallest tales, about meeting an itinerant
giant on the A14, is hilariously undermined by a sidekick who wants to
know how the story was missed by BBC *Points West*. And, towards the end,
we realise that Johnny's parasitic acolytes are capable of the deepest betrayal.

The brilliance of Rylance's performance lies in the contrast between the
public and private man. Surrounded by his disciples, Rylance epitomises the
glamorous, yarn-spinning outlaw. But there is a telltale moment in Ian
Rickson's perfectly judged production when Rylance is left alone and reaches
for a discreetly hidden pair of specs to read the eviction order. Later, in a
scene with the mother of his child, Rylance also implies that he knows the
game is up and there is no more room for him in today's world than there
was for Jack Falstaff in Henry V's ascetic realm. Mackenzie Crook, Tom
Brooke and Danny Kirrane are all impressive in supporting roles, but the
triumph belongs to Rylance for perfectly embodying Butterworth's vision of
a vanished demonic magic.

Enron by Lucy Prebble (World Premiere)
Royal Court, London: 23 September 2009

After the high praise earned in Chichester, there was always the lurking fear
that the *Enron* bubble might burst on transfer. But, although it had more
room to manoeuvre at the Minerva, Lucy Prebble's play and Rupert Goold's
production are so strong that they survive the move. What they vividly offer
is not a lecture on corporate madness but an ultra-theatrical demonstration
of it at work.

The play shows how the Texan energy giant, Enron, moved from a model
of the future to a bankrupt disaster with debts of $38bn. Prime mover is
Jeffrey Skilling: a Marlovian over-reacher who boldly announces "we're not
just an energy company, we're a powerhouse for ideas." His basic idea is to
trade in energy as well as supply it. But, as his dreams expand to include
video, internet and even the weather, the gap between stock market
perception and reality grows ever greater. As profits fail to materialise,
Skilling turns to his sidekick, Andy Fastow, to create shadow companies to
conceal mounting debts. Once the market loses confidence, however,
Skilling's schemes are revealed for what they are: a fraudulent fantasy.

It could all be dry as dust. But the pulse and vigour of play and production
stem from their ability to make complex financial ideas manifest. Everything is
made visually apprehensible. Thus the complicity of market analysts in Enron's
over-evaluation is captured by turning them into a close-harmony troupe. The
Lehman Brothers become Siamese twins locked into a single suit. Best of all is

the scene where Fastow explains his system for funnelling Enron's debts into shadow companies. Even financial innocents can follow this as Fastow shows boxes encasing ever smaller boxes lit by a flickering red light symbolising the basic investment. This is capitalism exposed as con-trick and illusion.

Goold's immaculate staging, Anthony Ward's design and Scott Ambler's movement illustrate the whirling kaleidoscopic energy that is part of the dream. But Prebble also creates plausible people, and Samuel West is hugely impressive as the self-deluded Skilling. It is difficult to feel sympathy for such a man, whose deregulation policies did so much damage, but West reminds us of the global complicity in money worship. Amanda Drew as his rival, Tim Pigott-Smith as Enron's avuncular founder, and Tom Goodman-Hill as the greed-driven Fastow, haunted by the scaly raptors which symbolise the shadow companies, are also first-rate. But the triumph of the evening is that it renders Enron's rise and fall in exciting theatrical terms, and leaves us with the feeling that, as the bonus culture thrives while others lose their jobs, the lessons of this vast collapse have still to be learned.

Critic's notebook: one of a number of periodic reflections commissioned by *The Guardian*.

10 September 2009

I lose track of the number of invitations I receive to discuss "the death of the critic." The subject came up again last weekend, at a conference in Stratford-upon-Avon entitled *Reviewing Shakespearean Theatre: the State of the Art*. I gave a talk which conceded that criticism, like Shakespearean production, is in a state of flux. Professor Peter Holland flew in from the University of Notre Dame in the US to tease both newspaper critics and bloggers for being confined to their own little bubbles. In a stimulating seminar session, Elle Collins argued that criticism should echo the collaborative nature of theatre: instead of a closed text, there should be a "dialogic confrontation" in the blogosphere.

Only a fool would deny that criticism has been affected by the rise of new technology. But I've spent my life arguing that a review is simply a way of starting a debate. I also think it's time to bury the myth that in the past critics were unaccountable, god-like figures. Criticism has always triggered meaty public debates. Years ago, I observed that we should have a UK Shaw festival, since he was our second-best dramatist after Shakespeare. The result was a blistering attack from John Osborne and a correspondence that raged, on our letters page, for weeks rather than days.

What has changed is the technology: any opinion is now open to instant, rapid rebuttal online. Sometimes this leads to fascinating discussions: this year, my own hesitant suggestion that there was a potential danger in theatre adopting the cinematic model of the "auteur" unleashed a host of contradictory opinions from readers. But it seems to me absurd to deduce from this that printed criticism is dead, dying or redundant. In any sphere of activity – be it politics, sport or fashion – there is a crying need for someone who brings to the subject a lifelong professional commitment: more than ever, I'd argue, in an age of spin and hype. You can attack particular critics – and it has been known to happen – as being out of touch or past their sell-by date. But I came away from the Stratford conference convinced that we still need critics, not least because they provide, in the excellent words of Shakespeare professor Carol Chillington Rutter, "a hedge against amnesia for the next generation."

Bright Spots in the Lost Decade: 2010–19

We can argue over whether the decade actually ended in 2019 or a year later. But, for convenience, I choose the earlier date. And what a turbulent decade it was even if we largely confine ourselves to Britain. It began with a General Election in May, 2010 that produced a Conservative-led Coalition government: one that immediately launched a programme of economic austerity that shrunk the public realm. The decade ended with another election in December 2019, dominated by the slogan "Get Brexit Done." in which the Conservatives had a majority of 80 and Labour recorded its worst result since 1935. In a book significantly entitled *The Lost Decade*, Polly Toynbee and David Walker charted the devastating impact of austerity politics on British life: for every £100 spent on public services in 2010 only £86, in real terms, was spent a decade later.

The theatre, especially in the regions, was hardly immune to the prevailing austerity: budgets were tighter, casts smaller, co-productions of necessity more frequent. Yet the commercial theatre actually did well over the decade and launched a number of massively popular money-spinners such as *Harry Potter and the Cursed Child* and, of course, *Hamilton*. A whole new genre, based on carefully calibrated mishaps, also took wing with *The Play That Goes Wrong* and it various follow-up created by Mischief Theatre. Even in the financially-challenged subsidised sector, there was a determination to respond to changes in the cultural climate. This was seen most clearly in two specific areas: diversity and gender equality.

For much of my critical life, I seem to have written about the crisis in Black, Asian and Minority Ethnic Theatre. There have always been companies – such as Talawa, Tamasha, Tara Arts, Eclipse and Yellow Earth – that have kept the flag flying but British stages rarely reflected the make-up of the British population. Gradually that began to change. Artists of colour – including Kwame Kwei-Armah at the Young Vic, Indhu Rubasingham at the Kiln, Roy Alexander Weise at the Royal Exchange in Manchester – currently occupy key positions as artistic director. It would now be offensive to stage a classical production without diversity of casting – indeed Trevor Nunn was attacked for precisely that reason when he directed an all-White *The Wars of the Roses* at the Rose Theatre, Kingston – and actors such as Sharon D. Clarke, Jenny Jules, Paapa Essiedu and Lucian Msamati have become amongst the highest-profile British actors of today. Policies within the big theatre companies have also shifted. The RSC, to its credit, has always championed actors of colour and when Rufus Norris succeeded Nicholas Hytner at the National in 2015 he immediately made it his aim to build on the work of his predecessor by creating a programme that acknowledged diversity: you saw that in productions like *Small Island*, *Barber Shop Chronicles* and *Three Sisters*. But, while substantial progress was made during the decade, actor Kobna Holbrook-Smith hit the nail on the head when he said that "things have got better but they were so damn bootleg before that nobody can afford to chill."

You could apply the same argument to gender equality. Utopia remained some way off but progress was at least made when it came to controlling the levers of power: the Royal Court, Donmar, Kiln (previously Tricycle) Hampstead, Shakespeare's Globe, Royal Exchange, Liverpool Everyman and Playhouse were all for much of the decade run by women. A whole generation of directors helped to undermine the myth of male supremacy: Deborah Warner, Katie Mitchell, Marianne Elliott, Lyndsey Turner were already established names but the decade saw Blanche McIntyre, Carrie Cracknell, Rebecca Frecknall, Nadia Fall, Eleanor Rhode, Kimberly Sykes, Ola Ince emerge as major figures. And while there was nothing unusual in seeing Maxine Peake play Hamlet or Glenda Jackson King Lear, of much greater significance was the growth of gender-blind casting in classical productions. Even if one occasionally quibbled with the results – such as the portrayal of Thersites in an RSC *Troilus and Cressida* as a scuttling female oldster – the principle was right.

One of the bigger surprises of the decade was seeing how a concern with domestic politics was augmented by an awareness of global crises. James Graham in *This House*, Laura Wade in *Posh*, Moira Buffini in *Handbagged* and Peter Morgan in *The Audience* still wrote about such matters as

Parliamentary infighting, the prevalence of bullying machismo and the occasionally fraught relationship between transient prime ministers and the well-entrenched monarch. But writers increasingly looked beyond home affairs. The most consistently internationalist playwright was Anders Lustgarten, a political activist, who in *Lampedusa* provided a stunning account of the merciless exploitation of those seeking refuge from tyranny. And at long last the British theatre began to address the most serious issue of our times: climate change. Steve Waters had led the way in 2009 with a powerful diptych, *The Contingency Plan*, staged at the Bush. More diffuse was the multi-authored *Greenland* (2011) at the National in which Moira Buffini, Matt Charman, Penelope Skinner and Jack Thorne offered a combined vision of catastrophe. Even more fascinating were Mike Bartlett's *Earthquakes in London* (2010) which dealt with the daily reality of global warming and Richard Bean's *The Heretic* (2011) in which a climate-change denier provocatively took centre stage. But it was two works, both staged at the Royal Court and adopting the form of a lecture, that achieved most impact. In *Ten Billion* (2012) Stephen Emmott left his audience stunned by his demonstration of the consequences to the climate of unchecked population. Two years later Chris Rapley in *2071* used his first-hand experience as a climate scientist to exhort the audience to action. Arguments as to whether or not what Emmott and Rapley were doing was theatre seemed to me spectacularly irrelevant: they were using a public stage to address the issue of the survival of the planet.

Climate change, mental health, the ethics of scientific experiment were among the topics debated on stage during the decade. But perhaps the most surprising development, during a time of economic austerity, was the public hunger for the epic. It was as if, having invested a good deal of time and money in going to the theatre, audiences craved a unique and demanding experience and it took many forms. In *The James Plays* at the Edinburgh Festival Rona Munro took us on a guided tour of Scottish history. In *The Apple Family Plays* at the Brighton Festival Richard Nelson charted a tight-knit group's response to the vagaries of American politics. Matthew Lopez's *The Inheritance* was a two-part, seven-hour play dealing with the bitter afterlife of Aids and the affirmative legacy of E.M. Forster-style humanism. And Stefano Massini's *The Lehman Trilogy* used a family saga, spanning 150 years, to explore the nature of Western capitalism.

Looking back, it is difficult to feel much affection for a decade that saw Donald Trump apply his own form of narcissistic gangsterism to the American Presidency, Britain totally consumed and irreparably divided by the debate about Brexit and lies superseding truth as part of the daily currency of politics. W.H. Auden called the 1930s a "low, dishonest decade." But, even if much the same could be said of the years from 2010 to 2019, the British theatre retained its integrity, made the work on stage more representative of the population at large and heightened our awareness of global issues. We were not to know at the time that one of the most prescient productions of the era was to be Neil Bartlett's revival at London's Arcola of Camus's *The Plague* which dealt with mass contagion.

2010

Off the Endz by Bola Agbaje (World Premiere)
Royal Court, London: 23 February 2010

Bola Agbaje has written a modern morality play. What she is attacking, in this 80-minute piece, are the self-delusional dreams of criminalised Black youth. And, even if her play is sometimes overly direct, Agbaje writes with the clarity, economy and street-savvy that marked her debut, *Gone Too Far.*

She presents us with a jarring triangular relationship. Kojo, a corporate suit, and his partner Sharon, a nurse, are aspirational, young, Black, planning a family and looking for a mortgage. Their lives are disrupted by the arrival of an old friend, David, just out of jail. Disdaining their bourgeois lifestyle, while battening on their hospitality, he treats work as a four-letter word and sets up as a drug-dealer. As well as driving a wedge between the couple, David becomes the fatal tempter who tries to seduce the debt-ridden Kojo with the prospect of quick money and a life of freedom.

At times Agbaje hammers her points home and is evasive on details: she never, for instance, explains Kojo's exact occupation. What she does very effectively is de-glamourise the romantic myth of the freebooting outsider. David has charm but is also a blatant chauvinist who insults a female secretary, behaves arrogantly to a jobcentre clerk and treats Sharon as a domestic slave. With great skill, Agbaje also shows the corrupting effect of male bonding in that Kojo increasingly allies himself with David.

As a moralist, Agbaje hits her target dead centre. In the play's best scene, she shows how David discovers that his old drug-dealing patch is now the property of terrifying 10-year-olds. And behind the play lurks the idea that young Black, high-flyers, such as Kojo and Sharon, are caught in a pincer-trap: in a White-created recession, they are the most vulnerable yet also feel a debt to the estate mates who shared their poverty.

Agbaje resolves the dilemma by pinning her faith, somewhat unfashionably, in the solid virtues of work and family. She is aided by Jeremy Herrin's fast-moving, well-acted production, played out against a spartan, white-walled design by Ultz. Ashley Walters endows David with enough charisma to explain his friends' concern, Daniel Francis brings out the spiritual weakness

of the success-driven Kojo and Lorraine Burroughs exudes angry resilience
as Sharon. And although the members of the gang are not individually
credited, the gun-toting 10-year-old leader is a potent reminder of Agbaje's
gift for telling uncomfortable truths.

Sweet Nothings by Arthur Schnitzler
Young Vic, London: 5 March 2010

I wish we saw more of Arthur Schnitzler. He was one of the great European
dramatists: at least the equal of Pirandello. And this revival of his 1895 play,
Liebelei, in a new version by David Harrower and an exquisite production
by Luc Bondy, offers a damning portrait of Viennese decadence without ever
reverting to overt moralising.

The central figure, Christine, is a Viennese archetype: "the sweet girl"
(*das süsse Mädel*) doomed to destruction by a social superior. In this case,
she is rapturously devoted to a handsome young drifter, Fritz, already
involved in an adulterous affair. In the first act we see Fritz and his friend,
Theo, hosting a wild party at which the romantic Christine and her more
realistic chum, Mitzi, are the guests. The air is filled with the promise of
orgiastic pleasure. But the party is interrupted by a dark-clad figure who
comes to challenge Fritz to a duel; and, in the second act set in Christine's
suburban home, we see the consequences for the innocent heroine.

Schnitzler's secret is that his framework is artificial but his people are
real. He makes, for instance, a sharp division between the guileless Christine
and Fritz and their cynical companions: Theo embodies a male, would-be
worldliness by announcing "our problem is we can't stand the women we
fall in love with" while the pragmatic Mitzi candidly tells him "you'll be
finished with us by August." And, if the people are real, so too is Bondy's
production which vividly captures the irresponsible hedonism of youth. The
first act foursome is a miracle of staging in which the characters seem
propelled by drink, lust and their own inner restlessness. Yet when the
mysterious stranger arrives, it is as if death has suddenly intruded on this
world of frenzied pleasure.

That sense of reality also pervades the sombre second half. Hayley
Carmichael, making a striking appearance as a neighbour of Christine, reeks
of the withering puritanism of the suburbs. And you learn everything you
need to know about Natalie Dormer's selfishly sensual Mitzi when she
casually plants her hat on Christine's carefully laid-out chessboard. But the
performances throughout are as impeccable as the production. Kate Burdette
makes Christine more than a simple victim: there is a determination about
the way she wrenches Fritz from Mitzi's grasp. Tom Hughes, in his
professional debut, captures the boyish helplessness of the frightened Fritz
when challenged to a duel. And there is fine work from Jack Laskey as his

friend who lives purely for the ecstatic moment. But this is the point that Schnitzler is making: that *fin de siècle* Vienna is a city of illusions haunted by the implacable shadow of death.

Ruined by Lynn Nottage (UK Premiere)
Almeida, London: 23 April 2010

Lynn Nottage's play arrives in London laden with American honours. And rightly so, since it offers a graphic portrait of women as perennial victims of war. More than that, it reminds us of the continuing conflict in the Democratic Republic of Congo, which rarely makes the front pages but has led to 5.4 million deaths.

Nottage's focus is very precise: she deals with a bar-cum-brothel in a small Congolese mining town on the edge of the rainforest. The bar's presiding spirit is Mama Nadi who believes, like Brecht's Mother Courage, that as long as business is good and she avoids taking sides, she can survive the war. But, in the course of the action, head and heart come into conflict.

Mama takes on board two new girls, Sophie and Salima, both of whom have been subjected to extreme sexual violence. Inevitably Mama discovers that, in trying to shield the girls from further cruelty and appease both government troops and rebel militia, she jeopardises both their lives and her own profiteering livelihood.

What Nottage brings out strongly is the multiple sufferings inflicted on women. Salima is a farmer's wife who describes how she was subjected to gang rape. As if that were not sufficient punishment, she is regarded as "ruined" by her husband who, she says, "was too proud to bear my shame but not proud enough to protect me from it."

But, although the play vividly depicts a war zone in which women's bodies are treated as battlegrounds, it has a glimmer of hope. Without minimising the pain, it becomes a tribute to women's endurance. Admittedly the climax lacks the ruthless logic of the Brechtian prototype. But, unusually for an American playwright, Nottage deals with global rather than purely domestic issues and raises our awareness of the use of rape as a military tactic.

Direction, design and acting are also first-rate. Indhu Rubasingham's production, aided by Dominic Kanza's music, depicts Mama Nidi's bar as a gaudy refuge from the horrors of war. Robert Jones's revolving, corrugated-iron set presents this louche, rainswept niterie in vivid detail. And Jenny Jules excellently captures all Mama's qualities: her arrogance and pride, her limited economic vision, and her maternal protectiveness towards her stable of girls. Pippa Bennett-Warner's vulnerable Sophie, Michelle Asante's defiant Salima, and Lucian Msamati as an ebullient salesman also hit the mark. It is not merely a good play. It jolts our conscience about a forgotten conflict. One emerges both shaken and stirred.

Religion and Theatre: a reflection in a godless age.

21 May 2010

We get plenty of sex in the theatre. Politics too. Religion, however, rarely surfaces in modern drama; and when it does, with rare exceptions such as David Hare's 20-year-old *Racing Demon*, it often fails to ignite impassioned debate. At a time when many religions seem to be facing internal crises and when faith constantly interacts with politics, it seems strange that the theatre has so little to say on the subject.

It wasn't always so. As a batch of revivals has proved, the 1950s was a decade in which religion was an animating force in drama. John Osborne's *The Devil Inside Him*, resurrected by National Theatre Wales, vigorously shows how bullying, fire-and-brimstone clerical rhetoric drives a young man to murder. Jerome Lawrence and Robert E. Lee's *Inherit the Wind*, at the Old Vic, dramatised the conflict between creationists and evolutionists. And Nigel Dennis's *The Making of Moo*, at Richmond's Orange Tree, offered a suave assault on the link between colonialism and Christianity. None of these plays was exactly a glowing advert for faith, but at least they assumed it mattered in people's lives.

Today that assumption no longer holds. So it came as something of a shock last week to find a new play at the National, Drew Pautz's *Love the Sinner*, that at least dealt with religious issues. I just wish it has been a better play. Pautz starts with a gang of Anglican bishops in heated debate at an African conference. But windy rhetoric replaces real argument over the big issue: the church's attitude to homosexuality. And Pautz spends far more time examining the private tensions of a bisexual lay volunteer than he does exploring the Anglican cultural divide between the conservative diehards and the progressive realists. The play is an opportunity missed.

But now it seems right for theatre to be engaging with religion. Militant secularism has produced a gnawing discontent and a reminder of the truth of Chesterton's dictum that, if people don't worship God, they will soon find something else to idolise. At the same time, we are confronted by a Catholic church experiencing the greatest crisis in its recent history through the cover-up of paedophile priests. Anglicanism faces a profound schism between its Eastern and Western adherents. And Islam is clearly facing the consequences of the age-old division between Sunnis and Shias, and the difficulty of accommodating itself to Western materialism. If this isn't the stuff of drama, I don't know what is.

Occasionally the theatre touches on these issues. Last year the Royal Court staged a very good play, *Shades*, by Alia Bano, about the dilemma faced by a secularised Muslim heroine who falls in love with an orthodox believer. Stephanie Street, who starred in that play, also recently created a fascinating verbatim-drama, *Sisters*, based on the testimony of Muslim women in Britain for whom religion was a shaping force.

But these plays are the exception. In the book world a fierce debate rages between polemical atheists such as Christopher Hitchens and Richard Dawkins and eloquent champions of faith like Karen Armstrong. Yet, for the most part, the theatre steers clear of religion or, as with Pautz's play, sidesteps big questions. Where is the modern equivalent of Brecht's *Galileo*, which pits science against religion? Or of Shaw's *Saint Joan*, which both puts the case for its heroine's direct access to God and explains the need for her political extinction? No one can write masterpieces to order. But since we are confronted by the tensions in organised religion and the vacuum created by unalloyed materialism, isn't it time faith made a comeback as a fit subject for drama?

The Persians by Aeschylus
Brecon Beacons, Wales: 13 August 2010

This is site-specific theatre with a vengeance. High up in the Brecon Beacons, in a mock-up village used by the military as a training-base, National Theatre Wales is recreating the oldest extant play in Western drama: Aeschylus' *The Persians*. The combination of the story and the setting is overwhelming.

The play itself is extraordinary. Produced in 472 BC, only eight years after the Persians had been routed at Salamis, it is the only Greek tragedy to be drawn from recent history rather than from legend. Obviously Aeschylus was celebrating Athenian victory. But what is astonishing is his sympathy for the vanquished. Atossa, mother of the defeated Xerxes, views the wreckage of her country with mounting horror. The ghost of Darius, her husband, rises from the grave to announce that grief is man's lot and must be borne. Even "war-lusting" Xerxes himself is finally seen as an abject object of pity.

What is impressive about Mike Pearson's production, however, is the totality of the experience. We assemble in a square in this deserted village where the four-strong male chorus is rejoicing in war and announcing "no one can withstand this tsunami of the Persians in full rage." We then march up a hill to sit in front of a four-storey house with the front cut away; and there we see, both in live action and on video, the tragedy enacted. There's a wonderful moment when Atossa arrives in a white car to a blaze of trumpets. But, once she is in the house, a hand-held camera moves in close to watch the disintegration of her hopes as the news from Salamis arrives.

Pearson puts the piece in contemporary clothes but makes no attempt to relate it directly to Iraq or Afghanistan. Instead he and the translator, Kaite O'Reilly, focus on how war destroys the very fabric of people's identity. At the beginning, the chorus praise Xerxes as "fierce as a dragon scaled in gold"; by the end, they are threatening to beat him to death with a hammer. Even Darius starts out in Paul Rhys's performance as a gently melancholy ghost, only to turn into a wrathful figure who talks of Xerxes as "a mortal playing God to gods." Sian Thomas also puts in a tremendous performance as the queen, a woman of fiery splendour reduced to ululating agony as the disasters mount.

This superb production literally takes one on a journey. And, as one went back down the hill after, strange lamentations emerged from the deserted houses. Shivering slightly, one moved on, still hearing the tragic aftermath of war in one's ears.

The Game by Harold Brighouse
Liverpool Playhouse: 27 September 2010

You don't find many plays about professional football. But Northern Broadsides has had the nous to revive this delightful "lost" work by Harold Brighouse. Written in 1913, two years before his famous *Hobson's Choice*, it's just as enjoyable as its successor, and uses football as a way of exploring class, money, the generation war and what we nowadays call gender politics.

Brighouse's plot is admittedly a bit contrived. Austin Whitworth, the cash-strapped owner of Blackton Rovers, has sold his star centre-forward, Jack Metherell, to a rival club on the eve of a crucial game. But what we see is Jack, the working-class hero, undergoing a series of moral tests. First, his integrity is severely challenged when Austin asks him to throw the match. And then Jack's manly independence comes under the microscope when Austin's elder daughter, Elsie, seeks to prize him away from the clutches of the domineering mother with whom he lives.

Part of the play's appeal today is nostalgic: it evokes an era when football reporters talked of "agitating the spheroid to the sticks" and when a star centre-forward, bent on self-improvement, could say "there's things in Browning I can't figure out and Walter Pater has me beat to atoms." But Brighouse also unsentimentally reminds us of the way soccer players were treated as little more than serfs by their employers and, even if he keeps the crucial game off stage, he makes up for that with a series of striking personal duels. My favourite comes when Elsie, the irresistible force, meets Jack's mum, the immoveable object, and, on offering to help in the house, is sternly told: "Jack's bed were made up this morning. Do you take me for a slut?"

Barrie Rutter's excellent touring production wrings every ounce of dramatic value out of these head-to-head encounters. He himself plays the bullying club owner at odds with his former star, whom Phil Rowson endows with the right working-class obduracy. And you get strong hints of the *Hobson's Choice* generational conflict when Catherine Kinsella's fiercely independent Elsie confronts Wendi Peters' Mrs Metherell. The latter is simply magnificent and at one point, I swear, uses her formidable bosom as a means of registering her indignation at seeing her territory threatened. You could pick holes in Brighouse's plot. But this is still a remarkable play that starts out by exposing the grubby chicanery of professional football and ends by revealing the terrifying power of English working-class motherhood.

Onassis by Martin Sherman (Revival)
Novello, London: 13 October 2010

First seen at Chichester two years ago under the title of *Aristo*, Martin Sherman's play poses a huge question: why on earth did people of taste and judgement bother to revive a piece as laughably awful as this? As a bio-play with pretensions, signally unfulfilled, to Greek tragedy, it falls between every available stool and makes one wonder why we should be bothered with the shenanigans of the super-rich.

Starting in 1963, and covering the last 12 years of the Greek shipping magnate's life, it shows him to be little more than a boorish megalomaniac. We see him dumping Maria Callas, for whose art he had nothing but disdain, for the supposedly more covetable Jackie Kennedy. It is also suggested, in conspiracy theory style, that his dubious financial dealings with shady Palestinians may have paid for the murder of Bobby Kennedy, whom he passionately loathed.

For good measure Onassis treats his perfectly decent son, Alexandro, with a bullying contempt which, in his macho world, apparently passes for love. Since he ends sad, lonely and widely detested, we are invited to see him as a classic victim of hubris.

Unfortunately, Sherman seems so mesmerised by this monster he has scarcely bothered to write a play. Of conflict, there is virtually none, since Onassis is surrounded by toadies, yea-sayers and financial dependents; and even if his son and his second wife briefly stand up to him, they are soon squashed by his daunting ego.

What gives the play a patina of absurdity, however, is the presence of a pseudo-Greek chorus who sit in a taverna and comment on the passing action. They periodically invoke Athena, Aphrodite and Poseidon and offer gnomic utterances such as "We have a future already written – it's called destiny." But just because Onassis liked to see himself as someone above common morality doesn't make him a demigod or a tragic hero. He was simply an immensely rich man who abused his power and privilege.

Sherman has written not so much a play as a part and it is one that Robert Lindsay fills to overflowing. But, as if to compensate for the emptiness of the dialogue, he is forced to lapse into an Anthony Quinn style of overacting which I'm tempted to dub Exorbitant The Greek. "Stillness always works," Onassis remarks at one point; but you would scarcely know

it from the restless, larger-than-life performance that Lindsay feels obliged
to give. He is a fine actor compelled by the lack of drama to put on a bit of
a show.

The best one can say of Nancy Meckler's production is that Katrina
Lindsay's sets have a certain marine charm and that the actors do what they
can – especially Gawn Grainger who, as Onassis's sidekick, has to heave up
large slabs of backstory, and Lydia Leonard who suggests something of
Jackie Kennedy's dressy steeliness. But this is a ridiculous play that treats a
delusional tycoon as if he were a figure of epic grandeur.

Men Should Weep by Ena Lamont Stewart (Revival)
Lyttelton, National Theatre, London: 27 October 2010

Ena Lamont Stewart's remarkable play was a big hit at Glasgow Unity in
1947, famously revived on the Edinburgh Fringe in 1982, and now it gets an
equally loving revival by Josie Rourke at the National. Rightly so: this play,
set in a Glasgow tenement in the 1930s, reminds us what economic hardship
really means, and yet has an ebullience that suggests a Scottish O'Casey.

There had been plays about working-class life before Lamont Stewart's.
What makes hers unusual is she views the subject from a woman's
perspective. Her heroine, Maggie Morrison, nourishes a brood of children,
an ailing mother-in-law and a jobless husband. And her troubles multiply.
Her youngest son is taken to hospital. Her eldest son, Alec, returns home
with his termagant wife when their house collapses. And her flighty grown-
up daughter, Jenny, stalks out of what she terms a "midden" to seek a better
life. As she camps out nightly on the living-room floor, Maggie wanly
remarks "I have na been in a bed since I was in maternity with Marina."

Yet what makes this a fine play is that Lamont Stewart neither
sentimentalises Maggie nor treats working-class life as unrelievedly grim.
Maggie herself may be tough, but she is capable of bursts of bilious anger.
And, although Maggie's husband says "all we've done wrong is to be born
into poverty," the play is filled with a wild humour. Lamont Stewart creates
a host of characters: a prim sister who views all men as "dirty beasts," the
mother-in-law who moans that her biscuit has chocolate only on one side,
and prying neighbours who might have wondered in from *Juno and the
Paycock*.

Rourke and her dazzling designer, Bunny Christie, also treat the play as a
tenement symphony in which we are reminded that the Morrison menage is
only part of the larger picture: we get a *Rear Window*-like perspective on
the whole block in which we see glimpses of all the adjacent lives. And, if it

takes time to tune in to the Glasgow dialect, the acting is uniformly superb. Sharon Small as the indomitable Maggie, Robert Cavanah as her ineffectual husband, Morven Christie as their hard-hearted daughter-in-law, and Anne Downie as the grumbling old woman inhabit this cluttered world as if it is their natural terrain.

This remains a landmark play in British drama; and, if men should weep, it is because Lamont Stewart was discouraged from ever writing a successor to a work that blends such indignation with theatrical exuberance.

2011

What's wrong with spoilers?

4 April 2011

Am I guilty of indecent exposure? I only ask because I am frequently accused by bloggers of revealing too much of a play's plot. I was even charged, rather weirdly I felt, with spoiling someone's enjoyment of the National Theatre's *Frankenstein*. Given that Mary Shelley's novel has been around since 1818 and subject to countless adaptations, I'd have thought it highly unusual for anyone to attend the production in a state of total innocence. But, in general, the accusation raises fascinating questions about the technique of reviewing and the undue primacy we give to narrative suspense.

How much should a critic give away? With a whodunnit, we are obviously honour-bound not to reveal the ending. It's a convention the London *Evening Standard's* Milton Shulman once broke by concluding his review of a 1950s Agatha Christie thriller with the fatal words: "George did it." The play closed within a week. But, even with non-genre pieces, there is often a problem. Many years ago, Richard Curtis wrote me a long, pained letter saying I'd spoiled Tom Stoppard's *The Real Thing* for him by revealing that the first scene was an artificial play-within-a-play; by the time he saw it, he knew Stoppard's narrative trick.

My answer now would be the same as then: any first-rate play transcends prior knowledge of its plot. Clearly, the critic has to withhold a certain amount of information for the sake of potential playgoers. But Stoppard's *The Real Thing* is so bubbly with ideas about the relation between reality and illusion, and the pain of infidelity, that it doesn't matter a damn whether you know it starts with a piece of deception – it could even be said to enhance the pleasure.

Pinter's *The Lover* reinforces the point. It hinges on the fact that a married couple play fantasy sex games, in which the husband returns every afternoon in the role of the wife's lover. Doubtless the original TV audience in 1963 was pleasantly bamboozled and shocked to discover the truth. But, once you know the twist, the play becomes an infinitely richer experience. Some years ago, I had the luck to direct it at Battersea Arts Centre with two first-rate actors, Sian Thomas and John Michie, and we discovered that every single line had a complex subtext. At the beginning, when the husband asks his wife, "Is your lover coming today?" a seemingly amiable inquiry conceals layers of anxiety and doubt; the more you know, the better the play becomes.

I wouldn't deny that suspense is a part of drama, and that there is a palpable excitement to seeing a play for the first time – you only have to sit with a young audience at its first *Hamlet* or *Macbeth* to realise that. But even suspense can operate in many ways. Instead of, "What happens next?" it's much more stimulating to ask, "How is it going to happen?" Hitchcock understood that when, in *Vertigo*, he revealed the crucial twist at an early stage in the film. And, although one could hardly have an artist further removed from Hitchcock, Brecht also grasped that prior knowledge allows an audience to focus on the rationale behind an action. There's a famous scene in *Mother Courage* where Brecht announces in advance that the heroine "loses her daughter," but we still watch, in a state of heightened anticipation, as the mute Kattrin sacrifices her life to warn of a military attack.

Those who complain that critics give too much away seem to want to approach a play in a state of paradisal innocence. I'd argue that, with a certain amount of prior information, you're free to concentrate on what really matters. Plot, for instance, is only the vehicle for the ideas and issues a play raises. Even though we know that Hamlet will die in the end, that Nora will make her dramatic exit in *A Doll's House*, and that Godot will never materialise, we go back to the plays time and again to experience the author's vision of life. In the end, character and language are every bit as important as plot. We attend the theatre to encounter magnetic, ambivalent people who seem to embody our own contradictions. And every first-rate dramatist, from Shakespeare to Chekhov to Pinter, is a poet at heart, who forges a diction that is not only engrossing in itself but the perfect means for expressing his or her purpose.

I'm not indifferent to my critics who accuse me of undue revelation, and I shall be more wary in future. I'd simply observe that it's impossible to pinpoint a play's strengths and weaknesses without citing chapter and verse. And if you look at the two most influential reviews of the last 60 years, Kenneth Tynan's of *Look Back In Anger* and Harold Hobson's of *The Birthday Party*, you'll find they tell you a surprising amount of what actually happens. But then Tynan and Hobson both realised that a sophisticated awareness greatly intensifies, rather than destroys, an audience's enjoyment.

The League of Youth by Henrik Ibsen
Nottingham Playhouse: 18 May 2011

Ibsen fanciers are in seventh heaven. In advance of the National's *Emperor and Galilean*, we get the British professional premiere of this 1869 prose comedy, although I did see it revived by the Guildhall School of Music and Drama 18 years ago with a young Damian Lewis in the lead. Then as now, I am struck both by the play's structural creakiness and its exuberant exploration of what were to become standard Ibsen themes.

Ibsen's hero, Stensgard, is a bumptious opportunist who has been aptly described as "a political Peer Gynt." He first sets a provincial town ablaze by his radical attack on privilege and his formation of an anti-capitalist League of Youth. But, courted by the community's conservative, all-powerful chamberlain, Stensgard changes tack and is happy, after a local electoral triumph, to be proposed by the old guard for a seat in parliament. What finally scuppers Stensgard is his sexual, rather than political, cynicism. Once it is discovered that he has proposed simultaneously to three women, and been comprehensively rejected, he becomes a local laughing stock.

Andy Barrett's new version does an excellent job in clarifying the plot and even explaining the complexities of the Norwegian electoral system. Barrett also allows us, without pushing the point, to savour the topicality of a play in which principles are sacrificed for power: the audience roars at a line where a right-wing bigwig observes that Stensgard is not weighed down by convictions "which makes it easy for him to be a liberal." But the main interest lies in seeing Ibsen flagging up ideas he was to explore more fully in his later, greater plays. Stensgard is the first in a line of frock-coated frauds, and when the chamberlain's daughter-in-law turns on her husband and says, "You dressed me like a doll, you played with me like you play with a child," we all hear intimations of the domestically trapped Nora.

Although the play strains the resources of a regional theatre, Giles Croft's production adroitly makes use of non-professionals to embody Stensgard's supporters, and allows the teeming action to spill out into the auditorium. There are also good performances from Sam Callis as the overweening antihero, smilingly unfazed by temporary setbacks, Philip Bretherton as the easily hoodwinked chamberlain and David Acton as a suave conservative who sees through Stensgard's expediency. I was sorry to lose a concluding Napoleonic quote in which we're told that "double-dealing is the stuff of which politicians are made." But the production, presented as part of Nottingham's first European Arts festival, makes a strong case for Ibsen's play, and reminds us that the bewhiskered old buffer always had a great gift for comedy.

The Merchant of Venice by William Shakespeare Royal Shakespeare Theatre, Stratford-upon-Avon: 20 May 2011

What to do with this endlessly problematic play? Directors such as Peter Zadek and David Thacker set it in the stock exchange. But Rupert Goold, as is his wont, goes for broke by transporting it wholesale to modern Las Vegas, where showbiz fantasy meets speculative capitalism; and the result is, by turns, brilliant, outrageous and excessive.

At first I had difficulty working out the logic of the setting: why, in particular, should Patrick Stewart's multi-millionaire property-owning, semi-assimilated Shylock feel an "ancient grudge" towards the local Christians? But, scene by scene, the concept begins to make sense: we realise that wealth is no barrier against ingrained anti-Semitism and Stewart's Shylock is secretly despised and reduced, presumably because denied access to the local golf clubs, to putting shots in his office. And, the greater his isolation, the more Shylock reverts to his ancestral religion.

Where Goold's production really breaks the mould is in its treatment of Portia. The casket-scenes are turned into a TV game-show called *Destiny* in which Susannah Fielding's stunning Portia dons a blonde wig and southern accent; she becomes, as it were, the hostess of a preposterous lottery in which her marital future is being decided. This not only provides wonderful comedy with the Prince of Morocco turning up as an avaricious contestant in golden boxing-shorts. It also achieves a startling final payoff when Fielding's Portia confronts the reality behind the make-believe; which is that Bassanio is more truly in love with Scott Handy's seductively melancholic Antonio than he is with her.

This is a dazzling production that gathers strength as it goes along. It may seem a gimmick to have Launcelot Gobbo played by Jamie Beamish as an Elvis impersonator, but it yields a handsome return when Portia's climactic breakdown is accompanied by the strains of *Are You Lonesome Tonight?*

And the full force of both the persecution of "aliens" and Shylock's concomitant revenge emerge in a remarkable trial scene: an underground, quasi-legal proceeding in which Antonio wears the orange suit of a political prisoner and the duke is surrounded by pistol-packing henchmen. It becomes a vision of the American nightmare; but the whole point of this daring and innovative production is that Shakespeare's play itself takes us into an imaginary dreamscape in which reality eventually intrudes. And, although Goold's production is bound to cause argument, Las Vegas seems a perfect metaphor for a world of financial and romantic fantasy.

truth and reconciliation by debbie tucker green (World Premiere) Royal Court, London: 7 September 2011

I would say debbie tucker green has carved out her own special niche at the Royal Court: partly through her insistence on lower-case name and titles, but more significantly through her ability – as in *random* and *stoning mary* – to create provocative dramatic poems. Now she has come up with a play that covers five countries and 22 characters, yet still only runs for 60 minutes. The result is powerful, but overcompressed.

The play offers vignettes of the aftermath of violence, sometimes genocidal, in the years from 1976 to 2007. In South Africa, a Black family testily awaits a white witness at a formal hearing. In Rwanda, a Tutsi widow angrily confronts her husband's Hutu killer. In Zimbabwe, a man deals with the fatal consequences of his wife's political outspokenness. In Bosnia, two Serbian ex-soldiers come face to face with a pregnant rape victim. And in Northern Ireland, two mothers, both of whom have lost their sons, vehemently argue about where responsibility lies for their deaths.

If one point emerges strongly from this kaleidoscope of suffering it is that women, as well as being victims of violence, are tireless in pursuit of truth. The Rwandan widow ceaselessly harries her husband's killer; a South African mother obdurately refuses to sit until the policeman who murdered her daughter shows up; the transgressive Zimbabwean tells her husband, "Somebody had to speak." That last episode is especially telling since, as in Pinter's *One for the Road*, the protagonist's fate is revealed through a change of tense. But, while green suggests that some crimes are so grievous that reconciliation is virtually impossible, her play suffers from its very compactness: we have barely grasped the impact of one scene before we are whisked off to the next. I would seriously suggest that the piece be played twice over so that audiences can absorb its meaning – a device that worked with Beckett's *Play*.

Staged by the author herself in the Theatre Upstairs, with the spectators sitting on hard chairs that replicate those endured by the characters, the piece is cryptic, fragmented, unsettling and well acted – especially by Wunmi Mosaku as the Rwandan widow, Petra Letang as the zealous Zimbabwean and Clare Cathcart as a defiant Northern Irish mother. But, although the play raises the issue of whether truth and reconciliation can ever be compatible, it feels strangely incomplete. I wanted either to hear the piece again or attend a post-play discussion to learn whether the author's political pessimism was justified.

Othello by William Shakespeare
Crucible, Sheffield: 21 September 2011

It's been billed in advance as a classic encounter between two stars of *The Wire*, Clarke Peters and Dominic West. But what first impresses about this much-touted event is the direction by Daniel Evans. He has come up with one of those increasingly rare Shakespeare productions: one that, without embracing any outrageous concept, suffuses the text with a wealth of psychological detail.

The long-range planning is evident from the start when Brabantio spurns his daughter Desdemona, by hurling her to the ground in a manner that Othello will later echo. The play's central problem, which is not making Othello himself look a credulous ass in believing in his wife's infidelity, is also partially solved by turning Cassio into a bit of a rake: one who warmly hugs Desdemona when he greets her in Cyprus and who later smothers Iago's wife in lascivious kisses. Even the long, lingering look that Desdemona gives the disgraced Cassio is enough to arouse any husband's suspicions. In short, Iago in this production has plenty to work on.

But it is the stars people have come to see and Dominic West's fine Iago benefits greatly from the production's scrupulous attention to detail. West gives us a plain, blunt Yorkshire-accented ensign who says of Othello right from the start, "in followin' 'im, I follow but myself." There is also a revealing touch when West publicly taunts Emilia, his wife, with failing to produce an heir: a gesture that leads her to bury her head in shame and that says a lot about his own misogyny and a decaying marriage. West is not, like some Iagos, a surrogate artist or a matador playing with a bull-like Othello. What he offers us, with driving energy, is a bluff, dirty-minded NCO who is filled with a rancorous, destructive negativity that least him to detest Othello for his "free and open nature" and to loathe Cassio for the simple reason "he hath a daily beauty in his life that makes me ugly." I've seen more visibly malignant Iagos; but what is excellent about West is that he has a surface honesty that makes him dramatically plausible and that yields a lot of laughs.

In contrast, Clarke Peters' Othello is wildly erratic. He makes a good impression at the beginning: dignified, noble, heroic in his appearance before the Venetian senate and even sounding the right Shakespearian music in a line like "she gave me for my pains a world of sighs." But, as the evening progresses the performance loses focus and, in the terrifying scene of Othello's epileptic fit, textual accuracy. Peters' flaw is he tends to act the emotion rather than allow it to emerge through the language and, although he recovers his poise, I felt of this Othello "I understand the fury of your words but not the words."

For a prize piece of Shakespearean acting you have only to look to Alexandra Gilbreath's Emilia. She offers us a complete character: a professional soldier's raunchy, sex-starved wife with an eye for a young lieutenant but also a deep attachment to Desdemona. You see the growing guilt on Gilbreath's face when she realises that, through the stolen handkerchief, she has hardened Othello's suspicions about his wife and it seems fitting at the end that the dead Emilia should take her place on the bed alongside Lily James's spirited Desdemona.

But that is typical of the care of Evans's production. It looks good with an octagonal platform set against a back wall that evokes both the watery corrosion of Venice and the sun-bleached world of Cyprus. And, although there is an imbalance in the central partnership, you get all the intensity of Shakespeare's most domestic and time-bound tragedy. Sheffield is lucky to have a production of this calibre.

Tribute to playwright Shelagh Delaney: born 25 November 1938, died 20 November 2011.

22 November 2011

Shelagh Delaney, who has died aged 71, was almost as important for what she symbolised as for what she wrote. She was, as Jeanette Winterson wrote in *The Guardian* last year, "the first working-class woman playwright." And even if nothing she later wrote achieved the success of her first play, *A Taste of Honey*, Delaney proved that an 18-year-old Salford girl could breach the walls of what, even in 1958, was still a mainly middle-class, male-dominated British theatre.

The story of how *A Taste of Honey* came to be written is well known. Delaney had been taken to see Terence Rattigan's *Variation on a Theme* at Manchester's Opera House and came away convinced she could do better. So, in little more than a fortnight, she banged out a play about a feisty Salford girl, Jo, who is left alone by her flighty mum one Christmas, goes to bed with a transient Nigerian sailor, gets pregnant and is lovingly tended by an effeminate art student. Having written the piece, Delaney had the nous to send it to the director Joan Littlewood, who had turned the Theatre Royal in Stratford East into a vibrant home of new drama.

In her autobiography, Littlewood made no bones about the fact that a lot of work was needed to knock Delaney's play into shape. She liked the sparky dialogue, but felt many of the scenes were undeveloped and the plot anecdotal. So she got Avis Bunnage, as Jo's mum, to use her talent for direct address and brought in a jazz quartet of trumpet, drums, guitar and sax to set the mood. Delaney's slightly artless script quickly became a critical success.

"There are plenty of crudities in Miss Delaney's play," wrote Kenneth Tynan in the *Observer*. "There is also more importantly the smell of living." He also pointed out that Delaney would have plenty of time in the future to worry about words such as "form," which mean something, and concepts like "vulgarity," which don't. That question of "form" is fascinating. After the success of *A Taste of Honey*, Littlewood tried to offer her young playwright concrete guidance. "Read a good play," Littlewood wrote, "an Ibsen for example, then analyse it, note the construction. Playwriting is a craft, not just inspiration." As far as we know, the advice went unheeded: Delaney's second play, *The Lion in Love*, made little impact and her theatrical career quickly petered out. Delaney did, however, write a number of short stories, several radio scripts and a handful of good screenplays including *The White Bus* for Lindsay Anderson, and *Charlie Bubbles*, directed by and starring Albert Finney.

I've not seen the latter since it first came out in 1967 but I have a memory of an extraordinary film in which Finney plays a successful writer who makes a pilgrimage back to his northern roots. As Finney, like Delaney, hailed from Salford, the film had a strong personal favour. But Delaney also pinned down the idea of a writer insulated from reality by success. There is a particularly good scene in a hotel where the waiter asks Finney: "Are you still working, sir, or do you just do the writing now?" Objectively, you could say Delaney's career never fulfilled its initial promise. But she opened a door for succeeding generations; and if we now think there is nothing unusual about women dramatists making a mark in their teens or coming from a working-class background, we have her to thank for it.

Foxfinder by Dawn King (World Premiere) Finborough, London: 6 December 2011

In a wan year for new writing, Dawn King's play shines out like a beacon. Winner of the Papatango playwriting competition, it may display the influence of Arthur Miller's *The Crucible* and have echoes of Kafka, but it remains an arresting and individual work that haunts the mind long after you've seen it.

King's setting is an English countryside on the brink of crisis and subject to rigorous official inspection. One farming couple, Samuel and Judith Covey, who are already troubled by the death of their son and failing crops, find themselves under investigation by 19-year-old William Bloor, a designated foxfinder. For Bloor, the fox is the deadly enemy of mankind, with the power to contaminate farms, influence the weather, unsettle the mind and kill children. We see how Bloor's fox fixation leads neighbours to betray each other, and drives the innocent Samuel into a state of deluded guilt.

Clearly the play is a parable, but one that works because of the openness of King's central symbol. At times, the fox represents a wild, untamed sexuality of which the monastic, self-flagellating Bloor is keenly aware. But the fox also symbolises the irrational search for scapegoats to explain the ills that haunt mankind. If I had to pin it down, I would say the play is an attack on the danger of fundamentalist certainties. What stops it toppling into gothic absurdity is King's sharp sense of humour, narrative drive and realism: she locates her dark fable in a plausible world where cattle have to be fed, leeks harvested and meals cooked.

Director Blanche McIntyre follows last year's dazzling Finborough revival of *Accolade* with another first-rate production. She keeps the staging stark and simple, and makes chilling use of prolonged silences. There are fine performances from Gyuri Sarossy as the quietly truculent Samuel, Kirsty Besterman as his anxious, raw-boned wife and from Tom Byam Shaw, who has the wit to play the foxfinder not as a raging hysteric but as a conscientious official terrified of his own repressed emotions. Any rural tragedy has to overcome the memory of *Cold Comfort Farm*, but King's play easily transcends that and – along with Mike Bartlett's *13* – is the most compelling new work I have seen this year.

The Animals and Children Took to the Streets by Suzanne Andrade (Revival) Cottesloe, National Theatre, London: 12 December 2011

A year ago this second show from a group called 1927, which mixes live actors and animation, won high praise at London's BAC for its visual ingenuity. What few could have foreseen, even its writer, director and co-performer Suzanne Andrade, is that its portrait of street riots and social disruption would turn out to be grimly prophetic. It's not just a clever show; it also has its ear close to the ground.

At first you gawp at the sardonic wit with which Andrade, Esme Appleton, musician Lillian Henley and animator Paul Barritt evoke life in a seedy tenement block, Bayou Mansions, on the fringe of a big city. This is like a murky version of Fritz Lang's *Metropolis*, which first appeared in 1927, populated by rats, cockroaches and all manner of social outcasts. But the sharply subversive script shows how a gang of child-pirates go on the rampage, take over a middle-class park and even kidnap the mayor's cat before being whisked off in black ice-cream vans and effectively sedated. But their cry of "we want what you have out there" strikes a chill chord after this summer's riots.

The 70-minute show makes its points with visual and verbal humour rather than heavyweight hectoring. A live, do-gooding liberal mum descends on the estate with her cartoon daughter to set up an art club only to retreat when the going gets tough. And the idea that we seem to be permanently stuck with grotty sink-estates is perfectly counterpointed by the lightning transformations of Barritt's brilliant animations, where coffins turn into telephones and cockroaches. Performed by a quick-changing, white-faced female trio, the show feels like a heady mix of Berlin cabaret, silent movie and social commentary. I only hope this astonishing company doesn't get permanently sucked into the international festival circuit and takes time out to apply its beady satirical eye to our growing discontents.

2012

29 February 2012

In all the recent controversy about whether British theatre has become more risk-averse as a result of the recession, one fact has been overlooked: the virtual disappearance of the truly bad play. This has happened for a simple reason. Production costs are now so high that commercial theatre can no longer afford to mount the kind of rubbish that was a staple part of my early reviewing life. And why would anyone go out and see second-rate theatre when they can stay at home and watch second-rate television?

Lousy plays used to come in two forms: drawing room comedies and thrillers. The former were an anaemic aftermath of the great Noel Coward tradition, and dealt with such pressing matters as debs seeking ideal spouses, dispossessed gentry slumming it in a Belgravia mews, or butlers standing up for conservative values against mildly progressive employers. Even worse were the whodunnits and thrillers which, if English, took place in snowbound country houses and, if American, in isolated Nantucket beach residences. After the success of the genuinely good *Sleuth* by Anthony Shaffer and *Deathtrap* by Ira Levin, one thing was also inevitable: no corpse would take death lying down ever again.

But, even if the bulk of new writing now comes from the subsidised sector, it is still in danger of breeding its own cliches. Following humbly in the wake of the great American critic George Jean Nathan, who once produced a list of the portents of a bad play (e.g. "When, as the curtain goes up, you hear newsboys shouting Extra!, Extra!"), I append my own list of contemporary signs, whether in new plays or classic revivals, that audiences are in for a rough evening:

1   Any play in which a character aggressively masturbates within two feet of the front row.

2   The moment a child emerges from an upstairs room to describe, in graphic detail, his or her bad dreams.

3   Any site-specific show that seeks to intimidate the spectators by asking them to pose as concentration-camp victims or inmates of an institution to be pursued down darkened corridors by chainsaw-wielding figures.

4   Plays that treat sad divas (Judy Garland, Maria Callas) less as specific examples of showbiz misfortune than as tragic emblems of suffering humanity.

5   Plays that invoke memories of Fred West, Josef Fritzl, the Soham murders or the abduction of Madeleine McCann as an excuse for titillation without offering any compensating psychological illumination.

6   Any revival of a period comedy in which it takes approximately seven-and-a-half minutes to get to the delivery of the author's first line.

7   Productions that start with an ear-splitting burst of pop music to announce their urgent contemporaneity.

8   Plays in which a run-down, travelling circus becomes a metaphor for cultural decay.

9   Family dramas in which parental sexual abuse is saved until the denouement, and produced like a rabbit from a hat, to explain the preceding two-and-a-half hours of unrelenting misery.

10 Any play in which defecation is used to cover up dramatic defects.

This is a highly personal list, to which I'm sure you can add. But it's a reminder that, even in an age when rank bad plays are far rarer than they were in the age of commercial profligacy, the type is not wholly extinct.

Julius Caesar by William Shakespeare
Royal Shakespeare Theatre, Stratford-upon-Avon: 7 June 2012

This, of all Shakespeare's plays, badly needs a shot in the arm – and it receives a powerful one in this production by Gregory Doran, the RSC's artistic director designate, who has transposed the action to modern Africa. To see it played by an all-Black British cast is also to be reminded of the wealth of classical acting talent in this country.

Africa has no monopoly on dictators but the play acquires fresh urgency in its new setting. This, after all, is a work about the encroachment of autocracy on a republic; and, although the evening begins with a street fiesta celebrating the return of a military hero, the looming bronze statue of Caesar shows the dictatorial threat. But the African setting doesn't simply give new edge to the ethical debate about political murder. It also reminds us that this is a play filled with prophecies, portents, dreams and, incidentally, leonine images. Even if Africa is not alone in its belief in spirits, the soothsayer here becomes a magical force who acts as a ubiquitous shaman.

The real strength of Doran's production lies in its attention to character. Ever since the late John Wood played the part at Stratford 40 years ago, the myth of Brutus as the noblest Roman in a batch of envious conspirators has been systematically demolished. Paterson Joseph goes much further than most by showing Brutus to be a man of quixotic temper swathed in self-regard. Joseph proudly beats his breast when he talks of "my ancestors," makes a series of catastrophic tactical errors, and self-deludedly announces of Caesar's killing that "we shall be called purgers, not murderers." I used to think Brutus was the idealist in a world of realpolitik: Joseph excellently shows him to be a self-righteous blunderer.

What makes this doubly effective here is that everyone knows Brutus to be wrong, no one more so than Cyril Nri's admirable Cassius, who is clearly the brains behind the conspiracy. Everyone looks on in disbelief when Brutus announces that Mark Antony is to be spared; but, in one breathtaking moment, Nri looks ready to stab Caesar's ally after the assassination, only to find his hand stayed by Brutus.

Not even Doran can disguise the anticlimax of the battle scenes; and once or twice, for all the production's vigour, I felt that vocal volume was replacing subtlety. But there is a superb Caesar from Jeffery Kissoon who, with his fly whisk and white suit, evokes memories of a whole line of African potentates.

And, in a male-dominated play, there are strong cameos from Adjoa Andoh and Ann Ogbomo, who, as the wives, respectively, of Brutus and Caesar display a vehement sense of reality denied their deluded husbands.

No one production can ever make total sense of this slippery play. But Michael Vale's set, with its sun-drenched stone steps, gives it a physical reality; Akintayo Akinbode's music moves from the carnivalesque to the ominous and Doran's production gives the play a new immediacy. In a year that has already seen an abundance of visiting Shakespeare, it is good to be reminded that we haven't lost the power to radically reinvent the plays ourselves.

Ten Billion by Stephen Emmott
Royal Court, London: 20 July 2012

This is one of the most disturbing evenings I have ever spent in a theatre. Stephen Emmott, an acclaimed scientist, stands in a re-creation of his cluttered Cambridge office and delivers, under Katie Mitchell's astute direction, an illustrated 60-minute talk on the consequences of overpopulation. He tells us that we are facing "an unprecedented planetary emergency" and, under his calm exterior, you sense a concealed fury at our failure to address the crisis.

Emmott uses an array of statistics to reinforce his argument that the current global population of seven billion will grow to ten billion, maybe more, by the end of the century and that is unsustainable. We are facing a crisis with ecosystems being destroyed, the atmosphere polluted, temperatures rising and a billion people facing water shortage. "Things," Emmott sombrely reminds us, "will only get worse" as the demand for food doubles by 2050, climate change intensifies and the transport system that sustains our needs grows.

Describing himself as "a rational pessimist," Emmott says there are two solutions. We can "technologise" our way out of trouble, through building solar shields, or we can change our behaviour – by consuming "less food, less energy, less stuff." Emmott sees little chance of this happening. I think he is too scornful of energy-saving gestures. He tells us he's fed up with reading about celebrities giving up 4x4s in favour of an energy-saving car and says it's not going to affect the world's water supply if we wee in the shower rather than the loo. But at least every little helps.

Emmott is on surer ground when he castigates politicians and world leaders. "Thirty years of words and inaction," he predicts, "will be followed by another 30 years of words and inaction." As one of Emmott's many public roles is as scientific adviser to the Chancellor of Exchequer, I'd love to know what happens when he tells George Osborne what he is telling 80 people a night in the theatre. Some will argue this is a lecture, not theatre. But the distinction seems nonsensical. David Hare gave us his perception of Israel and Palestine in *Via Dolorosa*. London's Tricycle Theatre has staged edited versions of public inquiries such as those into the Met's handling of the Stephen Lawrence case. And the Finborough in Earl's Court is presenting *The Fear of Breathing* based on reports from Syria. What is impressive is that Emmott argues his case with an implacable logic. He is quiet and concerned and when he says, at the end, "I think we're fucked" you have to believe him.

Three Sisters by Anton Chekhov
Young Vic, London: 15 September 2012

Textual tinkering with the classics rarely works. Better to go the whole hog, as Benedict Andrews does in this radical new *Three Sisters*, which is set in today's Russia, peppered with four-letter words and has the cast singing a Kurt Cobain number. For all its strangeness, I found Andrews' production true to the spirit of Chekhov's great play and, in the end, profoundly moving.

Shocks and surprises come early. Designer Johannes Schutz strips the Prozorovs' provincial household down to a bare platform backed by a mound of earth. The young Irina naively dreams of being a road worker; the aristocratic Baron Tuzenbach talks of lying at home in St Petersburg in front of the telly; and the philosophising battery commander, Vershinin, warns that, while happiness is a "marketing ploy," we still have to envision a golden future. You could argue that Vershinin's optimism sits ill with the current sense of economic and environmental decline. But Andrews' production catches perfectly the Prozorov sisters' yearning for escape and Chekhov's portrait of the need for endurance in the face of dashed hopes. All the play's great moments are still there: the prolonged silence induced by a spinning top, the exhausted chaos of the town fire, and the final fading sound of a military band as the soldiers depart.

This is Chekhov refreshed and reimagined – and acted with total lack of inhibition. What you might call the Andrews sisters are vividly played by Mariah Gale, Vanessa Kirby and Gala Gordon. There is striking work from Danny Kirrane as their tubby, unbuttoned brother Andrey; Emily Barclay as his brash Aussie wife; William Houston as a Vershinin who uses his conceptualising as a sexual come-on; and Michael Feast as a manic doctor. Something of the play's everyday realism may be sacrificed, but this is a production that gets to the drama's heart and made me realise, all over again, why I love Chekhov.

This House by James Graham (World Premiere) Cottesloe, National Theatre, London: 10 October 2012

Having written plays about the Suez Crisis and Thatcher's childhood, James Graham now turns his attention to the Labour government's precarious ability to survive a hung parliament and a wafer-thin majority from 1974 to 1979. This is a play about the daily process of politics rather than big ideas, but it recreates, with startling vividness, the madness of life in the Westminster village during five action-filled years.

The audience sits on replica Commons benches but Graham's focus is not on the debates but on the wheeling and dealing that goes on in the offices of Labour and Tory whips. In February 1974, after Heath has been ousted, Labour forms a minority government and we see Bob Mellish and his fellow whips offering sweeteners to the Liberals, the Scot Nats and the Northern Irish in order to stay in power. But, although Labour ends up with a slender majority of three after the October 1974 election, things get rougher and tougher. The party changes leader in mid-stream, the Tories cancel all pairing agreements after alleged cheating, fighting breaks out in the Commons, the sick and dying are wheeled in to vote. This, incredibly, is British democracy in action.

For all that, Graham's play adds up to an implicit endorsement of the system: when Humphrey Atkins, the Tory chief whip, reminds his new opposite number, Michael Cocks, that the gap between Government and Opposition benches is exactly the width of two drawn swords, it sounds like a recommendation of adversarial politics. Identifying MPs by their constituencies, Graham also suggests that, in the days before expenses scandals, they honourably performed an unglamorous task. Above all, the play unlocks a whole era and reminds those alive in the 1970s of the volatility of the period's politics: Michael Heseltine swings the mace in the Commons, a Labour MP carefully stages his own disappearance, another is ready to bring down the Government when the Chancellor proposes over £1bn worth of spending cuts.

That is a rare excursion into policy. Mostly the play is about pragmatic survival and my only complaint is that Graham gives the impression that dodgy parliamentary arithmetic virtually crippled the business of government. It is perfectly true that Labour had to go cap in hand to the IMF in 1976 during a sterling crisis. But the late 1970s wasn't all bad news: inflation and unemployment fell, progressive legislation, such as the Sex Discrimination Act, was passed, and it was widely assumed that if James Callaghan had called an election in 1978, Labour could still have won.

But Jeremy Herrin's production recaptures, with abundant theatricality, accompanying music and choreographed movement, the mayhem of Westminster politics. And, in a large cast, Philip Glenister, Vincent Franklin and Andrew Frame as working-class Labour whips, Julian Wadham, Charles Edwards and Ed Hughes as their smooth-suited Tory equivalents and Christopher Godwin and Rupert Vansittart amongst the role-swapping ensemble are outstanding. It may be a bit of an anoraks' night out but, as a relic of the period, I had a thoroughly good time.

All That Fall by Samuel Beckett
Jermyn Street Theatre, London:
12 October 2012

"It is a text written to come out of the dark," said Samuel Beckett of this radio play first broadcast by the BBC in 1957. But, although not conceived for the stage, it adapts perfectly to it in Trevor Nunn's production, which retains Beckett's orchestrated sound effects while giving the actors motion and visibility. And, in the case of Eileen Atkins as Beckett's heroine, it allows us not merely to hear but also to see a great piece of acting.

The play itself is Beckett at his most Irish and accessible. Springing out of memories of his native Foxrock, near Dublin, it charts the journey of an old woman, Maddy Rooney, along a country road to the railway station to meet her blind husband off a train. In the course of her travels, she meets a carter, a businessman, a racecourse clerk and a stiffly Protestant spinster. But the train she has come to meet is delayed. And, when it finally arrives and

Maddy accompanies her husband home, we learn that a child fell out of a carriage in an accident for which Mr Rooney may have been responsible.

Beckett, Cyril Connolly wrote, is the poet of terminal stages; and what starts out as a comedy turns into a threnody on death, dissolution and decay. And the miracle of Atkins's performance is that she implies this from the beginning in her long, silent, sorrowful gaze. That doesn't diminish our laughter as Mrs Rooney, a self-styled "hysterical old hag," puts everyone's back up. There's a hilarious episode when Mrs Rooney accepts a lift from the racecourse official in his limousine and has to be shunted into the vehicle, urging her helper to "get your shoulder under it." And when the religious Miss Fitt describes the ecstasy of being alone with her maker, Atkins throws her a look that would make hell freeze over. What is moving about this performance is that it contains all the tetchiness, sadness and sorrow, as well as occasional bawdiness of old age. And when, in the play's closing passages, Atkins supports Michael Gambon's sightless but stentorian Mr Rooney as they stumble along the highway, one is reminded of a later Beckett line about marriage: "Alone together, so much shared." Even the final revelation of the child's death, which dismayed some critics when the play was first broadcast, no longer seems a gratuitous plot twist but a reflection of the couple's loss of their own daughter.

The play introduces us to a whole gallery of Irish characters here vividly embodied by Frank Grimes as the bicycling bill broker, Gerard Horan as the car-owning clerk, James Hayes as the fretful stationmaster and Catherine Cusack as the desiccated Miss Fitt. Nunn's luminous production, while making good use of Paul Groothuis's sound score, also allows Beckett's richly allusive words to do the work. The Rooneys, one notices, are no simple country folk but able effortlessly to refer to Dante, Descartes and Theodor Fontane as well as the New Testament. This is Beckett at his most beguiling; and, although the production's impact depends upon the intimacy of the space, I just wish it could be televised so that both the play and Atkins's performance could be relished by the many as well as the lucky few.

Red Velvet by **Lolita Chakrabarti**
(World Premiere)
Tricycle, London: 18 October 2012

Indhu Rubasingham makes a strong start to her tenure at the Tricycle with this new play about the pride and prejudice that greeted the pioneering African-American actor Ira Aldridge in nineteenth-century London. Lolita Chakrabarti's text has some minor flaws, but opens up a fascinating subject and gets a major performance from Adrian Lester that whets the appetite for his Othello at the National next year.

Chakrabarti starts in 1867 when the dying, internationally renowned Aldridge is preparing to play Lear in Lodz . A persistent young Polish interviewer harps on about the fact that Aldridge never returned to Covent Garden after his debut there in 1833, and the bulk of the play explains why. We see how, after rival actor Edmund Kean's on-stage collapse when playing Othello, the theatre's French manager propelled Aldridge into the role. Although Aldridge was well known on the provincial circuit, his arrival prompts dissension in the company, dismays hidebound critics and leads to the theatre's temporary closure.

Although Sartre pulled it off in *Kean*, writing about great actors of the past is never easy, and there are times when Chakrabarti's play overdoes the calculated anachronisms: it sounds odd to hear nineteenth-century actors describe Aldridge as "charismatic." But the play deftly reminds us that Aldridge's London Othello took place in the context of fierce debates about the abolition of slavery, and that his casting acquired inescapable political overtones. We may view as history the green-room divisions his presence caused and shudder at the blatant racism of the reviews. Yet Peggy Ashcroft once told me that when she played Desdemona to Paul Robeson's Othello at the Savoy in 1930, she received hate mail, and that Robeson was unwelcome in the next-door hotel; the issues *Red Velvet* raises have never entirely gone away.

What is striking about Lester's performance is its emphasis on the novelty of Aldridge's approach: it was his insistence on direct physical and emotional contact with his Desdemona, as well as his colour, that caused consternation. This remarkable evocation of a legendary actor is well supported by Charlotte Lucas as his Desdemona, Ryan Kiggell as Edmund Kean's priggish son and Eugene O'Hare as the theatre's Gallic manager. Rubasingham's production, with its blend of permanently visible actors and nineteenth-century footlights, shrewdly underscores Chakrabarti's point that theatre is forever upset by the shock of the new.

The Effect by Lucy Prebble (World Premiere) Cottesloe, National Theatre, London: 14 November 2012

How do you follow a big hit? Just as Jez Butterworth succeeded *Jerusalem* with the more modest *The River*, so Lucy Prebble follows her spectacular *Enron* with an intimate four-hander that examines love, depression and the limitations of neuroscience. It's an absorbing, if slightly diagrammatic, drama immaculately directed by Rupert Goold in a joint production between Headlong and the National Theatre.

Prebble's setting is a posh clinic where paid volunteers take part in pharmaceutical drug trials. We meet two of the guinea pigs: Tristan, a boisterously flirty Ulsterman, and Connie, a bright psychology student. As they take ever stronger dosages, they are closely monitored by a psychiatrist, Lorna, who is herself being supervised by another doctor, Toby, with whom she enjoys an edgily tense relationship. But, escaping Lorna's policing, Tristan and Connie start to fall in love. What they are not sure of is whether their newfound passion is instinctive or a by-product of dopamine.

Prebble uses the situation to explore some big questions mostly articulated in the debates between the two doctors. Toby passionately argues that we are witnessing an epidemic of depression which is the result of a chemical imbalance that can be cured by medication. Lorna takes the opposite view: that "so-called depressed people have a more accurate view of the world" and that the cause of their illness often lies in external factors. Prebble herself clearly leans towards the latter view just as she shows that the love between Tristan and Connie depends on something deeper than artificial stimulants.

It is a fascinating debate, but I feel Prebble overstresses the parallels between the two couples. For a play that supports the validity of the heart's affections, it often seems strangely cerebral; and there is a certain structural neatness about the way Tristan's instinctive ardour is matched by Lorna's own long-standing depression. But at least the play is questioning and profoundly wary of what Steven Poole in the programme calls the idea that neuroscience "has a right to become the ultimate arbiter of any human activity."

The piece is also beautifully staged by Goold in a Miriam Buether set that turns the Cottesloe into a clinical institution filled with beige banquettes. And the acting is excellent throughout. Billie Piper, as she proved in *Treats* and *Reasons To Be Pretty*, has a strong stage presence, and endows Connie with a glowing warmth and palpable hunger for love. Jonjo O'Neill is equally good as the volatile Tristan, who is randy, funny and disobedient, even if I found it difficult to believe that the character's susceptibility to seizure wouldn't have been checked in advance. But Anastasia Hille and Tom Goodman-Hill carry the main burden of the play's argument, and do so with utter conviction. There is a wiry tenseness to Hille that makes her confession of the character's depression totally plausible. And Goodman-Hill has the right mix of assurance and guilt that comes from a man who believes that antidepressants are a universal cure-all.

It's not a flawless play, but it's a palpably intelligent one that proves *Enron* was not a flash in the pan and that Prebble is one of the long line of dramatists who view medical practice with a rational scepticism.

2013

The Audience by Peter Morgan (World Premiere)
Gielgud, London: 6 March 2013

Peter Morgan struck box-office gold with his movie *The Queen*. He's likely to do so again with this play based on the private weekly audience given by the monarch to the prime minister. But I'd say that in both cases, PM owes a great deal to HM: in other words, Helen Mirren, who once again gives a faultless performance that transcends mere impersonation to endow the monarch with a sense of inner life and a quasi-Shakespearean aura of solitude.

As a dramatist, however, Morgan faces two problems. One is that no one ever knows what is said at these weekly tête-à-têtes since they are un-minuted. The other, more serious, is that in a constitutional monarchy, the Queen has no authority to contradict policy: simply, in the words of Walter Bagehot in the nineteenth century, "to be consulted, to advise and to warn," which would seem to rule out dramatic conflict. I'd say that Morgan counters these problems with varying degrees of success.

In a play that zigzags back and forth over 60 years and shows eight of the 12 prime ministers the Queen has dealt with (though not Tony Blair), Morgan is obviously free to speculate about what was said. He does this entertainingly enough, showing the Queen often acting as a surrogate shrink to her harassed ministers: she offers a hanky to a tearful John Major (a very funny Paul Ritter) and counsels sleep and rest to a paranoid Gordon Brown (a highly plausible Nathaniel Parker). But Morgan's right to exercise dramatic licence goes way over the top in his portrait of Harold Wilson. This is no fault of Richard McCabe, who plays Wilson with a nice pawky humour. But I cannot believe that Wilson, the most calculating of politicians and an Oxford don before he acquired power, would ever have breezed into Buckingham Palace posing as a working-class "ruffian"; and, however chummy he later became, I find it unlikely that he would have cheeked the Queen about her Germanic origins, saying that at Balmoral, instead of the bagpipes, "you should have someone playing the accordion in lederhosen."

The more serious question, however, is how you inject conflict into a situation that, constitutionally, precludes it. Morgan does this in artful ways by showing the Queen using her position to speak truth to power. In 1952, as a nervous young monarch, she stands up to an ageing Churchill (Edward Fox, gallantly taking over the role at short notice). And in 1956 she smokes out the pretence of Anthony Eden (an excellently twitchy Michael Elwyn) that our invasion of Suez was a response to Israeli aggression rather than the result of military and diplomatic collusion.

But, in demonstrating the Queen's practical wisdom, Morgan limits the scope for conflict; and only twice, in a perky panorama of political history, did I feel the dramatic temperature rise. Once was in the 1992 scene when John Major relays Princess Diana's scathing views about the monarchy and puts the Queen on the back foot by questioning royal expenditure. The other was the moment when Mrs Thatcher (Haydn Gwynne in a tearing temper) storms into the palace to attack, with some justice, leaks over royal dislike of her policies. The virtue of this scene is that it leads to the one serious political debate over Thatcher's determined refusal to apply sanctions to South Africa.

However hard Morgan tries, the evening can't help but seem like a series of revue sketches: a kind of *1956 And All That*. What holds it together is Stephen Daldry's adroit production and Helen Mirren's luminous performance, which, even in a non-linear script, pins down the Queen's steady growth in confidence and authority. Daldry has had the witty idea of allowing many of the costume changes to take place on stage so that we see Mirren, like an upmarket Gypsy Rose Lee, shedding her layers of costume: in a trice she moves from being Major's solid, elderly comforter to the lissom newcomer coping with a patronising Churchill 40 years earlier. Mirren also captures the Queen's mix of the extraordinary and the ordinary. Like HMQ in Alan Bennett's *A Question of Attribution*, she has the capacity to see through all forms of pretence. And, in her dialogues with her younger self, she conveys the sense of entrapment and loneliness that co-exists with a life of royal privilege. I have a theory that all plays about monarchy, from Shakespeare's *Henry V* to Howard Brenton's *55 Days*, end up as studies of solitude. That's exactly what happens here. But if Morgan's speculative and essentially static high-class political gossip – what you might call Pepys behind the scenes – acquires emotional resonance, it is largely thanks to the naturally majestic Mirren.

Chimerica by Lucy Kirkwood (World Premiere) Almeida, London: 30 May 2013

I complained of Lucy Kirkwood's last play, *NSFW* at London's Royal Court, that it was too short: no such problems with this gloriously rich, mind-expanding three-hour play, which explores the complex relationship between China and America. Co-produced by the Almeida and touring company Headlong, it has the extravagant scale and swagger of the latter's version of Lucy Prebble's *Enron*.

Kirkwood's play takes the form of a quest. Joe Schofield, a fictional American photojournalist who snapped the lone protester confronting a tank in Tiananmen Square in 1989, gets a tip-off that the man may now be living in the US: this leads him on a journey through America's Chinese community, in the course of which he jeopardises his job, his friendships and his affair with a British market researcher. In Beijing, meanwhile, Joe's chief contact, Zhang Lin, has problems of his own. Outraged at the death of a 59-year-old neighbour through smog poisoning, Zhang Lin leaks the story to Joe, only to find himself being tortured by the authorities and losing the love of his factory-foreman brother.

"Chimerica" was a term coined by economist Niall Ferguson to indicate the global dominance of the dual country that is China and America. But Kirkwood's play highlights the sharp differences, as well as the similarities, between the twin superpowers. In America, Joe's bolshie individualism as a photographer who records world events is ultimately celebrated; in China, Zhang Lin, who has already suffered for his involvement in the Tiananmen protests, pays a heavy price for inciting unrest. Kirkwood goes further in examining the nature of capitalism in both countries. China may be open to Western investment and apparently enthralled by its products; at the same time, Joe's girlfriend Tessa, in a brilliant presentation speech to her clients, explains that the only way into its markets is to understand that China is a country that values the supremacy of its culture.

Among a host of other issues, Kirkwood deals with the ethics and practice of photojournalism; this is dazzlingly reflected in Es Devlin's design, in which blown up, contact-sheet images are projected on to a revolving cube. Lyndsey Turner's astonishingly filmic production keeps the action driving forward through 39 scenes and boasts an impressive array of performances. Stephen Campbell Moore precisely captures Joe's mix of reckless idealism and self-absorption, Benedict Wong eloquently conveys Zhang Lin's private grief and public defiance, and there is exemplary work from Claudie Blakley as the sharp-tongued Tessa and Sean Gilder as a battered reporter. If we see a better new play this year, we'll be extremely lucky.

A Season in the Congo by Aime Césaire (UK Premiere)
Young Vic, London: 17 July 2013

The turbulence following Congolese independence inspired John Arden to write the unjustly forgotten *Armstrong's Last Goodnight* in 1964. Two years later, the Martinique poet and dramatist, Aime Césaire, tackled the same events in this astonishing play now having its British premiere in Ralph Manheim's translation and Joe Wright's rousing production. It should attract all lovers of political theatre; and, given that it contains a tremendous performance by Chiwetel Ejiofor, anyone who simply relishes fine acting.

Césaire's purpose in this big, ambitious play was to trace the decolonisation process and to create a tragic hero in Patrice Lumumba. We first see Lumumba in 1955, when he's a beer-seller and political activist in Belgian Congo. By June 1960, he has become the first prime minister of the newly independent state. Lumumba instantly attacks Belgium's colonial record and installs his old ally, Joseph Mobutu, as army chief. But he also faces secession by the mineral-rich province of Katanga, intervention by Belgian troops and the collapse of his dream of a united Congo. By 1961, Lumumba is dead, leading eventually to Mobutu's 32-year-long dictatorship.

Those are the broad outlines of a play that shows post-colonial ideals poisoned by tribal conflicts, predatory international bankers and the competing interests of the Soviet Union and US. But what gives the play its power is its surprisingly nuanced portrait of Lumumba, who is magnificently embodied by Ejiofor. Along with Kenneth Branagh's Macbeth, it's the second major performance I've seen in the past 10 days. Ejiofor gives us all of Lumumba's dream of transforming a country he describes as "garbage rotting in the sun" into a place of democratic freedom. But Ejiofor also captures the leader's vanity and political naivety: in a scene directly cribbed from *Julius Caesar*, we see him ignoring his wife's prophecies of physical danger and, in yet another Shakespearean parallel, promoting Mobutu to military supremacy with the whimsicality of Richard II dispensing personal favours. Between them, Césaire and Ejiofor provide a complex portrait of a flawed hero.

Some things Césaire leaves unclear: the alleged involvement, for instance, of the CIA in Lumumba's assassination. But Wright's production and Lizzie Clachan's design prove political drama can also be intoxicating theatre. We get masks, puppetry, dance and music – some of it supplied by Kabongo Tshisensa, who acts as a shaman-like chorus. In a large cast, there are standout performances from Joseph Mydell as Congo's smooth-talking president, and Daniel Kaluuya as the Macbeth-like Mobutu. And, when the military seize power from a democratically elected government, Césaire's attack on colonialism's tainted legacy suddenly acquires a chilling contemporary resonance.

Handbagged by Moira Buffini (World Premiere) Tricycle, London: 2 October 2013

The Queen and Margaret Thatcher are becoming a familiar theatrical double-act. They provided the sparkiest encounter in Peter Morgan's *The*

Audience. Now Moira Buffini has expanded a short piece she wrote for the Tricycle's 2010 project, *Women, Power and Politics*, into a full-length play; and the result, if occasionally overstretched, provides a very funny portrait of a relationship between monarch and prime minister that clearly wasn't made in heaven.

Buffini's brightest idea is to double the central roles. So we get an older and younger Queen, respectively known as Q and Liz. Equally we get an older and younger Thatcher, identified as T and Mags. Add in two male actors playing 17 other roles, ranging from Kenneth Kaunda to Rupert Murdoch, and you have what sounds like a recipe for confusion. In fact, Buffini's device gives the whole evening a buoyant, meta-theatrical playfulness. The older Q spends much of the play trying to hustle the action along in order to get to the interval. And the two Thatchers, while consistent in their detestation of socialism, often lapse into a good cop bad cop routine that says a lot about the late PM's contradictory techniques.

The difficulty is that no one knows what transpired at the weekly meetings of sovereign and minister. But Buffini creates a wholly plausible conflict of values between two radically different women. In July 1986 the *Sunday Times* published a big front page story itemising the monarch's dismay at her "uncaring" government. And, given the Queen's attachment to the Commonwealth, it seems highly likely that she discreetly expressed her views on such subjects as Thatcher's foot-dragging acceptance of majority rule in Zimbabwe or unwillingness to apply sanctions to apartheid South Africa. The play is obviously speculation. But behind the jokiness lies a tight-lipped collision between two women who entertained opposing ideas of Britain's role in the world.

As in all plays about the monarch, from Alan Bennett's *A Question of Attribution* onwards, the Queen comes out on top. Precisely because her constitutional powers are limited, she has to express herself obliquely. And Marion Bailey is quietly hilarious as the older Q, whether showing her displeasure at being lectured or slyly pointing out that it was a Murdoch paper that splashed their supposed antipathy. Even if Clare Holman as Liz has less juicy lines, she also registers an unforgettable stony blankness at being asked if she's read Hayek's *The Road to Serfdom*.

Fenella Woolgar as Mags and Stella Gonet as T also join the long list of expert Thatcher impersonators. The former combines dogmatic certainty with a low-register voice that seems to be filtered through a vat of honey: the latter is the more familiar later Thatcher who grows more strident as she feels power slipping away from her. Neet Mohan and Jeff Rawle play the plethora of male characters in a production by Indhu Rubasingham perfectly pitched between the comic and the serious. The play has odd duff moments, especially in the scenes involving the broadly caricatured Reagans. It offers, however, a fascinating fictional portrait of two women who had much in common, but who were also separated by what seems like an unbridgeable chasm in which monarchical emollience regularly confronted ideological inflexibility.

The Scottsboro Boys. Music and Lyrics by John Kander and Fred Ebb (UK Premiere) Young Vic, London: 30 October 2013

One of theatre's most potent weapons is an ironic contrast between form and content. It was used by Joan Littlewood in *Oh, What A Lovely War* and, more recently, by Stephen Sondheim in *Assassins*. It is also the chief instrument of this fine musical, with music and lyrics by John Kander and the late Fred Ebb, that deploys a minstrel show format to expose the racist bigotry that pervaded the case of The Scottsboro Boys.

The story is not that well known so a few facts may be in order. In 1931 nine Black youths were hauled off a freight train in Scottsboro, Alabama, and accused of raping two white women. In those days of rough justice, the youths were swiftly tried and sentenced to the chair. They were reprieved only because of a campaign but their case dragged through the courts and it was 1937 before the four youngest were released. It is bitterly ironic that, while the others suffered a more protracted fate, the four freed young men went straight into a variety act at Harlem's Apollo Theatre.

I don't know if that was at the back of the minds of Kander, Ebb and the book-writer, David Thompson, when they conceived the idea of a minstrel show, but it was an inspired choice. The essence of such shows was that white actors blacked up to reinforce African-American stereotypes. Here a company of Black actors, supervised by a white Interlocutor, reverse the process to reveal the rooted prejudice at the heart of The Scottsboro Boys' story. But it is the contrast between the jauntiness of the songs and the injustice suffered by the story's victims that is stunning. My favourite Kander-Ebb song, Southern Days, starts as a hymn to the stereotypical American South of mint julep and banjos and elides subversively into a chorus about "the fire that makes those crosses burn."

The big question is whether an entertainment show can arouse retrospective indignation. This one definitely does. The cast, including five from the original production, is exceptionally strong. Colman Domingo and Forrest McClendon have the vaudevillian bounce of Mr Bones and Mr Tambo, James T. Lane flounces amusingly as a confessional prostitute and Kyle Scatliffe has an overpowering presence as the most resilient of the incarcerated youths. As the sole white actor, Julian Glover as the Interlocutor also exudes a tainted authority.

What staggers me is that, although nominated for 12 Tony Awards, this dazzlingly daring show was defeated in virtually every category by *The*

Book of Mormon. It just goes to prove that in the world of showbiz, as in the American South of the 1930s, there ain't no justice.

Looking back at 50 years of The National Theatre which began its life at the Old Vic in October 1963.

19 October, 2013

"There is no such thing as Shakespeare's Hamlet," Oscar Wilde resonantly declared in *The Critic as Artist*. By that he meant that the role was defined by the personality of the actor. In a similar vein, I'd argue that there is no such thing as the National Theatre. That may seem an odd claim when Denys Lasdun's South Bank building is a concrete fact, when Rufus Norris has just been appointed as the next director and when we prepare to celebrate the 50th anniversary of the founding of a National Theatre company.

My point is that the National Theatre is as much a flexible concept as a permanent institution. It is also shaped by several factors. The cardinal ones are obviously the taste, temperament and talent of the people who run it. And even though four of its five directors – Peter Hall, Richard Eyre, Trevor Nunn and Nicholas Hytner – are Cambridge English graduates, there is still enormous diversity within that group. But I'd go further and argue that the National reflects the changing nation. The Britain of 2013 is a vastly different place from that of 1963; and, in tracing the trajectory of the NT over the past 50 years, one is inevitably drawn into examining the state of the country.

For all the ludicrous prevarications that attended the creation of a National Theatre, I'd say it was good timing that a company was finally formed, under the direction of Laurence Olivier, in 1963. It was a momentous year in myriad ways. There was a sense of an old order crumbling: the pathetic charade of the Profumo scandal, with its lies, evasions and hints of orgies in high-class places, made the British establishment into a laughing stock. But it was also a period of creative excitement: of, as Philip Larkin famously noted, the Beatles' first LP; of Joan Littlewood's *Oh, What A Lovely War*, which saw the 1914-18 conflict from the perspective of the common soldier; of a new view of the Cold War reflected in Le Carré's *The Spy Who Came in from the Cold*.

In short, the National Theatre company at the Old Vic kicked off in culturally expansive times. Olivier, who possessed the instincts of a paternalist actor-manager, also had the good sense to surround himself with younger lieutenants. His two resident directors, John Dexter and William Gaskill, were effectively poached from the Royal Court. His literary manager, Ken Tynan, was the most radical, internationalist critic of the day. And those early years at the Old Vic look, in retrospect, like something of a golden age. Olivier himself, in the days when few balked at the spectacle of a white man blacking up, burned up the stage as Othello. Old rep standbys, such as Coward's *Hay Fever* and Brighouse's *Hobson's Choice*, were intelligently re-discovered. New plays emerged in the shape of Peter Shaffer's ritualistic *The Royal Hunt of the Sun* and the far better *Black Comedy* in which Shaffer, borrowing a trick from Chinese theatre, reversed the patterns of light and dark.

Olivier made an excellent case for the National by showing us just what we had been missing: I remember being struck, on my first visit, by something as simple as the elegantly informative programmes. To his credit, Olivier also led a company brimming with young talent: the names of Michael (then Mike) Gambon, Derek Jacobi, Anthony Hopkins and Ronald Pickup leap out from the cast lists. But there was inevitably a downside to the early success. People noted that Olivier's great contemporaries, such as Ralph Richardson and John Gielgud, were conspicuous by their absence. And, when the company took over the New Theatre in the West End for a season in 1971, it began to look dangerously overstretched. I was one of the few critics who loved *Tyger*, a kaleidoscopic celebration of William Blake by Adrian Mitchell and Mike Westbrook. In the end, the company's dwindling reputation was restored only by Michael Blakemore's revival of O'Neill's *Long Day's Journey Into Night* in which Olivier gave a magisterial performance as James Tyrone. For a truly great actor to play a thespian might-have-been was a stunning achievement.

A corner had been decisively turned; and company credibility was given a boost with a string of hit productions at the Old Vic in 1972–3 including Stoppard's *Jumpers*, Moliere's *The Misanthrope* in a new Tony Harrison version and Shaffer's *Equus*. But, by then, it was too late. A combination of Olivier's poor health and a grumbling dissatisfaction with a string of failures at the New Theatre led to a search for a new director. And, at this point, the story gets somewhat murky. What seems to have happened is that the NT's chairman, Max Rayne, and that Richelieu of the London arts scene, Lord Goodman, sounded out Peter Hall as a successor to Olivier. Hall, sworn to secrecy, behaved perfectly honourably and said he would take over only with Olivier's consent. But, in the end, Olivier was confronted with a *fait accompli* and felt he had been stitched up. It's a situation that rankles to this day as is clear from a first-rate, two-part BBC Arena documentary (showing on BBC4 on 24 and 31 October) in which Joan Plowright (Lady Olivier) talks darkly of "treachery of the highest order."

It was no way to treat Olivier. It also meant that Hall took over in the worst possible circumstances. On the one hand, he formally succeeded Olivier in November 1973 when the country was in crisis: the economy was in free-fall because of rocketing oil prices and a succession of strikes meant there were limited fuel supplies. That led, early in 1974, to the imposition of a three-day working week. It was hardly the time to be talking of opening a new National Theatre, already in halting construction on the South Bank. As if that were not enough, Hall faced lingering resentment from some of Olivier's old associates and his initial 1974 season was a string of disappointing duds. I remember beginning one review with the words: "What on earth is going on at the National Theatre?" only to learn that the piece had been pinned up on a backstage noticeboard by internal sympathisers.

As so often happens in theatre, a single production transformed morale. Hall's own 1975 version of Ibsen's *John Gabriel Borkman*, with a stellar cast headed by Ralph Richardson and Peggy Ashcroft, had an icy brilliance; and it was swiftly followed by other successes including Shaw's *Heartbreak House*, Beckett's *Happy Days* and Pinter's *No Man's Land* with Richardson and Gielgud looking like two sides of the author's own subconscious. At least Hall had a bank of productions on which to draw when he began the arduous, stage-by-stage process of occupying the still-incomplete Lasdun-designed National Theatre in the spring of 1976.

Looking back, it is astonishing to recall the hostility that greeted the opening of the National. We had waited more than a century for it to be built. Now that it was finally there, the media constantly moaned about an unsustainable white elephant. Leading theatre professionals wrote angry letters to *The Times* complaining that it would denude them of writers, actors and technicians. And, as Michael Blakemore makes plain in his book *Stage Blood*, he was deeply critical of Hall: especially his alleged lack of collegiate policymaking and his preferential treatment of his own productions. What I think Blakemore misses is that the very qualities he so disliked in Hall – above all, his ambition, voracious energy and readiness to take independent decisions – were exactly those needed to get the National up and running. It could no longer be the kind of close-knit company over which Olivier patriarchally presided. It was now a massive, three-theatre operation opening at a time of national nervous breakdown.

My contention that the National Theatre reflects the character of its director is, however, borne out by Hall's 15-year tenure. There were many ups and downs, but Hall's National was characterised by its insatiable appetite for the new and its responsiveness to living writers. At the RSC, Hall had argued that the Shakespearean tradition could only be kept alive if it were challenged by new work. And at the National he didn't merely welcome established dramatists such as Pinter, Ayckbourn, Bond, Shaffer, Stoppard, Storey, Wesker, Gray and Frayn. He also championed the provocative young. In 1977, Stephen Poliakoff's *Strawberry Fields*, starring Jane Asher and Stephen Rea, provided an eerily prophetic portrait of fast-rising, quasi-fascist groups. In 1978, Hall nursed David Hare's *Plenty*, a fascinating analysis of postwar British decline, so that it found a growingly appreciative audience. And when Howard Brenton's *The Romans in Britain* in 1980 provoked Mary Whitehouse into launching a private prosecution against its director, Michael Bogdanov, Hall stood both by the play and its interpreters.

Hall's signal achievement was to make the National a natural home for new writing. He was also generous, despite Blakemore's criticism, in providing scope for other directors. Richard Eyre's 1982 production of *Guys and Dolls* not only put down a marker for the future but confirmed Frank Loesser's show as the most literate of 1950s Broadway musicals. Bill Bryden created a distinctive company within the National that, in 1985, brought together the three parts of *The Mysteries*, fashioned by Tony Harrison ("a Yorkshireman who came to read the metre") out of medieval craftsmen's plays and turning a predominantly secular audience into awayday Christians. And no one who saw it will ever forget Alan Ayckbourn's 1987 production of *A View from the Bridge* or Michael Gambon's titanic performance as a passion-fuelled Brooklyn longshoreman.

When Eyre took over the National in 1988 he faced very different challenges from those that confronted his predecessor. The country itself was bitterly polarised after nearly a decade of Thatcherite government. Internally, Eyre inherited an organisation that seemed to be running smoothly but that needed a bit of a shake-up: in particular, it had to make a more conscious effort to represent the nation at large. One of Eyre's least-remarked innovations was to promote women directors in a way Hall notably failed to do. During Eyre's reign, Deborah Warner, Katie Mitchell, Phyllida Lloyd, Di Trevis, Annie Castledine, Jenny Killick, Julia Bardsley, Fiona Laird, Brigid Larmour and Paulette Randall were among those who breached the idea of the National, directorially at least, as an exclusive male club.

But Eyre's success lay not merely in pursuing Hall's devotion to new writing. He also saw that the National was uniquely well placed, because of its resources, to address the state of the nation. This was most obvious in Hare's accumulating trilogy of *Racing Demon* (1990), *Murmuring Judges* (1991) and *The Absence of War* (1993). Hare's inspiration came partly from going to see an all-day RSC production of Shakespeare's history plays under the title of *The Plantagenets*. If Shakespeare could do it, why not a modern dramatist? The ambition was extraordinary. And, even if the central play became a bit of a legal soap, the outer two still resonate. Although ostensibly about the Anglican Church, *Racing Demon* really exposes the division inside any institution between fiery evangelicals, gradualist reformers and innate conservatives. And *The Absence of War*, underrated at the time, stands up as a prophetic vision of a Labour Party that realised it could only regain power by becoming more like the Tories.

Eyre also backed to the hilt Tony Kushner's *Angels in America*: a fantasia on political themes that embraced Aids, Mormonism, the approach of the Millennium, the growing power of both the right and the righteous in the supposed melting pot of the disunited States. Even if Eyre's National might have done more to redefine the classic repertory – though I do remember brilliant productions of Lope de Vega's *Fuente Ovejuna*, Sophie Treadwell's *Machinal* and Ernst Toller's *The Machine Wreckers* – it always seemed to be in touch with Britain as it actually was. And never more so than when Stephen Daldry turned Priestley's *An Inspector Calls* into a quasi-expressionist assault on the culture of individualistic greed that was Thatcher's toxic legacy.

Matters took a very different turn when Trevor Nunn became director of the NT in October 1997. But his five-and-a-half year tenure offers a perfect illustration of my point that the National is defined by the taste of its director and the tenor of the times. Nunn arrived at the National six months after Tony Blair took office and, exactly like the Labour leader, instantly pursued a policy of fiscal prudence. When I complained that straight runs of *Oklahoma!* in the Olivier and *The Prime of Miss Jean Brodie* in the Lyttelton were not what the National was created for, Nunn's emissaries told me it was necessary to balance the books. My counter-argument was that, even if caution dictated straight runs, a balance of *Hamlet* and *Rosencrantz and Guildenstern Are Dead*, for instance, would have made for a more ambitious programme.

I never questioned Nunn's credentials as a director: he did magnificent productions of *The Merchant of Venice*, *Summerfolk* and *Anything Goes* during his time at the National. His Stakhanovite workload was also impressive. But Nunn's two prime obsessions as a director are Shakespeare and musicals; and I still believe the latter occupied too much stage time. I was periodically accused of a vendetta against Nunn. That was totally untrue. My concern was simply that the National, in so closely reflecting Nunn's personal predilections, was losing sight of its duty to offer a spectrum of world drama. Good things happened under his watch, including Pinter's Proust adaptation, Pinter's own stunning revival of *No Man's Land* with John Wood and Corin Redgrave and the premiere of Nicholas Wright's *Vincent in Brixton*. But Daniel Rosenthal in his invaluable book, *The National Theatre Story*, objectively records that six musicals accounted for more than a fifth of South Bank attendance during Nunn's tenure. To some of us, that remains an alarmingly high proportion.

By the time Nicholas Hytner took over the National in April 2003, yet another redefinition of the institution became urgently necessary. For a start, with the arrival of a form of devolved government in Scotland and Wales, the whole question of "nationhood" was up in the air. Cultural diversity was also a more vital factor than it had been in the days when Olivier blacked up to play Othello. In addition, Britain was supporting an American invasion of Iraq based on the existence of presumed weapons of mass destruction. With all those factors in mind, it was an inspired idea for Hytner to choose *Henry V* as the first production he directed. Shakespeare's play is based on a legally questionable war, throws together English, Welsh, Scottish and Irish soldiers and sets them arguing about national identity and, in Hytner's version, they were led by the magnificent Adrian Lester who is a fine classical actor who happens to be Black. If ever there was a play for the moment, this was it.

Hytner was also shrewd enough to recognise that he was taking over the National at a time when not only Britain but the theatre itself was rapidly changing. While still adhering to the need to present a mix of classic and new work, he encouraged the National to co-produce immersive events with companies such as Punchdrunk and Shunt. He gave Katie Mitchell the chance to freely experiment with video-based work such as *Waves*, *Some Trace of Her* and *Attempts on Her Life*. A succession of plays by Kwame Kwei-Armah, Roy Williams and Ayub Khan-Din went some way to acknowledge the realities of a multicultural society. And in place of routine obeisance to Broadway's golden oldies, Hytner recognised the emergence of a new kind of music theatre with Tony Kushner's *Caroline, or Change* and the stunning *London Road* in which Adam Cork's score was based on the speech patterns of people interviewed by Alecky Blythe in the wake of serial murders in Ipswich.

Not everything has been pure gold: I've felt, in recent years, there was a nervousness about the great classics as if period plays by Marlowe or Goldsmith need to be gussied up with the aid of interpolated songs or hand-held cameras. And I know one or two actors feel that Hytner's National is too much a "director's theatre." But there have been some outstanding successes – *The History Boys*, *War Horse*, *One Man, Two Guvnors* – and two innovations of paramount importance. The first was the Travelex £10 (now £12) ticket scheme, which brought in new audiences and confirmed the truth of Peter Brook's dictum that "the future of theatre is cheap seats." Even more revolutionary is the development of NT Live, which broadcasts productions worldwide from the South Bank. At a stroke, this makes the best work instantly available and rescues the National (and other theatres as well) from the old charge that public subsidy is devoted to supporting the passion of a metropolitan elite.

Hytner has emerged as a pragmatic visionary who has not only made the National a source of debate – not least with a show like Hare's *Stuff Happens* – but who has also helped to change the process by which theatre is transmitted. I realise, of course, that in putting so much stress on Hytner and his predecessors, I am burying the huge contributions made by an army of supportive administrative and backstage staff. But I still believe the National does not exist in the abstract. It is defined by the character of its leaders and the temper of the times. Rufus Norris, when he takes over in April 2015, will inherit a bustling institution. But he – and one hopes that soon might be "she" – will also have to confront a lot of questions.

What is the job of the National Theatre? How can it truly represent a country that is now one of the most cosmopolitan on earth? Given the existence of the peripatetic National Theatre of Scotland and National Theatre Wales, is it effectively the National Theatre of England rather than of Great Britain? Are there still more ways in which new technology can be used to broaden its appeal?

The National may be 50 years old. It remains, however, an ongoing, evolving, gloriously uncompleted project whose future will be determined by a whole host of factors: by Norris's own strengths and weaknesses, by the quality of the team around him, by the vagaries of the British economy and, not least, by the mad unpredictability of society itself.

2014

Ellen Terry With Eileen Atkins. Adapted by Eileen Atkins (World Premiere) Sam Wanamaker Playhouse, London: 22 January 2014

Actors are often the sharpest judges of Shakespeare: a point proved by Ellen Terry, who in 1910 started touring a series of informal lecture-demonstrations on Shakespeare's characters. Eileen Atkins has now adapted them into a 75-minute show which offers the delirious pleasure of seeing one great actor inhabiting the mind and spirit of another.

Terry's constant theme is that Shakespeare's plays are a vindication of women, and that his female characters have more moral courage than his men. Her technique was to illustrate this through performance. It's something that Atkins, clad all in blue and sporting a gown that gives her the look of a dashing don, follows to the letter. She steers us from the serious wit of Beatrice ("At least I didn't make the mistake of being arch or skittish," said Terry) to the lyrical ardour of Rosalind and the compassionate cleverness of Portia, whose speech on "the quality of mercy" is here delivered with a quiet sincerity that justifies comparison with the Lord's Prayer.

But this remarkable evening is at its best when Atkins, following Terry, takes us into unexpected territory. She gives Mistress Page in *The Merry Wives of Windsor* a rough, semi-rural burr and, having proved Terry's point that Desdemona is no ninny, goes on to make the unflinching, outspoken Emilia the real heroine of *Othello's* final scenes. The two heart-stopping moments, however, come towards the end.

First Atkins, by widening her eyes and lightening her voice, recreates Juliet's terror at awakening in the family vault. She then goes on to play both a gruff-voiced Lear and a youthful Cordelia at the moment of their reunion: through the alchemy of acting, Atkins moves you to tears by her ability to inhabit both characters simultaneously. Once or twice, Terry's observations on Shakespeare betray their period: the idea, for instance, that Shylock gets no more than he deserves in *The Merchant of Venice*. But Terry had a fresh, questing intelligence that allowed her to characterise Lady Macbeth as "a delicate little creature with hypersensitive nerves" and to declare that, in acting, "it's imagination first and observation afterwards." That maxim is perfectly borne out by Atkins, who possesses not just an immaculate technique but an imagination that allows her effortlessly to transcend the limitations of age and gender. If the BBC does not instantly go and send a film crew to record this masterclass in the art of acting, I shall go and chain myself to the portals of Broadcasting House in protest.

King Charles III by Mike Bartlett (World Premiere) Almeida, London: 11 April 2014

Mike Bartlett has written a speculative play about the future of the monarchy. Even if based on a questionable premise, it eventually acquires a moral grandeur through its Shakespearean form and a tragic dimension through the performance of Tim Pigott-Smith.

Bartlett starts with the funeral of the present monarch and the accession to power of Charles, who proclaims, in the blank verse that is the play's dominant mode, "My life has been a ling'ring for the throne." But, even before he is crowned, he suffers a crisis of conscience. Formally asked to sign a bill restricting the freedom of the press, he refuses to give royal assent and thereby ignites a constitutional storm that brings the country to the brink of civil war. Meanwhile, his son Harry falls in love with a republican art student and begs to be allowed to become a commoner.

If I question the play's premise, it is for this reason. Although, as Prince of Wales, he has been famous for writing to ministers and scrutinising legislation, I cannot believe that within a month of becoming king Charles would be so naive as to seek to block a parliamentary bill. It is also a weakness that Bartlett never provides any details of the proposed press regulation. But, once we are past these hurdles, the action acquires an unstoppable momentum. There is also a what-if fascination to seeing how a future king might exercise long-dormant powers, invoke army support and leave the country bitterly divided.

Bartlett's makes greater use of Shakespearean resonances as it proceeds. There are echoes of *Macbeth* in the idea of Diana's ghost as an instrument of prophecy and by the end we are into *Richard II* territory with the prospect of usurpation. As happens in most plays about kingship, the beleaguered monarch even provokes a grudging sympathy. Isolated, insomniac and haunted by his mistakes, Charles turns from an abuser of his legitimate power into a desolate and cornered figure. It is all, of course, a fantasy, but it is one that raises fascinating questions about the future of the monarchy.

The casting of Pigott-Smith also gives the play weight and substance. He starts by deploying familiar Caroline mannerisms such as the nervous shooting of the cuffs and the rotating of his signet ring, but goes on to skilfully show us a man of principled anxiety who declares: "Without my voice and spirit, I am dust." Rupert Goold's production, played on a raised, empurpled dais, is also a model of dignified restraint and gets strong performances from Oliver Chris as a filially loyal William propelled into action by Lydia Wilson's feminist Kate. I couldn't believe any of it would happen. But at least the play has the courage to raise the all-important question of how much British support for the monarchy is a reflection of admiration for its current incumbent.

Khandan (*Family*) by Gurpreet Kaur Bhatti (World Premiere)
Birmingham Repertory Studio: 29 May 2014

Ten years ago, Gurpreet Kaur Bhatti's *Behzti* provoked angry protests that led to the play's premature withdrawal on the grounds of public safety. Now Bhatti is back in Birmingham with a piece about the tensions and tenacity of family life that not only got the warmest of receptions but that also says a lot about the peculiar predicaments facing British Asians.

Bhatti presents us with a Sikh family living comfortably in the suburbs. The widowed matriarch, Jeeto, who came to Britain in 1969, dreams of retiring to the Punjab and spending her final years on a sunlit verandah. But first she has to deal with her son, Pal, who wants to sell the thriving family store and set up a nursing home, even though he has insufficient capital. Pal and his British wife, Liz, also seem incapable of providing Jeeto with the grandchild she craves. And when Reema, the abandoned wife of a Punjabi cousin, turns up, she adds to the turbulent atmosphere of a family in which no one ever quite fulfils their hopes and desires.

Some of the plot points are a touch predictable and I couldn't work out why Pal's sister, who runs a tacky beauty parlour, was quite so unhappy. But Bhatti writes excellently about the double-edged nature of inheritance. For this family, it involves an ancestral attachment to the Punjabi land and the work ethic of previous generations; it also yields a pressure to procreate that is destructive to marriage, and brings obligations to distant relatives, such as Reema, that prove disruptive. Just as Bhatti shows family ties are both a blessing and a curse, she also creates complex characters: when you've decided Pal is a ruthlessly egotistic materialist, you learn that he bathed and tended the dying father whose thrifty values he has jettisoned.

Roxana Silbert's production, jointly presented by the Royal Court, nicely conveys the contradictions within this divided family, and there are good performances all round. Sudha Bhuchar is fierce and tender as domineering

Jeeto, who never stops reminiscing about how she cleaned toilets when she first came to Britain, and there is fine support from Rez Kempton as the reckless Pal, Lauren Crace as his child-hungry wife and Preeya Kalidas as the intrusive catalyst under this particular suburban roof. If the play prompted first-night demonstrations, it was only of hearty approval.

Wonderland by Beth Steel (World Premiere) Hampstead Theatre, London: 3 July 2014

Once identified with domestic drama, Hampstead Theatre has lately become the home of big public plays. After studies of the English Civil War and the partition of India, it now brings us Beth Steel's re-creation of the miners' strike of 1984; and what is impressive about Steel's play is that, while her emotional sympathies are with the miners, she also shows how they were totally outmanoeuvred by the Thatcher government.

Initially, the miners start with the advantage of a close-knit camaraderie: something vividly registered in Steel's portrait of a Nottinghamshire colliery where two squabbling apprentices are told never to forget that "down here, your life is always in another man's hands." In Whitehall, however, there is a visible tension between the energy secretary, Peter Walker, who wants graduated pit closures, and the more draconian Ian Macgregor, an American-Scottish industrialist brought in to run the National Coal Board.

As the 12-month strike drags on, however, we see the fracturing of the miners' unity and the solidifying of Government intransigence. Neither Arthur Scargill, the miners' leader, nor Margaret Thatcher appears in the play, but their presences are strongly felt. By failing to call a national ballot, Scargill leaves the way open for division within the coalfields: for her part, Thatcher plays a long game by stockpiling coal supplies and sanctioning an undercover agent to encourage the formation of a breakaway union. But the overwhelming impression left by Steel's play is of the unhealed scars left by the strike. Steel goes to great pains to show the physical danger of mining and the communal spirit it engenders. But there is an immense sadness to the way strikebreaking severs old friendships.

While the hyperrealism of Edward Hall's production and Ashley Martin-Davis's design, with its pit cage, is admirable, it means that clarity is initially sacrificed to activity. But individual dilemmas gradually emerge and there are strong performances all round. Paul Brennen as a pitman with a ferocious belief in the group ethic, Gunnar Cauthery as a reluctant strike-breaker, Andrew Havill as the emollient Walker and Dugald Bruce-Lockhart as the forgotten figure of David Hart, a Cowardesque smoothie deployed to subvert the miners' unity, are all excellent. What is remarkable is not only Steel's skill in resurrecting the divisions of the 1984 strike but also in showing the destruction of a proudly defiant community.

Ballyturk by Enda Walsh (World Premiere)
Black Box, Galway: 22 July 2014

There's plenty of ballyhoo around *Ballyturk*. Written and directed by Enda Walsh, and with a cast comprising Cillian Murphy, Stephen Rea and Mikel Murfi, it is the hottest ticket at this year's Galway International Arts Festival. And deservedly so, because it combines manic physical comedy with a meditation on the brevity of our earthly existence.

As so often in Walsh's plays the main characters inhabit a hermetic world – almost a womb without a view. In this case, they are two men, simply identified as One and Two, who pass the time in speeded-up, silent-comedy rituals and speculating about daily life in an imagined Irish town called Ballyturk. When the character Three turns up, he not only breaks up the partnership but invites one of the duo into the outer world, en route to inevitable extinction.

It is not the last surprise Walsh springs, but it is as if Beckett's Godot had unexpectedly materialised. The whole play could, in fact, be seen as an illustration of a potent Beckettian image: "They give birth astride of a grave." I was less struck by the play's philosophy than by its sheer physical and verbal exuberance. Much of it consists of a fantasy vision of Ballyturk's daily existence that makes astonishing demands on the two actors: at one point, Murphy leaps like a gazelle on to a high ledge to become the town's lager-sipping female storekeeper, while the more granite-jawed Murfi is called on to embody 17 characters in the space of about 30 seconds. Imagine *Under Milk Wood* interpreted by Buster Keaton and you get the picture.

With the arrival of Stephen Rea, as a cigarette-smoking *deus ex machina*, the writing acquires a poetic richness that matches its earlier physical mania. When he talks of the transient beauty of life – "for everything is here and we are here to lay down legacy" – the effect is strangely moving. There are a dozen other ways you could interpret the play; I even wondered if it was a dramatisation of the eternal dilemma of the writer creating imagined worlds while enduring partial seclusion.

However you analyse it, *Ballyturk* offers a richly theatrical experience and is impeccably acted. Cillian Murphy shows he's a formidable comic athlete, while Mikel Murfi reveals the mimetic skill of a graduate of the Lecoq theatre school in Paris, and Stephen Rea exudes a compellingly louche omniscience. The great thing is that it's a play you don't have to understand in order to enjoy.

The James Plays by Rona Munro
(World Premiere)
Festival Theatre, Edinburgh: 12 August 2014

"What's the news from Edinburgh?" asks a character in Rona Munro's trilogy. The good news is that the three plays about James I, II and III are a resplendent feather in the joint caps of their co-producers, the National Theatres of Scotland and Great Britain. They also confirm, not that one ever doubted it, that Sofie Grabol, who appears in the third play, is every bit as compelling a stage actor as her appearance in the TV series, *The Killing*, suggested.

The main thing to say about Munro's plays is that, while telling us a lot about Scottish history from 1421 to 1488, they are also full of topical resonance. You see this especially in the opening play, *The Key Will Keep the Lock*. It shows James Stewart, after being kept a prisoner by the English for 18 years, finally assuming the Scottish throne that is rightfully his. As he does so, James McArdle's wonderfully nervous king gives a speech to his aggressive nobles in which he pours scorn on England's financial predatoriness, claiming that a future Scotland "will be assaulted but it will never be broken." It's a good line that could easily be appropriated – and probably will be – by the SNP's Alex Salmond.

But Munro is too good a writer to be simply providing seven-and-a-half hours of nationalist propaganda. In many ways, she shows fifteenth-century Scotland as a place that was barely governable, with kings under constant threat from fractious feudal lords and national unity hard to achieve.

Very amusingly, Munro implies in the third play, *The True Mirror*, that some things haven't changed much. Grabol, as the Danish wife of the defecting James III, tells the Edinburgh parliament that she is ready to occupy the power vacuum, but denies any personal ambition. "Who," asks Margaret of Denmark, "would want the job of ruling Scotland?" The biggest laugh of the evening occurs when, looking directly at the audience, she adds: "You know the problem with you lot? You've got fuck-all except attitude." Even Alistair Darling wouldn't dare go that far.

These are unequivocally plays for today. If I quote extensively from the first and third, it is because the middle one – *Day of the Innocents* – lacks something of their political urgency and emotional intensity. It focuses on the traumatic inheritance of James II, who became king aged six, had a fearful childhood and relied heavily on his companion, William Douglas. But the Douglases were an ambitious, throne-threatening lot and in the second part of the play we see Andrew Rothney's newly confident king savagely turning on the treacherous, two-faced William.

"A king has no friends," says James II. And one theme that emerges strongly from Munro's trilogy, as it does from the history plays of Shakespeare and Schiller, is the inescapable solitude of monarchy and the loneliness of power. That's why you nearly always end up feeling a measure of sympathy for a theatrical king. It is also why one of the best scenes in the whole trilogy occurs early on, when James I only gets to meet his arranged bride, Joan Beaufort, at their formal wedding ceremony. Played by McArdle and Stephanie Hyam, it is an immensely touching picture of two young people tentatively getting to know themselves and each other.

Throughout, Munro skilfully interweaves the personal and the political, something that you see clearly in the final play where the gift of a full-length Venetian mirror by Jamie Sives's rackety James III to his separated queen affects both private lives and public attitudes. Grabol is both sexy and funny as she gazes at herself in the mirror declaring: "I like this woman." But later, she crucially uses the mirror's power to demoralise the king's young mistress and thereby hasten the destabilisation of the kingdom.

I have left little space to praise Laurie Sansom's production, which constantly propels the action forward and even camouflages the odd moment of stasis in the second play. Jon Bausor has also devised a striking design dominated by a firmly embedded giant sword shaped like a cross, which reminds one of the omnipresent violence in fifteenth-century Scotland. And aside from the actors mentioned, there is fine work from Blythe Duff as a power-hungry Stewart, Peter Forbes as the land-grabbing senior Douglas and Mark Rowley as his devious son – who even plays dirty at football where an opponent gets bitten on the neck. That, if nothing else, confirms Munro's trilogy is very much in touch with the living present.

Gypsy. Book by Arthur Laurents, Music by Jule Styne, Lyrics by Stephen Sondheim
Chichester Festival Theatre: 16 October 2014

If proof were needed of the power of the traditional Broadway musical play, one need look no further than *Gypsy* (1959). Composer Jule Styne, lyricist Stephen Sondheim and book-writer Arthur Laurents are partners in a coalition of equals that has one overriding aim: to tell the tragi-comic story of Momma Rose, whom Sondheim called a "showbiz Oedipus."

Momma Rose's flaw is self-delusion: she believes she can turn a terrible family act into headliners on the vaudeville circuit of the 1920s and 1930s and achieve a surrogate fame through her daughter, June. The ironic twist is that it is June's sister, Louise, who gives Rose a vicarious glimpse of stardom, by becoming the celebrated stripper, Gypsy Rose Lee. It's a good story that views the iron mother with a persistent ambivalence, and Styne's score and Sondheim's lyrics preserve a perfect balance between passion and pastiche, self-revelatory solos blending with a glorious evocation of the tackiness of American vaudeville.

The specific joy of this production is that it reunites Imelda Staunton with Jonathan Kent, who directed her so memorably in *Sweeney Todd*; and the first thing to say about Staunton's Momma Rose is that it is a superb piece of acting. With her piratical hat and bustling gait, Staunton captures all of the character's determined jauntiness. But it is in the two big arias that close each act that Staunton shows her hand. In Everything's Coming Up Roses, Staunton displays a rhapsodic, teeth-baring glee only just this side of mania, and in Rose's Turn, in which she mimics the kind of striptease that has made Louise a burlesque star, she suggests a woman on the verge of a nervous breakdown.

I found Kevin Whately a touch dour as Rose's long-time lover, but Lara Pulver as Louise graduates immaculately from the overlooked sibling to the coldly calculating stripper. Georgia Pemberton, one of two youngsters playing Baby June, gives an astonishingly assured display of bright-eyed precociousness. Everything about Kent's production slots perfectly into place. Anthony Ward's design uses a false proscenium arch to remind us how the characters' lives are confined by theatre; Stephen Mear's choreography, especially in the elbow-jutting Together Wherever We Go, pays hymn to the showbiz past; and Nicholas Skilbeck's pit band has a magnificent, brassy ring. We go to modern musicals seeking sensory stimulus. Gypsy shows that the form, at its best, can also be an exploration of character.

2015

Oppenheimer by Tom Morton-Smith
(World Premiere)
The Swan, Stratford-upon-Avon:
23 January 2015

"Oppenheimer's stature is not in question, but do we have a playwright big enough to depict him?" That was the question posed by critic Eric Bentley in 1969. The answer has been found in the shape of Tom Morton-Smith, a 34-year-old dramatist with a handful of fringe credits, who has come up with this massively impressive three-hour play for the RSC: one that shows the father of the atomic bomb and leader of America's Manhattan Project to be a genuinely tragic hero.

Oppenheimer's tragedy, in Morton-Smith's version, takes many forms. The most obvious is that this visionary scientist, who led the team that created the bombs released on Hiroshima and Nagasaki, had to live with the moral consequences of his discoveries: "I feel," he says, "like I've dropped a loaded gun in a playground." But Oppenheimer is also tragic in that his espousal of communism in the 1930s forces him, once he is employed by the US military, to either abandon or, in the case of the academic Haakon Chevalier, betray his former colleagues. And, in terms of his own nature, Oppenheimer is a man in whom professional pride is accompanied by "a core of cold iron."

What is striking is the panoramic sweep of a play that explores big issues through character and action. Starting in 1934, Morton-Smith alternates scenes showing the anti-fascist fervour of the American left with others exploring theoretical physics. One of the play's signal virtues is its ability to convey the intoxicating excitement of the initial experiments at Berkeley: the chain reaction that follows when a neutron splits an atom is explained with a clarity that even a lay audience can understand. But Morton-Smith never loses sight of Oppenheimer's mix of missionary zeal and personal detachment: he swaps lovers as casually as if changing suits and, when recruited by the military to work on the Manhattan Project at Los Alamos, sheds his communist past like a snake sloughing its skin.

Morton-Smith neither eulogises nor condemns Oppenheimer: he simply shows him as a flawed human being aware that he has the scientific capacity "to murder every last soul on the planet." I also can't imagine him being better played than by John Heffernan, whom the role elevates to star-status. This is no portrayal of the scientist as crazed genius. Instead Heffernan, with his hooded, Mitchumesque eyes and wary gaze, shows us a man who always seems isolated in a crowd. Heffernan also captures perfectly Oppenheimer's mix of social unease and professional ego, not least in his angry confrontations with Edward Teller, obsessed with pursuing the possibilities of a hydrogen bomb. It's a performance that brings out the complexity of a man, forever haunted by the destructive power of his achievement.

Angus Jackson's production catches the propulsive excitement of a play that takes us from a Berkeley campus to a Pacific airbase and Robert Innes Hopkins's design, with the aid of overhead girders, even brings on stage the bomb – the so-called Fat Man – about to be dropped on Nagasaki. And, in a large cast, there are outstanding performances from Jamie Wilkes as Oppenheimer's most loyal subordinate, Catherine Steadman as his flaky lover, Ben Allen as the arrogant Teller and William Gaminara as the poker-backed General Groves. The result is the most fascinating play about the moral issues surrounding nuclear physics since Michael Frayn's *Copenhagen*.

The Hard Problem by Tom Stoppard (World Premiere) Dorfman, National Theatre, London: 29 January 2015

Tom Stoppard famously uses drama to explore problems, and in his absorbing new play he tackles some pretty momentous ones. How does consciousness come about? Is our identity the product of what Francis Crick calls "a vast assembly of nerve cells"? And how much is human behaviour the product of egoism or altruism? Although there is almost too much to take in at a single 100-minute sitting, the competing arguments always have a strong emotional underpinning.

Stoppard starts with the advantage of a vibrant central character, Hilary, who when we first meet her is a psychology student at Loughborough university. Having got a coveted research post at a swanky brain science institute, she is free to conduct experiments on adult motivation and to sanction others on child behaviour patterns. But Hilary herself is unusual in many ways: she has a hidden longing for the child she bore when she was 15 and gave up for adoption, and she prays to God, to the evident scorn of the brilliant scientific minds that surround her.

So what is Stoppard up to? Through the character of Hilary, he is suggesting consciousness cannot be explained in purely mechanistic terms and that there are intrinsic values that depend on an overall moral intelligence. In previous plays such as *Professional Foul* and *The Coast of Utopia*, Stoppard has implied that those values are instinctively to be found in children. It is significant that Hilary is partly driven by a thwarted love for an absent child. Even more striking are the limitations of the scientific materialists around her – in particular her occasional lover, Spike, who seems phenomenally clever but deficient in a sense of beauty, and the moneyman behind the institute who might best be described as a hard-hearted philanthropist. Although the play occasionally suffers from information overload, it is still a rich, ideas-packed work that offers a defence of goodness whatever its ultimate source. The play also works because we are made to care about Hilary, who is excellently played by Olivia Vinall. She brings out every facet of a woman who is altruistic, questing and vulnerable and who asks all the right questions even if she doesn't know all the answers. She is strongly supported by Jonathan Coy as her anxiety-ridden department boss; Damien Molony as her armour-plated lover; Vera Chok as her dazzling protege; and Anthony Calf as a financial titan wrestling with the unpredictability of the markets. Nicholas Hytner, in his final production as the National's head, directs with the stylistic clarity that has long been his trademark and Bob Crowley's design skilfully evokes the labyrinthine complexity of the human brain.

Stoppard's play may not solve the hard problem of human consciousness. But it offers endless stimulation and represents, like so much of his work, a search for absolute values and a belief in the possibility of selfless virtue. For all his reputation as a cerebral writer, Stoppard has always possessed a strong faith in the power of the irrational.

Nicholas Hytner's 12-year-reign as Director of the National Theatre from 2003 to 2015.

10 March 2015

When Nicholas Hytner took over the National Theatre in 2003, it felt like an institution settling into comfortable middle-age. After making some critical remarks about the pre-Hytner regime, I remember being taken to lunch by the then executive director. I told her I didn't quite know what the National stood for any more. "Funny you should say that," she replied. "We ask ourselves that question, too."

Hytner didn't mess around in seeking to answer it. Right from his opening press conference, he made it clear his mission was to define what the words "national" and "theatre" meant in twenty-first-century Britain. Any National worthy of its name obviously had to do more, through play-choice and casting, to embody the idea of diversity. Since Hytner's first season included new plays by Kwame Kwei-Armah and Roy Williams, and his final one has boasted two epic works on Asian themes, *Behind the Beautiful Forevers* and *Dara*, he has clearly dented the idea that the South Bank complex is the exclusive property of the white middle class.

More controversial has been Hytner's attempt to redefine what we mean by "theatre." His point was that dance theatre, music theatre, devised theatre and physical theatre were now challenging the supremacy of the solo-authored play. Hence, over the years, Hytner's National has played host to a variety of companies including Complicité, Kneehigh, Improbable Theatre and DV8. The results have been artistically mixed. But it says a lot about the changing times that two of the biggest popular hits of the Hytner years have been shows in which text is only one feature of a total theatrical experience: *War Horse* and *The Curious Incident of the Dog in the Night-Time*.

Hytner also made two structural changes that will leave a massive legacy. The first is NT Live, which initially transmitted plays from the South Bank to 80 screens in the UK. The number is now around 500, with many more abroad. It's the most revolutionary thing to have happened in theatre in my lifetime and I'm not sure we have yet grasped all its implications. Clearly, it gives virtually everyone access to the National's work and thereby reinforces the case for subsidy. NT Live has also become a facility that broadcasts work from other houses, including the Young Vic and the Donmar. The question yet to be faced is this: if it is cheaper, easier, more comfortable, and sometimes even aesthetically preferable, to watch plays transmitted on a screen, will the day come when the number of people going to a live performance starts to dwindle? Already, I see that a decline in audiences at New York's Metropolitan Opera is being blamed on the success of their live broadcasts.

One way to get people in, of course, is to make theatre affordable, which Hytner has done through the £15 ticket scheme (sponsored by Travelex). As long as I can remember, people have been talking about the issue: over two decades ago, I heard Peter Brook, in a talk at the Donmar, say: "The future of the theatre is cheap seats." Hytner, partly through cutting production costs and changeover-times for expensive sets, has made it happen. Where the National led, others have automatically followed.

But if Hytner has restored the National's sense of purpose, it is mainly through the work – more particularly, through the idea that the National should not leave comment on the big issues of the day to newspapers and TV. So we've had plays about Iraq (*Stuff Happens*), the financial crisis (*The Power of Yes*), climate change (*Greenland*), immigration (*England People Very Nice*) and press and police corruption (*Great Britain*). Clearly, the National is not alone in seeing itself as a forum for debate: two Royal Court shows about environmental catastrophe – *Ten Billion* and *2071* – knocked spots off the muddled and incoherent *Greenland*. But I don't know of any comparable theatre on the continent, certainly not the Comédie Française, that feels a need to tackle the headline crises affecting our daily lives.

Given the overall success of the Hytner years, what have been the areas of failure? A colleague suggested he has not done enough to promote women dramatists in the way that his successor, Rufus Norris, palpably plans to do. I'm not sure the charge is entirely fair. Rebecca Lenkiewicz' *Her Naked Skin*, Moira Buffini's *Welcome to Thebes* and Alecky Blythe's *London Road* were all seen in the Olivier; Tena Stivicic's *3 Winters* has just closed in the Lyttelton; and Lucy Prebble, Lucy Kirkwood and Tanya Ronder all had work produced in smaller spaces. Women directors – including Marianne Elliott, Katie Mitchell, Thea Sharrock, Polly Findlay, Melly Still, Josie Rourke, Nadia Fall and Emma Rice – have also done enough at the National to disprove the idea that the Hytner regime has been exclusively blokey.

A more serious accusation is that the classic repertory has not been sufficiently refreshed. We've had some notable Shakespeares (*Henry V*, *Othello*, *Hamlet*, *King Lear*, *Timon of Athens*), an occasional Jacobean or Restoration comedy (*The Alchemist*, *The Man of Mode*) and, thanks largely to director Howard Davies, some outstanding Russian plays (*Philistines*, *The White Guard*). Hytner even learned to overcome his aversion to Shaw. But, when I put it to Hytner last year that the classic repertory had not had enough attention, he said: "You'd be amazed at the number of planning meetings I've chaired where I've said, 'Will no one do *The School for Scandal*?'" If directors have to be bullied or browbeaten into doing Sheridan, that suggests a cultural problem that extends far beyond the South Bank.

But no national theatre can ever meet all expectations. In a time of national crisis, Hytner hasn't just kept the show on the road – he has expanded the possibilities. He has managed to retain the loyalty of an older generation of dramatists, including Alan Bennett, Tom Stoppard, David Hare and Howard Brenton, while embracing their successors such as Mike Bartlett, David Eldridge and Rebecca Lenkiewicz. He has got away from the kind of stereotyped thinking about the musical that, within a single year under the previous regime, gave us revivals of *My Fair Lady* and *South Pacific*; instead, he has provided shows as richly diverse as *London Road*, *Caroline or Change*, and *Fela!*. And, in purely physical terms, Hytner leaves behind an enlarged space with the newly opened Clore Learning Centre.

I'm not claiming he's St Nicholas. I know some older supporters who crave more classics. I also know some disgruntled actors who feel the talent pool has not been sufficiently widened. But set aside the grumbles and one can say the Hytner years have been exciting and provocative. In fact, I'd go even further. I'd say Hytner has done more than anyone since Peter Brook and Peter Hall in the 1960s and 1970s to change the face of British theatre. His advocacy of cheap seats and of live broadcasts will, I believe, be viewed by future historians as a major cultural turning point: the moment the National became a theatre for the nation and all the pious talk about reaching out to a new audience became a living reality.

Lampedusa by Anders Lustgarten
(World Premiere)
Soho Theatre, London: 17 July 2015

British theatre is full of plays about domestic politics. What makes Anders Lustgarten exceptional is that he thinks globally. After plays about Turkey's Roboski massacre (*Shrapnel*) and post-Mugabe Zimbabwe (*Black Jesus*), he now turns his attention to mass migration. But part of the power of this piece, his best yet, is that it links a subject of international importance to our own society.

Lustgarten achieves this through two interwoven monologues. One comes from Stefano, a former Italian fishermen who tells us "the Med is dead" and who now earns a living salvaging the bodies of migrants who have died making the perilous boat journey from north Africa to Italy. But Stefano's terrifying story – and last year more than 3,500 refugees drowned in the Med – is complemented by that of Denise. She is a mixed-race Chinese-British student who is financing her Leeds degree course by acting as a debt collector for a payday loan company. Forever an outsider in Britain, she claims the Chinese are "the last ones it's OK to hate."

Poverty and desperation are the themes. But what is striking is Lustgarten's ability to treat them not as lofty abstractions but to give them a concrete reality. He has clearly done his homework and writes with gripping precision about the fate of dead migrants as they drown in cold water. Handling their corpses, as Stefano graphically tells us, "is like oiled, lumpy rubbish bags sliding through your fingers." But Denise gives us an equally vivid account of how her 58-year-old sick mother is subjected to a work capability assessment, and how all the things people do to make a good impression, such as dressing well, are used as an excuse to deprive them of benefits.

Lustgarten draws instructive parallels between Stefano and Denise. Both are dealing with people in extremity. Both express the view that Europe is fucked. But, far from being a 65-minute litany of despair, Lustgarten's play is about the survival of hope. Stefano is befriended by a mechanic from Mali eagerly awaiting the arrival of his wife; and, in her own crisis, Denise finds a sympathetic companion in a debt-ridden Portuguese single mother.

Lustgarten's whole point is that systemic disaster is countered by individual kindness and, in the play's balance of opposites, I was reminded of something Harold Pinter said in his final TV interview: "I think that life is beautiful but the world is hell." That contradiction is very well caught in Steven Atkinson's production, presented in conjunction with the Hightide festival and Unity theatre, Liverpool. Played in the round on Lucy Osborne's bare, wooden stage, it allows the words and the acting to do the work. Ferdy Roberts as Stefano captures all the anger and resentment of a man who, even in his dreams, is haunted by death, yet who somehow struggles on and who is finally overwhelmed by a gesture of friendship. Louise Mai Newberry similarly conveys the wounded bitterness of the spat-upon outsider but also a willingness to surrender to an act of unexpected charity.

In a short play, Lustgarten has no room to explore the practical question of how European society balances its moral obligation to asylum seekers with its own economic problems. But Lustgarten in this brave, bold and moving play tackles the subject of mass migration seriously and, just as in *Shrapnel* he reminded us that bombs kill people, he here shows that behind the horrendous statistics of drowned refugees or scare stories in the press about supposed benefit scroungers lie tragic individual lives.

The Trial by Nick Gill based on the novel by Franz Kafka
Young Vic, London: 28 June 2015

Someone must have had it in for Michael B. He was dozing peacefully at home when a knock came at the door. Two men appeared telling him he had to attend a new production of Kafka's *The Trial*. "But I've done nothing wrong," he protested. "I've seen Steven Berkoff's version on stage. I've also seen a film directed by Orson Welles and another written by Harold Pinter." He was forcefully told that was not enough. This time everything would be radically different.

Watched by his guards, he arrived at the theatre to find a crowd excitedly milling around. To get to the auditorium people were led down long corridors and admitted through keyhole-shaped doors. Once inside, Michael B was seated on a judicial bench and at first astonished by what he saw. As his guards had promised, this looked like no other version of *The Trial*. The designer, Miriam Buether, had constructed a travelator that bisected the theatre and that whisked us from Josef K's bedroom to the bank where he worked and labyrinthine legal offices. Michael B was perplexed that the opening image was of Josef K watching a scantily-clad lap dancer but, as Nick Gill's adaptation unfolded, he began to recognise scenes from the novel. Only the names of the people had been changed.

Michael B was intrigued and puzzled: everything seemed familiar but, at the same time, oddly unreal. Rory Kinnear was brilliant as Josef K. He had a look of thickset normality yet, left alone, spoke a strange, dislocated language ("ee musten trial focus") that seemed like a mix of James Joyce and Stanley Unwin. Kinnear was never off stage and mesmerisingly showed a man reduced to desperation as he tried to find out why he had been arrested and with what crime he was charged.

If Kinnear was a modern everyman, Kate O'Flynn was equally remarkable as the various women – including Rosa who occupied an adjacent flat and the lap-dancing Tiffany – who haunted his imagination. But, as two hours passed without a break, Michael B began to feel a nervous sense of guilt. Why was his initial delight turning to faint boredom? Was it because Kafka's novel, as Harold Bloom once said, was better in parts than as a whole? Or was it because Gill's stress on Josef K's sexual peccadilloes, as the character tried to recall his past sins, was strangely limiting? Michael B remembered that Kafka was critical of Freudian ideas and had called psychoanalysis "a helpless error." But Gill, by suggesting that Josef K was simply a heightened version of *l'homme moyen sensuel*, seemed to undercut the prophetic power of the novel. Wasn't this a book that Primo Levi said predicted the time when it was a crime simply to be a Jew and that others saw as an eerily accurate anticipation of communist bureaucracy?

Michael B became sweatily anxious. He knew this was a prestige production. He recognised the visual bravura of Richard Jones as a director. He was in awe of Mr Kinnear and impressed by his fellow-performers including Sian Thomas as a svelte lawyer and Steven Beard as a scruffy magistrate. Yet, clutching the side of his seat, Michael B found himself waiting for the evening to end and wondering why he had got more pleasure from the staging of Kafka's short stories. Was the fault in him or in the concept of adapting *The Trial*? Like everyone else, he applauded the performance loudly but wondered if others secretly shared his guilt. Ashamed and uncertain, he slunk away to die like a dog.

Hamlet by William Shakespeare
Barbican, London: 26 August 2015

After all the hype and hysteria, the event itself comes as an anticlimax. My initial impression is that Benedict Cumberbatch is a good, personable Hamlet with a strong line in self-deflating irony, but that he is trapped inside an intellectual ragbag of a production by Lyndsey Turner that is full of half-baked ideas. Denmark, Hamlet tells us, is a prison. So too is this production.

What makes the evening so frustrating is that Cumberbatch has many of the qualities one looks for in a Hamlet. He has a lean, pensive countenance, a resonant voice, a gift for introspection. He is especially good in the soliloquies. "To be or not to be," about which there has been so much kerfuffle, mercifully no longer opens the show: I still think it works better if placed after, rather than before, the arrival of the players, but Cumberbatch delivers it with a rapt intensity. He is also excellent in "What a piece of work is a man" and has the right air of self-doubt: in the midst of his advice to the First Player on how to act, he suddenly says "but let your own discretion be your tutor," as if aware of his presumption in lecturing an old pro.

It is a performance full of good touches and quietly affecting in Hamlet's final, stoical acceptance of death. The problem is that Cumberbatch, rather like the panellists in *I'm Sorry I Haven't A Clue*, is given a lot of silly things to do. He actually opens the show, sitting in his room poring over a family album and listening to the gramophone, which denies us the propulsive excitement of the Ghost's first entries on the battlements. Later, in assuming an "antic disposition," Cumberbatch tries on a Native American headdress and then settles for parading around in the scarlet tunic and peaked helmet of a nineteenth-century infantryman. At one point he even drags on a miniature fortress – where on earth did he find it? – from which he proceeds to take potshots at the court.

Whimsical absurdity replaces genuine equivocation about Hamlet's state of mind and the effect is not improved by having him later strut about Elsinore in a jacket brazenly adorned on its back with the word "KING." All this is symptomatic of an evening in which the text is not so much savagely cut as badly wounded and yet which crudely italicises what remains. A classic example comes in the inept staging of the normally infallible play scene.

The whole focus should be on Claudius's reaction to this mimetic representation of his murder and Hamlet's eagle-eyed observation of his uncle. Instead, Turner starts the scene with the spectators in shadow and their backs to the audience. Even when they turn round to face us, Turner has Cumberbatch himself act out the lines of the villainous Lucianus. In consequence, Claudius's abrupt departure seems less the product of residual guilt than a hasty response to Hamlet's rude intervention.

The real problem, I suspect, is that visual conceits have taken the place of textual investigation. Es Devlin is a fine designer, but she and Turner have succumbed to the kind of giantism that marked their recent collaboration on *Light Shining In Buckinghamshire* at the National, which was rather like seeing Samuel Beckett reimagined by Cecil B. DeMille. Here, Devlin has created a massive permanent set in which Elsinore resembles a decadent, baroque palace filled with wrought-iron balconies and Winterhalter portraits. I remember a similar design for a visiting Romanian production, but where that evoked the sleazy opulence of the Ceausescu period, this one falls apart in more blatant fashion. In the second half, the palatial set is filled with mounds of rubbish and overturned chairs, just in case we'd missed the point about Claudius's collapsing tyranny.

One or two effects are striking, such as the gale-force torrent of leaves that invades Elsinore at the end of the protracted first half. But that is no substitute for the exploration of relationships. To take the most obvious example, just who are Claudius and Gertrude? For a couple supposedly bound together by reckless sensuality, Ciarán Hinds and Anastasia Hille show a remarkable lack of interest in each other and suggest nothing so much as a frigidly elegant pair used to giving cocktail parties in the Surrey hinterland.

Aside from Cumberbatch, there is only a handful of interesting performances. Leo Bill's Horatio is a stalwart, backpacking chum, Jim Norton makes Polonius an anxious fusspot who even reads out his carefully prepared advice to Laertes, and Sian Brooke is a genuinely disturbed Ophelia, with an equal devotion to Hamlet and the piano. But it says much about the evening that its single most memorable moment is a purely visual one: Ophelia's scrambling final exit over a hill of refuse, watched by an apprehensive Gertrude.

I am not against radical new approaches to Shakespeare. But this production does nothing more than reheat the old idea that Hamlet is the victim of a corrupt tyranny and is full of textual fiddling. To take one tiny example, Gertrude here tells us that Ophelia drowned herself where a willow "shows his pale leaves in the glassy stream" as if we were too dumb to work out the meaning of the original text's descriptive epithet, "hoar."

The pity of it is that Cumberbatch could have been a first-rate Hamlet. He is no mere screen icon, but a real actor with a gift for engaging our sympathy and showing a naturally rational mind disordered by grief, murder and the hollow insufficiency of revenge. He reminds me, in fact, of a point wittily made by George Eliot in *The Mill on the Floss* that, if his father had only lived to a good old age, Hamlet might have got through life with "a reputation of sanity, notwithstanding many soliloquies and some moody sarcasms towards the fair daughter of Polonius." Cumberbatch, in short, suggests Hamlet's essential decency. But he might have given us infinitely more, if he were not imprisoned by a dismal production that elevates visual effects above narrative coherence and exploration of character.

Hangmen by Martin McDonagh
(World Premiere)
Royal Court, London: 21 September 2015

Martin McDonagh has lost none of his power to shock. After more than a decade since his last London premiere with *The Pillowman* (2003), he returns with a savagely black comedy that reminds us it is exactly 50 years since the end of hanging in England, Wales and Scotland. But the question his play poses is whether the professional need to kill, with its potential for injustice, can be abandoned overnight.

The bulk of the action, after a brief prologue showing a judicial execution, takes place in 1965 in an Oldham pub belonging to Harry Wade. As a former deputy to the official hangman, Albert Pierrepoint, Harry is a local celebrity who attracts a gang of bar-room cronies, and who unwisely gives a newspaper interview bragging of his past prowess. But, when Harry's daughter goes missing, he begins to suspect a brash young visitor from London, Mooney, may be involved.

It would be criminal to say more, but the play reveals all of McDonagh's talent for eclectic playfulness. Mooney, who describes himself as "vaguely menacing," is a cryptic piss-taker strongly reminiscent of Lenny in Pinter's *The Homecoming*, which first appeared in 1965. Mooney's presence also introduces a whole string of metropolitan gibes which remind us of the 1960s vogue for movies and novels set in the north of England.

Above all, the play invokes a world where capital punishment camouflaged serious miscarriages of justice. Matthew Dunster's superb production matches McDonagh's mix of dark laughter and fearsome excitement, Anna Fleischle's pub set has just the right smoky fug, and there are pitch-perfect performances from Johnny Flynn as the cocky intruder, David Morrissey as the arrogant ex-hangman, Reece Shearsmith as his creepy assistant and Bronwyn James as his shy daughter. It makes for a compelling evening that confirms McDonaghs's prodigal, pluralist talent.

Tribute to playwright Brian Friel: born 9 January 1929, died 2 October 2015.

3 October 2015

Brian Friel, who has died aged 86, was the finest Irish dramatist of his generation. His work covered a wide variety of themes: exile and emigration, the political Troubles of Northern Ireland, the subjective nature of memory. But Friel's diverse output, spanning a 50-year period, was bound together by his passion for language, his belief in the ritualistic nature of theatre and his breadth of understanding.

Not surprisingly Chekhov, whose work he often translated, was the biggest influence on him as a dramatist. Having started as an accomplished short-story writer, Friel was alerted to the possibilities of theatre by spending two months in 1963 watching the great Irish director Tyrone Guthrie at work in Minneapolis. That led directly to one of his most innovative plays, *Philadelphia, Here I Come!* (1964), in which he gives voice to the alter ego of a young man about to leave small-town Ireland for the joys of America: a stock situation is given vivid new life by showing the public caution and private fantasies of the split-level hero.

Although Friel was always fascinated by the Irish dream of escape, he also responded directly to the Northern political crisis. People tend to forget now that in 1973 he wrote *The Freedom of the City* which was an expression of outrage at the whitewash of the Widgery tribunal, which effectively exculpated the British paratroopers who killed 13 unarmed civilians in a march in Derry that became known as Bloody Sunday.

Friel pursued his preoccupation with public issues in *Volunteers* (1975) in which a group of political prisoners agree to work on the erection of a corporate monstrosity on a valuable archaeological site. But, never a writer to be pigeonholed, he changed direction in 1979 with *Faith Healer* which many consider to be his greatest play. Comprising four monologues for three characters, it offers different angles on the story of an itinerant healer who returns to his native Ireland to restore his failing powers. This was as clear a statement as the interview-shy Friel ever made about the dilemma of the writer, always dependent on the accident of inspiration and never sure whether an artistic gift was a curse or a blessing.

In 1980 Friel joined forces with Stephen Rea to found Field Day with the intention to tour plays that responded to Northern Irish violence and eventually to publish anthologies of Irish writing. This led to a number of very fine Friel plays including *Translations* (1980), which explored the use of language as an instrument of colonial power, and *Making History* (1988) which dealt with a Gaelic revolt against British power in the sixteenth century and showed how the interpretation of history is conditioned by the needs of the present.

Moving away from Field Day, Friel proceeded to write a number of more personal plays about myth and memory. The most internationally popular was *Dancing at Lughnasa* (1990), based on Friel's own recollection of five Irish sisters who at one point unforgettably overcome the repressions of their rural existence to break out into an ecstatic pagan dance. In *Molly Sweeney* (1994) Friel, who was suffering from eyesight problems, wrote a haunting play that records its heroine's terrified journey from blindness to partial sight. A bit dismissive of the play when it first appeared, I still treasure a postcard from Friel expressing his surprised delight that I had undergone a change of heart on seeing it revived in 2013.

On top of his original work, Friel did a beautiful adaptation of Turgenev's *Fathers and Sons*, translated most of Chekhov's major plays and dramatised many of his short stories. He was always understandably in thrall to the Russian master. But his great achievement was that, in a vast variety of plays, he explored the condition of Ireland and embodied the idea of theatre as a vital secular ritual.

Elf the Musical. Book by Thomas Meehan and Bob Martin, Lyrics by Chad Beguelin, Music by Matthew Sklar (UK Premiere) Dominion, London: 6 November 2015

What do you call it when an elf takes a snapshot of himself? An elfie. Where does an elf go shopping for nutritious food? An elf store. Who was the most famous elf pop-singer of all time? Elfish Presley.

I should make clear these terrible jokes do not appear in this musical version of the much-loved 2003 movie starring Will Ferrell. They are emphatically not the work of Thomas Meehan and Bob Martin, who wrote the show's book, of Chad Beguelin who did the lyrics or Matthew Sklar who composed the music. The jokes simply popped into my head as a way of diverting myself from the musical's predictable plot and as a defence mechanism against its carefully calibrated Christmassy charm. I don't in the least mind having my heartstrings plucked, but I back off when I can see people doing it.

Fans of the movie will know what to expect. As an orphaned baby, Buddy crawled into Santa's sack and was inadvertently whisked off to the North Pole. Reared as a toy-making elf, the 30-year-old Buddy is now sent back to his native New York. With his honking voice, beaming merriment and pixie costume, he naturally stands out among Gotham's preoccupied residents. But Buddy gives Walter, his grumpy birth-father, who works for a children's publishers, a lesson in humanity and restores the spirit of Christmas to a heartless city.

Imagine an early Norman Wisdom movie combined with *A Christmas Carol* and you get the general picture. But, while there is nothing wrong with the idea of the innocent abroad, the musical offers a curious mix of the naive and the knowing. We are meant to warm to Buddy's unsophisticated niceness. At the same time, the show is full of insider references to *Annie*, Billy Crystal and even *The Iceman Cometh*. There is also something strangely self-regarding about the story. At one point the Scrooge-like Walter faces the sack unless he can come up with an instant bestseller. Needless to say, Buddy saves the day by telling his own story. You can either call that a clever piece of metafiction or a way of patting oneself on the back.

The saving grace for me is Ben Forster, winner of ITV's talent-spotting *Superstar*, as Buddy. He bounds through the evening with an anarchic glee that suggests he would be a perfect Puck in *A Midsummer Night's Dream*, sings the mostly anodyne songs with total conviction and has the priceless knack of getting on terms with an audience. That gift has sadly not been conferred on Kimberley Walsh who, for all her fame with *Girls Aloud*, cuts a curiously distant figure as Buddy's joyless girlfriend, Jovie. But there is staunch support from Joe McGann, who bears an astonishing resemblance to Harold Evans, as the waspish Walter. The score boasts one really good song, in which a group of department-store Santas bemoan the smartness of modern kids. Otherwise, this is a show that doesn't so much invoke the spirit of Christmas as market it. And while the musical, efficiently directed and choreographed by Morgan Young, won't do anyone any harm, I certainly wouldn't recommend it on the National Elf Service.

2016

Escaped Alone by Caryl Churchill
(World Premiere)
Royal Court, London: 29 January 2016

As dramatists get older, less is more. Caryl Churchill follows Beckett and Pinter into the field of fertile minimalism. Her last play, *Here We Go*, was a 45-minute meditation on death and dying. Her new one, running for an hour, juxtaposes two sharply contrasting worlds: a sunlit garden, where four women sit pleasurably conversing, and a rapidly disintegrating planet. Like all late Churchill, it packs an amazing amount into a modest frame.

The starting point could hardly be simpler. The nosy Mrs Jarrett pops through a fence into a back garden to join three women she vaguely knows. But Churchill shrewdly characterises the septuagenarian trio through their afternoon chats. Vi, an ex-hairdresser, is the most vituperative and has a criminal past it would be a pity to enlarge upon. Sally, who worked in medicine, is haunted by a fear of cats that you might call her pet aversion. Lena, meanwhile, is a one-time office worker afflicted by an agoraphobia that makes a trip to the supermarket a big deal. Over the course of the hour you get to know and like the women, who chat about everything under the sun, from families to the future.

Their talk is punctuated, however, by a series of monologues in which Mrs Jarrett, against a sizzling electrified frame, delivers a vision of global catastrophe. She starts with a terrifying image of cannibalistic underground communities. She later dwells on the devastating consequences of flood, fire, thirst and starvation, although the picture of dystopian disaster is sometimes shot through with a macabre humour. At one point, she imagines a world in which the hunger began when 80 per cent of food was diverted to TV studios and "commuters watched breakfast on iPlayer on their way to work."

This is not the first time Churchill has used drama to jolt us into an awareness of apocalypse. In *The Skriker* (1994), there is a moving speech about the erosion of our faith that spring will always return even after we are gone. And *Far Away* (2000) ends with a picture of the natural world in chaos. But, while the title of Churchill's new play derives from the book of Job and raises the question of whether our planet's decline is manmade rather than divinely ordained, I find Mrs Jarrett's speeches less effective as they go along. There are seven of them in all and, although they are excellently delivered by Linda Bassett without any colouring of hysteria, the law of diminishing returns sets in.

The overwhelming strength of the play lies in its portrait of the women in the garden. They talk inevitably of old times: of vanishing corner shops and TV soaps. At one point they even break, with glorious spontaneity, into a rendering of the old Crystals hit from 1973, Da Doo Ron Ron. But these women are not stuck in the past. They relish the benefits of living today: "whole worlds in your pocket," says Vi of mobile phones. Churchill also realises the old have aspirations, too – at one point they dwell on the joys of flight – and are not without a mocking humour. "Always wanted to go to Japan," says the hermetic Lena, to which Sally sharply retorts: "Get to Tesco first." This is Churchill at her best, observing with wry compassion how people actually talk.

James Macdonald's production also brings pitch-perfect performances from all the women. The great June Watson invests Vi with a wonderful mixture of tart-tongued vigour and hunger for knowledge. Kika Markham as Lena has just the right air of withdrawn shyness, though resentful of any reference to her affliction. Deborah Findlay as their host, Sally, exudes both panic and charm and, like all grandparents, casually boasts about her progeny. These garden scenes beautifully counterpoint the prophecies of disaster and lead me to think that the ever-adventurous Churchill, in her exploration of contradictions, would endorse a late remark of Harold Pinter : "Life is beautiful but the world is hell."

Cleansed by Sarah Kane (Revival)
Dorfman, National Theatre, London:
24 February 2016

Even by her own standards, Sarah Kane's 1998 play is an unusually punishing experience that posits a world in which licensed cruelty tests love to its limits. But while it has an undeniably serious purpose and is imaginatively staged by Katie Mitchell, I find its escalating horrors have a sense-numbing effect that outweighs its redemptive lyricism.

Kane's stage directions tell us we are in a university. Mitchell's direction and Alex Eales's design suggest more a run-down laboratory in a totalitarian institution where human beings are guinea pigs. Under the sadistic gaze of the self-loathing Tinker, the inmates are subjected to controlled experiments. We wait to see how far Grace, the central figure, will go in her fierce passion for her heroin-injected brother, Graham. At the same time, the 39-year-old Rod finds his commitment to his younger lover, Carl, rigorously examined as the latter undergoes progressive bodily mutilation. An illiterate boy, Robin, also attaches himself to Grace. Tinker is sexually hypnotised by an erotic dancer in a portable booth. Yet, in this chamber of horrors, love precariously survives.

Kane clearly borrowed from Büchner's *Woyzeck*, which she once superbly directed, in which a soldier submits to ruthless medical experiments. Her play also invokes memories of Orwell's *Nineteen Eighty-Four* and Pinter's *The Hothouse*. But all these works, in different ways, suggest the reduction of human beings to lab rats derives from a repressive society that punishes dissent. In Kane's play, there is no clear political framework or any indication of the source of Tinker's authoritarian power: in the end, the action takes place within a social void.

While the play is not without a residual optimism, it dubiously implies that love is only truly manifested when associated with extreme pain and suffering. For me, the play is a stage in Kane's tragically aborted dramatic development rather than the fully achieved work her admirers claim. Mitchell, taking a radically different approach from James Macdonald's semi-stylised original production, plunges us into a nightmare world of graphic violence and institutional frenzy, full of ringing bells, hurtling trolleys and scurrying, hooded attendants.

Everything in Mitchell's production is clear and explicit. We see Carl's tongue cut out, a pole inserted in his rectum, and his hands and feet brutally mangled. Grace undergoes an operation in which she mutates into her brother with visible genitalia. All this has proved too much for a handful of audience members who have, according to reports, fainted. But I would absolve both the play and the production, in which the sex is as graphic as the violence, of the charge of easy sensationalism. Kane is ultimately making a moral point about sanctioned butchery. My particular problem is that such relentless exposure to man's inhumanity to man produces a sense of fatigue rather than of horror.

In a play that makes exceptional demands on its actors, Michelle Terry gives an outstanding performance as Grace, turning her into an endlessly watchful figure, prepared to sacrifice anything for the sake of sibling love. Tom Mothersdale implies that Tinker's voyeuristic cruelty is the product of self-hatred, and there is unsparing support from Natalie Klamar as the writhing object of his lust and from Matthew Tennyson as the innocent Robin. But, for all the play's visceral power, it left me feeling drained rather than shocked into new awareness.

Hamlet by William Shakespeare
Royal Shakespeare Theatre, Stratford-upon-Avon: 23 March 2016

There is something spiritually refreshing about this new RSC *Hamlet*. It is not merely that the highly expressive 25-year-old Paapa Essiedu leads a predominantly Black ensemble. It is that the director, Simon Godwin, has taken a play conventionally wreathed in what a senior critic once called "baffled half-lights and glooms" and staged it with a vivid Technicolor brightness.

Even if the text has not been radically altered, it is clear from the start we are in for something different: the opening image is of Hamlet getting his degree at Wittenberg University, Ohio. A fascinating parallel is drawn in the programme with Ghana's first president, Kwame Nkrumah, who on returning to Africa in 1949 after studying in London, dwelt obsessively on mortality. How much more extreme is Hamlet's dilemma in that he comes home to confront familial murder, a ghost and incitements to revenge. Godwin's production might, in fact, do more to define the precise nature of Claudius's regime: a military tyranny is implied but, when Hamlet holds up a copy of *Time* magazine with Claudius on its cover, we are never quite sure whether this is because the leader is a Western puppet or a dangerous despot.

The focus is less on politics than on the predicament of a prince who finds himself an outcast in his own land. Essiedu is strikingly snubbed at court when Claudius turns immediately towards Laertes. Hamlet's wounded feelings are instantly clear when Essiedu later says to Gertrude: "I shall in all my best obey *you*, madam." This is a prince who is palpably isolated and bereft, even before the injunction to murder.

The prime fact about Essiedu, however, is that he is an intensely likeable Hamlet. He is young, quick-witted and, even in his rootless uncertainty, sportive: to convey his "antic disposition" he dons a paint-daubed suit and goes around doing subversive graffiti and big, splashy canvases like a mixture of Banksy and Jackson Pollock. For all his gun-toting, I never quite believed this Hamlet when he said: "Now could I drink hot blood." But Essiedu has a priceless vitality, speaks the verse intelligently and catches the contradictions of a prince who, even when knowing that his father is in spiritual limbo, heartlessly dispatches two fellow students, "not shriving time allowed."

But this is far from a one-man show. If Clarence Smith is an impressively composed Claudius, Tanya Moodie is an even more startling Gertrude: you see her shedding tears of outright contrition in the closet scene when she tells her son "thou hast cleft my heart in twain." Natalie Simpson excellently suggests that Ophelia, in her madness, poses a physical threat as she lunges at the onlookers with undisguised menace, and Marcus Griffiths's Laertes, arriving at court by helicopter, has a speech of fire that fain would blaze. But every part tells. A white Rosencrantz and Guildenstern arrive at court with patronising tourist gifts and the latter role is invested by Bethan Cullinane, herself a former Ophelia, with a deceptive chumminess.

What is heartening is to find the play so extensively rethought: we normally approach the graveyard scene expecting rustic gags from a wizened sexton, but here Ewart James Walters (who earlier plays the Ghost) and his assistant preface their daily rituals with a calypso. This is a reminder that the percussive music of Sola Akingbola makes a vital contribution to a production that makes you feel, even if you are seeing Hamlet for the 50th time, that you are experiencing it anew.

The Flick by Annie Baker (UK Premiere) Dorfman, National Theatre, London: 20 April 2016

Arnold Wesker in *The Kitchen* introduced us to the idea that work was inherently dramatic. This astonishing play by the US playwright Annie Baker is in the same tradition, in that it shows how work can be a way in to exploring human relationships as well as social and ethical issues. I should say straight off that this is a quiet play that slowly unfolds its meaning over three-and-a-quarter hours. By the simple act of not demanding our attention, however, Baker rivetingly compels it.

The two previous Baker plays seen in Britain, *The Aliens* and *Circle, Mirror, Transformation*, both dealt with enclosed worlds. In this play, her setting is a small movie house in Massachusetts: the audience is in the position of the screen, confronted by rows of empty seats and a projection booth. The three main characters work in the cinema. Sam is a burly 35-year-old whose job is to clear the debris from the auditorium and supervise the toilets. He is joined this particular summer by Avery, a 20-year-old African-American on a break from his studies at a college where his dad teaches semiotics. The third figure in this exquisite triangle is Rose, the projectionist in one of the few cinemas yet to switch to the digital process.

This last point is crucial. Among many other things, the play offers a passionate defence of films shot, in the digital age, on 35mm stock. Movies and cinema are central to the narrative; they work to reveal character, too. Avery's encyclopaedic cinematic knowledge, which enables him to work out the six degrees of separation between Michael J. Fox and Britney Spears, is a symbol of a profound depression. Sam's desire to learn the projectionist's trade is a sign of his unfulfilled longings. The plot also hinges on Avery's reluctant involvement in a scam concerning the resale of unused ticket stubs. I can vouch for the veracity of this element: as a student, I worked as a cinema usher at the Curzon in Mayfair and was roped into exactly the same, marginally criminal practice.

The beauty of Baker's play lies in its portrait of three quietly desperate people. It becomes clear that Sam has a yen for Rose who, in turn, fancies Avery. This, however, is a work in which deep passions are expressed as much through gesture as through words: Rose conveys her attraction to Avery with a hilariously wild dance in the cinema aisle and Sam's jealousy is shown by the way he calculatedly empties a bag of popcorn in Avery's path.

Baker's people are as driven by romantic need as characters in Racine – they just display it differently.

Sam Gold's hypnotic, silence-filled production was first seen in New York and retains two of the original cast. Matthew Maher is stunning as Sam, suggesting a man who, while destined to be a low-grade cleaner, is full of unarticulated desires: his slow-burn gazes are a joy to behold. Louisa Krause captures perfectly the baggy-trousered Rose's hidden Bacchic qualities and fear of her inability to sustain long-term relationships. Britain's Jaygann Ayeh, while new to the cast, is deeply moving as Avery, conveying both the character's isolation and use of movie expertise as a protective layer against life. This is like no other play in London. It moves at its own unhurried pace and magically exposes the souls of lonely people in danger of being left behind in our new, digitised age.

60 years of the English Stage Company at the Royal Court Theatre.

28 March, 2016

The Royal Court is much more than a theatre. It has been, during the 60-year-long tenure of the English Stage Company, both a battleground and a beacon. I only fully grasped its symbolic power when I was out of the country. In 1984 I was attending the annual new play festival in Louisville, Kentucky, when word came through that the Arts Council was considering withdrawing the Court's funding on the grounds that its commitment to new work had been overtaken by other theatres. The international theatre folk hastily drew up angry petitions protesting at the Arts Council's stupidity. As one delegate said to me, "there's hardly a new writing theatre anywhere in the world that doesn't owe its existence to the Royal Court." The Court has that effect on people: whatever its occasional lapses, it inspires a devoted loyalty. And, although I've had run-ins with various directors, that is certainly true in my case.

I was recently accused of a sentimental attachment to *Look Back In Anger* but, apart from the rather more crucial fact that it spurred a whole generation of dramatists into action, it shaped my own life. I've recorded before how, when I eventually got to see it as a schoolboy in 1957, I stood on the steps of the Court as people came out of the first-house performance on a Saturday night studying their faces to see if they had been changed by the experience: naive but true. When I came to live in London in the autumn of 1964, I also persuaded the Court's literary manager, Tom Osborn, to take me on as a script reader. After I'd filed several reports, Tom said that George Devine felt I wrote too much like a critic. My services, I gathered, were no longer required.

That was a reminder that in its earliest years critics were often seen as the principal enemy. In 1970 Lindsay Anderson took the extreme step of trying to ban the *Spectator*'s critic, Hilary Spurling, on the grounds that her reviews were not "helpful"; in this case the Arts Council, to its credit, stepped in and Anderson humiliatingly climbed down. In 1976 there was also a comic fracas between David Storey and the critics. Angered by the response to his play *Mother's Day*, Storey lay in wait for us on our next visit and proceeded to remonstrate. I was singled out for a hearty cuff round the ears, which was reported in the press as if I'd been savagely felled by a blow from Muhammad Ali.

I still respect Storey for his passionate defence of his play. The Court, however, was like that in those days. There was a sense, under the successive direction of Devine, William Gaskill, Anderson and Anthony Page, that they were carrying on a military campaign against the theatrical philistines and that you were either with them or against them. That shouldn't, however, disguise their achievements. Their dedication to the work of Osborne, Arden, Arnold Wesker and Edward Bond has been well documented. Less noticed was their early support of women writers such as Ann Jellicoe, Doris Lessing and Caryl Churchill. The Court also broke through the idea that British theatre was an exclusive white man's club: one of the best of its early plays was Barry Reckord's *Skyvers* (1963), dealing with life in a tough London comprehensive, and it introduced Wole Soyinka to London audiences with *The Lion and the Jewel* in 1966.

If the Court was a battlefield in its first quarter-century, it was for several reasons: it was an idealistic cause run by combative directors who often had to contend with fickle audiences and uncomprehending critics. I sensed a change of mood, however, in the years from 1979 to 1993 when Max Stafford-Clark ran the theatre. He had numerous battles to fight and had to deal with an unsympathetic Arts Council chaired by a Thatcherite appointee in William Rees-Mogg. Money was always tight. He made mistakes, such as the last-minute cancellation of Jim Allen's *Perdition* in 1987, under pressure from his board, because of the play's alleged anti-Semitism. But Stafford-Clark's approach to critics was much more emollient than that of his predecessors. He initiated an annual Christmas lunch in which the assembled hacks would be invited to play games, amounting to moral tests, such as deciding whether a hard-pressed theatre should accept vital sponsorship from tobacco companies.

But Stafford-Clark did much more than keep the show on the road in straitened times. He actively encouraged women dramatists, so that in 1989 the Court presented an unbroken run of plays by Timberlake Wertenbaker (*Our Country's Good*), Caryl Churchill (*Ice Cream*), Charlotte Keatley (*My Mother Said I Never Should*) and Winsome Pinnock (*A Hero's Welcome* and *A Rock in Water*), together with a reading of Clare McIntyre's *My Heart's a Suitcase*. As a graduate of Trinity College,

Dublin, Stafford-Clark also had a partiality for Irish dramatists, whether of the past like George Farquhar or of the present like Brian Friel, Thomas Kilroy and Anne Devlin. Stafford-Clark, like Othello, did the state some service; it's astonishing that his achievements have never been officially recognised.

Since Stafford-Clark's departure, the Court has undergone massive changes: for a start, the building itself has had a radical refurbishment. But, rather than chalking up the hits, and occasional misses, of successive directors such as Stephen Daldry, Ian Rickson, Dominic Cooke and now Vicky Featherstone, I would pick out one or two salient factors of the last quarter-century. One is the Court's progressive internationalism. This is very much the brainchild of Elyse Dodgson, who began running international workshops in 1989. In practice, that meant she'd get dramatists from all over the world to come to the Court each summer and put them through an intensive programme of theatre-going, lectures and playwriting. She also took Court dramatists around the world to offer practical advice. As part of the two-way traffic, the Court has staged plays by the German Marius von Mayenburg, the Russian Presnyakov brothers and the Spanish Juan Mayorga, among a host of others, that are the direct fruit of Dodgson's determination.

I'd also argue that the Court has lost none of its power to shock and disturb. The most famous example remains Sarah Kane's *Blasted*, which hit us all amidships in 1995 and left many of us reeling at its visceral horrors and failing to grasp its moral purpose. My own blindness over *Blasted* did not stop me reacting with similar horror in 2014 to Jennifer Haley's *The Nether*, with its vision of a digitalised paedophile fantasy world; my accusation of sensationalism was, however, vigorously rebutted by the play's director, Jeremy Herrin. It was quite like the old days, except possibly more polite.

All this, I suppose, raises the question of what the Court stands for in today's world, where the competition for new work is fiercer and more intense than it's ever been. At a time when other theatres, such as the Young Vic, the Almeida and even Rufus Norris's National, seem very much director-driven, I would say the Court still puts the dramatist at the centre of the theatrical event. It also strikes me as defiantly internationalist in tone and open to experiments with form, as proved by work as various as Stephen Emmott's *Ten Billion*, a dramatised lecture on population explosion, or Caryl Churchill's *Escaped Alone*, with its riveting mixture of the domestic and the apocalyptic. Over 60 years I've had a long love affair with the Court; and, as with all love affairs, there have been occasional rows and break-ups. But it remains for me London's most indispensable theatre because of its tenacious and single-minded belief that, whatever the interpretative skills of the director, designer, actor or sound engineer, in the beginning, and irreplaceably, is the dramatist's word.

Why Shakespeare lives on 400 years after his death.

22 April 2016

On Saturday the RSC marks the 400th anniversary of Shakespeare's death with a slap-up gala in Stratford-upon-Avon that will be broadcast live on BBC2 and boasts, as MGM used to say, "more stars than in the heavens." If you are in London, you could stroll from Westminster to Tower Bridge and see a sequence of short films produced by Shakespeare's Globe. Alternatively you could pop into a fascinating exhibition at the British Library titled *Shakespeare in Ten Acts*. To confirm Shakespeare's global reach, in Dubai you could catch an immersive *Romeo and Juliet* staged in a vast shopping mall, and in Warsaw there's a season of Shakespeare-inspired ballets with Polish dancers and Iranian designers.

This bombardment of Bardolatry prompts a series of questions. What is it about Shakespeare's plays that keeps them so constantly performed and studied at a time when the idea of a Western canon is in question? Is the hierarchical status given to Shakespeare's tragedies due for urgent reassessment? And how should we stage his plays in a period of rapid social change and shifting theatrical techniques?

Aside from the obvious richness of plot, language and character, two things especially strike me. One is that Shakespeare, like his contemporary Cervantes in *Don Quixote*, displays a pioneering freedom that anticipates many of the developments of his chosen form. Just as Cervantes gives us magic realism and a self-referential narrative *avant la lettre*, so Shakespeare plays with time, space, direct address, inner consciousness, cosmic despair and metaphysical absurdity in ways that prefigure future drama. When Peter Brook directed *King Lear* in 1962, critics commented on the Beckettian nature of the moment when Alan Webb's blinded Gloucester fell to the ground believing he was hurling himself off a Dover cliff. Brook wasn't, however, imposing Beckett on Shakespeare: the great modernist was always present in his predecessor.

A second key Shakespeare quality is an ambivalence that allows his plays to change their meaning according to when and where they are produced. *Hamlet* is the most famous example. As Oscar Wilde remarked, there is no such thing as Shakespeare's Hamlet: the role is defined by the temperament of the leading actor. The play also changes according to historical and geographical circumstance. The Western tradition is, by and large, to see it as a study of existential doubt. In contrast, at the Taganka Theatre in Moscow in the Soviet era, it became a portrait of obsessive state surveillance with characters constantly observed from behind a vast mobile curtain. As staged by the Bulandra Theatre in Bucharest during the

Ceausescu years, Elsinore was transformed into a decaying museum that became a symbol of a declining Romania.

Shakespeare's infinite adaptability is the source of his global popularity. In 1992 I gave a talk to a Shakespeare conference in Adelaide mischievously titled Was Shakespeare English? I heard recently that this is also the title of a forthcoming documentary which argues that Shakespeare's Italy-based comedies could only have been written by a native Italian. I wasn't, however, questioning the veracity of Shakespeare's origins. My point was that Shakespeare was too elusive, variable and pluralistic to be the exclusive property of one culture. It's a point that has been richly confirmed by international seasons at Shakespeare's Globe and the RSC. Even in English, the plays are brilliantly unstable. The great South African actor John Kani once told me a story about playing Othello at the Market Theatre in Johannesburg. To local liberals, the play was a tragedy about the hero's destructive credulity. To the weekend township audience, claimed Kani, the play suddenly became a topical drama about the eternal fraudulence of the white liar.

The examples I've quoted have all been from Shakespeare's tragedies and they retain their popular currency. This year you can hardly move without stumbling across King Lear. Don Warrington in Manchester and Michael Pennington in Northampton are currently playing the king. Later we will see Antony Sher in Stratford and Glenda Jackson at the Old Vic crazily dividing their kingdoms. Among the comedies, A Midsummer Night's Dream is also a perennial favourite. Erica Whyman's RSC production, billed as "a play for the nation," is now traversing the land, and Emma Rice shortly opens her reign at Shakespeare's Globe with a radical new version.

I relish Shakespeare's tragedies and comedies. But I question the inherited assumption that they represent Shakespeare's supreme achievement and speak to us most clearly today. Peter Brook once wrote that Shakespeare's plays are like planets which move closer to or further away from Earth at moments in their orbit: he cited Timon of Athens, which, in its bitterness and cynicism, seems peculiarly modern. My own claim would be that it is Shakespeare's histories which today seem more urgently apprehensible than even Lear or Othello.

It's a big assertion but one that is backed up by current performance schedules. The RSC is halfway through an epic history cycle. The BBC is about to unveil the second part of its Hollow Crown sequence, comprising the three parts of Henry V1 and Richard III and starring Benedict Cumberbatch, Judi Dench, Sophie Okonedo and Michael Gambon. This weekend, Ivo van Hove brings his acclaimed Kings of War, placing Shakespeare's histories in the war rooms of modern political leaders, from Amsterdam to the Barbican. In late May I will set out eagerly for America to see the Chicago Shakespeare Theatre's version of the histories, in which director Barbara Gaines promises to view the cycle from the perspective of the common man. Last year I saw Galway's Druid Theatre Company offer a radical take on the plays in which both Henry IV and Henry V were played by women.

So why is it that Shakespeare's histories speak to us so clearly today? One reason is that the plays are not, as often thought, simple exercises in Tudor propaganda, but penetrating studies of politics and power. James Shapiro's book, *1599*, reminds us just how subversive Shakespeare's *Richard II* was in the age of Elizabeth I: as Shapiro writes, the authorities were concerned that Londoners might draw lessons from a story about "the overthrow of a childless monarch who had taxed them ruthlessly and mismanaged Ireland." Today the play has lost none of its potency since it poses a perennially topical question: at which point does it become legitimate to unseat a leader who claims unquestioned authority whether it be divine, as in Richard's age, or democratic, as in our own? I don't imagine, for instance, that Dilma Rousseff would be keen to see the play revived in modern Rio.

But all Shakespeare's history plays deal with ever-pertinent issues. *Henry V* never ceases to astonish me with its capacity to reflect the mood of the moment. Laurence Olivier's 1944 movie was sanctioned as a morale-booster by politicians and dedicated to the fighting men liberating Europe at the close of the Second World War. And in 2003, at the time of the Iraq war, Nicholas Hytner chose the play to begin his tenure at the National Theatre and showed Adrian Lester's king launching a foreign invasion on questionable legal grounds and making chauvinist speeches to TV cameras and embedded journalists. The Polish academic Jan Kott once wrote a book called *Shakespeare: Our Contemporary*. If Kott's claim is still true, it is because it is repeatedly endorsed by Shakespeare's histories.

This, however, raises the question of how we stage Shakespeare's plays today. Do we heighten their application to the present? Or do we leave it to audiences to deduce the contemporary parallels? I don't believe there is a fixed solution. Everything hinges on the integrity of the approach and the insights it provides.

I would cite the case of Rupert Goold. When he set *The Merchant of Venice*, first for the RSC and later at the Almeida, in modern Las Vegas, he brought out brilliantly the gambling culture that pervades the play and highlighted the tragic solitude of Portia who ended up as a wealthy heiress belatedly realising she was tied to a husband whose sexual preferences lay elsewhere. But I was less struck by a Goold *Hamlet* set among 1940s Parisian existentialists: a bright idea that was not fortified by the text.

What is clear is that our approach to casting is changing rapidly, and has to go much further, in matters of race and gender. David Oyelowo has played Henry VI, Adrian Lester Hamlet and Henry V, Paapa Essiedu is the new, very good, Stratford Hamlet. But this is the first stage in reclaiming Shakespeare for Black and Asian actors. I can't think of a single Shakespeare play that wouldn't be reinvigorated by this process. And, although it may annoy some, I long for the day when a white actor can once more play Othello. If Jonas Kaufmann is permitted to sing Verdi's Otello at Covent Garden, why can't a white actor, without the obscene literalism of "blacking up," play the Moor?

Gender-blind casting is also refreshing and right. Acting is a feat of imaginative impersonation: a point made by Harriet Walter in an interview in the British Library Exhibition, where she says she has just as much, or just as little, in common with Brutus as she has with Cleopatra. I take that to mean that it requires the same feat of transubstantiation to turn herself into an anguished Roman senator as it does into an omnipotent Egyptian queen. My only observation is that mixed-gender casting works just as well, if not better, than single-sex productions. When Maxine Peake played Hamlet in Manchester, it made total sense for her to have a male Claudius and a female Polonius.

Similarly, in the current Stratford Hamlet, it is intriguing to see a male Rosencrantz and a female Guildenstern. In gender, as with race, the only true test lies in the quality of the actor.

In the end, Shakespeare's plays will always be a mirror for the times. But, while I applaud the cyclical re-invention of Shakespeare, I also believe that should not preclude a microscopic attention to the text. If I have any fear, it is that more attention is sometimes paid to ostentatious design than to the excavation of meaning. For me, a great Shakespeare production is one where I emerge with a new understanding of the play achieved through acting and direction. If we are to make the festivities surrounding Shakespeare's 400th anniversary something more than a ritual gesture, it will be through a renewed focus on his language. The best way to mark his death will be by giving his words renewed and vigorous life.

Father Comes Home from the Wars by Suzan-Lori Parks (UK Premiere) Royal Court, London: 23 September 2016

Suzan-Lori Parks's three-part play is epic in every sense. It deals with the US civil war and the concept of freedom. It evokes memories of Homeric myth. It is also the first stage in a projected trilogy that will, like the work of August Wilson, offer a historical perspective on the African-American experience. It runs for three hours, and I found it totally compelling.

In the first segment, Parks presents its leading character, Hero, with an agonising moral dilemma. As a slave on a west Texas plantation in 1862, he is offered the promise of freedom if he joins his Master in fighting with the rebel Confederate army. At the same time, his wife, Penny, and many of his fellow slaves urge him to stay at home. But, in the great tradition of classic drama, the present is shadowed by the past, not least the fact that the Master has reneged on previous promises of liberty. The dilemma is made more acute by the fact that Steve Toussaint as Hero admirably combines a massive physical presence with a morally flawed character: he is also exquisitely torn between his duty to his pleading wife and his pragmatic father, played with great force by Nadine Marshall and Leo Wringer.

Parks's second section is even more directly political. Set in a wooded enclave not far from a southern battlefield, it deals with the implications of freedom. By now Hero has joined his Master (convincingly played by John Stahl as both brutish and sentimental) who has a Union soldier (Tom Bateman) as his prisoner. But where do Hero's loyalties lie? And what does freedom (which is consistently capitalised in the text) actually mean? Parks vividly illustrates the crude materialism of a culture that assesses slaves according to their financial worth. But she also suggests that, even with emancipation, people of colour will always be branded with what the Union soldier calls "the mark of the marketplace."

The final section is the one most riddled – sometimes to the point of excess – with classical allusions. Hero returns from the war, like Odysseus, to find his wife has been wooed in his absence, and there is even a touch of Aeschylus's *Oresteia* in his homecoming. But Parks successfully lightens the mood by having Hero's talking dog, wittily named Odd-See and played with sprightly vigour by Dex Lee, fulfil the role of a messenger reporting on past events.

The excellent cast is British, but the production by Jo Bonney was first seen at New York's Public Theater in 2014. What is striking is its rapt attention to Parks's words and ideas and its ability to seamlessly incorporate her songs, beautifully performed by Steven Bargonetti, into the action. It may be an unfashionably long evening – but it captures the complexity of a civil war where Black Americans found themselves fighting on opposing sides and where, although freedom was the ultimate goal, its achievement was fraught with hazards that continue to this day.

Oil by Ella Hickson (World Premiere)
Almeida, London: 16 Oct 2016

The old idea that women dramatists tend to shun the epic form has emphatically been given the lie in recent years. After Lucy Prebble's *Enron*, Lucy Kirkwood's *Chimerica* and Beth Steel's *Labyrinth* we now have Ella Hickson's new play, which takes on a vast range of subjects, including empire, energy and the environment, as well as mother–daughter relationships. The result may be uneven but the piece is bold, playful and scorchingly ambitious.

Spanning more than 150 years, Hickson's play focuses on a woman called May who travels effortlessly through time. We first see her as a nineteenth-century Cornish farmer's wife for whom the newly invented kerosene lamp becomes a source of personal illumination. Later, we see May working as a servant in 1908 Tehran, at a time when the British are desperate to exploit Persia's natural resources. By 1970, she has risen to become CEO of an international oil company threatened by Libya's proposal to nationalise its assets. But, as May rises in the world, difficulties with her daughter, Amy, intensify and become deeply problematic as they head into a nightmarish future.

Hickson suspends the normal rules of realism to pursue big ideas. One is that there is a parallel between the imperialist instinct of countries and corporations and that of parents. This is most vivid in the scene where May, on one crisis-ridden evening, simultaneously seeks to retain control of her company's Libyan oil wells and of her teenage daughter's love life. But Hickson is equally fascinated by the price that has to be paid for living through a century-and-a-half of accelerating progress: in particular, she shows the career-driven, uncompromising May becoming habituated to loneliness and to a sense of estrangement from the activist Amy who, as her three-letter name implies, represents her other self.

Hickson strives too hard for cyclical neatness. The level of the writing also varies from one scene to another. But she has created a remarkable play that, aside from an opening scene that is as impenetrably dark as a Georges de la Tour painting, is very well directed by Carrie Cracknell and contains one of the best theatrical mother–daughter relationships of recent years. Anne-Marie Duff excellently catches all May's contradictions: her sensuousness and solitude, her curiosity and curmudgeonliness and the oppressive nature of her maternal love. Above all, Duff, with her taut, expressive features, is very good at suggesting hardship overcome. When May says: "There is still blood on my hands from hauling myself up, from clinging on," Duff makes you believe every word.

Yolanda Kettle is equally good as daughter Amy: defiant, angry, passionate about the environment, yet imbued with a faint touch of self-righteous certainty. The men are less multi-dimensional, but there is good work from Tom Mothersdale as May's abandoned husband, Patrick Kennedy as her regimental pursuer and Nabil Elouahabi as a Libyan emissary. And even if Hickson's play is about the ultimate exhaustion of our oil reserves, it has a renewable energy of its own.

The Intelligent Homosexual's Guide to Capitalism and Socialism by Tony Kushner (UK Premiere) Hampstead Theatre, London: 28 October 2016

"Have you seen the play?" "No, but I've read the title." So ran an old joke about the original 26-word name of the work now known as *Marat/Sade*.

But, while you could apply the same gag to Tony Kushner's prodigious three-and-a-half-hour play *The Intelligent Homosexual's Guide to Capitalism and Socialism With a Key to the Scriptures* (also known as *iHO*), its full title reveals a lot: this is a work about sex, politics and religion. While it bulges at the seams, it is bracing, in an age of mini-dramas, to find a play that throws in everything from Karl Marx to modern materialism.

In contrast to the spiralling fantasy of *Angels in America*, Kushner has written a piece that relies on the tradition of American family drama. The setting is New York in 2007 and Gus, a retired Brooklyn longshoreman and devout communist, has called his clan together to announce his plan to sell his house and then kill himself. This causes varying degrees of shock to his three offspring. Empty (short for Maria Teresa) is a labour lawyer with a pregnant lesbian partner. Pill (otherwise Pier Luigi) is a gay teacher torn between his long-term academic lover and a young Yale-educated hustler. V (short for Vito) is a hetero building-contractor and much the angriest. Watching over proceedings with eerie calm is Gus's sister, Clio, a one-time nun and Maoist.

It is easy to itemise the flaws in Kushner's concept. At one point, he resorts to a plot device straight out of *The Cherry Orchard*. The religious element, in that the partners of both Empty and Pill study faith without practising it, often seems tacked on. And you wonder how many lovers discuss commodity fetishism in the heat of passion. But the play, which makes constant use of overlapping dialogue to convey family tensions, has a furious energy and deals with the disillusion in an Italian-American community, and by implication a whole society, whose dreams have not been realised.

For me, Kushner is at his best when he deals directly with politics in a series of father–child exchanges. The most powerful comes when Gus is confronted by Empty over his planned suicide. He may have Alzheimer's but it is clear that his death wish is driven by despair over revolutionary failure: as a union man, he fought for a guaranteed annual income for longshoremen only to find it never achieved the radical change he longed for. Meanwhile Empty is an ardent revisionist who cites the numerous incremental benefits brought about by political action. It is a classic battle between the revolutionary and the reformer and has echoes of the father–daughter conflicts in Shaw's *Major Barbara*.

Kushner's play, which is both vivid and untidy, is given a terrific production by Michael Boyd. David Calder's Gus has the right mix of gravitas and rumbling embitterment. Tamsin Greig as Empty is sharp, witty and passionate in her gradualism and there are equally strong performances from Richard Clothier as the chronically indecisive Pill and Lex Shrapnel as the recklessly impulsive V. But the performance that draws the eye in this tumultuous family battle is that of Sara Kestelman as the ironically watchful Clio. There are many better-organised plays around, but Kushner's has the rare capacity to make ideas fizz.

King Lear by William Shakespeare
Old Vic, London: 5 November 2016

It would be easy to regret Glenda Jackson's 25-year absence from the stage but she has lost none of her innovative instinct. I suspect her experience of political life and the world's injustice has enriched her understanding of Lear. Even if I jib at the conventional pieties surrounding Shakespeare's flawed tragedy there is no doubting that she is tremendous in the role. In an uncanny way, she transcends gender. What you see, in Deborah Warner's striking modern-dress production, is an unflinching, non-linear portrait of the volatility of old age. Jackson, like all the best Lears, shifts in a moment between madness and sanity, anger and tenderness, vocal force and physical frailty.

Her great gift, however, is to think each moment of the play afresh. She enters, without undue ceremony, hand in hand with her beloved Cordelia. But there is irony when she announces, in a self-mocking drawl, that she will "crawl" unburdened towards death. Having routinely given Goneril and Regan their share of the kingdom, she ecstatically cries "Now our joy" on turning to Cordelia, and initially greets her refusal to play the game with incredulous laughter. But instantly this turns to violence as she hurls Cordelia to the floor and rushes at Kent with one of the blue chairs that adorn the set. Yet, even here, the mood swiftly changes as Jackson registers the banished Kent's departure with a derisive regal wave.

Even Jackson cannot reconcile me to the gobbledegook of the hovel scene but she is superb in the play's later stages. The pathos of the confrontation with the blinded Gloucester is overshadowed by Lear's rage at the world's inequity: Jackson gives especial force to "The strong lance of justice hurtless breaks," reminding me of Michael Pennington's observation that Lear becomes a socialist. Right to the end, Jackson embodies Lear's contradictions: while tenderly clutching the dead Cordelia, she spits with vengeful fury at "you murderers, traitors all." If I describe the opening scene in detail, it is because it lays the ground for everything that follows. It shows Lear's fatal partiality, capricious waywardness, even wild humour. All these qualities come into play in Jackson's brilliantly jagged reading of the part. Scorned by her elder daughters, she parodies her supposed decrepitude while quietly winking at the Fool. Yet there is ferocity in the vulpine claws she extends towards Goneril. And when Regan asks why she needs even one follower, Jackson makes "O reason not the need" less an earth-rending cry than a simple utterance of despair, delivered head in hands, at human incomprehension.

Warner's production offers a clear framework for a shattering performance. She and Jean Kalman have created a simple design composed of rectangular white flats: at one point, one spins round to reveal the beer-stocked fridge at Goneril's house. The storm is evoked through billowing black sheets, looking like large bin liners, and a projected rainstorm. A perspective of distant blue sea tells us we are in Dover. Some of the details are decidedly peculiar: both Edmund and Edgar display their buttocks to the audience making me wonder if mooning is a family trait. And when Regan hurled part of Gloucester's gouged eye into the audience, I worried that, as the panto season approaches, someone might throw it back.

The surrounding performances are also variable. Rhys Ifans over-colours every line of the Fool, even venturing into a cod Bob Dylan tone when he sings a snatch of folk: I began to think nostalgically of the way Paul Scofield's Lear and Alec McCowen's Fool simply sat side by side on a bench in Peter Brook's celebrated production. But Celia Imrie's grimly determined Goneril and Jane Horrocks's sexually excitable Regan are sharply distinguished. Morfydd Clark as Cordelia intriguingly suggests a belated passion for Sargon Yelda's Kent. And although Edgar's argument that he fails to reveal himself to Gloucester to save his father from despair strikes me as nonsensical, Harry Melling lends the role a believable integrity. Even if *Hamlet* and *Macbeth* are greater plays, Jackson's performance catches perfectly the zigzag patterns of Lear's mix of insight and insanity. This is "reason in madness" to the very life.

Hamlet by William Shakespeare
Almeida, London: 1 March 2017

By a strange irony, Andrew Scott is the first major Hamlet London has seen since Benedict Cumberbatch. Even odder is the fact that, while both have starred in TV's *Sherlock*, the two actors suffer a similar theatrical fate in that their Hamlets transcend the productions that surround them.

Robert Icke's version at the Almeida is cool, clever, chic and has some good ideas but also some that strike me as eccentrically wrong-headed. Icke and his designer, Hildegard Bechtler, make it clear that we are in a contemporary world. Newsreel images display the state funeral of Hamlet's father and his Ghost makes his first appearance as an image on closed-circuit screens of the Danish security guards. Surveillance is, in fact, a key part of this world. Polonius is wired up so that he can report the latest news of Hamlet's mental state, Hamlet himself eavesdrops on Claudius and Gertrude's post-honeymoon canoodling, and hand-held cameras track Elsinore's leaders on all public occasions. No one is ever quite alone in this corrupt kingdom.

Scott's performance fits the quiet, non-declamatory tone of the production. He is, for the most part, soft-spoken and gently ironic with a perceptible Irish lilt. There are flashes of genuine rage, as when, observing his mother cuddling up to Claudius, he roars: "Frailty, thy name is woman." Confronting Laertes over Ophelia's grave, he also goes into ranting mode. But I shall remember Scott's Hamlet for its charm, self-mockery and ability to speak directly to the audience. With "To be or not to be" you feel Scott is engaging us individually in his own moral dilemma about the pros and cons of self-slaughter. Scott's Hamlet also has the ability to send himself up. I've always been puzzled by Hamlet's clearly bogus assertion that he has been in "continual practice" at fencing: here it becomes a conscious joke about his own palpable unfitness and secret death wish.

In short, this is a good performance. Icke's production also has some highly intelligent touches. I loved the staging of the play scene so that, with

Claudius sitting in the Almeida front row, a camera tracks every shade of his reaction to the mimetic re-enactment of his own crime. And it was also fascinating to see Ophelia in the mad scene played as a hospitalised patient rather than as someone licensed to do a peculiar cabaret turn. But one or two of Icke's ideas strike me as dotty. I cannot fathom why Claudius should make his confession of murder not to an unseen divinity but to a Hamlet standing in front of him holding a pistol. Why, if the king came clean, wouldn't his nephew shoot him?

Even if there are odd features, the performances are generally fine. Angus Wright and Juliet Stevenson for once present us with a Claudius and Gertrude who are physically wrapped up in each other and lose no opportunity for making love, even when there is a diplomatic mission on the doorstep. Jessica Brown Findlay, though she occasionally drops her voice at the end of lines, charts the progressive stages of Ophelia's downfall. Peter Wight as a sinisterly snooping Polonius and David Rintoul, doubling as the Ghost and Player King, both exude great authority. It's a long, four-hour production and one that mixes insight and occasional absurdity, but it is Scott's sweet prince I shall remember best.

Consent by Nina Raine (World Premiere) Dorfman, National Theatre, London: 6 April 2017

Aside from John Mortimer and David Hare, few dramatists have in the past tackled legal affairs. But Nina Raine, who wrote about a dysfunctional family in *Tribes* and the NHS in *Tiger Country*, here confronts the distinction between the law and justice. The result is a play of fierce moral intelligence that, for the most part, leaves the audience to weigh up the rights and wrongs of specific cases.

Explaining the legal system, one of Raine's barristers says: "Basically, it's a fight between two opposing narratives." We see that in operation in a rape case where a complainant finds her allegations destroyed in court: what seems unjust is that her own depressive history is used against her, while the past sex crimes of her assailant are never mentioned. But Raine goes on to show how the private lives of lawyers are also the source of contradictory narratives. Is the adulterous Jake right to be jettisoned by the punitive Rachel? When the cold-hearted Edward is accused of marital rape by his wife, Kitty, we see the adversarial debates of the courtroom transformed into domestic agony.

The play is critical of the law without being cynical. It shows how lawyers acquire a professional carapace that enables them, off-duty, to talk light-heartedly about their cases. It also shows, not unsympathetically, that their own lives are often as muddled and chaotic as ours. Behind the play lie some big questions: in particular, whether constantly dealing with violent, dishonest people has a corrupting effect on lawyers, and whether rape cases should be subject to point-scoring battles. But while the play is always lively and engrossing, it occasionally tilts the evidence. It is not hard to condemn the smugly promiscuous Jake, whereas the case of Edward and Kitty is genuinely complex. We get a plausible portrait of a disintegrating marriage in which neither partner can claim the moral high ground.

Consent is a play that stimulates debate rather than stifles it. It is beautifully directed by Roger Michell, in a co-production with Out of Joint. Hildegard Bechtler's design turns the stage into an opulent arena, and the performances match the vigour of the writing. Ben Chaplin, fresh from *Apple Tree Yard*, skilfully shows how Edward's professional callousness has pervaded his private life, while Anna Maxwell Martin deftly suggests that Kitty's lively humour conceals a long-nursed bitterness. The other couple are less vivid, but Adam James and Priyanga Burford invest them with a history. Meanwhile, Pip Carter as a perennial bachelor and Daisy Haggard as an actor who, while playing Medea on stage, yearns for happiness off it, are instantly recognisable. Heather Craney, doubly abused as the woman who unsuccessfully brings a rape case to court, also makes her character the emotional pivot, even if I couldn't quite believe her intrusion into lawyers' Christmas revels.

This is a very good play that reminds us that drama, like the law, depends on antithetical narratives in which we become judge and jury.

The Ferryman by Jez Butterworth
(World Premiere)
Royal Court, London: 3 May 2017

The combination of Jez Butterworth as writer and Sam Mendes as director has inevitably turned this play into a hot ticket. But behind the box-office glamour of a work co-produced with Sonia Friedman and almost certainly destined for the West End lies a rich, serious, deeply involving play about the shadows of the past and the power of silent love. Only in the final moments of a play that runs well over three hours did I question Butterworth's mastery of his material.

You could say the play combines the gangland politics of his first hit, *Mojo*, with the rural rituals of his later work including *Jerusalem*. That, however, would be to do Butterworth an injustice, since there are big issues at stake. The year is 1981. The setting, except for a brief prologue, is a 50-acre farm in County Armagh, Northern Ireland. In the Maze prison, ten republican prisoners die after a hunger strike. But, down on the farm, Quinn Carney, a reformed IRA activist, is celebrating the annual harvest with his extended family. Two events, however, show the inescapability of the past.

One is the discovery of the body of Quinn's brother, who disappeared 10 years earlier after Quinn's defection from the IRA. The other is the arrival on the farm of a leading republican power figure.

Butterworth is not the first person to dramatise the intersection of politics and private life in Northern Ireland: coincidentally the same theme is explored, from a Protestant perspective, in David Ireland's *Everything Between Us*, currently at London's Finborough Theatre.

But what gives Butterworth's play such shattering force is its Hardyesque love of rural rituals and its compassionate exploration of unspoken love. At the heart of the play lies the tender relationship between Quinn, whom Paddy Considine endows with an unflinching integrity, and his brother's wife, Caitlin, beautifully played by Laura Donnelly. The idea of secret passion extends to two aunts who, in different ways, lost their loved ones. It reaches its fulfilment, however, in the captivating moment when a slow-witted English factotum reads Sir Walter Raleigh's poem *The Silent Lover* at the harvest home.

There are many other themes coursing through this abundant play: one, hinted at in the title with its reference to the Virgilian ferryman, Charon, is of unburied souls roaming the earth. But the power of Mendes's terrific production, which I saw at the final preview, lies in its ability to combine scrupulous naturalism with a sense of the mysterious. Astonished gasps greet the presence of real rabbits, a goose and even a baby on stage. But one tiny moment illustrates Mendes's microscopic approach: the way Genevieve O'Reilly, as Quinn's ailing wife, quietly averts her gaze as Donnelly's Caitlin bustles about their communal kitchen speaks volumes about the plight of two women in love with the same man. All the performances, like Rob Howell's set with its antique beams and time-weathered walls, are invested with the same intense detail. Bríd Brennan as Aunt Maggie Faraway, whose name says it all, is as eloquent in her watchful silence as in her rare moment of speech. Dearbhla Molloy as Aunt Patricia, meanwhile, is filled with the inextinguishable rage of the politically militant. Des McAleer as a loquacious uncle with a love of the classics, John Hodgkinson as the lone Englishman with his own hidden desires, and Stuart Graham as the inflexible IRA leader anxious to bury the sins of the past are equally fine.

If, however, Butterworth's engrossing and haunting play tells us anything, it is that the violent past can no more be suppressed than the private passions that we are afraid to articulate.

An Octoroon by Branden Jacobs-Jenkins (UK Premiere)
Orange Tree, Richmond: 31 May 2017

If I say that this bizarrely brilliant play is the work of a 32-year-old Black American dramatist called Branden Jacobs-Jenkins, I am already subscribing to an idea the piece seeks to subvert: that our identities can be defined by convenient labels. Even the notion of what makes a "play" is up for grabs, as this tumultuous piece is both an adaptation of *The Octoroon*, a popular nineteenth-century melodrama by Dion Boucicault, and a postmodernist critique of it.

The evening starts with a confrontation between the two "authors." One, simply called BJJ, explains the dilemmas facing a writer of colour whose every word is mined for its racial significance, the other figure, representing Boucicault, is a drunken showman who has no such self-doubt. We then launch into a condensed rewrite of Boucicault's original: a mortgage melodrama in which the Peyton family's Louisiana plantation seems destined to fall into the unscrupulous hands of its former overseer, M'Closky. The crunch comes when the good-hearted George Peyton has to choose between his love for Zoe, of one-eighth Black ancestry, and his need to save the estate by marrying a rich heiress.

That, however, is only the bare outline of a work that is infinitely playful and deeply serious and which dazzlingly questions the nature of theatrical illusion. The actor who plays BJJ – in this case, the astonishing Ken Nwosu – goes on to don whiteface and appear as both the heroic George and the villainous M'Closky. This leads to a hilarious scene in which he switches between the two characters engaged in a fight to the death. But white actors assume blackface and even, in the case of a Native American, redface in order to reinforce a key point: that, while Boucicault's original was progressive in its anti-slavery message, it also traded on racial stereotypes that are still deeply embedded in today's consciousness.

The tension slackens slightly in the second half when Jacobs-Jenkins summarises Boucicault's sensational climax. By uprooting every plank in the stage to create a pit for a slave auction, Ned Bennett's inventive production and Georgia Lowe's ingenious design also create a needless hiatus. Otherwise, the execution perfectly matches the quicksilver skill of the writing. In addition to the resourceful Nwosu, who deserves to be honoured in end-of-the-year awards, there is a host of fine performances. Kevin Trainor as the bombastic Boucicault, Vivian Oparah and Emmanuella Cole as a pair of closely bonded slaves, Celeste Dodwell as a cracked Southern belle and Iola Evans as the eponymous heroine are all first-rate.

Significantly, the character of Zoe loses the definite article she has in Boucicault's title to become simply "an octoroon": one of many rather than a symbol of her race. That is very much the point of an extraordinary play, first seen at New York's Soho Rep, that defies categorisation and that proclaims Jacobs-Jenkins as an exciting new dramatist who questions what it means to be dubbed "a Black playwright."

Barber Shop Chronicles by Inua Ellams
(World Premiere)
Dorfman, National, London: 9 June 2017

Bijan Sheibani's exuberant production begins and ends with a party in which audience members dance with the cast or even go on stage for a quick trim. That seems in keeping with the spirit of Inua Ellams's invigorating play, which shows how barbers' shops run by and catering for African men combine the roles of pub and political platform, social centre and soapbox. It makes the average white British male's belief that you simply go in for a quick haircut look decidedly dreary.

Ellams switches between six shops in two continents on the day in April 2012 when Chelsea beat Barcelona in the Champions League semi-final. The main focus is on a London barber's where a family drama is played out as a young hairdresser discovers the truth about his father's imprisonment. It is, however, typical that the place is also a talk shop where cutters and clients debate the propriety of using the N-word, the subversive power of pidgin English and the supposed differences between Black and white women.

The action embraces five other shops spread across Africa, but what is fascinating is how Ellams finds common threads in the geographical diversity: not only soccer, but an obsession with fathers and sons and even the same bar-room anecdote told with variations. What also hits one is the way the barber's becomes a place where African men can safely let off steam. In Kampala, they talk about the way discrimination against gay people is hitting Ugandan exports. In Harare, we see a generational clash about popular music. Most telling is the rage of a man in Johannesburg who argues that Nelson Mandela failed his people and that the perpetrators of apartheid got off scot-free.

The role of women in African life is hardly touched on and you have to be pretty nimble to keep abreast of so many stories. But the acting is first-rate and Sheibani skilfully uses music and dance to knit the episodes together. Each man in his time plays many parts, and there are fine contributions from Cyril Nri as a patriarchal London Nigerian, Patrice Naiambana as a jaundiced Jo'burger and Hammed Animashaun as a randy youngster who never allows racial politics to impede his sex life. Co-produced by the National Theatre, Fuel and West Yorkshire Playhouse, it's a richly enjoyable play.

Donald Trump and Shakespeare

13 June 2017

Sponsorship, a British director once told me, is implicit censorship. As if to prove the point, Delta Airlines and Bank of America have pulled out of funding a New York Shakespeare in the Park production of Julius Caesar on the grounds that the Roman dictator is played as a blond-haired bully with an American tie-pin and a Slavic wife. A spokesperson for one of the sponsors said the portrayal of Caesar was clearly designed "to provoke and offend," which some of us thought was one of theatre's basic functions.

But is there scope for recasting other Shakespeare plays with Trump lookalikes? Some may be tempted by the idea of a Trump Lear in that Shakespeare's monarch has a shaky grasp of reality, carves up his kingdom among his family and is confronted by his daughters' ingratitude but, although Ivanka Trump allegedly tried to persuade her father not to pull out of the Paris climate agreement, the mad Lear has a tragic grandeur entirely missing in Trump.

It is easier to envisage a Trump-like Richard III. After all, the character is a satanic joker who systematically wipes out all obstacles to ultimate power, puts on a false face to deceive the populace and is ultimately confronted by his own hollowness. As he says on the eve of battle: "There is no creature loves me and if I die, no soul shall pity me."

But there is one character who shows that Shakespeare had an uncanny understanding of the Trump type, and that is the lying braggart Parolles in the rarely revived *All's Well That Ends Well*. Parolles has a repugnant chauvinism that leads him to accost Helena with the words, "Are you meditating on virginity?," and go on to assail her sexuality by claiming that virginity is like a withered pear in that "it looks ill, it eats dryly." That sounds very like a Trump chat-up line. Moreover, Parolles poses as a military hero but is exposed as a treacherous coward when he is ambushed by his fellow soldiers and tricked into revealing their strategies: this could almost be Trump subverting the FBI or engaging in reckless dialogue with the Russians. There's even a shamelessness about Parolles that allows him to survive exposure and declare: "Simply the thing I am shall make me live." I wait eagerly to see Parolles played as a bombastic backcombed bully. In the meantime, there is bound to be a big laugh next time we hear Timon of Athens ask: "What means that trump?" It's a question to which we would all like to know the answer.

Fatherland by Simon Stephens (World Premiere) Royal Exchange, Manchester: 7 July 2017

The scene: a wine-bar close to the Royal Exchange, Manchester. Two critics have just emerged from a verbatim piece, *Fatherland*, staged as part of the Manchester International Festival. One critic, a baggy-eyed oldster, is called Michael. His younger, sharp-witted colleague, is Helena. They have form in that their previous fictional encounters have been recorded in a book called *The 101 Greatest Plays*.

M: Well that was nice and short at 90 minutes and I'll say this for it: as verbatim pieces go, it was a damned sight better than *Committee*, which I've just seen in London, in that it really does integrate text, movement and music. Simon Stephens, Scott Graham and Karl Hyde not only put themselves into the story but genuinely seem to have worked as a team. I just had one problem. The piece is based on interviews about fathers and sons conducted in the creators' respective home towns – Stockport, Corby and Kidderminster – but I didn't feel it told me anything new. It also ducked the fact that we are, in most cases, the product of two parents, not one.

H: Funny you should say that. I thought I'd object to the predominance of testosterone but I found it a change from all the mother–daughter plays I see so often. It's also thrillingly staged. There's one brilliant scene where the guys interview a fireman called Mel. His story about having to retrieve the corpse of an old man who'd been left alone to melt into the bedclothes in his flat is overwhelming in the light of what happened at Grenfell Tower. The director, Graham, also makes marvellous use of stage space by showing Nick Holder as Mel ascending a ladder levered out of the stage floor, and Hyde's music, as it does all evening, perfectly echoes the rhythms of people's speech.

M: I'd agree, that episode was the highlight, but it's only tangentially related to the main theme. I also felt I knew all about the sense of guilt, shame and lack of emotional contact that characterises many father–son relationships. And, although the piece is called Fatherland, it tells you hardly anything about Britain as a whole.

H: You must have cloth ears! Mel describes the referendum as "an opportunity to kick Westminster in the bollocks," another character rails against the PC nature of modern Britain, and there's a constant sense of wrecked lives and economic struggle. I actually learned a lot more about who and what we are than I did from that National Theatre post-Brexit play, *My Country: A Work in Progress*.

M: Fair enough. But I feel you can't generalise about the supposed crisis in masculinity or the state of the nation from a handful of interviews carried out by a trio of guys making a rare visit back to their home towns.

H: Gotcha! That's exactly the point made by one of the characters they interview, Luke, who is sceptical about the whole project, wants to know how much money they'll make, and finally withdraws his support.

M: Strange you should mention Luke, since I wondered how genuine he was. I assumed he was an invented character planted in the story to voice all the stock objections to verbatim theatre. At one point, he says: "Why don't you just make it up?" and that thought frequently crossed my mind. I kept thinking of all the plays that tackle father–son relationships with much greater depth and intensity than you will find here. Just think of great American plays such as O'Neill's *Long Day's Journey Into Night* or Miller's *Death of a Salesman*. Or, if you want a local example, how about John Mortimer's *A Voyage Round My Father*? And I learned far more about masculine violence and emotional cowardice from Stephens's earlier play about Stockport, *On the Shore of the Wide World*, which I saw at the Royal Exchange in 2005, than I did from this collaboration.

H: But you're falling into your usual trap. Fact doesn't preclude fiction and verbatim theatre doesn't stop people staging the great classics. What is refreshing is to hear the language of real people on stage, and even an old grump like you must admit this piece is beautifully done. There's a great moment when Hyde's dad, played by Neil McCaul, says his son wasn't a "pretty child," and then gets swept up in the air as he describes his thrill at seeing him on stage.

M: I'm not denying the piece is excellently staged, I loved Hyde's music and all the actors – including Ferdy Roberts, Emun Elliott and Bryan Dick as the show's co-creators – are very good. But I still didn't feel as emotionally moved as I have been by imaginative works about fathers and sons.

H: So how many stars would you give it?

M: Three, I think.

H: I'd give it four for the boldness of the concept and the skill of the execution.

M: Perhaps we should split the difference. Now how about one for the road?

Girl From The North Country by Conor McPherson (World Premiere) Old Vic, London: 27 July 2017

This is the second time in a week I've seen an Irish writer create a remarkable fusion of text and music. Woyzeck in *Winter* at the Galway arts festival unites Büchneruchner and Schubert. Now Conor McPherson has written and directed a play incorporating 20 diverse songs by Bob Dylan. Set in

Dylan's home town of Duluth, Minnesota, in 1934, the piece uses the songs to reinforce the mood of desperation and yearning that characterised America in the Depression era.

It was the Dylan team who approached McPherson with the idea and they knew what they were doing since his work, from The Weir onwards, has been marked by a sense of unfulfilled longing. Here, that is located in a run-down guesthouse where everyone is staring into a bleak future. Nick, the owner, has to deal with crushing debt, a wife with dementia, a layabout son, and he is trying to marry off an adopted, pregnant, Black daughter to an elderly shoe salesman. His guests include a ruined family, a fugitive boxer, a blackmailing preacher-cum-Bible salesman and Nick's lover, who is awaiting a legacy in vain.

Yet for all their failures they still manage, gloriously, to sing.

The use of a local doctor as narrator reminded me of Thornton Wilder's *Our Town*. The interweaving of multiple stories suggests Arthur Miller's mosaic of the Depression, *The American Clock*. But it is the constant dialogue between the drama and the songs that makes this show exceptional. The songs are drawn from every decade of Dylan's extensive catalogue, and are presented as visible "numbers," with the actors often singing into stand-microphones.

At the same time, they articulate the characters' innermost feelings. The preacher and the boxer unite in Slow Train (1979), from Dylan's born-again Christian period. Nick's son and his departing girlfriend express their shared frustration in I Want You (1966), dating from the time when Dylan was revolutionising rock. On the eve of Thanksgiving, the whole cast rousingly unite in You Ain't Goin' Nowhere (1975), which perfectly catches the mood of hope endlessly deferred.

Because the songs are so good, it is easy to overlook the economy and skill with which McPherson evokes the mood of 1930s America: the racism that leads the Black boxer to be alternately insulted and exploited, the poverty that has highways lined with people living in tents. As director, McPherson has created an astonishingly free-flowing production and the 19-strong cast, which includes three musicians, is so uniformly strong it is tough to pick out individuals.

Shirley Henderson as Nick's wife gives a mesmerising portrait of a woman unshackled by social convention. But Ciarán Hinds as the stoically suffering Nick, Stanley Townsend as a bankrupt factory owner and Bronagh Gallagher – very handy on drums – as his pill-popping wife are equally striking. And there is fine work from Sheila Atim as Nick's desolate daughter, Arinze Kene as the fleeing pugilist, Ron Cook as the choric doctor and Jim Norton as the shoe merchant who, lamenting his widowed solitude, says: "You remember a warm light and a smile from long ago." That's a deeply poignant line, and it says much about the fruitful creative marriage of McPherson and Dylan that it might have been written by either of them.

Tribute to Sir Peter Hall: born 22 November 1930, died 12 September 2017.

13 September, 2017

Peter Hall was a man of infinite contradictions. In public, he exuded confidence, authority and the gift for leadership that enabled him to both found the Royal Shakespeare Company and overcome the manifold crises surrounding the early days of the National Theatre. Yet, having interviewed Hall countless times over the past 40 years, I also saw that he was vulnerable, sensitive and even sometimes strangely solitary. I have a vivid memory of travelling to Athens in the mid-1980s with a party of critics to see Hall's production of *Coriolanus*, with Ian McKellen, staged in the Herod Atticus theatre. One morning we announced we were going to Athens's National Archaeological Museum. "Do you mind if I come with you?" Hall asked, almost apologetically.

It was a sudden glimpse into the loneliness of a director once the task of getting the show up and running has been achieved.

Long before I got to know Hall, or even write about his work, I had followed his career. I first saw his work at Stratford in the late 1950s when a slightly chilly *Love's Labour's Lost* was followed by a blissful *Twelfth Night*, a symphony in russet staged in Caroline costume, and an overwhelming *Coriolanus*, this time with Laurence Olivier.

Given the two men's chequered relationship when Hall succeeded Olivier at the National, it is fascinating to recall how much the young director brought out of the great actor. This was vintage Olivier who gave us a Coriolanus full of emotional power, physical audacity and withering irony. When Hall created the RSC, the production that defined the ensemble spirit of the company was undoubtedly *The Wars of the Roses*, which offered a conflation, achieved by John Barton, of the three parts of Henry VI and Richard III.

Today we expect to see the plays given in their entirety. But Hall's production was exactly right for the early 1960s. Its cynicism about power-politics coincided with a year of Tory disarray in which Harold Macmillan's sudden resignation provoked a period of unseemly backstabbing. Its chauvinist portrait of the perfidious French reminded us of De Gaulle's peremptory veto of British membership of the EEC. Even the assassination of President Kennedy seemed to chime with the work's portrayal of power as something subject to arbitrary extinction.

Hall's work for the RSC was vibrant, urgent and exciting. In 1965, against the advice of all his colleagues, he staged Harold Pinter's *The Homecoming* in the large Aldwych theatre: a production of meticulous precision, in which actors such as Paul Rogers, Ian Holm and John

Normington applied their Shakespearean expertise to the ambiguities of Pinter's text. That same year, Hall directed a Stratford *Hamlet* in which a young David Warner seemed to echo the baffled alienation of a whole 1960s generation. In between these productions, Hall directed Schoenberg's opera *Moses and Aaron* at Covent Garden with a cast of 300 and an on-stage orgy that induced me to get a standing ticket for the first night.

Hall later confessed to me that he left the RSC too early, in 1968: his work was not done but he was exhausted and he had found, in Trevor Nunn, an ideal successor. Unlike King Lear, Hall always had the capacity to relinquish power and to discover talent in the next generation. On that trip to Athens for *Coriolanus*, I remember Hall gave me an extraordinarily candid interview in which he said he was aiming to leave the National and wanted Richard Eyre to succeed him. "My only fear," he said, "is that the board may think he is too left-wing." Happily, Eyre became the duly appointed heir.

Hall's tenure at the National from 1973 to 1988 is a subject in itself and encompasses a wide range of work. I intemperately loathed his opening masque-like production of *The Tempest*, when the company was still at the Old Vic, and said it was one of the worst Shakespearean productions I had ever seen: a rash statement given some of the dreck of recent years. Hall went on to do masterly productions of Ibsen's *John Gabriel Borkman*, Pinter's *No Man's Land* and Marlowe's impossible *Tamburlaine the Great*. His work later went into decline with oddly neutral, unimaginative productions of *Volpone*, *The Country Wife* and *The Cherry Orchard*. It may have been because he was spreading himself too thinly or because of the pressures in his private life.

But he brought all his operatic instinct to Peter Shaffer's *Amadeus* in 1979 and thereafter recovered his lost form. Hall's final achievement was a sequence of Shakespeare's late plays that were very good at the National and even better when I saw them on tour in Tbilisi where they were stripped of their original set and costumes because of Soviet transport problems. It was a measure of Hall's rapt attention to the verse, as well as to the resourcefulness of the actors, that they transcended the dearth of decor.

But what I most admired about Hall at the National was his tenacity in withstanding industrial action, persistent attacks from disappointed members of the Olivier regime and media abuse. This came to a head in 1986 with a lead story in the *Sunday Times* – headlined Laughing all the way to the bank – alleging that Hall at the National and Trevor Nunn at the RSC were, in effect, exploiting their privileged position for their own commercial advantage.

In fact, I think there were loopholes in directors' contracts that the 1986 Cork inquiry into English theatre, of which I was a member, sought to address: we proposed that no director should ever make more money from a commercial transfer than the producing theatre. But what struck me at the time, and does so still, was that the *Sunday Times* story was intended as an assault on the subsidised sector and used Hall and Nunn as convenient whipping boys.

Shortly after this I made a long TV profile of Hall with Derek Bailey that gave me many insights into the man himself. I remember a rainy day filming at Hall's Sussex home where his young daughter, Rebecca, showed a remarkable capacity to entertain herself. Hall was also highly critical of his early work: especially his famous 1955 *Waiting For Godot* which, he said, was over-decorative and filled the silences with wispy fragments of Bartok. But Hall also struck me as a mixture of the adventurous and the conservative: passionate in his belief in new writing but ultra-cautious when I challenged him on the National's failure to promote women directors.

After he left the National, Hall's career was peripatetic and periodically productive: he seemed like a director in need of a stable financier. He occasionally found one and did wonderful productions such as a West End *Wild Duck* in 1990 with Alex Jennings. But the great dream of Hall in his later years was to revivify the Old Vic, and there was a time in the mid-1990s when this started to happen. He initiated a seven-day operation, created a regular company and, with the aid of Dominic Dromgoole, made new plays part of the repertory alongside established classics. It was a bold, imaginative idea and when it fell apart, because the Old Vic's owners decided to sell the building, Hall was palpably crushed.

Fortunately he later found a permanent home at the Theatre Royal, Bath, where he approached the standard repertory with fresh insight: never more so than in a *Much Ado About Nothing* that brought out the latent homosexuality in Don John's relationship to Claudio. Inevitably, there was a sadness to Hall's later years. I remember a public interview with him at the Galway International Arts Festival in 2009. It was suggested we should meet for lunch in advance to map out the territory: something unheard of with the highly articulate Hall. All went well until we touched on the subject of Shakespearean verse-speaking. "People sometimes accuse me of being . . ." said Hall and then suddenly words failed him. "An iambic fundamentalist?" I prompted and Hall, recovering his nerve, said: "Yes, that's it." It was a small moment but a hint of the onset of dementia.

When I last interviewed him on his 80th birthday, he was mellow, reflective and told me he had a lot of luck in his life and been blessed with doing the job he adored. What he didn't say was that he had also made his own luck and left the British theatre, through his work at the RSC and the National and his unremitting championship of the subsidy principle, infinitely richer than he had found it.

Albion by Mike Bartlett (World Premiere)
Almeida, London: 18 October 2017

Gardens often acquire a symbolic value in drama. Since the one in Mike Bartlett's fascinating, complex new play is called Albion, and is attached to a rambling Oxfordshire house, it is pretty clear we are watching is state-of-the-nation stuff. But what makes the play so enormously intriguing is that, as in his *King Charles III*, Bartlett shows us as a deeply divided people torn between the urge to preserve the past and to radically reform it.

Bartlett focuses on a woman called Audrey who embodies the play's contradictions and who is superlatively performed by Victoria Hamilton. Audrey is a mover and shaker in her mid-50s who sells up in London to live in a seven-bedroom rustic pile she knew as a child. Its prize feature is a famous garden that represents "the chaos of nature in a formal setting," and Audrey's big dream is to restore it to its former glory and to use it to memorialise the son she recently lost in a pointless foreign war. In the process Audrey alienates her daughter, her son's lover, her oldest friend and the entire village. In her mixture of romanticism about the past and restless hunger for change, she seems to epitomise the nation's neurotic divisions.

Like most dramatists who adopt rural settings, Bartlett can't keep Chekhov out of the picture. The fourth act palpably evokes *The Cherry Orchard*, and with Audrey's daughter an aspiring writer who falls for a famous novelist and harshly jettisons another would-be scribe, the echoes of *The Seagull's* triangle of Nina, Trigorin and Konstantin are thunderous. Yet for all its Russian reverberations, Bartlett's play accurately pins down a peculiarly English confusion. This is a world where Audrey's historical vision is juxtaposed with a creeping contemporary fascism, where a building's national character is restored with the aid of Polish efficiency and where privileged country-house parties are contrasted with raucous, rock-driven village revels.

Bartlett throws almost too much into the mix and some of the relationships are not entirely convincing: although they are old college chums, I could never quite believe that Audrey and the now-celebrated novelist would have kept in touch. But Rupert Goold's production orchestrates the action perfectly, Miriam Buether's design creates a garden that blossoms before our eyes and Hamilton, too long absent from the stage, is breathtaking. She shows us exactly why Audrey is a success in business yet a failure in her personal relations. Hamilton strides into the garden as if nature and people can be brought to order, yet she also seems quietly tragic in her incuriosity and lack of empathy. In short, she gives us every facet of Bartlett's multi-layered character.

There is outstanding support from Helen Schlesinger as the rueful novelist, Charlotte Hope as her adoring acolyte, Vinette Robinson as the dead son's obsessive lover and Margot Leicester as a mutinously resentful cleaner. Among the men Nicholas Rowe is striking as Audrey's complaisant husband. It all makes for a long evening, but a rich one: a modern equivalent of Shaw's *Heartbreak House*. But, as well as analysing England's current identity complex, it also suggests, along with *The Ferryman*, *Girl from the North Country*, *Ink* and *Labour of Love*, that this is turning into a vintage year for new writing.

Ken Dodd at 90. A celebration of a great comedian.

4 November 2017

Is theatre the best rejuvenating pill on the market? I've recently talked to a sprightly, 92-year-old Peter Brook and seen the 90-year-old playwright Peter Nichols hold an audience spellbound. I'm also recovering from two extraordinary encounters with Ken Dodd who turns 90 next week: one was a private lunch in Liverpool, the other a public lunch in London where Sir Ken was lauded by members of the British Music Hall Society. On both occasions, I got a glimpse into the transformative power of comedy. As Ken said to me: "I'm told that before I go out on stage, I look my age. Once I'm there, I suddenly turn into a 32-year-old."

I've reviewed and interviewed Ken – I find it hard to call him Dodd – many times over the years but I'd never before been to his home in Knotty Ash, Liverpool. That, in itself, is a revelation. The house, built in 1782, is a rambling mansion that has been in the family for generations and is currently having a new library-cum-study added. It's a stone's throw from the church where Ken's partner, Anne, plays the organ every Sunday and where he worshipped as a boy. "I was in the church choir," he says, "till they found out where the noise was coming from." Although Ken still tots up 50,000 miles a year performing around the country, his roots are as firmly planted in Knotty Ash as the oak trees in his garden. Indeed, only in Liverpool do you realise that he is seemingly loved by everyone. He is warmly greeted by passers-by and returns their affection. When one man, who ardently pumps his hand, tells him he's a postman, Ken instantly replies: "It's better than walking the streets."

Ken seems to have a gag for every occasion. In the course of the brief ride from Knotty Ash into the city centre, he is a constant source of merriment. He talks fondly of his old agent, Dave Forrester, who died a few years back aged 90. "Actually," says Ken, "he was 100 but he kept 10 per cent for himself." When the conversation turns to football, Ken swears he is not prejudiced – "I don't care who beats Manchester United" – and almost persuades me that the Liverpool manager, Jürgen Klopp, has a glamorous daughter called Klippetty.

But there is infinitely more to Ken than the face that launched a thousand quips. He is a thoughtful, highly intelligent man who, having got a scholarship to grammar school at 11, still treasures the advice given to him by his headmaster: "You have not come here to be educated – you have come here to have your minds opened." You could say that mind expansion has been part of his lifelong comic mission.

Over lunch, in what he calls his Autumn Statement, Ken divides the conversation into past, present and future. Much of the past is well documented: his early induction into comedy in being taken by his dad to the Shakespeare's Theatre of Varieties in Liverpool, where he saw greats such as Wilkie Bard and Randolph Sutton; his early comic apprenticeship that saw him doing the rounds of dockers' soirees and funeral directors' dinners; his professional debut in 1954 in the guise of a wild-haired eccentric known as "Professor Yaffle Chuckabutty, Operatic Tenor and Sausage Knotter." *The Manchester Guardian* was quick to spot his talent, claiming: "The trammels of gentility still cling to the splendid down-at-heel madness as portrayed by Mr Ken Dodd at the Hippodrome."

"I was 10 years out on the road learning my craft," says Ken. "But I then made it to the Palladium, the temple of show business, in 1965, and that changed my life. I did 13 shows a week, including three on Saturdays, for 42 weeks and broke box-office records. But I remember a terrible attack of stage fright on opening night. I had to go on stage and sit in a yellow Rolls-Royce and wait for five minutes while there was a dance routine in front of the curtain. I was almost quaking with fear. But the moment the lights came up and I stepped out of the car, I was astonished by the wall of warmth and goodwill that greeted me. I realised that fans who'd seen me all over the country had come to London for the opening. In fact, I came on to more applause than when I went off."

Ken was back at the Palladium in 1967 for another 38-week season and that prompts a story about one of his childhood heroes. "Being at the Palladium meant you automatically did a spot in the Royal Variety Show. We were doing the Sunday night dress rehearsal, directed by Robert Nesbitt, who was a legendary figure. At the end, Mr Nesbitt tottered down majestically from his desk in the stalls, where he always had a glass of champagne to hand, and was confronted by 200 of the finest variety talents in all the world. But I've never forgotten the great Arthur Askey puncturing the pomp of the occasion by suddenly piping up, 'In your opinion, Mr Nesbitt, which one of us stood out?'"

In the 50 years since then, Ken has done just about everything: annual Blackpool summer seasons, pantomimes, nationwide tours, TV and radio. Given that he was a very fine Malvolio in a 1971 Liverpool Playhouse *Twelfth Night*, I am puzzled he has not done more Shakespeare. "I suppose," he says, "the chance never arose but I did play Yorick in Sir Kenneth All-Bran's film of *Hamlet*. I could never quite see why we all had to be in the studios at 5.30 in the morning, but I remember Ken gave me a long explanation of my function in the film to which I said, 'What you mean is I don't have any lines.' What I had to do was be seen entertaining the court, so I just came up with spur-of-the-moment gags to keep them chuckling. I remember saying to Brian Blessed 'I hear you had a crucial role in *Chariots of Fire* – you were a wing nut'; and to Derek Jacobi that he was very big in *The Barefoot Contessa* – he was a verruca.' Anyway, it got them all going, and I remember saying to Ken, 'You're directing and playing Hamlet but who directs you?' He pointed to a figure in the corner and said, 'He was my old tutor at RADA'"

Returning to the present, I can't help asking Ken about the prodigious length of his shows. Anne, his partner, says: "We've got it down to four-and-a-half hours." It's also a source of endless jokes at the Music Hall Society lunch a week later. Bernie Clifton, the veteran comic, says that, at his age, he doesn't go and see a Ken Dodd show without putting his affairs in order. Lord Grade suggests Ken's knighthood was "for services to timesheets all over the world" and that Chairman Xi Jinping's recent lengthy address to the Chinese party faithful was secretly scripted by Ken. My own theory is that Ken rarely abandons tried-and-trusted gags but simply likes adding new ones. When I ask him bluntly why he goes on so long he says: "Because I can."

But he is most revealing when he talks about a comic's relationship with an audience. "You're like a gladiator," he says. "You buckle on your sword and helmet and you have to take on the audience. I reckon you've got 30 seconds in which to build a bridge to them. You can't do a show *at* an audience – you have to do a show *with* an audience and structure the act so that you start with the 'hello' gags, then the topicals, then the surreal stuff. Eventually, you can go wherever you want and say whatever comes into your head: 'How many men does it take to change a toilet roll? I don't know. It's never been done.' You play an audience like you play a musical instrument. But, in the end, it's not enough to be creative. A performer has to have something in his or her psyche I would call 'a comic imp'. That imp is always with you sitting on your shoulder or in your shadow."

Ken is an endlessly exploratory comic but in many ways an old-fashioned, quietly religious, man. He literally thanks God for having been given the chance to make the most of his gifts. He plans to carry on performing but expresses a deep wish that Andrew Lloyd Webber would turn the London Palladium back into a proper variety theatre and give room to the nation's comedians, singers and speciality acts, from jugglers and acrobats to mind-readers and magicians.

As we part company, it strikes me I've been lucky enough in my lifetime to see two performers kissed with genius. One was Laurence Olivier who could enthral an audience with his animalistic power and interpretative originality. The other is Ken Dodd, who has the capacity to take a roomful of strangers and, through a fusillade of verbal and visual gags that never lets up, induce in them a spirit of collective ecstasy. You can't ask much more of a 90-year-old.

2018

The Inheritance by Matthew Lopez
(World Premiere)
Young Vic, London: 31 March 2018

This is quite something: a two-part, seven-hour play by Matthew Lopez dealing almost exclusively with New York gay men. You could say it's like *Angels in America* crossed with *Howards End*, in that it deals with the bitter inheritance of Aids and the spiritual qualities of a house. That bald summary does scant justice, however, to a play that, in Stephen Daldry's crystalline production, pierces your emotional defences, raises any number of political issues and enfolds you in its narrative.

Lopez's debt to E.M. Forster is palpable. There is even a character called Morgan who kickstarts the play by addressing a group of young men and urging them to look in their hearts and write. This prompts a story about a young couple, Eric and Toby, that ripples outward. Eric is a kindly, humane lawyer who lives in a posh Upper West Side apartment. Toby, his long-time lover, is a sharp-tongued writer whose success is based on the denial of his past. Their impending marriage is threatened both by Eric's loss of the family apartment and by Toby's fixation on Adam, the charismatic star of his play.

This leads to the same clash of values that animates *Howards End*. The liberal Eric is drawn to a real-estate developer – named Henry Wilcox, like the embodiment of materialism in Forster's book – who has recently lost his own partner, Walter. One of the best and funniest scenes shows Henry shocking a roomful of Eric's left-leaning friends by declaring he is a Republican. As in Forster's book, a property is pivotal. Walter always wanted Eric to have an upstate house he owned that, at the height of the Aids epidemic, he turned into a refuge for the dying. We wait to see whether Eric will ever come into his rightful inheritance.

While Lopez's play has a literary framework, it teems with life and incident: watching it is like binge-watching a boxset. It tells multiple stories. One of the most intriguing shows the success-driven Toby becoming involved with a rent boy, Leo, who is not only a lookalike for Adam but also tests the moral probity of all who encounter him. Lopez is also unafraid to periodically stop the plot and clear the stage for an impassioned debate: one of the most intense is about the status of gay culture which, having fought so long against oppression, now finds itself in danger of being co-opted. It is Eric who cuts through the swirling opinions by urging the need to honour the past while living fully in the present.

This, in a nutshell, is the Forsterian message that emerges from the play. I admired its roller-coaster energy and high entertainment value, but I found its exclusive maleness limiting. The only woman we meet does not appear until the end, when Vanessa Redgrave makes a moving appearance as a mother who belatedly learned to love her gay son. I also occasionally felt, as with Adam's graphic description of his orgiastic experience in a Prague bathhouse, that Lopez was exhibiting his own virtuosic writing at the expense of the character's believability.

In Daldry's production, staged on a Bob Crowley set that looks like a stripped Japanese table, the prime emphasis is on narrative clarity. The performances are also exemplary. Kyle Soller conveys every ounce of Eric's instinctive decency and Andrew Burnap all of Toby's sad selfishness. Samuel H. Levine switches brilliantly between the fast-rising Adam and the sinking Leo, and John Benjamin Hickey as Henry embodies the emotional isolation of the stinking rich. But the performance that best epitomises the play's values is that of Paul Hilton who, as Morgan Forster and Walter, exudes a quiet humanity that suggests respect for the dead needs to be balanced by a love of the living.

The Writer by Ella Hickson (World Premiere) Almeida, London: 28 April 2018

Ella Hickson struck gold with her last play, *Oil* (2016), which spanned 150 years of female history. Her new play may look at first like a Pirandellian box of tricks but is no less ambitious in its attempt to address the purpose of art, the nature of gender and the need for the mythic in a society governed by fixed, male-determined rules. Playful and impassioned, it keeps one riveted for two hours.

It starts with a bruising encounter in a deserted theatre. The woman (Lara Rossi) is an angry 24-year-old who detests the hidebound conventions of modern drama and whose driving ambition is to "dismantle capitalism and overturn the patriarchy." The man (Samuel West) is a part of the theatrical establishment governed by a cautious pragmatism. The woman's view of theatre as a sacred space with a political purpose is met with amused condescension and a vain attempt to co-opt her fury. It sets the tone for much of the ensuing action.

But Hickson quickly asks whether we are watching real people, or characters created by the Writer (Romola Garai) and manipulated by the Director (Michael Gould)? What we see over the following four scenes is an extension of the initial debate. Garai's Writer is a fervent idealist wrestling with the compromises demanded by her boyfriend and her director. This leads her into a quest for a more tribal way of living and a rejection of the polarised fixities of gender.

Above all, the play is asking: do we need new theatrical forms to reflect a society in the midst of a sexual revolution? Hickson's approach is witty, clever and keeps the ground shifting under our feet – Rossi's character attacks the kind of play that introduces real-life babies only for Hickson's to do precisely that.

But while Rossi questions the power of "old white guys" to set the critical rules, I have two reservations. Hickson portrays the two key men in the play as implacable materialists: she seems to deny the possibility that men can unite with women in overthrowing the existing order. And in placing so much stress on the solitary anguish of the Writer, Hickson is in danger of endorsing the privileged despair of the lucky few.

Still this is a play about big issues, and Blanche McIntyre's superbly inventive production and Anna Fleischle's ingenious design reinforce how Hickson's play practises what it preaches: it adopts precisely the provocative, non-naturalistic form it is asking for. Garai is a wonderful mix of the tentative and the assured and nothing in the play is better than her realisation that, in her sex life, she has achieved the domination she deplores in men. Rossi captures perfectly the blazing intensity required in the opening, and West and Gould, who hovers on the edge of the action like a puppetmaster, convey the male desire for control.

In the end this is a play about a Writer's desire to change the world, and it leaves us urgently debating whether theatre itself is a potential instrument of revolution or a bastion of the status quo.

Nine Night by Natasha Gordon (World Premiere) Dorfman, National Theatre, London: 5 May 2018

There is a key moment in Natasha Gordon's highly impressive debut play when Aunt Maggie leaves the nine-night funeral wake that is part of her Jamaican heritage to go home to watch EastEnders. "Big tings are gwan in the Queen Vic tonight," she announces. For me, that neatly sums up Gordon's theme – which is the ability to inhabit two cultures and to acknowledge one's ancestral past while living fully in the present.

Gordon's play acquires extra resonance in the light of the Windrush scandal: the same Aunt Maggie gets a big laugh when she says that her Freedom Pass is "the only decent ting me get from this teefing government." But the play is less about living in a hostile environment than about the tensions that erupt in the wake of loss.

The dead woman, Gloria, came to Britain from Jamaica as a young woman, leaving behind a daughter, Trudy. She then had two children by another man and their differences drive the action. Lorraine, who gave up her job to look after her dying mum, is the eternal coper supplying the food for the traditional nine-night celebration. Robert, married to a white teacher, is an entrepreneurial go-getter impatient with the claims of the past.

Gordon deals very well with the different layers of grief: one of the sharpest scenes shows the family arguing over the practical problems of the funeral. But the joy of the play is that it is exuberantly funny while arguing that it is possible to dwell in seemingly antithetical worlds. Even Anita, Lorraine's graduate daughter, who initially views the whole nine-night wake with a rational scepticism, is sufficiently moved by her gran's funeral to momentarily believe in God.

Cecilia Noble, who plays Aunt Maggie, steals every scene she is in and along with the newly returned Trudy (played by Michelle Greenidge) she carries out a climactic ritual that supposedly releases the spirit of the dead woman. Whether we believe in its efficacy is irrelevant: Gordon's point is that you do not – nor should you – abandon inherited customs simply because you inhabit a materialistic, metropolitan culture. The family history takes a bit of sorting out and I wish Gordon had told us more about Anita's self-empowerment. But Roy Alexander Weise's production has real momentum and underscores Gordon's gift for raising big issues through laughter. The magnificent Noble is inescapably dominant as the dogmatic Aunt Maggie, who has a belief in the equally restorative powers of chicken and Jesus and who, reacting with horror to the idea of Gloria being cremated, roundly declares: "We don't cook our people." Franc Ashman as Lorraine captures perfectly the sadness of the dutiful daughter who was never wholly loved and, without shouting it from the rooftops, makes the point that England never really wanted the immigrants who have for so long sustained the country economically.

Oliver Alvin-Wilson as Robert and Hattie Ladbury as his wife, Sophie, also make a totally plausible couple: it is a sign of the play's subtlety that while she is unequivocally embraced by her inherited Jamaican family, he is angrily resentful at his rejection by Sophie's mother. This is a play, dealing with Jamaican life but easily applicable to others, that says a lot in 105 minutes. It also proves the National's belief in its mission to portray the multicultural Britain we live in.

Red by John Logan (Revival)
Wyndham's, London: 19 May 2018

"Make something new," the painter Mark Rothko urges his young assistant in John Logan's play. One is tempted to say the same to the play's director, Michael Grandage, except that there are several justifications for reviving this piece. In 2009, it moved straight from the Donmar to Broadway, bypassing the West End it enshrines a towering performance from Alfred Molina and it is one of the few plays that offers a plausible portrait of an artist at work.

We are in Rothko's Bowery studio in the late 1950s after he has been commissioned to paint a series of murals for the ritzy Four Seasons' restaurant in New York's Seagram Building. His assistant, Ken, is there to mix paints, stretch canvases, fetch coffee and listen to Rothko's dogmatic utterances and raging paranoia about the art establishment.

"Ten per cent of one's time," says Rothko, "is putting paint on canvas – the rest is waiting." And while they wait, we see the gauche apprentice turn from humble sounding board into fierce spokesman for the future. Just as Rothko's paintings are about the tension between blocks of colour, so the play itself is about opposing views of art. The rabbinical Rothko stands for a belief in the quasi-religious, tragic, timeless nature of painting Ken argues for the urgently contemporary and rashly embraces the emerging pop art of Lichtenstein and Warhol. While this leads to fruitful debate, and yields telling aphorisms such as Rothko's "To surmount the past you must know the past," it also raises serious doubts. Seeing the play again, I wondered if Rothko would really have tolerated an assistant who attacked his "titanic self-absorption" and cultural irrelevance. The delight of the piece, however, is its ability to balance theory and practice. In Christopher Oram's design, the studio really does look like a workspace, and the highlight of Grandage's production is still the moment when Rothko and Ken take a blank canvas and slap on an undercoat. The two men go at their task like demons.

Returning to the role of Rothko, Molina also suggests flickers of self-doubt beneath the iron certainty. Molina has a bullish physique, lays down the law like an aesthetic tyrant and, at the mere mention of Warhol, averts his gaze with silent disdain. But the virtue of Molina's performance is in suggesting Rothko knows that, in painting murals for a swish eatery, he is betraying his own ideals. The performance is as layered as a Rothko.

Alfred Enoch captures exactly Ken's progress from sorcerer's apprentice to articulate opponent, and wittily scores off Rothko by reminding him that, just as the abstract expressionists waged brutal war on the cubists, so they too are now being overturned. Even if I couldn't always believe that the studio would have housed such suavely phrased arguments, the play offers an invigorating 90 minutes and shows Rothko's ability to paint the town his own sombre form of red.

The Jungle by Joe Murphy and Joe Thompson (World Premiere)
Playhouse, London: 7 July 2018

This is that rare thing: a necessary piece of theatre. It is the work of Joe Murphy and Joe Thompson, who created Good Chance Theatre in the Calais refugee camp known as the Jungle. It not only offers, in a superb production by Stephen Daldry and Justin Martin, a vivid re-creation of lived experience but leaves you pondering how the migrant crisis should be addressed.

First seen at the Young Vic, the production has moved into the West End with its vital organs intact. Miriam Buether's design transforms the stalls into the camp's Afghan Cafe, where we sit round tables that are walkways for the actors. Starting with a funeral and threatened camp eviction in 2016, it goes back to trace the site's growth to see a multinational mix of refugees turn into a town of 6,000 citizens living with hope and desperation. The play is built on opposites. Optimism is embodied in Safi, a former student from Aleppo, who finds in the camp "more hope than you've seen in all lifetimes." That is offset by the harrowing memories of 17-year-old Okot from Darfur, who declares "a refugee dies many times." The two are left to compete for a place in a smugglers' lorry.

The Jungle raises a host of issues and seems a mix of the structured and the spontaneous. It is also powerfully performed. Ammar Haj Ahmad (Safi), John Pfumojena (Okot) and Ben Turner (Salar) speak for the residents Alex Lawther, Rachel Redford and Jo McInnes for UK volunteers who are initially resented but in the end gladly received. The result is a priceless evening that enlarges our understanding while appealing to our emotions.

The Lehman Trilogy by Stefano Massini (UK Premiere)
Lyttelton, National Theatre, London: 14 July 2018

What an astonishing evening! Spanning 150 years and running three-and-a-half hours, Stefano Massini's play traces the trajectory of Western capitalism by following the fortunes of a single family. But where previous European stagings have deployed a vast cast, Sam Mendes's production of Ben Power's adaptation uses just three actors: Simon Russell Beale, Ben Miles and Adam Godley. The result is an intimate epic that becomes a masterly study of acting as well as of the intricacies of high finance.

For most of us the name of the Lehman Brothers stirs memories of the financial crash of 2008, when this Wall Street institution filed for bankruptcy, an event that had global consequences. But Massini's play traces the family's progress from the arrival of three brothers from Bavaria in the America of the 1840s.

Starting with the opening of a general store in Montgomery, Alabama, the Lehmans move into buying and reselling raw cotton and expand into banking, the coffee market and the railway business. Power passes from one generation to the next but a decisive shift comes in the late 1960s with the creation of a trading division run by non-family members. Eventually this leads to the firm's demise with the collapse of the mortgage bond market.

You can see the story in many ways: as a dynastic drama, as a study of the decline and fall of an immigrant Jewish family, as a parable about the dangers of market deregulation. Although Power's adaptation avoids lectures, it is hard not to see the play as an account of the shifting definition of the American dream. To the original Lehman Brothers, arriving in what one of them dubs "that magical music-box called America," it meant enterprise and hard work would be rewarded by success. By 2008 it has dwindled into delusions of infinite riches based on financial services.

The real joy of Mendes's impeccable production, however, lies in watching the actors at work as they switch genders and ages to evoke multiple characters. Russell Beale starts out as the solid, senior Henry Lehman but, at different times, turns into a sprightly tightrope walker, a decrepit rabbi, a flirty divorcee. It not only reveals a versatility we have not seen in Russell Beale before: one scene where, as Henry's nephew, he assesses potential brides on a points system, also brilliantly demonstrates the limitations of the business ethos. Godley is no less extraordinary. He starts as the patronised youngest of the Lehman siblings, Mayer, and later transmogrifies, by donning dark glasses, into the ferociously entrepreneurial Bobbie: in the interim, he plays everything from blushing brides to recalcitrant toddlers. Miles, meanwhile, exudes an authoritative calm as the middle brother, Emanuel, but goes on to reveal the rebelliousness of later members of the Lehman clan and the rage of piratical traders. Es Devlin's set is also beautiful to look at: a rotating glass box backed by Luke Halls' stunning video designs that provide a black-and-white panorama of a changing American landscape.

The final stages of the firm's collapse are rather hastily handled. It would have been fascinating to know more about the subprime mortgage scandal and the way the firm removed liabilities to create a misleading impression of its stability. Otherwise, this is an engrossing evening. Not the least of its virtues is that it shows how, even at the height of Lehman Brothers' success, the key players all had nightmares prophesying doom. But Mendes and Power are not offering a wise-after-the-event hindsight saga. As in all the best plays about finance – such as Caryl Churchill's *Serious Money* and Lucy Prebble's *Enron* – they capture the dubious excitement, as well as the danger, of high-risk capitalism. It makes for a remarkable evening, which offers a kaleidoscopic social and political metaphor while reminding us that one of the reasons we go to the theatre is to watch superb acting.

Caryl Churchill at 80.

2 September 2018

Caryl Churchill, who will be 80 on 3 September, was once compared by a fellow writer to Pablo Picasso. At first, it seems a bizarre coupling: a bull-like Spanish painter-sculptor and an intellectual British dramatist. But, as you think about it, the comparison makes sense. Like Picasso, Churchill has an active political conscience, has had a big influence on succeeding generations and is a restless experimenter with form. That last quality is, for me, the key to an extraordinary career that has yielded close to 40 plays and made Churchill an iconic figurehead.

Given the surge in plays by women in recent years, one forgets just how isolated Churchill must have felt when she set out. She began writing at Oxford but, while raising a family in the 1960s, focused exclusively on short plays for radio. She had her first stage play, *Owners*, put on at the Royal Court Theatre Upstairs in 1972 at a time when there were scarcely any role-models for women dramatists. Ann Jellicoe, another experimental dramatist, was the only major woman writer to have emerged from the Court's chauvinist culture, Shelagh Delaney had flared like a rocket with one hit and then fizzled out and Agatha Christie had her secure niche in the West End. Otherwise, that was just about it. To whom was a young woman dramatist to turn for inspiration?

I suspect it was that combination of her isolation, the imaginative freedom she had learned from radio and her inquisitive intellect that made Churchill strike out on her own. Even as a fledgling dramatist in the 1960s she had said that "whenever conventions of subject and form outlast the impetus that formed them they are felt to be inadequate to expressing life." That could be seen as the mantra that has governed her whole theatrical career, from *Owners* to *Escaped Alone* in 2016. James Macdonald, who directed *Drunk Enough to say I Love You* at the Royal Court in 2006, put it succinctly when he said "Caryl is always ahead of the game ... She would only hand something in as a new play if for her its form and content were new in the theatre."

If today Churchill is lauded for her novelty, and all dramatists – men as well as women – feel free to experiment, it wasn't that easy at the start. I liked *Owners*, in which Churchill anticipated the rampant individualism of the 1980s through the figure of a ruthless female landlord but complained that "she throws everything in bar the kitchen sink." Others were more severe. One critic said that the play failed for want of elementary disciplines, "namely unity of action and unity of tone – those much despised classical standards." Yet who was to say that Aristotelian rules were still applicable? Churchill's achievement was to break through that kind of conservative, male thinking to capture the fragmentation of life and show that each new play was an adventure into the unknown.

A sign of Churchill's capacity for innovation was her readiness to engage in a radical new way of writing plays involving collaborative research. That sprang from her association with Max Stafford-Clark who in 1974 had created, with William Gaskill, the Joint Stock company as a theatrical collective. By the time Churchill joined, the company had already had a striking success with David Hare's *Fanshen*, but it was with Joint Stock that Churchill wrote *Light Shining in Buckinghamshire* (1976), *Cloud Nine* (1979) and *Fen* (1983). Although it wasn't a Joint Stock show, the same techniques were also used to create *Serious Money* (1987), which became a Royal Court and West End mega-hit.

Even with the Joint Stock method, the dramatist is still the undisputed author of the finished play: the difference is that he or she is part of the research process. *Light Shining in Buckinghamshire*, which dealt with the millennial movements bred by the English Civil War, was an obvious eye-opener. "I'd never seen an exercise or an improvisation before and was as thrilled as a child at a pantomime," Churchill said of the first day in rehearsal. But, while obviously benefiting from the group approach, the play stands up today as one of Churchill's very best: a study of the way the utopian dreams of the Levellers and Diggers had been crushed by Cromwell's army evoking parallels with the disillusion that followed the collapse of the revolutionary hopes of the 1960s. As always, Churchill also tries new techniques. Anticipating the kind of Tribunal Plays that were to become popular at the Tricycle Theatre in the 1990s, Churchill incorporates the Putney Debates of 1647, in which arguments for liberty and equality were outmanoeuvred by the unyielding English faith in the sanctity of private property.

Churchill has never stopped experimenting with form. The danger is that one sometimes overlooks what she is saying in our fascination with the way she is saying it: what I see in her work is a socialist-feminist perspective that has expanded to embrace a vision of impending catastrophe. But what Churchill gets little credit for is detecting early on that it is no sign of progress for women simply to replicate a ruthless male success ethic. It was there in *Owners* when the protagonist announced her philosophy: "Be clean, be quick, be top, be best." That is also the credo of Marlene in the magnificent *Top Girls* who runs her own thriving employment agency but presides over a company simmering with discontent and finally confronts the vacancy in her own life.

This is vintage Churchill in that radical form and content coalesce. Churchill, who had been struck in America by women boasting of boardroom promotion as the ultimate goal, is arguing there is no such thing as right-wing feminism. At the same time, the play's action is a series of revelations. It starts with Marlene hosting a dinner-party for famous women of history and myth who emerge as both pioneers and victims, goes on to give us a satiric vision of office-life and climaxes in a painfully naturalistic study of the drudgery and fear experienced by the sister and child Marlene abandoned. Forget unity of tone: this is Churchill showing that form follows function and that a play can be written in a miscellany of styles.

One consequence of being ahead of the game is that you sometimes leave the punters panting in your wake, and not all Churchill's experiments have worked. I recall being baffled by *Softcops*, which felt like a meditation on crime and punishment lacking Churchill's usual gift of narrative drive. *A Mouthful of Birds* was equally mystifying in its attempt to create a dance-drama suggesting that the violence and ecstasy of Euripides' *The Bacchae* were alive in modern Britain.

But anyone who takes as many risks as Churchill is bound to have her failures. Far more important is that, at an age when many writers are simply content to build on the territory they have already colonised, Churchill goes on exploring. In *Blue Heart* she played fascinating games with time and language while introducing surrealist touches: who, but Churchill, would import an SS officer, an emu and a gang of children into a modern domestic kitchen? *Far Away* transported us, in three short scenes, from localised fascism to cosmic destruction. And most recently in *Escaped Alone* she whisked us from cosy chat in a sunlit garden to Cassandra-like monologues about a disintegrating planet. I once thought there was a determinist gloom about Churchill's prophecies of disaster: I now believe that she is offering a necessary jolt to our shocking complacency.

There is another side to Churchill we often overlook: she is a reluctant interviewee but a ceaseless campaigner. She resigned from the English Stage Company's governing council in 1989 over the Royal Court's sponsorship deals, has come out fighting in defence of many other writers including a vilified Sarah Kane and only last week was co-signatory to a letter to *The Guardian* deploring the bombing of a cultural centre in Gaza. Some will not forget that she got into trouble in 2009 for writing a 10-minute play, *Seven Jewish Children,* which suggested that Israel's understandable preoccupation with national security was leading it into acts of indiscriminate slaughter. Without wishing to resurrect old arguments, that play was another sign of one of Churchill's key qualities: a total lack of fear. In my few brief encounters with her, she has struck me as a very modest, quiet person with a built-in reserve. As a writer, however, she has offered a critique of modern society from diverse viewpoints, opened doors for other dramatists and helped to dismantle antiquated, manmade notions of theatrical structure. If nowadays there is no consensus about form and a play can be whatever its author chooses it to be, then that is largely thanks to the pioneering, Picasso-like figure of Caryl Churchill.

Company. Book by George Furth, Music and Lyrics by Stephen Sondheim
Gielgud, London: 20 October 2018

A gender change can work wonders. It is no secret that Robert, the bachelor hero of this 1970 show with music and lyrics by Stephen Sondheim, has now become Bobbie. The transition makes total sense in today's world: my only reservation is that the musical, in Marianne Elliott's production, has lost some of its Manhattan identity.

The starting point is a surprise birthday party for Bobbie that both pinpoints her single status and enables her to view her married friends with an outsider's amusement and envy. The gender swap has a ripple effect on key numbers. You Could Drive a Person Crazy becomes the cry of three guys unable to comprehend the heroine's refusal to conform. Even more radically, Getting Married Today articulates the prenuptial panic of a gay man. If the show sharpens the dilemma facing the semi-detached woman, it also offers a hauntingly ambivalent study of marriage. You see that in one of Sondheim's finest numbers, Sorry-Grateful, in which three married men express the constant tug between security and freedom. The key idea behind Elliott's production and Bunny Christie's design is of Bobbie as a modern Alice In Wonderland exploring a set of sliding rooms that expose the foibles of married life. It gives the show a dreamlike quality but obscures the implied connection between Manhattan and marriage.

All else is heavenly. Rosalie Craig invests Bobbie with a warmth, curiosity and hunger for life, above all making the point that the stakes are higher for Bobbie because of her ticking biological clock. *Company* was the first musical I saw on Broadway and has always had a special place in my affections. It is gratifying to see it not just being revived but intelligently reimagined.

The Watsons by Laura Wade (World Premiere)
Minerva Studio, Chichester: 10 November 2018

I would seriously urge anyone planning to attend Laura Wade's adaptation of Jane Austen's unfinished novel to stop reading now since one of the play's many pleasures is its capacity to endlessly take us by surprise. We go in expecting a literary exercise and come out having seen a philosophical comedy.

Wade plays fair in briskly dramatising the events of Austen's fragment. Emma Watson, after being stylishly reared by a Shropshire aunt, returns after 14 years to the genteel poverty of the Surrey family home. Marriage, for Emma and her sisters, seems a matter of economic necessity and various candidates present themselves at a local ball. One, Tom Musgrave, is a conceited flirt another, Lord Osborne, is a diffident aristo a third, Mr Howard, is a sententious clergyman. Who will Emma choose in order to escape from her own discordant family? A lesser dramatist, seizing on hints from Austen's sister that Emma would reject the lord and marry the cleric, might have gone on to give us period pastiche. But, just as Wade turned the tables on us in *Home, I'm Darling* by showing the ersatz nature of the 1950s milieu, so here she upsets the applecart by making a writer called Laura pivotal to the action. Laura finds herself confronting a puzzled, angry Emma about her destiny. This has a ripple effect in which all the characters question Laura's authority and even threaten to take over the story.

The debt to Pirandello's *Six Characters in Search of An Author* is openly acknowledged but it is repaid with interest. Wade goes beyond the Pirandellian proposition that illusion is reality to launch a debate about the shifting status of a dramatic or literary creation.

In one sense, it is absurd to say that a character takes over from the author: all the words spoken here are written by Wade. Yet Austen's people and plots have a vigorous extratextual life, as John Mullan reminds us in the programme, with references to *Vampire Darcy's Desire* and an online video monologue, *The Lizzie Bennet Diaries*.

I loved Wade's approach because it is playful and serious at the same time. It wrestles with the impertinence of completing a literary fragment yet it rejoices in the limitless possibilities this affords. Even if it once or twice seems to be coruscating on thin ice, it is also given a beautifully bold, clear production by Samuel West and a fine design by Ben Stones. We start in a pristine Austen drawing room, which opens up to become a battleground of ideas embracing Hobbes, Locke and Rousseau.

The acting is also excellent. Louise Ford as Laura captures both the desperation and delight of a dramatist who finds her supposed omniscience challenged. Grace Molony as Emma shows how the lively wit of Austen's character translates into mutinous fury when she finds she is apparently entrapped in a fiction and there is rich support from Sally Bankes as a disarmingly knowledgeable Nanny, and Tim Delap as the archetypal poker-backed clergyman.

Writers sometimes tell you that a character has the capacity to dictate events. Wade has seized on this tension between authorial control and imaginative freedom to create a stunning play.

Sweat by Lynn Nottage (UK Premiere) Donmar Warehouse, London: 21 December 2018

Lynn Nottage, as she showed in *Intimate Apparel*, which was about a seamstress in the 1900s, has the capacity to dramatise work. In this breathtaking play she tackles the devastating impact of loss of work and of de-industrialisation on modern America. Based on extensive interviews with residents of the rustbelt town of Reading, Pennsylvania, it shows the anger and despair that helped fuel the election of Donald Trump.

The play takes place pre-Trump. It is bookended by scenes showing two young ex-cons confronting their parole officer, but most of the action is set eight years earlier, in 2000, in a bar where female workers from the local factory hang out. Divisions surface when Cynthia, an African-American, is promoted from the shop floor to supervisor over the head of her white oldest friend, Tracey. The sense of personal betrayal is exacerbated when it is left to Cynthia to reveal that the firm plans to ask everyone to take a 60 per cent pay cut to save the plant. This leads to a lockout, scabs crossing the picket line and an act of violence that explains the parole interviews.

What Nottage captures brilliantly is the way work gives people an identity and purpose. Tracey is a militant unionist but bereft without employment. "Do you know what it's like," she asks, "to get up and have no place to go?" For Cynthia, work is a means of advancement and her union card a symbol of racial acceptance. Behind the play's portrayal of the damage done to lives by what Nottage calls "the American de-industrial revolution" lies a wider picture of collapsing hopes and corporate ruthlessness.

In Lynette Linton's production, Frankie Bradshaw's impressive design sets the watering hole against a background of rusting girders. The acting is superlative. Martha Plimpton as Tracey and Clare Perkins as Cynthia suggest a lifetime of friendship, tragically sundered Patrick Gibson and Osy Ikhile show the heavy prices paid by their respective offspring and Stuart McQuarrie as the pacifying bartender and Leanne Best as a boozy dreamer reveal how everyone is blighted by a company town's decline. I can't think of any recent play that tells us so much, and so vividly, about the state of the union.

2019

Our Lady of Kibeho by Katori Hall (World Premiere) Royal and Derngate, Northampton: 17 January 2019

Katori Hall's astonishing play, dealing with the apparent visitation of the Virgin Mary to a trio of Rwandan schoolgirls in 1981, has some distinguished forebears. Like Shaw's *Saint Joan*, it explores the nature of miracles, and, like Miller's *The Crucible*, it raises the spectre of mass hallucination. But it is very much Hall's own work in that it roots religious ecstasy in a world of political tension between Tutsi and Hutu that was to lead to Rwandan genocide in 1994.

Hall's previous work ranges from *The Mountaintop*, which saw Martin Luther King as a flawed martyr, to the book for the Tina Turner musical *Tina,* which was a celebration of the pop icon. Here she examines the true story of how three village girls in a Catholic college claimed to have received messages from the "Mother of the Word." In the first half, the school's tolerant Tutsi head and his domineering Hutu deputy clash over their responses to this seemingly divine eruption. But the play becomes even more gripping in the second half with the arrival of a Vatican emissary whose task is to test the validity of the girls' visions, which climax in a prophecy of the appalling bloodshed that was to visit their native land.

In an age dominated by secular drama, it is rare to find questions of faith so explicitly raised. What is good about Hall's play is that it strikes a balance between respect for the girls' integrity and scepticism about the religious hierarchy. It is possible, especially when the girls suddenly levitate, that they are surrendering to hypnosis. Yet Hall suggests they could be vessels for a divine message that sees Rwanda's rivers running with blood. Their visions also expose both Rwanda's ethnic divisions and the expediency of the Catholic establishment. The diocesan bishop, who initially wants the story suppressed, comes to see it as a tourist attraction and even the school's priest covertly trains the girls in the liturgy so that they can pass the Vatican's tests.

Hall's virtue is that she puts a complete world on stage, one that embraces a cloistered college, a faith-hungry village and tribal hatred. James Dacre's production rises to the challenge with the aid of a community ensemble, a Jonathan Fensom set that shows the sun-kissed landscape beyond the hermetic school and an Orlando Gough score that blends a cappella singing with tingling accompaniments to the girls' visions.

Characters are also sharply delineated. Gabrielle Brooks brings out the artless wonder of Alphonsine, the initial visionary, while Yasmin Mwanza evokes the scholarly intensity of her fellow student Anathalie and Pepter Lunkuse the manipulative nature of the more mature Marie-Claire. There's a touch of Graham Greene about the waning faith of the school's Father Tuyishime, which Ery Nzaramba nicely captures. Leo Wringer pins down the worldliness of the local bishop, and Michael Mears as the Vatican's man shows how disdain for the idea of divine visions in remote Africa give way to shaken acceptance of the possibility.

Hall leaves it to us to make up our own minds about whether the Virgin Mary spoke to the girls of Kibeho. But this is a play that swims against the tide by asking us to acknowledge the miraculous while also exploring the historical context of the Rwandan violence that the West notoriously did nothing to prevent.

Rutherford and Son by Githa Sowerby
Crucible, Sheffield: 12 February 2019

The astonishing thing about Githa Sowerby's play is not that it is currently fashionable – the National also revives it this year – but that it lay neglected for so long. It was ignored between its premiere in 1912 and its rediscovery by feminist groups in the 1980s, yet in its passion, power and ability to relate domestic issues to the wider social landscape it more than matches the plays of its time by Harley Granville-Barker and D.H. Lawrence.

Rutherford himself is the patriarchal owner of a Tyneside glassworks who expects total fealty both at home and on the factory floor. His world is slowly crumbling, however. He alienates his two sons, one of whom has made a discovery that could save the tottering firm from collapse, and banishes his daughter, Janet, on learning of her secret affair with his foreman. At the last he is left alone with his daughter-in-law, Mary, who strikes a bargain that shows the balance of power to be radically shifting.

Ingenious as the climax is, I shall remember Caroline Steinbeis's production for two tremendous scenes, both involving Laura Elphinstone as Janet. In the first, she rounds on her father, accusing him of ruining her life: delivered by Elphinstone with a lifetime's banked-up fury, the speech is one of the most potent statements by a wronged woman in British drama. Elphinstone is equally hypnotic when, realising that her lover's ultimate loyalty is to his master, she sits on a chaise longue with head tilted in silent contemplation of a world awry. Owen Teale is excellent as Rutherford in that he neither rants nor blusters but speaks with the quiet authority of a man who expects to be obeyed. There is strong support from Danusia Samal as the despised daughter-in-law, Ciarán Owens as her weakly defiant husband and Brian Lonsdale as the foreman steeped in feudal values. I could have done without some artily choreographed movement between the acts. Otherwise this is a first-rate revival of a landmark play.

Betrayal by Harold Pinter (Revival)
Harold Pinter Theatre, London:
14 March, 2019

After a brilliant season of Pinter's short plays we now get his full-length study of the complex mathematics of betrayal. But, while Tom Hiddleston is the big draw and gives a fine performance, what is striking is the spartan purity of Jamie Lloyd's production. Of the many versions of the play I've seen over the past 40 years this one goes furthest in stripping the action of circumstantial detail.

Pinter famously reverses chronology so that we start with the bitter-sweet aftertaste of an affair and then backtrack in time to its beginnings. But Lloyd never lets us forget that there are three sides to an emotional triangle and that the absent partner is always there in the mind. So, as Emma and Jerry meet for a drink long after their relationship is over, we are aware of the gaunt, unforgiving presence of Hiddleston as Emma's husband, Robert, in the background. In the Venetian scene where Robert first learns of Emma's affair, Charlie Cox's Jerry is both physically and spiritually present. And when the two men later have a deceptively casual lunch at a London restaurant, Zawe Ashton's Emma sits in the shadows pensively munching an apple.

It's a device that nails several points in one go. It reminds us of the molten intimacy of the three characters. It heightens the fact that the play is about the labyrinthine nature of betrayal. It also confirms that, as in all Pinter's work, memory is a key factor. But what is equally startling is the absence of scenic detail: Soutra Gimour's design simply consists of pastel-shaded screens and a couple of chairs. This gives the action a dreamlike fluidity but occasionally I hungered for a touch of domestic realism: in particular Emma's attempt to convert the lovers' Kilburn flat into a surrogate home gets lost in such starkness.

The great gain, however, is that the focus is on the play's psychological intricacy and on the acting. Hiddleston, especially, is superb in conveying Robert's unhealed emotional wounds. His initial mocking superiority to Jerry is explained by the fact he has long been aware of his best friend's covert betrayal. In the Venetian scene, when he learns that Emma's affair has been going on for five years, he has the poleaxed stare of a man whose world has fallen apart. But there is a savage humour to the restaurant scene where Hiddleston stabs at a melon as if displacing his anger with Jerry.

Ashton also subtly brings out Emma's capacity to love two men simultaneously. She suggests a free spirit yet one capable of exquisite tenderness: even when forced to confess her adultery, her hand gently traces Robert's forearm as if softening the blow and reminding him that her passion is still intact. Cox's engaging Jerry, meanwhile, emerges as the least complex of the three characters: an affectionate sensualist who is able to compartmentalise his desires. Yet the revelation of this excellent production is its reminder that betrayal is never-ending and that the one deceived forever haunts the imagination.

Kunene and the King by John Kani (World Premiere) The Swan, Stratford-upon-Avon: 3 April 2019

How do you put a nation's history on stage? In this remarkable play, John Kani – as formidable a writer as he is an actor – does it through a confrontation between two men who represent polarised aspects of South African experience. Marking 25 years since the country's first post-apartheid democratic elections, the play becomes an exploration of race, class, politics, theatre and the potentially unifying power of Shakespeare.

Antony Sher plays Jack Morris, a cantankerous old actor who hopes to overcome severe liver cancer to get to Cape Town to play King Lear. Kani himself is Lunga Kunene, a retired carer assigned by an agency to tend this querulous thespian. While claiming to be apolitical, Morris embodies the reflex attitudes of white supremacy and consistently, when talking to Kunene, refers to "you people." Although refusing to be a spokesman, Kunene recounts how his own dreams of being a doctor were thwarted, not so much by his Soweto upbringing as by the vengefulness of "comrades" towards his storekeeper father for seeking to transcend the divisions of the apartheid era.

Bound together by medical necessity, the two men reveal much about South Africa's past and present. For all the talk of truth and reconciliation, it is clear that old antagonisms still persist: when Morris dwells on the country's continuing internal violence, Kunene recalls the long history of white oppression and asks, poignantly, when the long-promised "better future" will arrive. Yet, for all their radical differences, the men have much in common. Both are estranged from their children. Even more significant is their love for Shakespeare, one that Kunene acquired through an isiXhosa version of *Julius Caesar*, and something that is part of the fabric of Morris's life. Saturated with quotations from *King Lear*, Kani's play might even be an attempt to shadow it: not only is there a storm scene, but also a suggestion that through profound suffering comes enlightenment.

By its very nature, the play omits the story of South Africa's women, but it is directed by Janice Honeyman, in a joint production between the RSC and Cape Town's Fugard Theatre, with exquisite delicacy. It contains two great performances: Sher, shuffling round the stage in rubberised slippers and furtively snatching bottles of forbidden liquor from every conceivable hiding place, captures all of the old actor's testiness, insecurity and his Lear-like moral awakening. Kani is equally magnificent in showing how Kunene's dignified forbearance, even when he has a pair of soiled underpants hurled in his face, conceals a deep anger at the cruelty and injustice created by apartheid and at the persistent inequalities in South African life. The play runs for 100 minutes but in that short time it offers a rich portrait of a relationship and a society.

Small Island by Helen Edmundson, based on the book by Andrea Levy
Olivier, National Theatre, London: 2 May 2019

This feels like a landmark in the National Theatre's history: a tumultuous epic about first-generation Jamaican immigrants playing to a genuinely diverse audience. It is based on the novel by the late Andrea Leavy which Helen Edmundson has skilfully adapted into a three-hour-plus play directed by Rufus Norris with hurtling energy. If I was moved, it was by the occasion as much as the play, in that it showed theatre exercising a truly national function.

Levy's book allows big themes to emerge through the interwoven lives of four people. Edmundson focuses on just three. One is Hortense, a light-skinned Jamaican who, farmed out by her mother, becomes a prim schoolteacher who arrives in Britain in 1948 with great expectations. She is joining her husband, Gilbert, who, having served in the RAF, is part of the Windrush generation and equally buoyed by the false hope that postwar Britain will be a land of opportunity. The third figure is Queenie, the daughter of a Lincolnshire pig farmer, who becomes landlady to Gilbert and Hortense. We hear less about Queenie's husband, Bernard, whose reflex racism is partly explained in the book by his experience as a serviceman in partitioned India. Edmundson also takes a more linear approach than Levy and the play's first half, shuttling between Jamaica and Britain, is a helter-skelter affair charting the three main characters' urge to escape.

The second half, set in 1948, paints an unforgettable picture of postwar reality. We see Gilbert, working as a postal driver, routinely asked: "When are you going back to the jungle?" Queenie is ostracised by her neighbours for her hospitality to what they call "darkies." Yet we also see Hortense's shock at realising she and Gilbert have to coexist in a grimly spartan single room.

In the end, it is a play about lies; and the biggest lie of all is that Britain would both welcome and utilise the talents of its fellow citizens from Jamaica. But individual stories take precedence over messages and one of the virtues of Norris's superb production is its ability to focus on people while giving the action a panoramic sweep. Jon Driscoll's projections encompass everything from Caribbean hurricanes and burnished sunsets to the bustle of prewar Piccadilly and the echoing emptiness of Lincolnshire landscapes. Katrina Lindsay's sets also evoke multiple locales with minimal fuss.

In a vast cast there are outstanding performances. Leah Harvey precisely captures Hortense's stiff-backed pride in the face of prejudice. Gershwyn Eustache Jr expertly shows how Gilbert's anger at being denied self-fulfilment is being masked by a surface cheerfulness. Aisling Loftus touchingly pins down Queenie's working-class resilience and, even if Bernard is more shadowy than in the book, Andrew Rothney shows his initial shyness giving way to downright aggression. C.J. Beckford also lends a carefree glamour to Jamaican airman Michael, whose story intersects with that of Hortense and Queenie. From an aesthetic standpoint, there may be better plays this year. But, in showing how aspiring Jamaicans left one small island to land in another of diminished hopes, it will surely rank as one of the most important.

Rosmersholm by Henrik Ibsen
Duke of York's, London: 3 May 2019

This has been dubbed Ibsen's darkest and most complex play. It is also rarely revived but Ian Rickson's breathtaking production does justice to its passion and politics, and boasts stellar performances from Hayley Atwell and Tom Burke. They richly deliver on Shaw's notion of "the deep black flood of feeling from the first moment to the last."

Written by Ibsen in 1886, the play has echoes of its immediate predecessors. As in *Ghosts*, the dead weight of the past is made visible: John Rosmer, a widowed pastor who has lost his faith, is surrounded by portraits of his forebears. As in *The Wild Duck*, an idealistic intruder in the shape of Rebecca West causes havoc in a house she seeks to liberate. Duncan Macmillan's adaptation, while respecting Ibsen's structure, makes vital changes to the original. Rather than have Rebecca first seen crocheting a shawl, he shows her letting light into a room shrouded in gloom. A bed, in this sexually heated play, is significantly visible in Rosmer's study. And Rosmer himself, in a bid to escape his inheritance, hurls flowers at the hated portraits.

What is Ibsen's play ultimately about? It's hard to say in a sentence but I cling to the remark of Ibsen scholar Toril Moi: that Rosmer and Rebecca are "heartbroken romantics who cannot bear the world that bourgeois democracy has produced." They are Tristan and Isolde in a political setting – as this production makes abundantly clear. Rosmer's brother-in-law, Kroll, vividly played by Giles Terera, is a right-wing bigot whose views are disowned by his wife and children. But the left comes off no better. Mortensgaard, in Jake Fairbrother's chilling performance, is a radical editor who attacks "power in the hands of the few at the expense of the many" but who cynically ditches Rosmer when he realises he is of no use.

Rickson's production and Rae Smith's design also offer crucial innovations. One is the presence of servants desperate to enjoy the freedom Rosmer and Rebecca earnestly talk about. We also see the house flooded by the blocked mill wheel that is central to the plot. But it is the lead performances that motor the evening. Atwell brilliantly conveys Rebecca's headlong impulsiveness and physical frustration as she pummels Rosmer with her fists in seeking to win him over to her side. Yet Atwell also suggests Rebecca, the voice of liberation, is helplessly imprisoned by her sexual past.

Burke plays Rosmer with fierce intelligence as an honourable but lost soul who craves certainty and who is never more moving than when he cries: "I want my God back." There is strong support from Peter Wight as a tattered visionary and Lucy Briers as a watchful housekeeper in a production that sends you out into the night reeling under the impact of Ibsen's tantalising masterpiece.

Ian McKellen. A one-man show.

Everyman, Cheltenham: 9 May 2019

Scratch a great actor and you often find a born comic underneath and, watching Ian McKellen's itinerant solo show, I was more than once reminded of Ken Dodd. McKellen shares the late comic's total devotion to theatre so, to mark his 80th year, is touring that number of venues across the country. And, like Dodd, McKellen treats the audience not as passive spectators but as one half of a double-act in an evening that becomes a form of acted autobiography.

McKellen could hardly ignore Gandalf, and the show begins with a reading from *The Lord of the Rings* and an invitation to a young lad from the audience to wield the wizard's sword. But McKellen's heart and soul is in theatre and the first half of the show is an exploration of how the love affair began. We get stories of McKellen's early excursions to *Peter Pan*, Ivor Novello musicals (he claims that it was at *King's Rhapsody* "I had my first erection") and pantomime. This last leads McKellen to dip into the theatrical skip behind him, don a headscarf and instantly turn into a gossipy Widow Twankey, hurling sweets into the stalls before asking: "Anyone like a banana?" We hear naturally of McKellen's coming out and the burden that lifted from his shoulders.

While that's a now familiar story, I was struck by how it relates to the whole saga of the McKellen family. It is fascinating to learn that so many of his forebears were lay preachers and so many of his relations teachers. There is clearly in McKellen an inherited campaigning zeal, whether it takes the form of pursuing gay rights, championing live theatre or preserving the idea of companies. While he laments the passing of the permanent rep ensemble, he also demonstrates its shortcomings: evoking the 80-year-old butler he once played in Agatha Christie's *Black Coffee* he lapses into a form of quivering antiquity hilariously at odds with his own octogenarian vitality.

If the evening is a series of love letters to theatre, it is Shakespeare who gets the most mail. In the second half, McKellen asks us to shout out the names of all Shakespeare's plays and, as we do so, he gives us an anecdote, a reminiscence or an extract relating to each one. He is at his best, and his simplest, in the Seven Ages of Man speech: at one point, his voice even pipes and whistles in a way that signifies old age. But McKellen also proves the value of Irene Worth's comment that "when you're doing Shakespeare, you should jazz" and offers a series of riffs on everyone from Romeo to Macbeth. It is an extraordinary feat, and rather like watching a music-hall memory man with an obsession for the Bard.

I'd like to have heard more about McKellen's mentors and even about directors who have helped shape his career. But you can't have everything and, in just over two-and-a-half hours, McKellen takes us on an engrossing voyage round himself and the British theatre and, wherever he goes, donates the takings to a cause specified by the venue. At heart McKellen is a missionary with the technique of a vaudevillian.

The Cheviot, the Stag and the Black, Black Oil
by John McGrath (Revival)
Eden Court, Inverness: 21 May 2019

John McGrath's 1973 play is a legend in Scottish theatre. It both shocked people into a new awareness of the brutal exploitation of the country's natural resources and provided a pattern for future national touring. But, for all its iconic status, it is not that often seen, so it seems right that the National Theatre of Scotland – in association with Dundee Rep and Live Theatre, Newcastle – has revived and updated Joe Douglas's vigorous 2015 production. I got the sense that many in the Inverness audience, like myself, were seeing the play for the first time.

The story it tells, especially in the first half, is truly horrifying. It reminds us of the ruthlessness of the Highland Clearances, which took place roughly from 1750 to 1860, and which showed much of the land depopulated to maximise profits from the sheep trade: women, more than men, provided active resistance but, as houses were burned and heads split open, they could do little against the force of the Duke of Sutherland's factor, Patrick Sellar. McGrath's continuing theme is the power of capitalism, and he goes on to show how the Highlands were turned into a popular hunting ground for the Victorian ruling class and how the Scottish people never reaped the benefits of the oil boom that started in 1962.

It is a chastening tale but McGrath had the wit to tell it in popular style. Music is central to the show's appeal: the evening starts with a Canadian barn dance and includes song sheets and Gaelic ballads, and part of the show takes the form of a ceilidh. The enforced emigration of many Highlanders is also presented in panto terms and the arrival of American entrepreneurs to exploit North Sea oil becomes a Texas hoedown. Yet, as with Joan Littlewood's *Oh, What a Lovely War* the stylistic gaiety is used to counterpoint the subject's gravity: the point that really hit me was that the success of the Highland Clearances provided a model for other nations seeking to remove inconvenient native peoples.

Douglas's production wisely reminds us much has changed since 1973: in particular, this version suggests that oil should stay in the ground and that Scotland should be harnessing its winds and waves to confront the growing climate crisis. But, while it makes sense to refresh the text and while McGrath proved political theatre can embrace popular techniques, there is something a touch hortatory about the show that reminds us of its 1973 origins. It spells out its message – about the evils of international capitalism and the fact that "the people must own the land" – in ways that seem over-insistent in an age that likes to draw its own conclusions.

It is still a buoyant piece of theatre in which the cast of seven – Billy Mack, Jo Freer, Christina Gordon, Alasdair Macrae, Calum MacDonald, Reuben Joseph and Stephen Bang – switch roles with ease, sing and play a variety of instruments. "Show us your skills," was McGrath's original injunction to his actors – and the current touring troupe do just that with great elan. But, while it's good that the play will get its first-ever English showing in Newcastle, it remains a quintessentially Scottish piece of theatre that did much to explain the nation to itself and change the rules of the game.

Fleabag by Phoebe Waller-Bridge
Wyndham's, London: 28 August 2019

Six years after its debut on the Edinburgh Fringe Phoebe Waller-Bridge's one-woman play finally gets its West End premiere. In the interim it has travelled the globe, spawned two TV series and garnered shelf-fulls of awards. Seeing it on stage for the first time, I was struck by its subversive method, its inherent sadness and by Waller-Bridge's mimetic skill as a performer.

Everyone by now has a shrewd idea of who Fleabag is: a woman in constant crisis whose guinea-pig-themed cafe is going bust and who has the capacity to screw-up her sex life, alienate family and destroy friendships. Yet, although her story is familiar, and the first-night playing to a celebrity-packed audience felt like a coronation, Waller-Bridge still has the ability to spring surprises.

At one point she recounts how Fleabag, after seeing a drunk girl home, decides to have a nightcap. When she tells us that "a sweaty, bald man cups my vagina from behind at the bar," the audience gasps in suitable horror. Yet Waller-Bridge instantly pulls the rug from under us by smiling sweetly as she adds: "But he buys me a drink so – he's nice actually."

It is that ability to catch the contradictions in Fleabag's character that is, I suspect, the source of the show's success. Waller-Bridge says aloud the things that are normally kept hidden and has created a woman who is both caustic about men and avid for sex. But, although the show is often funny, I laughed less than I expected. Ultimately, it is less stand-up comedy than sit-down tragedy in that it is a study in female desperation. Fleabag craves human contact but her quick tongue and awareness of the absurdity of every situation repels those she would attract.

Waller-Bridge the performer, however, is indivisible from the writer. If I preferred the stage version to the Fleabag of TV, it is because Waller-Bridge is able to populate the stage with the characters of her imagination. When on the tube she meets a rodent-faced guy who tells a story "like he doesn't want to let the words out," she screws up her face so that his tiny mouth becomes a minuscule orifice. Equally when she recalls how her cafe-partner, Boo, took music seriously Waller-Bridge's head does little rhythmical jerks evoking the monastic absorption of those enslaved to a beat. If she can summon up a character at will, Waller-Bridge also makes expressive use of her body while barely moving from a stool: at one point she contorts her shape to show how she obliged an ex-boyfriend by taking intimate snapshots of her vagina.

Vicky Jones's production and Isobel Waller-Bridge's sound design enhance the performance by their essential simplicity and, although the show has been overhyped, it is still quirky and original. It offers a remarkable portrait of a modern woman who shamelessly bares her soul and in so doing reveals her essential solitude.

A Very Expensive Poison by Lucy Prebble
(World Premiere)
Old Vic, London: 6 September 2019

Watching Lucy Prebble's fascinating new play about the murder of Alexander Litvinenko on British soil, I was frequently reminded of her earlier hit, *Enron*. Prebble once again bases her play on fact, tells a complex story with great clarity and adopts a variety of techniques, including direct address, puppetry and song, to create a uniquely theatrical spectacle.

Prebble openly acknowledges her debt to *Guardian* journalist Luke Harding's book of the same name which exposed the astonishing details of the Litvinenko case but she goes her own way about recounting the story. The first half, largely seen through the eyes of Litvinenko's wife, Marina, reminds us how this former detective with Russia's FSB (successor to the KGB) died in a London hospital in 2006 of a radioactive element known as polonium-210. His offence was to have exposed the links between organised crime and the Russian government that forced himself and his wife to flee to Britain. Having meticulously explained the background, Prebble then allows Litvinenko's former boss Vladimir Putin to become the unreliable narrator while showing how two Kremlin hitmen were despatched to London to carry out the killing.

What is impressive about the play is its kaleidoscopic variety of tone. In part, it is the love story of the Litvinenkos, capturing their closeness, Marina's occasional criticism of her husband's dubious anti-Putin tactics in exile and her determination that the truth about his death should be told despite the evasiveness of the British government when Theresa May was home secretary. But Prebble is unafraid to show the black comedy behind a tragic story. The hitmen turn out to be hapless bumblers, one of them even mislaying the fountain pen that contains the poison. Even Putin, who seeks to control the narrative from the vantage point of a stage-box, becomes a smarmy puppetmaster concealing his menace under a mask of ingratiation.

If the tone is constantly shifting, so, too, is the style of John Crowley's exemplary production. Tom Scutt's design is a box that contains multiple locations including a London hospital, a Moscow flat, the swish hotel where the poison was fatally administered. But, as with *Enron*, it's the theatricality of the piece that constantly surprises: the history of polonium is told through a shadow-play fairy tale and the Russian entrepreneur Boris Bereszovsky bursts into song while dining in a swanky Mayfair restaurant.

The play offers a compelling portrait of Russian corruption and British vacillation – it took nearly a decade for a public inquiry to be launched – and its multifaceted approach is anchored by strong central performances. MyAnna Buring's Marina emerges as a woman of implacable determination and ferocious loyalty who shares her husband's obsession with truth. Tom Brooke captures the complexity of Litvinenko, whose moral zeal is accompanied by a desire to protect his family. There is also a gallery of fine supporting performances from Reece Shearmsith as the deviously dangerous Putin, Lloyd Hutchinson and Michael Shaeffer as the barely competent assassins, Peter Polycarpou as the glad-handing Bereszovsky and Thomas Arnold as Marina's staunch legal ally. It's an evening that instructs as it entertains and that leaves one appalled at Britain's initial reluctance to do anything that might antagonise Moscow.

Three Sisters by Inua Ellams (World Premiere) Lyttelton, National Theatre, London: 11 December 2019

Inua Ellams describes his new play, his first since *Barber Shop Chronicles,* as "after Chekhov." He has taken the characters of *Three Sisters* and relocated them from provincial Russia to Nigeria between 1967 and 1970 during Biafra's attempted secession.

The result is a startlingly vivid account of the civil war and a direct assault on British neocolonialism. I just wish Ellams had been less faithful to Chekhov. Structurally, the play stays close to the template. It is set in a village in Owerri, where three sisters think back longingly to Lagos. One of them, Lolo, is a hard-working teacher; the married middle sister, Nne Chukwu, has an affair with a military commander; the youngest, Udo, sees her dreams of happiness shattered. All of this is true to Chekhov. But we also see the brutal consequences of civil war, including death and starvation, and at the end we witness Biafra's doomed attempt to create a separate republic.

Ellams brilliantly uses the context to sharpen specific relationships. The hostility of the sisters to their brother's wife, which in the original seems like snobbery, is explained by the fact that they belong to the dominant Igbo ethnic group, while she is a Yoruba. The reason for the failure of Nne Chukwu's marriage also becomes clear when you realise it was arranged when she was 12. Above all, the play offers a searing attack on British responsibility for the war dating to the time when they created Nigeria out of 250 ethnic groups and languages.

While the play offers an eye-opening account of the civil war, Chekhov sometimes gets in the way. The point of the original is that, in the course of three years, nothing essentially changes. Here, however, we see a brave vision of Biafran independence being fatally shattered. Although Nne Chukwu attacks Udo for worrying about private problems during a period of public upheaval, her own affair with the commander also loses some of its dramatic significance as the country is being torn apart.

For all my cavils about Ellams grafting a new play on to an old model, Nadia Fall's visually impressive production contains a host of fine performances. Sarah Niles makes Lolo a politically vigorous figure who vehemently attacks both British colonialism and Igbo tribalism. Natalie Simpson movingly conveys Nne Chukwu's lifelong resentment at an enforced marriage and Racheal Ofori shows Udo's transition from naive optimism to acceptance of tragic reality.

But there is strength in depth throughout the company. Ken Nwosu hints at the vanity behind the commander's philosophising, Tobi Bamtefa disintegrates memorably as the sisters' once high-flying brother and Jude Akuwudike is all growing disillusion as the brigade doctor. Ronke Adekoluejo also has the right brashness as the brother's Yoruba bride, whose own clandestine affair actually ensures the family is fed, and Anni Domingo as an elderly retainer embodies the bolshy outspokenness of age. The production and the performances are first-rate, and the house rose spontaneously at the end of a long evening. Yet I still wish Ellams had been even more ruthlessly radical in rewriting Chekhov.

That wasn't quite my final review, as chief theatre critic, for The Guardian. *I closed my account a week later with a review of* Pippi Longstocking *in Northampton. Happily, however, I was given a freelance contract by the paper to write a minimum of 15,000 words per annum on theatrical matters. What I could not have foreseen was that by mid-March 2020 theatres across the country would have been forced to close because of a COVID-inspired national lockdown imposed by the Government. In fact many theatres, in advance of the Government diktat, had already ceased performing because of the danger posed by the virus. What followed was a period of prolonged uncertainty about the future of all the arts. In July, at the suggestion of my theatre editor at the paper, Chris Wiegand, I wrote an open letter to secretary of state for culture, Oliver Dowden, expressing the concern of the whole artistic community.*

The show won't go on without a proper plan.

4 July, 2020

Dear Oliver Dowden,

You presumably heard Boris Johnson, when asked at prime minister's questions this week about the future of theatre, declare that "the show must go on." I wonder what your reaction was. Did you let out a silent cheer? Or did you, like the rest of us, groan at Johnson's hollow bombast at a time when not only theatre but the whole performing arts sector faces decimation by December?

We are in a situation, like that in a Shakespeare history play, where messengers arrive hourly with bad news from all ends of the kingdom. The Nuffield Southampton, which combines a new city centre theatre with a long-standing campus playhouse, is closing with 86 roles made redundant. The Theatre Royal Plymouth has made its entire artistic team redundant and the Royal Exchange Manchester may have to make 65 per cent of its staff redundant. The story is much the same everywhere you look, be it Birmingham, Norwich or Perth. Even the big, seemingly well-protected institutions are not immune: the Royal Opera House, Covent Garden was reported in the London *Evening Standard* to be "facing closure."

So what are your team at the Department for Digital, Culture, Media and Sport doing to reassure the arts community and provide a concrete plan of action?

Well, so far you have come up with a five-phase roadmap for the performing arts that is worse than useless. Sam Goldwyn said that "a verbal agreement isn't worth the paper it's written on" and a roadmap that offers no clue as to how to get to one's destination is positively insulting.

What's most alarming is that it reveals a total incomprehension as to how the arts actually work.

Stage one, "rehearsal and training," supposedly leads to stages four and five, outdoor and indoor performances. But how can any theatre start rehearsing a production when it has no guarantee of financial support , nor any idea whether it will even exist in a few weeks' time? Wouldn't that be the height of irresponsibility?

It's time, Mr Dowden, that you faced up to a simple truth: artists know much more about the arts than politicians. So far the most practical plan for the theatre has come from Sam Mendes who has made numerous recommendation: increasing the theatre's tax-relief scheme from 20 per cent to 50 per cent; inviting the Government to become theatrical "angels" by investing in productions; challenging the streaming services, such as Netflix and Amazon, to put money into an industry from which they directly benefit.

Have you spoken to Sir Sam about his ideas? Have you co-opted him onto the cultural renewal taskforce you have set up? Or are you simply fiddle-faddling while Rome burns?

I also wonder if you have spoken to your European counterparts about protecting the arts from economic ruin. I am well aware that you are part of a Brexit-driven government that relies on the myth of British exceptionalism. But it is surely worth noting that the German government has pledged 50 billion euros to support the arts in crisis and that the French have, among other measures, created a fund of 7 billion euros for small businesses, including those that have had to cancel shows and film shoots. By comparison, our £160 million Arts Council emergency package looks like very small beer.

I've never met you and I'm ready to believe you are well-intentioned. But I wonder if you have even begun to grasp the scale of the crisis facing the performing arts – theatre, opera and dance as well as classical music – in this country. Unless you come up soon with a detailed, precise, properly financed plan of action soon, you will go down in history as the politician who presided over the dissolution of the arts in Britain. The only thing one can say for sure is that the show definitely won't go on.

Yours,

Michael Billington ·

As it happens, two days after this letter was published the Government announced a £1.57 billion rescue-package to keep the arts afloat. But, while the money was widely welcomed and saved a number of institutions from immediate closure, it did nothing for the thousands of freelance workers who are the lifeblood of the performing arts. What followed was a period of sustained anxiety with the Government adopting a stop-start approach to containing the COVID-19 virus: a desire to re-charge the economy was countered by the need to protect lives as the death-rate rose. Two further national lockdowns meant that theatres, initially encouraged to re-open to perform to socially distanced audiences, were once again closed down. In May 2021, they were finally given the green light to resume business. How long it will take for theatre both to recover its old buoyancy and take off in exciting new directions is an open question. I only hope this book offers testament to its enduring vitality.

INDEX